SORCERER'S
APPRENTICE

SORCERER'S APPRENTICE

AN INCREDIBLE JOURNEY INTO THE WORLD OF INDIA'S GODMEN

TAHIR SHAH

Arcade Publishing
New York

Arcade Publishing books may be purchased in bulk at special discounts for sales promotion, corporate gifts, fund-raising, or educational purposes. Special editions can also be created to specifications. For details, contact the Special Sales Department, Arcade Publishing, 307 West 36th Street, 11th Floor, New York, NY 10018 or info@skyhorsepublishing.com.

Arcade Publishing® is a registered trademark of Skyhorse Publishing, Inc.®, a Delaware corporation.

Visit our website at www.arcadepub.com.

10 9 8 7 6 5 4 3 2 1

Library of Congress Cataloging-in-Publication Data

Shah, Tahir.
 Sorcerer's apprentice : an incredible journey into the world of India's Godmen / Tahir Shah.
    p. cm.
 ISBN 978-1-61145-057-6 (alk. paper)
1. Shah, Tahir--Travel--India. 2. Magicians--Travel--India. 3. Magicians--India--Biography. 4. Occultism--India--History. 5. Swindlers and swindling--India. 6. Hindus--India. I. Title.
 GV1545.S29A3 2011
 793.8092--dc22
 [B]

2011002221

Printed in the United States of America

This book is dedicated to the memory
of my father, Sayed Idries Shah.

AUTHOR'S NOTE

Some names and locations have been
changed in order to respect privacy.

هيڅ شئ هغسي نه دي چې ښکاري

Hits shay haghase nu dai che khkari
Nothing is what it seems

Favoured Pashtu proverb
of Jan Fishan Khan

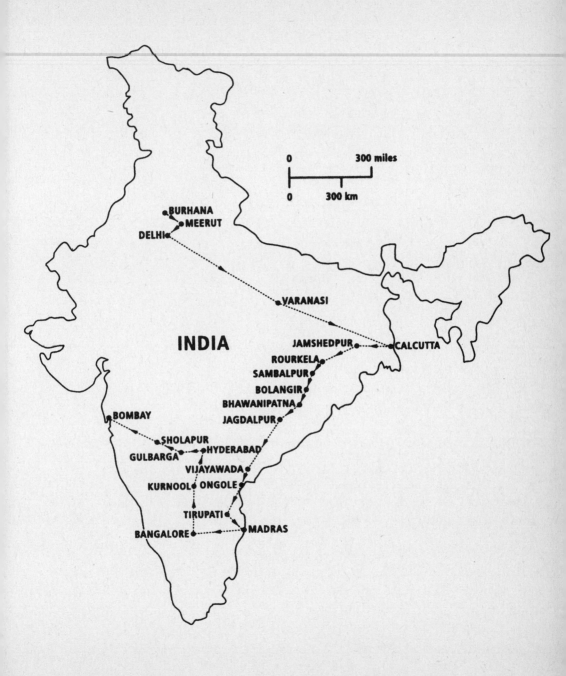

CONTENTS

PART ONE

Three things cannot be retrieved:
The arrow once sped from the bow
The word spoken in haste
The missed opportunity.

Ali the Lion, Caliph of Islam,
son-in-law of Mohammed the Prophet

He Who Scatters Souls

We failed to realise it was an omen when it came. Sunshine streamed down through an almost cloudless indigo sky, warming the dew-covered lawn. The gardener had fished out his dilapidated machine for the first mow of the summer. The great yew tree, basking in sunlight, threw long shadows across the grass. Squirrels dashed about in the monkey-puzzle and copper beech. A bank of azaleas perfumed the early-morning air. Then, quite suddenly, hailstones the size of conkers showered down from above, shattering the peace. A lone cloud in an unending blue sky had spawned the freak bombardment, which persisted for about three minutes. And, as the last nuggets of ice struck the lawn, the doorbell echoed the arrival of an unexpected visitor.

My family's home in an isolated English village was not unused to bizarre guests. The house was a magnet for the peculiar. One could never be certain whom the next to arrive would be. But, even by normal unpredictable standards, the man standing at the porch, waiting to be welcomed, was anything but typical.

The first thing that struck me about the towering Pashtun was his extraordinary bristliness. An immense bush of woolly beard masked much of his face. Hanging like an ink-black inverted candy-floss, it fanned out in all directions. His hands, ears, and the nostrils of his hooked beak of a nose were also thick with waxy hair. In the few places where the skin was bald – the fingertips, palms and below the eyes – it was creased and scaly as an armadillo's snout. The sable eyes spoke of honesty and the furrowed forehead hinted of an anxious past.

The giant bear of a man teaselled the froth of beard outwards with a scarlet plastic comb, and dusted down his filthy khaki *salwaar kameez*, shirt and baggy trousers – the preferred outfit in the Hindu Kush. Straightening the knotted Kabuli turban, which perched on his head like a crown, he peered down at the ground bashfully, as the front door was pulled inwards. My father, recognising Hafiz Jan, son of Mohammed ibn Maqbul, embraced him.

The Pashtun's luggage – a single sealed tea chest bearing the word 'ASSAM' in black stencilled lettering – was carried in ceremoniously. It was heavy as an elephant-calf and stank of rotting fish.

Although received at no notice, Hafiz Jan was welcomed with great decorum. Tea and refreshments were brought and pleasantries exchanged. Blessings and gifts were conferred upon him. According to Eastern tradition, my father expounded in detail the pedigree of our distinguished visitor.

His forefathers had fought alongside my own ancestor, the Afghan warlord and statesman Jan Fishan Khan (a *nom de guerre*, translating literally as 'He Who Scatters Souls'). None had been so courageous, or trusted, as the progenitors of Hafiz Jan. They had accompanied the warrior on all his campaigns. Many had died in battle, side by side with members of my own family. When, in 1842, their lord had travelled with his enormous retinue of soldiers from Afghanistan to India, they had escorted him. With his sudden death at the tranquil Indian town of Burhana, they had pledged to guard for eternity the mausoleum of their commander, Jan Fishan Khan.

More than a century on, Hafiz Jan was proud to have assumed the inherited position: keeper of my great-great-great-grandfather's tomb.

'The shrine of Jan Fishan,' he said in faultless English, 'is the shrine of shrines, and as noble as He who lies there. It will last ten thousand years and longer!'

A lengthy harangue followed, in which the Pashtun showered praise on the memory of Jan Fishan. Such orations, more familiar as the conclusion to a great Afghan feast rather than a dainty tea, are designed to verify well-established facts.

'His Highness Prince Mohammed Jan Fishan Khan, son of Sayed Qutubuddin Khan of Paghman,' began Hafiz Jan with deep, growling intonation, 'was pious, generous, chivalrous, honourable, and the greatest horseman that ever lived. Known as Shah-Saz, "the King-Maker", he was a tactician, diplomat, philosopher and leader of great wisdom. Still today,' continued Hafiz Jan, working himself into a frenzy, 'the descendants of his opponents tremble on hearing that legendary name – Jan Fishan Khan, the Soul-Scatterer!'

Suddenly, as if ordered to do so, Hafiz Jan fell silent. His face contorted with anxiety, he led my father into the garden. Twenty minutes later, the two men returned. My father was taciturn at first. Hafiz Jan was equally reserved.

'Our brother, Hafiz Jan,' began my father hesitantly, 'has crossed continents to be with us. He left the tomb of our forefather and hurried here. His journey was inspired by a disturbing dream.'

His brow ridged in thought, my father related the dream of Hafiz Jan. Prolonged and elaborate, it had depicted many things. At the core of the tale, fringed by a series of confusing and interlinked events, was one gruesome incident. It centred on my own future.

Deceived by a concealed well-shaft, the dream had shown me meeting a sudden, undignified end. Hafiz Jan had hastened across land and sea to protect me from what he could only assume was a premonition. Rising up to his full height, the Pashtun thrust an arm in the air,

'Rest assured,' he barked, 'that I shall not stir from this place until the threat is vanquished!'

The sudden arrival of a gallant and honourable Pashtun, pledging to defend an eleven-year-old boy, might have seemed incongruous. However, a precedent gave the visitor's dream greater significance.

At the time of the British retreat from Kabul, an insurgent had crept into Jan Fishan Khan's sleeping quarters. As he drew his dagger to murder the warlord, one of Jan Fishan's most trusted men stepped nimbly from behind a screen and severed the throat of the intruder. The incident, which had passed into legend, is a favoured tale in our family. Jan Fishan's defender – himself a forebear of Hafiz Jan – had been alerted to the murder plan by a premonition.

Refusing all further hospitality, Hafiz Jan strode from the sitting-room, and hauled his tea chest up the four flights of stairs to the landing outside my attic bedroom. Removing the lid, he plucked out a mattress and set it down in front of my door.

'Be at ease,' he whispered, as he lay down on the bedroll. 'I will seize the danger and tear it limb from limb!'

I would constantly remind Hafiz Jan that he was not waiting for a mortal assassin, but an uncovered well-shaft – a hazard I was unlikely to encounter on the upper-most floor of the house. Filling his lungs sharply with air, thrusting his fists upward like pistons, the Pashtun would reply:

'Never underestimate the slyness of *Shaitan*, the Devil!'

With summer stretching out before us, Hafiz Jan and I spent a great deal of time together. I would teach him tongue-twisters, and he would recount the many remarkable exploits of Jan Fishan Khan. These tales, as with all Hafiz Jan's conversation, were peppered with Pashtun proverbs.

'An intelligent enemy,' he would say, stroking his beard as if it were a bristly pet, 'rather than a foolish friend.' Or, 'He learnt the language of pigeons, and forgot his own.' Or, the favourite of Jan Fishan Khan: '*Hits shay haghase nu dai che khkari* . . . nothing is what it seems.'

Only when he had done justice to the memory of my ancestors would Hafiz Jan agree to reveal a little more of his bewildering excursion from northern India to our small village. The voyage comprised a series of journeys by container ship and tramp steamer. It had taken in an astonishing array of distant and exotic ports. Aboard ships loaded with alfalfa seeds, pinking shears, salted ox tongues, and hypodermic syringes, Hafiz Jan had earned his passage by peeling potatoes and amusing the crew.

Entertainment, I soon discovered, was the Pashtun's forte.

Over the weeks he stayed, Hafiz Jan disinterred a variety of apparatus and oddities from the depths of his tea chest. The deeper his stout, hairy fingers delved into the crate, the greater the reward. The more I saw, the more alarmed I became that HM Customs at Southampton would have permitted such hazardous belongings ashore.

At the bottom of the tea chest, below a Webley and Scott Mark VI revolver, twin sets of buffalo-hide bandoleers, a flare gun with six distress beacons, and a large dented tin of *naswar*, a green narcotic snuff, nestled a selection of oversized antique moss-green glass bottles. Speckled with miniature bubbles, plugged with waxed glass stoppers, the collection had been packed in straw. Removing them one at a time, like priceless eggs from a great auk's nest, Hafiz Jan held them up to the light. Each was embossed with skull and crossbones and bore a label advertising a virulent solution.

Arsenic, cyanide and sodium; strychnine, phosphorous and nitric acid: their names read like the tools of a homicidal maniac. So enthralled was I with the newcomer's fine clutch of poisons that I never questioned his motives. For all I knew, Hafiz Jan had resolved to slay us all, to break his ancestral slavery to the tomb. With his tea chest of chemicals, nothing would have been simpler.

But the Pashtun had an unexpected and abiding passion, for which he required all his lethal chemicals. Hafiz Jan loved conjuring tricks.

If not for his hereditary role as guardian of a shrine, he would certainly have become a full-time stage magician. Until the death of his father, five years before, he had studied conjuring and illusion under one of India's greatest masters. Yet now, with a career as a warden already staked out for him, Hafiz Jan was forced to perfect his illusory skills in his spare time.

After breakfast each morning, having wiped his beard like a hand-towel over the full expanse of his face, our guest would lead me into my bedroom and close the door firmly. An assortment of concoctions and equipment would be fished from the crate. Hafiz Jan would, for protection, tuck his swath of beard beneath his shirt. Then, in the silence of my attic retreat, we would begin work.

Each day brought a new conjuring skill. 'Sleight-of-hand' – an act of deception through a furtive movement of the wrist and hand – formed the basis of so many tricks. Under Hafiz Jan's impromptu tuition, I would often practise the basic movements until dawn. 'Sleights' were essential for demonstrating to my parents the new and *harmless* skills I had acquired. But they lacked the daring, heinous effect which the leaf-green bottles could so effortlessly provide.

Hafiz Jan had noticed my keen interest in chemicals and severe procedures. Within the makeshift laboratory which my bedroom had become, bottles and jars were readied for use. First, a handful of potassium permanganate was sprinkled over a sheet of card on the floor. Pour on a few drops of glycerine and flames were soon licking upward. Then came the 'Bloody Battle' experiment, as Hafiz Jan liked to call it. He always used the word 'experiment', rather than 'illusion', for he felt that it added importance to what we were doing. The Bloody Battle transformed old-fashioned conjuring into high art.

A solution of ferric chloride was painted on to my leg. Before the liquid dried, Hafiz Jan seized a carving knife and surreptitiously dipped it into a solution of sodium sulpho-cyanide. Forcing the knife against the coated section of skin, he motioned melodramatically, as if slicing into my thigh. As I tumbled about, feigning death, Hafiz Jan would roar with delight. Crimson streaks were left where blade had met skin. The Pashtun demonstrated how the scarlet liquid could be wiped away without leaving a mark. Magicians throughout the world, he said, used the experiment to prove they had the power to make wounds vanish at will.

Hafiz Jan's ceaseless stream of chemical enlightenment continued. My family rarely saw me. Brief sightings every so often assured them I had not yet succumbed to the well-shaft. As days turned into weeks, my parents began to consider the hirsute Pashtun's lessons as a malign influence on their prepubescent son.

When collared by either parent on the landing, where he insisted on living, Hafiz Jan would mumble Pashtu aphorisms. His great lugu-brious eyes would seem meek and trustworthy. The parent would leave with renewed confidence in our guest. As if by magic, Hafiz Jan would materialise a bottle of mercuric chloride, and grinning a broad conjuror's grin would lead me back to work.

'Now you are ready to mesmerise an audience,' said Hafiz Jan at breakfast one morning. 'We will bewitch them with our magic.'

'*Them?*'

Smiling broadly, the Pashtun pointed at my parents who were sitting in the garden. Surely he was forgetting that in the circumstances public exposure was unwise. I voiced my apprehension.

'Don't be so modest,' roared Hafiz Jan, 'I want to show you off, my little apprentice!'

'But . . .'

'We'll put on a grand display of our work. How about next Saturday night?'

For days I practised sleights and chemical feats, perfecting the new skills. Every spare moment was devoted to magical study. One session took us into the field behind the house. I led the way to a secluded spot in a copse at the far end of the field, where a cottage had once stood. First, Hafiz Jan demonstrated 'burning water'. The magician pours some water into a tin mug, and takes a sip to prove that it's ordinary water. He pours another mug of water from the same jug. As soon as the cup has been filled, the water catches fire. Hidden at the bottom of the second mug is a pea-sized nugget of potassium and three tablespoons of ether. When the water is poured into the mug, the potassium ignites, setting fire to the ether, which surges to the surface of the liquid.

'Now,' announced Hafiz Jan, 'I'll teach you a trick with my magic ring.' He twisted the gold-flecked lapis lazuli ring off the little finger of his right hand. 'But first I'll need three wild mushrooms, can you find some?'

I tramped over to a scrub thicket in search of fungi. In the undergrowth I uncovered an old plimsoll, a coil of rusty wire and a brown beer bottle. No mushrooms in sight. I was just about to report back to Hafiz Jan when my foot caught in an overgrown dip in the ground. I tripped, cutting my knee.

The Pashtun heard my cry and hurried over. He bandaged my leg with a rag ripped from his turban. Then he excavated the mesh of sticks, leaves and soil to see what had cut me. I looked on as his hands tore away at the earth. When the debris had been cleared, we both found ourselves staring at the ground in stupefaction. I had tripped on what appeared to be a disused well.

Filled in long before, the concealed shaft had not posed a life-threatening hazard. Even so, the Pashtun, who was triumphant with his find, spent two full days sealing it with cement.

'*Shaitan*,' he said, 'will be hungry in Hell tonight!'

The great day of our exposition arrived. A row of chairs was laid out in the kitchen. Hafiz Jan groomed his beard, trimmed his nostril hair. The various chemicals and apparatus were installed in the tea chest, which doubled as a conjuror's cabinet. My parents, sisters, the gardener, housekeeper and secretary were ushered to their seats. The audience waited politely for the show to commence.

As Hafiz Jan clapped his giant hands together like cymbals, alarm bells were sounding in my mind. Fortunately, I had managed to tone down the inventory of illusions at the last minute. The Pashtun had intended to burn a section of mysterious coarse grey bark during the show. He had explained that the bark, of the Indian *chaitan*, 'devil's tree', is used by Eastern magicians to stun an audience. Some say the bark's hallucinogenic smoke is the secret behind the fabled Indian rope trick.

Hafiz Jan began by performing a selection of sleights; materialising objects from thin air. The gardener was invited up to the front. His wristwatch vanished as the Pashtun shook hands with him. A moment later, the watch was pulled from my sister's pocket. I scanned the room. My parents seemed relaxed. So far, so good.

Next, a pot of boiling vegetable oil was taken from the stove and placed before me. Without hesitation, I thrust my left arm into it. The audience breathed in deeply, tricked by the simple illusion. Lime juice is added to the oil before it's heated. The juice boils when only tepid, sending a cascade of bubbles to the surface, and giving the appearance that the oil is boiling.

As I wiped the oil from my arm, Hafiz Jan pulled a fired poker from the oven, and began to lick it. An alarming sizzling sound, and the fragrance of barbecued flesh billowed outwards as tongue met iron. Hafiz Jan had washed his mouth out moments before with liquid storax, which absorbs the heat.

My parents seemed impressed. I wondered how long their enthusiasm would last. Bloody Battle came and went, as did a variety of inoffensive illusions.

The next trick was austere by any standards. An ordinary light-bulb was materialised from nowhere by Hafiz Jan. Placing it in a handkerchief, the Pashtun crushed it with his right foot. He handed me a banana, which I ate. He ate one, too, then placed a shard of glass on his tongue and began to chew. Then it was my turn. Positioning a jagged piece of glass in my mouth, I began to munch.

My father looked on in disbelief, overwhelmed that his son had been taught to eat glass and relish it. The shock quickly turned to anger, but he suppressed his rage for fear of insulting the visitor. The tiny fragments of glass, which get embedded in the banana, pass easily through the body. Hafiz Jan had taught me to always use clear light-bulbs, as the opaque ones contain poisonous mercury oxide.

Moving swiftly along, the Pashtun got ready to perform the *pièce de résistance*. It was a brave decision. He lit a large beeswax church candle, placed before our stage. Its wick was at the audience's eye level. Then, pulling a fistful of dust from beneath his shirt, he murmured a magic phrase, and hurled the fine powder at the candle. Covering his eyes with the end of his turban, Hafiz Jan winced with pleasure as a golden fireball rocketed sideways towards my family and their associates.

The conjuror had not anticipated the remarkable force of the combustion. He had been more used to igniting powdered camphor outside. As the spectators rubbed at their singed hair and blackened faces, I wondered what to say. Silence seemed safest.

Hafiz Jan was up at dawn the next day. I could hear him moving uneasily about the landing on tiptoe. By seven o'clock the tea chest was packed with his possessions. Padded with the horsehair mattress, the half-filled bottles of poison sloshed about as the crate was hauled downstairs.

The front door was pulled inwards once again. The great Pashtun lifted me by the cheeks and smiled sombrely.

'Now that the well-shaft – that vile tunnel to Hell – is covered over,' he said, 'I ought to be on my way. I must return to the mausoleum, it's there that I belong. Jan Fishan,' he said softly, 'will be waiting for me.'

As Hafiz Jan, son of Mohammed ibn Maqbul, prepared to retrace his wayward route back to northern India, I made my own pledge. One day – although I did not know when – I would seek him out, and continue with my magical pupillage.

Snake-Jugglers and Liposuction

Almost twenty years had passed since the inimitable Hafiz Jan had blasted the vast fireball at my family. Despite reliving the performance over and over in a recurring nightmare, my interest in conjuring had never waned. The vanilla odour of liquid storax still haunted my olfactory nerve. The idea of chewing glass caused my pulse to race. And the deep, secret longing to study illusion was always there. But the spark to rekindle my motivation was wanting.

That spark arrived late one night in an ill-lit, smoky flat somewhere in west London. A roomful of supposed friends jabbered on about their sensible cars, their sensible jobs, and their sensible plans for a sensible future. Theirs was a world of ruched curtains, floral print wallpaper, asparagus soufflé and French cuff shirts.

Such preoccupations were at odds with my own. I yearned to rediscover the thrill of spontaneity, once fostered so intensely by Hafiz Jan's magic. I longed for adventure, for discovery and wonder. The idea of a secure, planned future was severely disturbing.

My sensible friends swivelled to face me. Would I at last buy a sensible pad, with ruched curtains and florid wallpaper? Could I be counted on to fall into line? Why didn't I take up golf, or learn to dish up an asparagus soufflé once in a while? Surely the time had come to get some decent shirts with proper French cuffs?

Swilling their port, the inquisition awaited my answer. I mulled over my position. Why should I adopt their bourgeois lifestyle? Their materialistic trappings were nothing but illusion. The blood-red port whirled about like one of Hafiz Jan's precious chemicals. *Illusion . . . Hafiz Jan . . .* my mind set to work. Why not escape? Why not leave all this behind, and embark on a great adventure?

'You can keep your sensible cars, clothes and prim little houses!' I bellowed. 'I'm off to India to become a magician!'

*   *   *   *

Hotel foyers across the Indian capital were resounding with restless anticipation. Throngs of visitors were pouring into the city, all in a state of high excitement. They swanned about greeting long-lost friends, laughing, weeping, embracing triumphantly. I wondered what was going on. Then, at one large hotel, I noticed an impressive daffodil-yellow banner, slung like a washing-line between a pair of chandeliers. It read: 'ALL INDIAN ASTROLOGERS' CONFERENCE'.

The event, which had drawn seers from all corners of India, explained why every hotel bed in New Delhi was full. Palmists and horoscope-readers brushed shoulders with numerologists and tarotists. Crystal-gazers, face-readers and dream diviners – they had come to swap secrets, to tell tales, and to be seen.

Pushing my way out past the bustle of crystal balls, dog-eared tarot cards and hand-reading charts, I waited for an auto-rickshaw. Mediums were still arriving in droves, many weighed down with phrenological busts and new-fangled fortune-telling machines.

All the hotels on my list were full to bursting with astrologers. Where would I find a spare bed? Then I had an idea. When a rickshaw pulled up, I told its driver to hasten to the most misfortunate, accursed establishment in the city. Such unlucky lodgings would surely ward away the superstitious astrologers. Without questioning my request, the driver rubbed his hands together and headed north to the Old City.

With the vehicle charged up to full speed, we careered through Old Delhi's back-streets, swerving to miss incense-sellers and sacred cows. Past the colossal Jami'a Masjid and the noble Red Fort. Left down Chandni Chowk, fabled Silver Bazaar of Shah Jehan. An abrupt left again into Dariba Kalan – 'Street of the Incomparable Pearl' – where *jalebis* boil like lobsters in foaming oil-filled urns. Reining in his rickshaw, the driver wrenched its handlebars sharply to the right. A moment later we were skidding to a halt in the Kinari Bazaar.

A small, quiet market, Kinari peddles wedding brocades, tinsel, and garlands fashioned from rupee notes. An air of jubilation surrounded all the stalls. The bazaar was packed with happy people.

Tapping the driver on the shoulder, I asked him if this spirited lane was home to the damnedest, most ill-fated hotel in all of Delhi. The driver pulled his coarse blanket tighter about him and nodded earnestly. Then, cringing as low as he could, he pointed upwards.

Looming over on the south side of the bazaar stood the dilapidated hostel. A rusting signboard publicised its unfittingly optimistic name, 'Hotel Bliss'. Its walls were caked in lizard-green slime, its windows broken, and its corrugated iron roof pocked with holes. A curse of doom and catastrophe hung over the place like a death-cloud. It was the sort of place whose door is marked by a bloody cross in times of plague. But there was no door. As I took in the features of the wretched shelter, a chill surged down my spine. The rickshaw driver, who appeared anxious to leave, unloaded my bags. I handed over the fare. Then I presented him with a large tip. He had done himself proud.

The shock of the building's exterior continued inside. The ground floor, which was well below street level, was two feet under water, presumably the result of a leaking pipe. I waded through the flood. A vomit-strewn staircase led to the reception desk, which had been relocated to the third-floor. Cautioning myself to be bold, I ascended the steps. The hostel's walls were soot-black, scorched by fire. The rotting floorboards were as soft as wet clay; the stench of drowned, decomposing rats was suffocating.

Lolling back in a wicker chair, the manager picked his teeth with a *neem* stick. His closely cropped hair was seal-brown, his eyes were wily and foreboding. I introduced myself, declaring I'd heard of the residence's fine reputation. The man carved the *neem* twig between the gap in his front teeth. He could tell I was lying, for he knew as well as I that the hotel had no reputation at all.

'Are there any astrologers here?' I asked cordially.

'No one here,' came the reply.

'Do you have a room for a few days?'

'Why not?'

Hotel Bliss, with its less than charming aura and rising tide, encouraged its patrons to spend their days off the premises. After a vile night spent in room two, even a lunatic would have satisfied a craving for self-punishment. In the dead of night, the rats which had survived the flood could be heard nibbling cockroaches in the dank corridor outside my room. Bedbugs swarmed about the prison-issue blankets, relishing their banquet of foreign blood.

The manager had lied when reporting that his hostel was empty. From the cubicle opposite mine came the intermittent, echoing groans of a heroin addict. As I tiptoed past the unfortunate's room, preparing to breach the floodwaters, I pondered whether the entire place was a dope fiend's den.

Were it not for the cheery atmosphere of the Kinari Bazaar, I would have abandoned Hotel Bliss right away. The street provided a welcome distraction from the reality of room two. Its fabulous stalls brimmed with colourful ornaments. At one were piles of cherry-red plastic bunting, coconuts and panniers of rose petals. Another offered heaps of pink balloons: fashioned in the form of Ganesha, the elephant god. Sandalwood incense smouldered in burners, warding away the flies. Rich brocades and glass bangles, sachets of *mehendi*, henna powder and silver tinsel glowed in the bright December sunlight.

Behind the bustling Chandni Chowk, adjacent to the Jain Bird Hospital, I rested at an open-air tea stall to watch the world go by. A glass of sweet *chai-i-sabs*, green tea, was poured and placed before me by the young waiter. Sipping the refreshing drink, I focused on the Old City's teeming blend of life. Cyclists and auto-rickshaws raced ahead, swooping through the traffic like eagles. A group of women tottered past, baskets of fish on their heads. A blind leper led by an infant appealed for alms. Hawkers came and went: touting ball-point pens and gingham dishcloths; crêpe-paper party hats and bundles of fenugreek.

As I requested a second glass of *chai-i-sabs*, a middle-aged Western woman approached the tea stall. A full-length red fox fur protected her from the winter cold; a patterned Gucci scarf was tied over the confection of bleached-blonde curls. She sat on a chair across from me. Her complexion was anaemic, her face tired and wan. I wondered what a well-dressed woman was doing at the type of low tea stall I like to frequent.

Without waiting for her order, the waiter – who seemed to recognise the woman – poured a glass of tea and set it before her. I straightened my back and tried to appear respectable. Without looking at me, the lady struck up a conversation.

'I come here every Friday,' she said in a strong, unfamiliar accent. 'You see, I adore to hear the Muslim call to prayer. We do not have it in Moskva. It is so romantic. I adore it . . . you hear me? I adore it!'

Pulling a packet of imported American cigarettes from her purse, she lit one. Then, waving her hands through the smoke with exaggerated movements, she told me why she had come to the sub-continent.

Her native land had, I learned, a limited supply of surgeons, private hospitals and human livers. India, on the other hand, has many skilled surgeons, several exclusive hospitals, and best of all, an unending supply of livers.

'Finding a nice fresh leever is a problem in Russia,' she intoned darkly.

'Is that so?'

'A juicy, tender leever is a wonderful thing,' she continued, licking her lips like a hungry borzoi.

Forced to agree that we take our livers for granted, I hoped that we might move on to a less morbid topic. But the Russian had more to say. She lit another cigarette, filled her capacious lungs to bursting point with dense smoke, and exhaled.

'You see,' she hissed, 'we Russians drink too much. That is the problem. Too much vodka and not enough leevers!' The Muscovite chuckled at her joke, rubbing a smear of lipstick from her glass. 'I am waiting for my new leever now,' she seethed, glancing at her watch. She said it in such a way that I half-expected a man to turn up right then with a polystyrene carton marked 'Fresh Liver'.

I wondered what luckless person would have their organ hacked out on the Russian's account. In India, the body parts business is thriving. That very morning, *The Hindustan Times* had carried a typical story. Days before his beloved sister's wedding, a young man in southern India had committed suicide. Beside his body, a note was found in the boy's handwriting. It asked for his organs to be sold, to pay for his sister's dowry. But even if the organs were to be traded, there was no hope. Without refrigeration, donor organs spoil within hours of death.

Eyes, livers, kidneys, even hearts and lungs, are transplanted in New Delhi's private hospitals – nicknamed the 'body parts bazaar'. Attracted by the prospect of no waiting lists, and inexpensive treatment, more foreigners than ever are travelling to India for transplants. They arrive drawn and ill. When they leave they quite literally take a part of India with them.

The Muscovite opened her purse a crack, removed a Chanel lipstick, and coated her lips with fire-engine red. The silver stick moved easily around the perimeter of her mouth. As it painted her lips, it reminded me of a supposedly true story – possibly an urban legend – when the sub-continent fought back.

A woman from Chicago had some time to spare while in Karachi, in neighbouring Pakistan. Rather overweight after too many heavy *tandoori* meals, she had considered taking up a new dieting regime. As she rambled through Karachi's crowded streets, a billboard caught her eye. It publicised the services of a local cosmetic surgeon.

More eager than ever to shed a few pounds, she entered the building and apprehended a surgeon. Could he remove some extraneous fat through liposuction? The physician seemed uneasy for a moment. But then, shrugging his shoulders, raising his palms in the air, and smiling broadly, he replied, 'Why not?'

A modest fee was agreed and the woman arranged to return for the operation the next day.

Insisting that a full general anaesthetic was necessary for a procedure of this kind, the surgeon scrubbed up and went to work. Some hours later, as the effect of the anaesthetic wore off, the American patient began to revive. Sensation gradually returned to her fingers. As it did so, she reached out to touch her new fat-free thighs. Were they as slim-line and elegant as she hoped? It was then that her distress began.

Even the most proficient physicians, she thought to herself, have to bandage a patient's thighs after removing fat through liposuction. The woman tried to whisper her concern to the nurse. Then the full horror of her new condition became apparent. Her lips were missing.

Although baffled as to why a woman with pretty lips would want them surgically removed – *lip-o-sucked* away – the doctor had agreed to perform the strange operation, if only to make the foreign patient happy. To him, sucking away the lips must have seemed like the latest in American chic. Distraught at her loss, the woman claimed that without lips, her gums dried out and insects flew into her mouth. Robbed of even the weakest smile, she returned to Chicago, lipless and in considerable pain.

I decided not to share the tale with the Russian. Instead, I wished her luck with the second-hand Indian liver, and wandered back through Chandni Chowk to the odious Hotel Bliss.

*   *   *   *

Next day, before the stalls of Kinari Bazaar had opened their shutters to the light, I took my bags and waded from the hotel. Outside, the residents of the street were performing their ablutions and bathing at the standpipe. The scents of soap and hair oil were heavy in the air.

Down a passage off the back-street, behind a booth selling aromatic herbs, a wizened figure was making ready to perform. Emaciated and lame, with cataracts that had stolen his sight many years before, the man stretched his arms before him. His fingers were bent with arthritis, their skin creased with wrinkles. Lifting the cover from a cool stone jar, he removed a heaving mass of entwined miniature vipers. As the infant reptiles squirmed about, coiling with displeasure, the serpent-handler paused to drink three mugs of water. Then, tilting back his head and opening his mouth very wide, he swallowed the snakes one by one like ribbons of emerald liquorice.

The veteran performer rubbed at his blind eyes, scratched his nose, and coughed. As he did so, a helix of five twisting regurgitated snakes, interwoven like mangrove roots, spewed anxiously from his mouth.

The tiny serpents were returned to the jar. Then a second, larger container was opened. Three adolescent pit vipers were jerked from their rest. Propping himself against the low wall, the blind serpent-handler began to toss the reptiles up into the air, juggling them. The two-foot snakes rotated silently. As gravity snatched them earthward, each was caught by the head and hurled up again.

Indifferent to the spectacle, the residents of the lane continued with their chores, without turning. In the twisting alleyways of Old Delhi, Amjed the blind snake-juggler hardly merited a second glance.

Juggling snakes, murmured the ancient when he had finished his routine, is no easy task. Decades of practice are vital to cultivate the skill. But alas, time is an ingredient that novices inevitably lack – most drop dead during the first weeks of practice. Die-hard snake-jugglers like Amjed frown on those who sap the venom from their serpents. Milking instils an alarmingly carefree attitude which is incompatible with the career. Amjed rubbed his fingertips together in reflection. Juggling snakes, he agreed remorsefully, is a dying art.

With the straps of my two cases cutting into my shoulders, I marched out from the Kinari Bazaar towards the Red Fort. By late morning I was aboard a bus bound for Ghaziabad – first stop en route to my reunion with Hafiz Jan.

The vehicle pushed eastwards, across the border into Uttar Pradesh. I took time to think about Hafiz Jan: that black fleece of beard, the eagle's beak, and those gigantic hands. The Pashtun had made a deep impression upon me. Whether it was his features, his dress, or his bearing that had affected me most, I was not certain. Now, after almost two decades, I was to be with him again.

As we left the outermost suburbs of Delhi, the auto-rickshaws died away. Instead, a stream of tangerine-coloured Ashok Leyland lorries shot past in the other direction. In an endless caravan of merchandise, they heaved sugar cane and calico, water melons and live chickens towards the capital.

Beside me sat a gangling young man with wetted-down hair. He was as keen as a whippet. His olive eyes stared agog at the world. His shoes were well-polished, his shirt free of stains, and trousers pressed with razor-edge creases.

We began talking. The man's name was Maruti, which is one of the names of Ganesha, the Hindu elephant god. He had recently qualified as a professional *mahout*, and was now travelling to a job interview in Ghaziabad. The position was for a junior elephant driver at an elephant 'taxi' service in New Delhi. Hired by the city's wealthy for weddings, parties and ceremonial journeys, the elephants could be provided painted with elaborate colours, or decorated with religious motifs.

Maruti rattled on about the training course he had done in the enchanted forest of Pecci, near Kerala's Malabar Coast. A hardback manila envelope on his lap contained the graduation certificate.

'Down there in Kerala,' said Maruti enthusiastically, 'people love elephants very much. A *mahout* from Pecci will see to his elephant's well-being before that of his eldest son. You see, for a *mahout*, an elephant is a father, brother, son and best friend, all rolled into one. Give an elephant love and respect, and he will return it ten times over.'

Maruti glanced out of the window. But he didn't see the traffic jam which now gripped the bus, or the roadside guava-sellers. He saw elephants instead.

'When sitting in position, steering with his feet,' the youth continued, 'a *mahout* from Pecci will never order his elephant to do anything. You would never order your best friend to do something. No . . .' said the young man pointedly, 'the *mahout* will invite the elephant courteously to move.'

In late spring each year, as a cooling breeze streams in eastward from the Malabar Coast, the Pooram Festival takes place at Thrissūr, in central Kerala. At the town's *maidan*, central park, beside the ancient Vadakkunnatha Temple, a crowd of many thousands gathers. Then a cavalcade of thirty great tuskers marches out of the Pecci Forest towards the magnificent temple. Richly adorned in ceremonial finery, the elephants – ridden by students from the *Mahout* School – have colossal Hindu idols strapped to their backs.

The procession of caparisoned elephants parades forward. Music blares from loudspeakers, children caper about in the moonlight, and fireworks shoot into the night sky.

'Pooram is our moment of glory,' said Maruti sentimentally. 'But the elephants also love the grandeur just as much. They may take slow, dignified steps towards the temple, but inside they are dancing!'

On a self-imposed crusade to teach all *mahouts* to be friendly to their steeds, Maruti had much to say about evil elephant-handlers.

'Some *mahouts* beat their elephants and goad them with sharp spikes,' he said. 'If they won't get up, the *mahouts* will make them go without food. The saddest thing of all,' continued Maruti, anxious to share his knowledge, 'is that over time even the most abused elephant will begin to love its master.'

With no easing of the traffic jam, I wondered how much more elephant talk I would be able to stand. My own deep fascination, conjuring, had made me realise that an obsession is often a good thing. Everyone should be obsessed about something. In the hope of redirecting our conversation to my own interest, I told Maruti that I was heading for Burhana to begin an apprenticeship in conjuring.

Staring out of the scratched window, Maruti clasped his long spindly fingers together, and sighed loudly. It was not a sigh of boredom. For he had not heard a word I had said. It was a sigh of true love. Love for his elephants. His fixation seemed to run very deeply. Here was a man whose whole life had been mapped out – steered by a single devotion.

Maruti prodded me eagerly in the stomach. He had more trivia to vent and was in need of a captive audience. I was that audience. He revealed to me that elephants are the only animals to have four knees; they have 'fingerprints' like humans, and they make different sounds to express their emotions. It seemed as if there was little to tell us apart.

But then, enough of the trivia. Maruti had a more pressing message to pass on.

'Innocent wild elephants are being attacked daily in Assam,' he reported mournfully. 'When I have enough money, I'm going to go and protect them.'

'Why are they being attacked?' I asked.

Lowering his head like a vulture, the lanky-framed youth told me of the conspiracy.

'People say the elephants are drunk – that they're out of control and stampeding in massive herds!'

'Is it true? Are they drunk?'

'Well, it's no secret that elephants – like all mammals – enjoy a drink from time to time. They don't mean any harm. Humans don't behave well when they're drunk either.'

'How do they get the alcohol?' I asked, picturing a smoky saloon bar filled with tuskers, slurping stout from gallon glasses.

'They come across illegal stills hidden in the forest, and they have a little sip,' Maruti replied, sniffing. 'One misdirected foot, the still falls to pieces, and liquor's all over the place. They're thirsty, so they drink it up. It's not their fault if they become a bit delinquent.'

Some time later an Indian newspaper headline caught my eye: 'DRUNK ELEPHANTS RUN AMOK'. Maruti had severely underestimated what had become a national problem. A herd of three hundred and fifty inebriated elephants had descended on a small Assamese village, trampling thirteen people to death, and causing destruction on an unknown scale. The report said the creatures had pilfered a vast quantity of rice beer from a 'tea garden', and that alcoholic elephants were ravaging communities across India's north-east every week.

At long last, as the knot of traffic cleared, we sped toward Ghaziabad. At the bus stop in the town centre, Maruti clasped his brown manila envelope to his chest and set off in search of his interview. Just before he disappeared into the frenzy of bobbing heads, he turned. Then, sweeping his right arm in the air like a bull elephant's trunk, he saluted.

Land of Warriors

The bus jarred its way towards Meerut. Sprawling *pipal* trees lined the route, their whitewashed trunks hinting at the days when the region was a cornerstone of the British Raj. It was hard to imagine that May morning in 1857 when discontent led the Bengal Army to revolt. It was harder still to believe that the great Indian Mutiny had begun right here, in the city of Meerut.

History records that the rebellion began when a batch of new Lee Enfield rifles arrived for the Indian troops stationed at the Meerut barracks. When the cartridges were handed out – smeared as they were with pig and cow fat – the troops couldn't contain their fury. The ranks, comprised of a large number of high-caste Hindus and pious Muslims, saw the fat as a direct insult to their religious beliefs.

Once north of Meerut, the bus turned left, detouring on to a minor road. Thirty miles further along, heading north-west towards Karnal, and we arrived at the small settlement of Burhana.

Without wasting time I hurried from the bus stop through Burhana's back-streets towards the sepulchre of my ancestor. Hafiz Jan had described the town in extraordinary detail. But there had been no order to the information. He had reported what he remembered, in random sequence. I fought to piece together the best route to the shrine.

I crossed a grassy paddock to the right of the main street. Beyond that, buried in a copse of date palms and encircled by a low wall, stood a large square building. Despite the surrounding foliage, I could make out its basic structure. Fashioned from dandelion-yellow stone, and replete with Mughal-style arches, it was capped by an exquisite dome. This was the mausoleum of Jan Fishan Khan.

Approaching slowly, I made my way to the entrance of the tomb's enclosure. The tall wrought-iron gates were open. A sudden gust of wind moved the fronds of the surrounding date palms. Several Islamic tombstones poked out from the undergrowth around the main memorial. Inching forward, I walked down the narrow path to the shrine's portal.

On a stool in the doorway sat a figure dressed in a khaki *salwaar kameez* and buffalo-hide *chappals*, with innumerable bandoleers and a black cotton turban. His face was dominated by familiar features: a hooked, aquiline nose, deep-set eyes and ears brimming over with tufts of hair. And longer than ever was the profusion of now greying beard. I stood silently, observing my childhood hero, the incomparable Hafiz Jan.

The Pashtun was honing a bayonet on a smooth block, gritting his teeth as the knife's edge rasped again and again across the surface of the whetstone. So engaged was he with sharpening the blade that he had not seen me. I continued to stare, capturing the moment.

Unsure of what to do, or how to greet him, I shuffled my shoes firmly on the cement path. The sound rose above the rustle of palm leaves and the scrape of metal on stone. Hafiz Jan stopped grinding. Jumping to his feet, he snatched the bayonet to his chest. Then he looked me full in the face. His mouth opened wide and gasped for air. His features seemed to knot together. I said my name. Still mute, he nodded, dropping the bayonet, his black eyes brimming with tears. In slow motion he struggled to push forward, like a man moving underwater. Then, in a single, awkward movement he picked me up and tossed me into the air.

It was some time before Hafiz Jan recovered from the shock of the reunion. We sat quietly for several minutes as he hyperventilated with satisfaction. I apologised for not providing advance notice of my visit, but the ancestral guardian waved my apologies aside.

'This is your home,' he said over and over. 'Why should you tell the humble guardian of your plans to come? Welcome to this land; *your* land – the Land of Warriors. Welcome! I have waited for this day for so many years.'

I replied that I, too, had long dreamt of making the journey to the mausoleum of my great ancestor.

Hafiz Jan was eager to serve refreshments and introduce me to his wife and sons. But more important duties came before the pleasantries. moving his *chappals*, the guardian led me inside the great sepulchre. my bare feet took their first steps on the cool stone floor, I sensed a of energy. The chamber was illuminated by light, streaming the latticed windows set into the wall opposite the door. head backwards I scanned the room. As I did so, I sensed a

As my bare feet took their first steps on the cool stone floor, I sensed a wave of energy. The chamber was illuminated by light, streaming through the latticed windows set into the wall opposite the door. Tilting my head backwards I scanned the room. As I did so, I sensed a

great, unyielding force. It seemed to help me collect my thoughts. Perhaps it was the spirit of Jan Fishan.

The Pashtun pointed at the broad rectangular cenotaph in the centre of the chamber, beneath which lay the crypt. The carved marble was inscribed in Persian lettering.

Hafiz Jan read the legend:

The Prince, Lord of Magnificence, exalted and full of virtue:
From whose aroma itself Paghman was swelled with pride;
He was of the Children of Ali Musa Raza,
A resplendent sun following an auspicious dawning.
From Kabul he came to visit India –
His steps turned Burhana into a garden of paradise.
When the inner urge of a return to Heaven took hold of him:
He left this abode of mortality, taking nothing.
For the date of his going, O Sidq, weigher of words,
Say: Sayed Mohammed Jan Fishan Khan.

As dusk fell over Burhana I sat and reminisced with Hafiz Jan on the veranda of his house. His teenage sons served us with pomegranate juice and *kishmish*, a mixture of fruit and nuts. His wife busied herself arranging an elaborate feast of welcome. The evening *muezzin* rang out over the rooftops, and as it did so, Hafiz Jan grabbed his older son by the cheek.

'Mohammed is now fifteen,' he said, as the boy withstood the vice-like grip of his father's hand. 'And what do you want to do when you grow up, Mohammed?' he probed.

'I want to guard the tomb of Nawab Jan Fishan Khan,' came the reply.

Hafiz Jan raked his huge fingers through his beard, satisfied that his son was prepared to continue the family tradition.

A meal of leviathan proportions followed. Three enormous mounds of *pilau* rice were brought in on brass trays. Chunks of mutton were buried in one, chicken in another, fish in the last. Hafiz Jan's sons invited me to eat. Their mother remained in the kitchen. An Afghan *naan*, the size of a lambskin, was ripped up and also set before me. The Pashtun would pick out the largest chunks of meat and hand them to me one by one, like nuggets of gold. Only when I had finished my third helping did my hosts begin to eat.

'This is a blessed day!' Hafiz Jan repeated continually. 'Every anguish passes but the anguish of hunger! You are honouring us. Eat! Eat! Eat!'

Although desperate to ask whether the great conjuror would take me on as a trainee, I bit my lip. The time for such questions would come once the prolonged formalities were at an end.

When the lavish meal was over, Hafiz Jan rubbed his fingers in his beard in his own inimitable fashion. He stretched backwards and thanked God again that I had come. Then he thanked Jan Fishan Khan for drawing me here.

I replied by saying that Jan Fishan Khan had been one of the two magnets that led me to Burhana. The other, I confirmed, had been Hafiz Jan himself.

Then I seized the moment. Charged with as much enthusiasm as I could muster with several kilos of assorted meats digesting inside me, I enquired about the Pashtun's fascination for magic and illusion.

Hafiz Jan seemed confused for a moment. Then, twisting his ear tufts anti-clockwise, he replied:

'Oh, those old tricks. Silly, weren't they?'

'What do you mean, *silly*? They were incredible! You taught me how to do so much – how to eat glass . . . how to suck red-hot pokers as if they were lollipops . . . how to . . .'

The Pashtun cut me short:

'How to almost kill the great-great-grandson of Jan Fishan with a giant ball of fire.'

Silence pervaded as we both thought back, reliving the horror of that moment.

'That was an unfortunate miscalculation,' I said weakly.

'The blunder brought shame on my family,' asserted Hafiz Jan. 'From that moment forth I vowed never to perform another illusion. What if something had happened to your father?'

'*Aga*,' I continued, 'I have come here to Burhana to ask you to teach me all you know about illusion and conjuring. Please consider accepting me as your pupil.'

Thrust into an uncomfortable position, the Pashtun rubbed his beard between his palms. Only when it had furled into one long, rope-like fibre did he reply.

'Tahir Shah,' he said, 'you honour me by requesting any favour. Ask me to be of any service, however great, and it is truly a privilege. Make any request – however impossible, I will rise to the challenge. But *sahib*, you are asking me to break a solemn oath which I swore on the grave of Jan Fishan Khan. Nearly twenty years have passed since I made my pledge. I have married since, and brought up two sons. I have forgotten – forced myself to forget – all that I knew. I am sorry.'

We sat in silence for several minutes. I understood Hafiz Jan's position and respected his sense of honour. The hush was awkward. Not because I felt any vein of condemnation – but because, selfishly, I wondered what to do next.

Again thanking God for bringing me to his home, the Pashtun whispered to his younger son to fetch the tea. I attempted to revive conversation by asking about trivial matters. Hafiz Jan did not answer. He was in deep thought.

A magenta porcelain Gardiner teapot, filled with *chai-i-sabs*, was brought from the kitchen. With great ceremony the tea was poured as if it were a magical potion. Only when he had swallowed three mouthfuls of green tea did Hafiz Jan speak.

'When you were eleven years old,' he said in a rather solemn tone, 'I came to your village in England. Together we practised many illusions and I explained how I had myself been a student of conjury.'

I nodded, rounding my lips upwards in a smile. When the Pashtun had seen that I was listening, he continued.

'Tahir Shah, when I was a child, I wanted to be the greatest stage magician in the world. I thought about nothing else. I dreamt, ate and talked nothing but illusion. My father thought I was insane, for no member of our family had ever been interested in such a subject before. A doctor was summoned. He looked deep into my eyes. Fearful that I had contracted some potent disease, he ran away. My parents grew more and more worried. They begged God for guidance.

'In the months that followed I searched for a teacher. Only after much hunting did I find a brilliant tutor at Ghaziabad. He was an expert illusionist and conjuror. He was reputed to be the finest of his kind in Asia. I stayed with him and learnt from him. But, as my father's eldest son, I knew I could never embark on a career in that profession.'

Hafiz Jan swallowed a second glass of tea in a single gulp.

'Do you understand?' he asked.

'Yes, I do.'

Then, as I resigned myself to the prospect of an early return to Europe, Hafiz Jan addressed me again.

'I have an idea,' he said. 'It is a humble, worthless idea, but you may consider it.'

'What is it?'

'In those days when I was fascinated with conjuring,' he said reflectively, 'I knew that nothing could satisfy my craving but hard study with a tutor.'

Faltering, as if resolving whether to continue, Hafiz Jan inched his way forward.

'My teacher . . .' he went on, 'left Ghaziabad many years ago. He travelled east and made his home there. I think he now lives in Calcutta. Go to him. He will teach you every trick and illusion ever devised. His name is Hakim Feroze.'

*   *   *   *

That evening another sumptuous meal was borne forth from the modest kitchen of Hafiz Jan. But my mind wasn't on food. I was considering the Pashtun's suggestion that I trace his own teacher. I would have preferred to remain at Burhana rather than embarking on what was sure to be a wild-goose chase. Even though the prospect of studying under such a renowned magician was intriguing, would he accept me as a pupil?

On each night that followed, as I deliberated harder, the feasts grew more opulent. The Pashtun insisted that every meal was another special occasion: honouring yet another battle which our forefathers had waged side by side. By the fourth night, the platters of *pilau* were so heavy that Hafiz Jan's sons could barely lift them. Beneath the great mounds of rice were buried whole marinated pigeons, an Afghan delicacy. On the fifth evening an entire roasted sheep was trundled in, still attached to the spit. The chunks of tender meat were served on a bed of special rice, flavoured with saffron, pine kernels and cardamoms.

On the sixth day my concern had almost reached fever pitch. Hafiz Jan's wife was now cooking day and night. I noticed she had dragged her bedding roll into the kitchen and was sleeping in there, too. The Pashtun's family would be bankrupted for generations if something were not done immediately. I pleaded with my hosts, begging them not to cook such absurd quantities of food. But when I questioned the catering arrangements, Hafiz Jan would rear up like a king cobra preparing to strike.

'How can we mere mortals not salute the triumphs of our ancestors?' he would demand.

I feared that Hafiz Jan might be tempted to replicate the fabled Muslim feast of his Bedouin antecedents. The meal, which is customary at great desert weddings, holds the world record for comestible extravagance. Cooked eggs are stuffed into fish, which are packed into whole chickens, which themselves are stuffed into a roasted ewe's carcass. The sheep is then crammed into the belly of a female camel and borne by stewards to the awaiting guests.

Unable to stand such rich food any longer, I sought refuge in the tranquil surroundings of Jan Fishan's shrine. A week of feasting under my belt, and I could at last consider the future of my journey. Hafiz Jan's teacher seemed more appealing all the time. Another week in Burhana and I would be unfit to walk. Although fearful that this man Feroze might have nothing to do with me, I vowed to travel eastwards to Calcutta.

As I sat in the doorway of the tomb, planning my next move, Hafiz Jan approached. He seemed restless. Before I could ask him what was wrong, he voiced his concerns:

'Tahir Shah,' he began with his characteristic greeting, 'I know that you have been thinking about my suggestion of Hakim Feroze.'

I nodded.

'I recommend him. He is an excellent tutor. Indeed, there's none finer . . . But beware!'

The Pashtun widened his eyes until they were as large as chestnuts. 'Feroze is a merciless teacher,' he said. 'If he accepts you, he'll crush you – that's his method. He expects his students to toil without rest . . . destroying them thrills him. Don't call on him unless you're certain this is what you really want.'

'But surely a simple course in stage magic would be harmless?'

Hafiz Jan's cheeks turned milky white, his eyes became bloodshot, and his lower jaw dropped in trepidation. I waited for his advice. As I did so, the Pashtun thrust his arms like rockets towards the sky.

'Are you out of your mind?' he bellowed. 'You have no idea who you're talking about! Hakim Feroze is no ordinary teacher. His training is no simple course for someone with a passing interest in conjury. It's not a *course* at all – it's a way of life . . . a tortuous regime – drill after drill under a sadist. As he torments those in his clutches, you wonder what act of insanity brought you to his door. Most of the time he makes you study absurd subjects. You hardly learn any "magic" when you're studying under him. Now that I think about it, you must *not* make contact with him. You are too precious to be mishandled by that man!'

'But respected Hafiz Jan,' I protested, 'I can't believe that your teacher – Hakim Feroze – could be so stern.'

The Pashtun cupped his head in his tremendous hands, and emitted a demonstrative shriek. I feared that recalling his former teacher had driven the man to hysteria.

'Hush!' he wailed. 'Hush . . . don't say another word and don't ever say that name aloud!'

'What name?'

'Hakim Feroze's name, of course!'

'Why? What's wrong with saying his name?'

Grooming his beard, Hafiz Jan peered to the left and to the right.

'*He* has spies, that's why. Feroze knows what everyone's doing. I may not be certain where he is at this very moment, but he certainly knows every minuscule detail of my life.'

'But you haven't been in touch with him for more than twenty years.'

'Irrelevant!' spat the Pashtun. 'Like I said, he's no ordinary mortal. He is a magician!'

Feroze sounded more like a monster than a master. Could he really be that bad? There was only one way to find out.

Again and again Hafiz Jan begged me to forget his 'foolish' suggestion. He strove to terrify me from engaging in the course. 'Spend one day with him and Feroze will turn your blood cold!' he would say. Or, 'He will tear you apart . . . that's his way. He thrives on others' misfortunes.'

The more counselling I received to turn back, the more I longed to go forward: to meet the Master, to meet Hakim Feroze.

I am not sure when it happened, but the point came at which Hafiz Jan ended his outbursts. He came to me late one morning, as the sun's rays rose up above the tomb of Jan Fishan. I had been reading at my usual spot in the shrine's doorway. Without a word, the Pashtun held out a clenched fist. The hand opened, revealing a ragged leather pouch. Inside was a curious reddish stone.

'I am giving this to you,' he said, 'as Feroze gave it to me. Present it to him and he'll believe I sent you.'

'What's this inside?'

'It's a *bezoar*.'

'What's that?'

Hafiz Jan held the stone to the light.

'A healer of poisons, an amulet, and the symbol of a searcher for knowledge – this *bezoar* is said to have come from the stomach of an eagle.'

As I tied the locket's leather thong around my neck, the Pashtun pulled me out beyond the enclosure's gates. There, on a large Afghan rug, a picnic lunch had been arranged. But this was no frivolous snack of crustless cucumber sandwiches. It was a meal of dangerous proportions.

Hafiz Jan dug both hands into the mound of rice, pulled out a charred waterfowl, and passed it to me, wincing. It seemed to be a mallard duck, its annual migration terminated by a hunter's gun.

'Khalifa Ashpaz!' cried the Pashtun, as he rammed the back end of another mallard into his mouth. 'Khalifa Ashpaz!' he called again. 'The famous master-chef of the Hindu Kush – this is his recipe!'

Four hours of eating came and went. By late afternoon, mutton, mallards, chickens and immeasurable quantities of *pilau* had been consumed. I wondered if I would ever need to eat again. By the end of the meal I felt exonerated of any further duty. Hafiz Jan had obviously gone mad. He had decided that we were both to eat ourselves to death. Determined to put an end to this insanity of feasting, I protested vehemently – the food had to stop before someone was injured.

Hafiz Jan stared at me. The furrows of his brow deepened. But then, grinning broadly, he wrung his hands together, exclaiming:

'*Imshab chi pukhta bekunem* – what shall we cook tonight?'

4

City of Light

The mere mention of the Farakka Express, which jerks its way eastward each day from Delhi to Calcutta, is enough to throw even a seasoned traveller into fits of apoplexy. At a desert encampment on Namibia's Skeleton Coast, a hard-bitten adventurer had downed a peg of local fire-water then told me the tale. Farakka was a ghost train, he said, haunted by ghouls, Thuggees, and thieves. Only a passenger with a death wish would go anywhere near it.

As I passed over a wad of rupee notes, the clerk at Delhi's railway booking office paused. Without looking up, he mumbled, 'Yamuna Express or Farakka Express?' The question was innocuous enough. But the locomotive's name had triggered a violent subconscious reaction. I started to choke uncontrollably.

The clerk asked again. The next man in the queue was nudging me to decide. '*Jaldi*! Hurry up!' As always happens in India when you're deliberating under duress, a crowd gathered. They took it in turns to call out suggestions: 'Farakka very nice,' said one, 'No, no, too noisy,' replied another. '*Sahib*, you like to buy handkerchief?' asked a third.

Apologising aloud to the Namibian adventurer, I whispered, 'Farakka Express, please.'

Later that afternoon I was installed in the second-class carriage, eager to begin the journey to Calcutta, in search of Hakim Feroze. With the *bezoar* locket hidden beneath my shirt, and a formal letter of introduction from Hafiz Jan, I felt that I was in with a real chance of securing the apprenticeship.

Peering around the compartment, I wondered what all the fuss had been about. The train seemed clean and orderly. Silly old travellers, I thought to myself, they deserve all they get. A knock from outside pulled me back to reality. The door slid away. A boot-boy with stark, beady eyes, dressed in a smart calamanco shirt, stood in its frame. In a single, expert movement, he scanned the cabin.

'Shoe cleaning, *Sahib*?'

'No thanks, I had them cleaned yesterday.'

'Dirty now, I do good job?'

He motioned in circles with a large patterned rag. I shook my head and he scurried back into the corridor, closing the door firmly behind him.

Ten minutes later, as the train was due to depart, the door slid back once again. A well-dressed couple entered and took their seats. The woman was wearing a fine crimson-coloured south Indian *sari*; her wrists were tinkling with glass bangles. Her hands and feet had been ornately decorated with *mehendi*. The extent of the pattern, like an exquisite filigree mesh, suggested she was recently married. Beside her sat a rather scrawny, unshaven figure – presumably the groom.

I broke the silence.

'Newly-weds?' I asked.

'Yes, we were married yesterday,' said the woman.

'You better be careful with your jewellery,' I warned. 'I've heard horrible stories about this train.'

'I told you,' the bride protested to her husband boisterously, 'we shouldn't have brought my trousseau!'

Unable to contain myself, I expounded the ill-favoured legends of the Farakka Express. I spoke of the ghouls, the Thuggee insurgents and the cunning thieves.

'The Farakka Express supposedly has its own breed of brigand,' I summed up. 'They even dress up in disguises – or pretend to be blind – to win the other passengers' sympathy.'

'Why did *you* take this train?' asked the bride.

'Well,' I said, 'I don't believe all that rubbish – look around. This train's as safe as anything. There's no getting me, I know all the tricks!'

At eight p.m. a modest vegetarian supper was supplied by a bearer. After a week of gigantic meaty meals, it was a positive delight.

The newly-weds cooed to each other lovingly as I wolfed down my vegetables. When I had finished, the bride peeled a ripe juicy *chakotra*. She offered me a segment. The perfect way to round off a meal. I accepted gratefully. As the section of fruit slid down my throat, I sprawled out on my bunk. Then, taking care to wish the kind-hearted couple a comfortable night, I fell into a deep trance-like sleep.

Just before dawn I woke up. The train had stopped at a station to pick up supplies. Still half-asleep, I foraged for my travel alarm clock. My fingers fumbled like a blind person reading Braille. The clock wasn't there. Expecting it to have fallen on to the floor, where I had left the smaller of my two cases, I peered down. The timepiece was not on the floor. Nor was the case. I lurched upwards. Wiping the sleep from my eyes, I called out to the newly-weds; had they too fallen victim to the vile curse of the Farakka Express?

But no one answered. The newly married couple were gone.

Five minutes later, I was huddled on the floor in a ball, my legs hugged up beneath my chin, my hands over ears, my face pressing in against my stomach. My passport, most of my money, and half my luggage were gone. I thanked God that the *bezoar* locket was still fastened around my neck, and that the letter of introduction in Hafiz Jan's hand had not been stolen.

The Farakka Express sped towards the rising sun. I shunned the breakfast when it came. And when, at Allahabad, a new passenger entered the compartment, I shunned him, too. Screwing up my face miserably, I gazed out at the agricultural heartland of Uttar Pradesh. Workers were already toiling away, sprinkled across the landscape like peppercorns on a sheet of cloth. Some were busy winnowing grain, others combing ploughs through the sienna-red soil, straight-backed, carrying water-pots on heads, or dragging great spiders of kindling homeward.

I would have continued to stare at the paddy fields and palm-thatch houses, but I sensed the cabin's new passenger watching me. Twisting round, I gawked back at him. His stout frame was topped by an egg-shaped head. Its face, rough as a loofah, was dominated by overgrown mustachios. His hair was matted with dirt, his clothes were tattered as a scarecrow's. The figure emitted an odour similar to ripe Camembert.

Rather than glancing away as I scrutinised him, the man gaped back. We leered into each other's eyes like duelling hypnotists. Neither blinked. Tears rolled down my cheeks as I strained to carry on.

'Been robbed, have you?' asked the man, swivelling abruptly to face the window.

'How did you guess that?'

'Remember what train you're on. This is the Farakka Express – or don't you know the legend of the Farakka Express?'

'I know all about this bloody train, thank you very much!'

'How did it happen?'

'I think I was drugged.'

'Was it fruit or Bengali sweets?'

'Fruit.'

'*Chakotra* or banana?'

'*Chakotra.*'

'Clever stuff,' hissed the man. 'The taste masks diazepam very well indeed.'

'I feel so stupid. Especially as I'd been warning the couple about the dangers of this train. They must be paralysed with laughter.'

Rising to his feet, the man opened the cabin door and leant out into the corridor. He seemed to be examining its outer glass.

'Before the train left Delhi Junction,' he said quizzically, 'did a shoe cleaner come by?'

I agreed that one had.

'How did you know that?'

The man pushed the tip of his right index finger towards me. On the end was an ochre-brown smear.

'The shoe cleaner was in league with the fruit person,' the man explained. 'It's teamwork. First the boot-boy comes scouting for suitable prey. Seeing that you were a lone foreigner, he marked the door with a shoe polish thumbprint. The person with the drugged *chakotra* just follows the trail.'

'Ingenious,' I said weakly.

'Brilliant!' he corrected. 'But then again, I wouldn't expect anything less than brilliance on the Farakka Express.'

In the hours that followed, the portly, moustached passenger opposite revealed much to me. A private detective by profession – known as 'Vatson' to his friends – he put the myth of the Farakka Express down to a few simple scams.

'Well before a train linked Delhi to Calcutta, the route was lined with thieves,' he noted. 'Between these two important cities is Varanasi: holiest place in Hinduism. For three thousand years con-men of all kinds were drawn there. Everyone knows that pilgrims are trusting, naïve and easily duped.'

'Do they?'

'Of course,' said Vatson sharply. 'Look at your own situation. Although well aware of the dangers of this train, you were letting down your guard. Newly-weds, you thought. Instead of thinking, *How sweet*, you should have been thinking, *Newly-weds: can't trust them as far as you can throw them*!'

'Well, how do I know that I can trust *you*?' I asked.

'You don't,' said Vatson. 'You're learning already.'

A restless interval passed as I contemplated the problems caused by the grand theft.

'*Chakotra* fruit,' snapped the detective, clasping his cheeks after ten minutes of silence. '*How* could you have fallen for that one?'

'I was expecting far more sinister con-men,' I said defensively, puzzled that a complete stranger should be so reproachful.

Vatson was unimpressed at my gullibility. He seemed unable to discern that I required comfort not condemnation.

'Do you know how modern trickery developed in India?' he asked bluntly.

I shook my head.

'Thugs!' he clamoured. '*Phansigars*, "People of the Noose", "the Deceivers": they're the ancestors of these small-time charlatans. Theirs was a great tradition – it's sad to think they've been reduced to such pitiable acts of thievery.'

'This was a heist of considerable ingenuity,' I responded.

But the detective wasn't listening.

'Thuggee was a cult dedicated to ritual murder, in honour of the goddess Kali,' he declared. 'You see, Thugs considered murder an art form. They felt no guilt about killing.'

'How many people did they actually kill?'

Vatson cracked the knuckles of his left hand.

'Millions!' he cried out. 'Millions at least! In those days journeys were taking months, even years. By the time you realised your dearly beloved was late home, there was nothing to do!'

'So what happened to all the Thugs, then?'

'The Britishers realised they were destroying the country. You couldn't travel anywhere. The roads were far too dangerous to use. Then a chap called Sleeman set about wiping them out. Bit of a pity really. He taught himself Ramasi, the secret Thug language, and worked out their formula for death.'

'What formula was that?'

'Number One,' cooed Vatson: 'never let any member of a party escape alive – strangle them all with a *rumaal*, a knotted handkerchief. Number Two: always decapitate the victims, to make identification impossible. But most important, Number Three . . . prepare!

'Thugs would follow an intended victim for months, sometimes even years. They dispatched scouts, just like the boot-black who was sent ahead to find you. Then they would gain the trust of the servants by posing as holy men. But within thirty years they'd been broken. You

Britishers got them off knotting handkerchiefs, and on to knotting carpets. They made lovely rugs.'

Shortly before noon my jinxed passage on the Farakka Express came to an end. The prospect of spending another uncertain night on the train disturbed me. Resolving instead to leave with what few possessions I had left, I climbed down at Mughal Sarai, the alighting point for Varanasi. After reporting the loss of my passport and money, I would continue to Calcutta by road.

Vatson disembarked at the same station. He claimed to be on an undercover mission for a client in Allahabad. We shared an Ambassador taxi. As the ramshackle vehicle trundled the short distance towards the holiest city in India, Vatson divulged the most private details of his assignment.

'I used to get much more interesting cases,' he began despondently. 'Once I even had a murder case – I enjoyed that. But these days work is so humdrum. Most cases are involving checking if a groom's family have any skeletons in their cupboard.'

'What if you find any?'

'Show the boy's side have skeletons,' said Vatson, 'and the dowry gets reduced.'

Before we reached Varanasi – fabled 'City of Light' – the private eye disclosed, in a deafening voice, that he was now to assume a disguise and go to ground.

*　　*　　*　　*

For three thousand years, and longer, Varanasi has been the centre of the Hindu faith. Nestling on the western banks of the sacred River Ganges, the city attracts millions of pilgrims each year. Some stay a few days, praying and bathing in the waters of Mother Ganga. Others, once arrived, will never leave. They believe that to die within the boundaries of the ancient city – marked by the Panch Kosi Road – is to secure *moksha*, enlightenment. This state, of direct ascendance to Heaven, releases one from the perpetual cycle of reincarnation. Each day, thousands of pious Hindus are cremated on the banks of the Ganges at the 'burning' *ghats*, steep stone steps which lead down to the river. As the eerie silence of dusk descends across it, the ashes of the dead are scattered upon the sacred waters.

Walking through the labyrinth of back lanes, teeming with *sadhus* and mendicants, mischievous children and water buffalo, I heard the sound of coins jingling on a beggar's palm; the thumping of a funereal drum, and the cries of a cycle *rickshawalla* hurrying through. I smelled the sizzling *puris* on makeshift stalls, the heaps of turmeric, cinnamon and coriander, and the moist dung patties drying on shadowed walls.

Symbols were all around: swastikas painted above hidden doorways, *ghee* lamps burning at miniature shrines, and dense sandalwood smoke hanging like a thundercloud above the musty passages.

I probed forward little by little. Everyone but me understood the symbolism, everyone else knew the etiquette. Unable to grasp the inner meaning of it all, I was affected all the same. India's is the most refined, well-practised theatre of life, and Varanasi is the pre-eminent act on its stage.

*   *   *   *

I set off to the Dhobi Ghat where, I had heard, affordable accommodation could be found. After a night on the Farakka Express, lodgings at Varanasi would have to be cut-price. But the Dhobi Ghat had no guest houses at all. As the word *dhobi* – 'laundry' – suggests, the *ghat* is where the washing is done. Dozens of men were kneading clothes like great balls of soda-bread dough. They hurled the lathered laundry in time with each other on the steps of the *ghat*. Fifty thousand Brahmins live at Varanasi. Many employ special *dhobis* to do their washing, as it guarantees their clothes are kept apart from those of the lower castes.

One of the *dhobis* saw me looking around for a hostel and came over to where I was standing. His face was flat as a shovel, his nose splayed out towards each ear, and his arms were reddened, scalded to the elbows by his trade. When I asked if he knew of a place to stay, he led me to his own one-room home.

Resembling an upturned coracle in size and shape, the gloomy wattle-and-daub dwelling was thick with steam. Once inside, the *dhobi* motioned to a horsehair mattress and smirked.

'*Das rupia.*'

'Ten rupees a night for *this*?'

I examined the mattress. Rotting, flea-infested, and positioned beside a kettle, in which a Brahmin's shirt was boiling, it was the best feature of the room. A great deal of steam was generated by the constant cooking of clothes. The vapour had led to considerable rot. The decay was so extensive that I suspected it was actually holding the place up. Scrape away the rot and the walls would have caved in.

The lodgings were grim by any standards – far more basic, I mused, than those required for POWs by the Geneva Convention. But then, as the *dhobi* waited for an answer, I remembered that I was no prisoner of war. I might have feared my belongings would be filched, but I had very little of value left to steal.

'All right,' I said to the laundry-landlord, 'I'll take it, but I'm only doing it as a self-imposed penance – like Thomas à Becket's lice-infested horsehair shirt beneath his robe. While I think of it,' I joked, 'Becket would have been rather at home here.'

The *dhobi* had understandably lost my drift long before. He spoke no English. Grinning again, he licked his fingers and rubbed them together, indicating that payment was due in advance. I fished out a crumpled note and passed it over.

Outside the room, a few feet from the Ganges, a young *sadhu* was squatting. His naked body was caked in fresh ash; his hair was a mass of matted dreadlocks, his face painted with esoteric symbols. The *dhobi* greeted the holy man with respectful salutations. But the salutation was not returned. Instead, the godman took up his *chilam*, and inhaled deeply. The *chilam*'s embers glowed brightly for a moment, before the mystic puffed out a turbid cloud of marijuana smoke.

Later that afternoon, after being almost boiled alive when bathing in the *dhobi*'s great cauldron, I roamed around Varanasi.

A bank located in the foyer of a plush hotel agreed to help me have money transferred. For some inexplicable reason the funds had to be collected at their other branch, in Calcutta. After the bank, I proceeded to the police station to report the train robbery. It was a humiliating experience as thirty officers of all ranks crowded round to hear another tale of the Farakka Express.

Shortly before dusk I walked through the slender bazaars which lead down to the *ghats*, at the water's margin.

Down a secluded lane, off a larger passageway, I came across a series of cramped workshops. Huddled like hunchbacks over looms, sat a number of women. Some were young – in their early twenties – yet most were elderly and frail. They were all dressed in simple white *saris*; none wore jewellery. Some had shaven heads. I had heard of these forgotten women: the widows of Kashi.

Considered by most as untouchable, frequently regarded as witches, widows are outcasts in Hinduism. Disaster is said to befall anyone who talks with them. Thrown out by their families, shunned by their closest friends, thousands of widows journey to Varanasi each year to live out their days. Most will not consider suicide, for self-immolation will destroy their hope of attaining their dream of enlightenment.

Strolling about the busy passageways of the city, or sitting down by the steep steps of the *ghats*, you see them. They are everywhere. Some with cup in hand; others too proud to beg. A few take up employment. Those who do work toil long hours in sweat-shops for a fraction of the going rate. As if labouring in such conditions were not enough, many are raped or abused by unscrupulous employers.

At one of the looms crouched a young woman. Stony-faced and timid, with hennaed fingertips, a pronounced nose, and a crescent scar on her chin, she struggled to keep up with the other weavers. Her name was Devika. Married when she was thirteen to a man twenty-two years her senior, she became a widow young. When her husband died three years ago she was chased out of the house by her mother-in-law, who said she was a witch.

Like all the other widows at Varanasi, Devika, who was now twenty-three, longed for the day when God would call her to Paradise. In a society where widows rarely remarry, she knew that Varanasi could be her home for decades to come.

Ironically, widows are a relatively new sight in India. Until 1828, when the British outlawed the practice of *sati*, a widow would perish on her husband's funeral pyre. Although barbaric, the repulsive practice provided an immediate solution. Since sati's abolition, widows have journeyed like lost souls to the 'City of Light'. Once installed on the banks of the Ganges, they begin a new existence: a life waiting for natural death.

'My mother-in-law sold my belongings,' confided Devika, making sure her employer was not around. 'She gave me a third-class ticket to Varanasi. She swore if I ever returned, she would blind me.'

Her hazel eyes staring in concentration at the floor, Devika remembered the ordeal.

'When I arrived here it was as if I was a leper. People spat at me or shouted insults. Mothers whispered to their children, "Don't look at her, she is diseased!" I thank God for providing me with a job here. Of course it's hard work,' she added, 'but it is work. Each night I pray to Him to let me die soon.'

Would Devika ever marry again? Humoured by the inane question, she grinned.

'How could I wed a second time?' she asked in bewilderment. 'No, that's impossible. I am a widow.'

*   *   *   *

Darkness falls suddenly over Varanasi. As the widows' looms clapped away like crude printing presses in the candlelight, the back-streets bustled with new energy. It is after dusk that Kashi's ancient magic comes alive. With the silk merchants and barber shops shuttered up for the night, an endless procession of pilgrims issues forth. Barefoot, stooped and half-blind, they hurry to the great congregation of *mandirs*, temples, located in the tapering trails and along the waterfront.

Gas lamps hissing with fluorescent flames move forward on padded heads; the pungent scent of *mogra* flowers mingles with the shuffling of feet and the pealing of temple bells. Like a rendition of a Shakespeare play, the words and actions are known by all. Tight as a knot, the mélange of pilgrims, priests and sacred cattle divide for a moment to allow a funeral cortège by. The corpse, bound in a saffron-yellow shawl, is borne on a bamboo litter down to the Jalasayin, 'Burning Ghat'.

With impressive precision, the pallbearers negotiate their charge through an airport-style metal detecting frame. The haphazard contraption, decorated abundantly with orange garlands, was originally installed to deter terrorists from bombing Varanasi's Golden Temple. Long since out of order, the metal detector has assumed an alternative, religious role. Pilgrims hustling to the Golden Temple stumble with cringing reverence through the ornamented frame – perhaps believing that the transition bestows benediction upon them.

On a platform at the water's edge, more than a dozen funeral pyres send sparks crackling into the brisk night air. Behind them, great crests of timber – chopped into uniform lengths – lie ready for use.

Enlightenment, and the death which comes before it, is the primary business of Varanasi. But unlike elsewhere, death here is a wondrous, cheering event, so different from the Western preoccupation with hearses and tail-coated undertakers, shuffling forward in sensible shoes. There are no long faces, coffins, gravestones, cemeteries, or dramatic black veils. Instead, there's a pragmatic acceptance of what is simply transition.

The body is carried forth. A quantity of timber is weighed out and paid for. When the pyre is constructed, the corpse is positioned. The sacred fire is applied. Only when the ashes have cooled are they gathered up and cast into the black waters of Mother Ganga.

Affected by the subtle simplicity of the Burning Ghat, I made my way, by boat, home to the *dhobi*'s flea-infested bed. Little bigger than a canoe, the craft was more usually hired by grieving families. In the bows a hunched figure strained at the oars, his long ivory beard tied in a granny-knot. As we cut through the sacred waters, illuminated by a thousand bobbing leaf-boat lamps, I looked back. Funeral pyres lit up the night. Ferocious with life, raging like forest fires, the mountains of flame licked upward. It was a breathtaking salutation to the dead.

The *dhobi* simpered through broken teeth when I tried to explain my adventure at the Jalasayin Ghat. He handed me a mug of murky grey Ganga water with which to rinse my mouth. Then he pouffed the home-made pillow; a pile of dirty clothes wrapped in a sheet.

As I reclined on the vile bed I felt virtuous. It was a fine feeling, one that was quite new to me. No wonder Thomas à Becket had so relished his lice shirt. Perhaps I would do penances more often, I thought. Then, as I closed my eyes to imagine the blazing funeral pyres . . . the mattress' savage night-life began to feast.

By five a.m. the *dhobi* was already hard at work, boiling up another kettle of Brahmin clothes. Pulling the sheet around me like a toga, I sat up. It was still dark outside. A paraffin lamp provided a haze of platinum light. The *dhobi* seemed pleased I was awake. He handed me a neatly folded stack of clothes. Somehow, during the night, he had managed to wash and press my shirt, trousers, socks and even my underpants. They smelt of cinnamon. When I thanked him he crumpled up his nose, snorted twice, and grabbed my pillow, which was the next load of laundry.

Then, stooping over the cast-iron urn, he fished out a sock. Taking considerable care, he emptied out its contents – three very hard-boiled eggs.

As the darkness was gradually edged out by the first glimmer of light, I noticed a procession of women wending down to the water. Barefoot, and cloaked in plain white *saris*, they moved with slow, deliberate steps through the morning chill. Once at a secluded spot on the riverbank, they cleansed their bodies in the sacred Ganges.

With their bathing at an end, the widows seemed to pause in silent prayer. Immersed in the first rays of amber light, they stood motionless, their arms stretched towards the sun, as if supplicating God to summon them to Paradise.

*   *   *   *

Leaving Varanasi was remarkably difficult. Millions of people in all corners of India would do anything to visit the city. No one deserts Kashi unless pressing business elsewhere forces them to do so. After less than a day in town I found myself falling victim to traveller's inertia. My great plans of apprenticeship seemed to be ebbing away. I had been drugged, robbed, and was now holed up with a *dhobi*. What had happened to my dreams of studying magical science? Coming to, I remembered my priorities. Next day I would hurry on to Calcutta.

Enlivened by the decision, I trekked over to the Panchganga Ghat to dangle my feet in its water. With the ashes of countless dead flung into it – not to mention the half-charred bodies – you'd expect the Ganges to be filthy. Pilgrims and locals bathe in the river every day. They even drink Ganga water, considering it to be less tainted than the purest mountain stream. But given the abounding pollution, why aren't its devotees dropping like flies? Scientists may have discovered the reason. They say the Ganges has the ability to re-oxygenate and cleanse itself. When cholera microbes were put in a sample of Ganga water, they died within three hours. Put in a sample of distilled water, the same microbes lived for twenty-four hours. Sailors have long recognised the water's ability to stay fresh. Until recently, ships setting sail from Calcutta would stock up with as much Ganga water as they could carry.

When Jaipur's Maharajah Sawai Madho Singh II travelled to England in 1902, he commissioned two colossal silver amphora to be built. Considered to be the largest single silver objects in the world – holding almost two thousand gallons each – they were filled with the river's sacred waters and taken along.

At Panchganga Ghat I splashed about up to my shins in the hope of drowning some of the fleas. But the sense of sheer pleasure quickly turned to horror. A severed, badly charred human hand was floating my way. I tried to calm myself. As I did so, there was a tap on my shoulder. A plump robed figure held up a bottle of cloudy water and, in a thick accent, exclaimed:

'Saheeb, neyes Gaangaa varter . . . gut foor drinkeeng. Pifteeen rupee onlee.'

'No.' I recoiled. 'Leave me alone, I've just had a nasty shock.'

I looked away, but the tap came again.

This time, ready to berate the salesman, I turned round to face him. Pulling off his robe, I realised he was no salesman. It was Vatson Private Eye. He was in deep disguise.

'How did you know I was here?'

'What do you expect? I'm a detective!'

Vatson told me to lace up my shoes. A strange performance was about to begin. Still shaken by the experience with the severed hand, I was slower than usual on my feet.

'What's this all about, Vatson?' I asked, as we made haste through the endless maze of back lanes.

'You'll be seeing soon enough.'

'Did you dig up any skeletons in that family's closet?'

'Not an entire skeleton,' said Vatson, smiling. 'A skull, a few ribs . . . but not the whole thing yet. It will be needing a little more time.'

We scrambled aboard a bicycle rickshaw. Vatson directed the driver to the Rani Ghat. As the rickshaw rattled ahead, Vatson reported on the case at hand.

'Research is going well,' he began. 'This stakeout is going to take about two months. We've been busy checking all sorts of things.'

'Like what?'

'Oh, the usual,' retorted the sleuth casually. 'Whether the groom's school diplomas are the real McCoy; if he's seeing any other girls, or if he has any repulsive moles, warts, genital growths. You know . . .'

'Well, I'm not sure that I do.'

'Then we have to check for family feuds, criminal records, secret debts, drug addictions, hereditary abnormalities, unwanted half-brothers . . .'

Vatson broke off abruptly, and commanded the driver to stop. He led me to a deserted area behind the Rani Ghat. It seemed as if a building had recently been cleared from the land. A family of rag-pickers were recovering any odds and ends hidden under the stray bricks.

Sitting at the centre of the ground was a *sadhu*. He was in deep meditation.

His face was haggard, probably before its time. His beard was tangled and oyster-grey; his hands were weathered with ridges; his costume was nothing more than a *lungi* and a string of coral beads. Beside his right foot was the cranium of a human skull.

The object explained a great deal. The man was an Aghori *sadhu*. My interest in the trophy heads of the Naga head-hunters had led me to the Aghoris. Their beliefs are close to those of traditional shamans. The Aghoris, said to have the power to overcome evil spirits, were traditionally confirmed cannibals. Their libations, which once included human blood, are drunk from the bowl of a human skull. But to an Aghori, the skull is far more than a simple drinking vessel. It contains the spirit of the deceased. The soul remains the Aghori's prisoner until the skull is cremated. Such *jinns*, spirits, are tamed and put to work by the *sadhu* in his world of shadows.

The detective motioned for me to step closer to the holy man.

'What's he here for? What's going to happen?'

'Just watch.'

The ascetic continued to sit cross-legged in meditation. A few minutes later another man appeared, dug a shallow hole in the earth with his hands, and left. We continued to wait. A modest crowd, about fifteen people, turned up and circled around the Aghori. They appeared to know exactly what was going on. The godman stirred from his trance and rose to his feet. Then, having wrapped a rag shirt around his head, he leant over and pushed it into the hole. Sand was carefully filled in around the head, with the *sadhu* now balancing upside-down.

'Vatson, what's happening?'

'The Aghori is going into hibernation,' said the sleuth.

'Why?'

'Why not?' said Vatson.

'Human hibernation . . . I've heard about this . . . it's all an illusion!' I shouted.

Vatson gave me a stern look.

'I know it's illusion,' he whispered, 'but be quiet.'

An hour passed. The crowd watched the *pandit's* upturned body with great concentration. Another hour went by. A pye dog was warded away with a stick when it made a run for the Aghori's drinking skull.

After another hour of waiting I was mad with boredom. At last Vatson turned to me.

'Did you notice that very fine, dry sand was being filled in around the Aghori's face?'

'Yes, I did, it was different from the earth around it.'

'Exactly: look closely, and you'll see that the ground here is clay. The hole was filled with dry sand. The *sadhu* can breathe through it.'

Four hours after his hibernation had begun, the Aghori suddenly pulled his head from its sand-filled hole. He unwound the cloth from his face and took a sip of water from the skull. Vatson and I might not have been persuaded, but the crowd was visibly moved by the feat.

As Vatson Private Eye led me away, I told him about the most famous of all human hibernations, which I had once heard about.

In the 1830s, fabulous tales of hibernation came from a remote mountain community near Jammu. They told of a slight, dainty man with calculating eyes, named Haridas, and this soon reached the ears of the Maharajah of Lahore.

The Maharajah, who was a sceptic, sent for Haridas, requesting that he perform his feat under controlled test conditions. Haridas arrived, and the experiment began.

Various distinguished English physicians and soldiers were present at the Maharajah's palace. At the initial examination, one of the doctors noticed that Haridas had cut away the muscles beneath his tongue, allowing him to push it backwards, sealing his throat. In the days preceding the burial, Haridas took hot baths up to his armpits, flushed out his bowels, and consumed only milk and yoghurt.

The day before the burial, he swallowed a piece of linen, thirty yards long. Officials and courtiers looked on in stupefaction as, before their eyes, Haridas withdrew the bandage, dislodging any remaining material from his digestive tract.

At last, preparing himself for hibernation, Haridas sat in the lotus position, sealed up his nostrils and ears with dainty wax plugs, closed up his throat with his flipped-back tongue, and folded his arms.

His pulse was no longer traceable, and the European physicians were already at a loss for words. Haridas was placed in a great chest, fastened with a padlock embossed with the Maharajah's own seal.

The trunk was carried out ceremoniously into the palace gardens, a cavity was dug, the box was lowered down, and the hole was filled with earth. As a further precaution, a crop of barley was planted above where the hibernating *sadhu* lay. A towering wall was constructed around the entire area. Palace sentries guarded the spot day and night.

Forty days passed. The court was rife with anticipation. With the courtiers unable to stand the suspense any longer, the Maharajah gave the order for the wall, the barley and the soil to be removed. The chest was hauled from the hole, and the padlock was smashed away. Hesitantly, the box's lid was opened. To everyone's amazement, the godman was alive, sitting in the same position as when buried more than a month before.

A doctor removed the nostril and ear plugs, pulled the ascetic's tongue forward into position, and breathed air into his lungs. Within an hour he was as fit as ever before.

Haridas was lauded by the Maharajah, who presented him with a handful of diamonds. The people of Lahore rejoiced in the streets and followed the *sadhu* wherever he went. Further public hibernations took place in cities across India. Haridas became a celebrity, shunning his simple clothes for more resplendent attire.

Wined and dined, and courted by high society, Haridas forgot his humble birth. When complaints accumulated that the godman had seduced a number of high-ranking ladies, it was too much for the government. Haridas was sent back to his mountain village, and was never heard from again.

I asked Vatson for his impressions.

He thought hard for a few seconds. Then, looking me in the eye, and screwing up his face, he barked:

'Poppycock!'

5

Waiting Out the Jinns

Kipling called the Grand Trunk Road 'such a river of life as nowhere else exists in the world', and he was spot on.

Carving a route from Calcutta westwards, to the wilds of the Hindu Kush, the G.T. – pronounced 'Geetee' – is not for the faint-hearted. My decision to continue to West Bengal by bus was one inspired by lunacy. What kind of deranged simpleton would give up the gentle rocking of a locomotive for the jarring, back-breaking ride of an Indian bus? This was a question I asked myself many times, as the antique vehicle of the Express Bus Company strained to reach its cruising speed of nine miles an hour.

Seething forward in a savage whirlwind race to the finish line, the maelstrom was thick and furious. There were bullock carts loaded with towers of sugar cane, buses with passengers swinging from the windows; Ashok Leyland trucks piled high with baskets of rotting fish, cows with nowhere else to go; petrol tankers steered by chain-smoking drivers; taxis and rickshaws, steam-rollers and articulated lorries; a full travelling circus, complete with a wagon of clowns, a convoy of elephants, a cohort of cyclists with their families riding pillion; and a man on crutches trying to keep up. At the eye of the tornado's vortex, helpless amid the intense black fog of diesel fumes and blaring klaxon horns, was the Express bus.

After forty fearful hours, with other passengers and me bent double in the crash-landing position, the vehicle rumbled into Calcutta. I half-expected a welcoming committee, a brass band, and a commandant with medals of valour for each survivor's chest. But no one noticed us arrive. The bus slid to a halt in a lay-by on the banks of the Hoogly River. Before being spewed out, I patted the driver on the back and saluted. He was a man with iron nerves. Like comrades in a forgotten war, we now shared a special bond. I gathered my few belongings together and heard the other passengers murmuring, 'Geetee always drives someone crazy!'

* * * *

Calcutta has spectacular over-employment. In the West, where we're obsessed with slashing the numbers of workers for the sake of it, we drool at the idea of more, faster computers, fewer humans. But as we struggle to adopt an ever-changing technology, we lose sight of the satisfaction that only a finely tuned human system can provide.

As I toured the city's municipal bastions in search of Feroze, I marvelled at just how many people were engrossed with work. The General Post Office, situated on the site of the infamous Black Hole, is a splendid place. The Renaissance dome, Corinthian colonnades and traces of Baroque adorn what is an imposing building. Yet far more impressive is the postal system itself. Purchase a postage stamp, and the extended machine of clerks activates.

The first clerk calls out to the next customer in the queue, the second listens to the customer's order, the third writes it down, the fourth weighs the envelope in his hand, the fifth checks the price for that weight, the sixth explains to the seventh which stamp to select from the stamp folder, the eighth tears out the right stamp, the ninth applies glue to its underside, the tenth affixes it to the envelope, the eleventh takes the customer's money, and the twelfth makes out the receipt.

Heartened by such a meticulous procedure, I hailed a taxi and directed its crew to the bank, where I had arranged to collect my money. In Calcutta, the driver has an assistant who interacts with the customer. Sitting in the front passenger seat, he also navigates, takes the money, mumbles pleasantries and maintains the taxi's dashboard shrine. I reclined in the back seat safe in the hands of professionals. The hulk of a car veered into the fray like a battle tank on manoeuvres.

As we swerved from one lane to the next, I took a moment to inspect the lavish dashboard shrine. Crafted with rare workmanship, it possessed multiple moving parts. The centrepiece was a foot-high golden figurine of Kali, weighed down by garlands of skulls. Six cleaver-wielding arms flagellated rhythmically in time with the taxi's 1970s disco sounds. Every nine seconds the mouth of the black-faced goddess flew open. Like some fiendish cuckoo-clock from Hell, she retched crimson blood-like dye down her torso. A miniature receptacle at the base of the statuette collected the liquid, which was then pumped back to the mouth. Excellent stuff, I meditated, as the driver and his

subordinate swayed their heads to 'Night Fever', I wondered how many
people were involved in making that.

As he handed over the money, the bank manager suggested I search for
Feroze at Kalighat, Calcutta's temple of Kali. It seemed a peculiar place
to look but, being new in town, I took his advice.

With its rounded domes, lines of jostling beggars, widows, and
pilgrims with shaven heads, you might expect Kalighat to be like any
other of India's temples. But rather than being a sanctuary designed to
celebrate life, Kalighat is dedicated to venerating death. The overriding
association with Kali ought to have hinted it was no place to find
Hakim Feroze.

Non-Hindus are forbidden from entering Kalighat. But I went
unchallenged, proceeding through a low doorway into the main
courtyard. The first sight to greet me was that of infertile women tying
oyster-sized stones to the branches of an enchanted cactus. The
procedure is said to make any barren woman bear a child.

Despite the life-giving plant, a sense of gruesome debauchery hung
like a curtain over the shrine. Glaring images of Kali scrutinised every
footstep. Garlanded with decapitated heads of the vanquished, and
feasting on human blood, Kali's voluptuous form is far more ghoulish
than anything Hollywood has ever dreamt up. Her tongue hangs out,
lusting for death; her ten hands wield executioners' swords; and her
large, bloodthirsty eyes hypnotise her foes.

The temple was constructed in 1809 on the site of a former shrine.
Hindu scriptures tell that it was built at the exact spot where one of
Kali's toes fell to Earth. It was here that Thugs would pray before
rambling off to strangle unsuspecting travellers.

In one corner of the courtyard a goat was being tempted to a simple
enclosure with some lush leaves. The animal chewed away at the
foliage, green-eyed and trusting, content as all goats are. Greed
blinkered it to the garnet-red goat blood in which it was standing. But
even if the creature had attempted an escape, odds were against it.
Within seconds, an executioner's hand tilted its head east, and clamped
it tightly in a vice. The glint of a blade followed. Before it could bleat in
protest, the goat was dead.

At a second enclosure, opposite the first, a pair of butchers hacked up
the meat. Heaped at their feet like a pile of bloodied boots were the goat
heads.

Up to two dozen sacrifices to Kali are made at the shrine daily. Until
the last century, human immolations formed an important part of the

temple's busy routine. Before an animal is slain, a devotion is offered in honour of the mighty goddess – consisting of milk, blended with Ganga water and *bhang*, cannabis paste. The goat, or other offering, is washed and garlanded with *jabba* flowers, red hibiscus, before it's sacrificed. Then, as the ritualistic knife is made ready, the devotee whispers a prayer into the goat's ear. The message is taken directly to Kali by the goat's soul.

I suspected the bank manager had been well aware that Kalighat was a red herring of the most bloodthirsty kind. Splendid, I mused as I made my escape from the macabre shrine. Practical joking is very much alive in this town. I think I'll enjoy it here.

*   *   *   *

For five days I did nothing but hunt Feroze.

Calcutta is a large city, but within a week I felt certain I was searching for someone who did not exist. Had Hafiz Jan been wrong in directing me to Calcutta? Or had Feroze moved elsewhere? Both were strong possibilities. Yet I knew very well such questions were liable to remain unanswered.

I suspected that the harder I pursued him, the less likely I was to come across Hakim Feroze. In honoured tradition, the *jinns* had obviously seen me engaged in the chase. Having a bit of fun, as *jinns* like to do, they had hidden Feroze from me. In time, a virtuous spirit would pull back the shroud and reveal the teacher. Meanwhile, I would have to wait out the *jinns*.

Avoiding a tram rattling towards me like a hopper at a coal head, I crossed the road and turned left on to College Street. Famous for its hundreds of bookstalls, College Street must be the largest graveyard on Earth for out-of-date books. Faded by the sun, dampened by monsoon deluges, and eroded by the continuous abrasion of city life, all the books on sale have seen better days. I ferreted about in the skyscraper stacks. Half the books found on College Street are concerned with lost programming languages of early computers. The other half are romance. I inched my way down the central promenade and stumbled into the Mills & Boon Bazaar. Tussling over the squared-edge piles, businessmen and schoolgirls, office clerks and taxi drivers were searching zealously for a racy romantic read.

Peeking up from a disintegrating copy of *A Chance Encounter*, a stall-holder in the Mills & Boon Bazaar suggested I have coffee at his beloved haunt. Guide books like to tell you that the Albert Hall is Calcutta's answer to a café on Paris' Left Bank. It's a nice line which once – very long ago – might have been true.

Albert Hall Coffee Shop is a square second-floor room, where a high ceiling and steep walls hide beneath a thick layer of powdery soot. A score of antique fans rotate in slow motion, their sharp rounded blades slicing the air like scimitars. Inside the Albert Hall there were no vivacious intellectuals, debating important issues of the day. Nor was there the impenetrable silver smoke of Gauloises. The twenty or so tables were empty. Empty, that is, except for a single elderly, hunchbacked man at one end of the room, who was mounting stamps in an album.

The figure seemed lonely, a feeling which disturbed me. So I went over to his corner table and sat down. The hunchback's head was round, like an orb, his clothing shabby, ingrained with Calcutta's own indescribable blend of pollution. His complexion was so waxy it reflected the chipped pearl-blue vinyl tabletop over which he was leaning.

'Those are nice stamps,' I said admiringly.

'What? What is it you're saying?' replied the man, who appeared to be hard of hearing.

'I said those stamps are nice. Very colourful.'

I hoped to endear myself to the gentleman through praise.

'What stamps?'

We seemed to be having trouble getting a conversation going.

'The ones in your album . . . those ones are very nice and colourful . . . Brazilian, aren't they?'

'Oh, like stamps, do you?'

Marvellous, I thought, he's getting the hang of it. There's no stopping us now.

'Yes, I like stamps very much. Do you like stamps?'

The man's expression suddenly turned from one of angelic tenderness to one of extreme acerbity.

'No!' he bellowed. 'I hate stamps. Think they're wretched little things.'

'Then what are you collecting them for?'

'This isn't *my* album,' the hunchback confessed, lighting a cigarette. 'It's my friend's. He's in the lavatory.'

At that moment, a tall figure, suave as a toreador, with strong Pashtun features and turtle-green eyes, returned to the table and sat down. His zinc-grey hair was sculpted back with lavender brilliantine;

his face was clean-shaven, save for a neatly clipped moustache. Over a white sailcloth shirt, he wore a tan waistcoat, its last button undone. His fine beige twill-woven trousers, and expertly polished Oxfords, hinted of a stern, wealthy upbringing. His hands, with manicured nails and plucked of their hair, were flecked with liver spots, leading me to suspect he was in his mid-sixties. Seldom does one come across such a well-presented gentleman. But far more forceful than his appearance was the aura of solemn confidence which encircled him.

Turning to his friend, he said in an exquisite low, silky voice:

'Rublu, who is your new acquaintance?'

The hunchback replied, without looking up:

'Haven't any idea – he was interested in the stamps.'

'I couldn't help noticing – a wonderful collection you have, sir,' I said.

'Oh, thank you, young man, I have been collecting stamps for many years. I've got all the Indian ones, and most of the British ones, too, going back about . . .' he thought for a few seconds. ' . . . Going back about eighty-three years, I suppose.'

'Stamps are vile things . . .' the hunchback repeated pensively.

'Don't pay any attention to Rublu, he's jealous. You see, he doesn't have a hobby – never has had.'

The hunchback flicked cigarette ash into his coffee. Then he slurped the treacle-like liquid from a saucer, held to his lips. I watched with some interest.

'Why do you put ash in your coffee?'

The hunchback looked at me with contempt.

'It makes the coffee taste more bitter,' he said with loathing.

It was obvious that I had much to learn in the way of local etiquette. Allowing him to savour his caustic drink in silence, I turned to the hunchback's companion.

The gentleman seemed to be out of place in the dilapidated Albert Hall. Leaning back on his chair, he spoke about Calcutta's history; of its role in the nation's cultural life, of its peoples, and of its abiding artistic legacy. In return, I explained about my doomed journey on the Farakka Express. The gentleman appeared to know the accursed train well.

'Tell me,' he continued, as if ready to move the conversation on, 'what has brought you to our little city?'

'Oh,' I began to explain rather uneasily, 'I've come here to meet someone. But that's the problem, I can't find him.

'Who exactly have you come to meet?'

'Um,' I stammered, 'a well known illusionist, actually.'

'An illusionist, really?'

'Yes, that's right, it's a great interest of mine.'

'You mean, like Houdini and all that, conjuring?'

'Well, Houdini and many others.'

'What's his name . . . the man you are looking for?'

'Oh, I'm sure you've never heard of him . . .'

The suave figure smoothed back a stray hair with the index finger of his right hand.

'Give it a try,' he said.

'I'm looking for a man called Feroze . . . Hakim Feroze.'

The hunchback looked up in silence. The sophisticate studied my face for a few moments.

'Have you heard of him?'

'Yes, as a matter of fact I have heard of him. But tell me, how did you hear of this illusionist?'

'He was the teacher of a family friend.'

'Whose name is . . . ?'

I speculated why the gentleman was concerned with the precise details of my search.

'His name is Hafiz Jan.'

'If you find this Feroze,' continued the man, 'how will you prove to him all these things?'

'I've got a letter of introduction and a locket to show him.'

I was supplying information far too freely to these complete strangers, but the well-dressed man seemed to draw answers from me.

'How will you know Feroze when you find him?'

'Oh,' I said thinking hard, 'I'll know Feroze because he's the master of illusion. He can make things appear and disappear at will.'

I broke off to take a sip from my glass of tepid mint tea. But the glass was missing. So was the sugar bowl, the milk jug, the ashtray, my street-map of Calcutta, the stamp album, and even the miniature pile of Brazilian stamps. The hunchback slurped his coffee once again. As he slurped, his debonair friend burst into laughter.

'How do you do?' he smiled. 'I am Hakim Feroze.'

6

Renting Babies

'How *is* Hafiz Jan?' Feroze asked fondly. 'I hear the boys are growing up well, and that his wife's sciatica is no longer as painful as it was.'

'That's right; but how did you know? Hafiz Jan said he hasn't been in touch with you in years.'

'Quite so,' murmured Feroze. 'But you know how it is . . . I keep my ear to the ground.'

The hunchback stared across the table at his companion and raised an eyebrow.

'Hafiz Jan was one of my finest students,' Hakim Feroze persisted. 'Did he tell you that? Please show me the letter and the locket . . . it must be the *bezoar* I gave him.'

I passed over the letter and the amulet. Feroze opened the envelope with great care. Before deciphering the Pashtun's almost illegible writing, he touched the paper to his nostrils and inhaled lightly three times. Then, grinning through sharp teeth, he clasped the amulet in his fist and breathed in once again. I might, at first, have doubted that this was indeed Feroze. But having seen what the tokens meant to him, my doubts melted away.

Despite the one in ten million probability of such a chance meeting, Feroze – like any Indian I related the story to – was unfazed by the improbable encounter.

'So,' said the Master at length. 'What can I do for you?'

My heart throbbed a little faster as I anticipated how my single question would be answered.

'Respected Feroze,' I uttered nervously, 'I have heard you are the most accomplished illusionist alive. Sir, I would like to learn from you . . . Mr Feroze . . .' I faltered, 'I would like to become your student.'

Hakim Feroze seemed not to be listening. He was watching the waiter as he wove between the tables with S-shaped manoeuvres, like an ice-skater. He sighed twice. I waited for an answer.

'I regret to tell you,' he revealed softly, 'that I retired some time ago. I no longer take on students.'

'But I have come a long way to meet you,' I snapped selfishly. 'I have been drugged and robbed; have bathed in a *dhobi*'s cauldron, and am still suffering from severe trauma from the Geetee.'

'*Geetee?*' winced the hunchback, distorting his face. 'Very nasty.'

'Well,' rejoined the great conjuror, 'it sounds as if you've had quite an adventure already. But again, I must advise you that I am retired, and am enjoying my retirement.'

Any further outbursts seemed futile. I was at a loss for words. I cursed myself for having pursued the ridiculous quest for so long.

Leaning forward, making ready to storm out from the Albert Hall like a prima donna, something made me pause.

'Could I beg one small favour of you?' I asked.

'Of course you may,' answered Feroze, his green eyes staring at me like bottle-glass beads.

'As a favour to your old pupil Hafiz Jan, would you let me know if you change your mind?'

Feroze smiled. He withdrew an antique orange fountain-pen from the welt pocket of his waistcoat. Then, scribbling a few words on the back of my Calcutta street-map, he handed it to me.

'Come to this address tomorrow at noon,' he said. 'If I have changed my mind, I will tell you.'

*   *   *   *

While hunting for Feroze, I had pitched up at a guest house near the main Park Street area in central Calcutta. Dingy as an oubliette, the hotel was packed with a tour group of Glaswegians. Downing bottle after bottle of local beer in the reception, they disclosed that they had come to Calcutta on a pilgrimage in honour of their champion – the legendary Bengali film-maker Satyajit Ray.

Only one of the group stayed away from the drink. Unlike his companions, he was extremely reserved. As the others lurched about clinking bottles together rambunctiously, he perched primly on a high stool, like a cockatoo. His face was long and very pale, with bristly greying sideburns and a sharp nose; his eyes were magnified by clumsy black-framed spectacles. When I asked him if he was an admirer of Bengali films, he affirmed in a Yorkshire voice that he was. Leaning his torso towards me, he said his name was Horace, and that Calcutta was his passion.

A retired schoolmaster, Horace funded his annual trips to West Bengal by conducting cut-price tours for people with an interest in Bengali cinema. Surprisingly, there appeared to be no shortage of customers. He had spent years studying Calcutta's history – but Horace's preoccupation was with the present, not the past. In his twenty visits to the city, the former prep-school master had gained a rare understanding of Calcutta, one that eludes most foreigners.

'Calcutta's *indescribable*!' he called, clearing his throat. 'Not because it's reprehensible – it certainly isn't. But because it's an astounding mixture of every element of humanity. Westerners dwell on the sordid aspects, blinkering themselves to the city's secrets. Focus only on the beggars, the diseased, and the collapsing buildings, and you miss the sheer ingenuity.'

'Ingenuity?'

'It takes an Eastern mind to decipher Calcutta,' said Horace, peering over the black frames which had slipped down his nose. 'Ask a room full of Bengalis to look beyond the city's day-to-day routine and, without hesitation, they grasp its reality.'

'What about foreigners?' I asked.

'Calcutta has a strange effect on them,' said the schoolmaster, glancing nervously round at the group of rowdy Scotsmen. 'It tends to destabilise them.'

'What does?'

'Everything . . . but most of all the buildings. The sight of the once-majestic architecture, which now lies derelict, is too much for them. Haven't you seen tourists tearing their hair out in the streets?'

I shook my head. But Horace wasn't interested in feedback. He was only halfway through his lecture.

'Calcutta has moved on,' he mused. 'The façades may be crumbling, the streets may be a mass of pot-holes, and the traffic a frenzy of heaving buses and suicidal driving. And, granted, it may be dark as night at three in the afternoon – but this is Calcutta, the "genuine article".'

I gazed across to the guest house's front door and wondered how I could escape through it. The teacher clapped his hands to regain my attention.

'We British doted on a city which didn't really exist,' he said. 'We put up monuments to our heroes, whitewashed everything in sight, enjoyed our liveried servants and our airy bungalows on the banks of the Hoogly. We got everyone speaking English, and saluting our kings and queens: all in a desperation to create a Kensington in West Bengal. But as soon as we steamed away, after Independence, Calcutta – the real city – began to burgeon forth.'

Horace drew a deep breath. I sensed he was reaching the crux of his lecture.

'Fifty years on,' he said studiously, 'and the true character is still percolating forth. Every day Calcutta becomes a little more rounded, more lived in and loved. Spend time here, and what at first seemed like utter chaos reveals itself as quite methodical. Calcutta has a way of arranging systems. As they develop, they provide security for those who need it. Open the mind to the wider picture. Scan about for a minute or two, and these systems become visible . . . they're everywhere.'

*   *   *   *

As I sauntered past Flury's, a café which was the height of fashion in about 1922, I mulled over the schoolmaster's remarks. How could he see systems in what was, for me, a random jumble of people? I hoped that one day I, too, would learn to decipher the city's secrets. Although I tried to make sense of Park Street, all I saw was the endless blend of cars and beggars.

I did notice a respectable man fraternising with the beggars across from Flury's. He appeared to know them well. Feeling lonely, I went over and struck up a conversation. Calcutta's the only city I know where you are actively encouraged to stop strangers at random for a quick chat.

The man was dressed in a blue jacket, with leather braces, a silk handkerchief in his top pocket. His face was swarthy, his ears protruding, and his hair shiny as greasepaint. When I asked him about Calcutta's mysterious underbelly, he – like Horace – was eager to share his information.

Known locally as Nondan – everyone in Bengal goes by a nickname – he had made it his business to help out some of the beggars living in central Calcutta.

'The streets are a window into a million lives,' he recounted, poetically. 'Beggars are a part of our society. We mustn't shun them, but help them whenever we can. Who knows what will happen to us next week, or next month? We may end up out here, begging for a living, too.'

Nondan led me down Park Street. Outside the affluent shops and expensive restaurants, weaving between the yellow and black Ambassador taxis with their fish-mouth grills, or squatting in the deep monsoon gutters: there were beggars everywhere.

'Ask yourself why others don't come to beg here, too,' Nondan said, pausing outside the Moulin Rouge – Calcutta's version of the celebrated Parisian nightclub. 'No beggar would turn down the chance of working on Park Street. But you see, the homeless here aren't positioned randomly.'

'Of course they're random, they're wandering around!'

'No they're not,' contested Nondan firmly. 'Take that woman over there . . .' He pointed at an elderly woman, her head veiled with the end of her lilac-coloured *sari*. 'Like all of them, she stays within the area that she rents.'

'*Rents?*'

'That's right – she pays about half of the money she makes directly to the *Dadas*.'

'Who're the *Dadas*?'

'The "Big Brothers" – the men in control.'

'A Mafia?'

'Well,' said Nondan hesitantly, 'you could call it that. They demand protection money from all the beggars working this area. Anyone who doesn't pay is beaten up.'

'There can't be much money in it for the *Dadas*,' I said. 'Why don't they go and get into some more profitable line of business?'

Nondan rolled his eyes.

'*Not much money in it?*' he choked. 'Are you mad? Calcutta's beggars are a multi-million-dollar business.'

'Nonsense . . .'

'Do your sums,' said Nondan. 'Calcutta has at least eighty thousand full-time beggars. If each one's making about twelve rupees a day and, say, they're working every day of the year . . .' Nondan gesticulated wildly, counting on his fingers. 'Well, I make that about . . . about three hundred and fifty million rupees . . . that's about . . .' Nondan thought for a few seconds. 'That's about ten million American dollars a year between them. And that's only Calcutta – all Indian cities have lots of beggars.'

As I went over the figures myself, Nondan gave a stern caution.

'Be warned,' he remarked. 'When in Calcutta, never underestimate what looks simple.'

'What do you mean?'

'All right,' said Nondan, surveying Park Street. 'Take a look at that woman over there. What do you see?'

'I see a woman – like any of the others – holding a screaming baby.'

'How old would you say she is?'

'About fifty. That must be her grandson in her arms . . .'

'Wrong!' exclaimed Nondan.

'Then perhaps it's her friend's child.'

'Wrong again! Remember – in Calcutta, nothing's that simple. I know that woman. She hires the baby.'

'Impossible!'

Nondan regarded me with an austere glance.

'My friend,' he said gruffly, 'this is Calcutta. *Nothing* is impossible. That woman doesn't have young children, they're all grown up. It took her years to get a spot in this part of town. She knows that people pay more if you're crippled or have an infant – so she rents the baby. It costs her about three rupees a day. She looks after it very well.'

The arrangement seemed back to front.

'In the West,' I said, 'people pay to have someone baby-sit their child.'

Nondan shook his head from side to side, as if condemning such a primitive system.

'Does the woman have to feed the baby?'

'Of course not,' he declared, irritated at my stupidity. 'The baby has to wail – if it doesn't, no one will give money. What better way of ensuring a baby cries than not feeding it?'

One had to admit that, although a little on the ruthless side, the system was ingenious.

Nondan knew his way around the secret world of Calcutta's streets. His information was inspiring, yet one question bothered me.

'There's one last fact I need to know,' I said.

'What is it?' asked Nondan, greeting some street urchins.

'Where do the beggars hire their babies from?'

Nondan looked at me as if I were an imbecile. Then, answering what was to him the most elementary question of all time, he replied:

'From the baby dealer, of course.'

*   *   *   *

Throughout the night, the fleas gnawed at my ankles like hyenas ripping at a carcass. Unable to stand any more of the hostel, I rose early and went out into the sleeping city.

First, I explored the maze of New Market. Even at dawn the air was heavy with the aroma of breakfast, simmering on a hundred pavement stalls. *Puchkawallas*, Calcutta's fast-food merchants, were busy cooking up snacks to tout to the mass of commuters who would be along shortly.

Chowringhee Road, the main thoroughfare, which skirts the east perimeter of the Maidan, was virtually deserted. Like an eighteenth-century etching of imperial Calcutta, the scene was stark: with just enough locals to give perspective to the opulent buildings of the British Raj.

Indeed, at first glance, little seems to have changed. The occasional rickshaw, pulled by a barefoot Bihari, rattles past. A groomed yellow labrador strains at a servant's leash. A *bhishtiwalla*, water-carrier, pauses to fill his damp goat-hide sack from a hand-pump. But a second glimpse reminded me that the British left long ago.

The façade of a classical pavilion is now racked with billboards, advertising facial bleaching cream. Its Corinthian colonnades are crumbling; its walls are stained with algae, devoured by acidic rain, splattered with torn posters of Marx and Lenin; and the pair of granite lions which flank the gates are headless and forlorn. I felt a sudden pang of sorrow that such imposing buildings are in decay. But then, as Horace had made so clear, Calcutta is a city with a firm agenda of its own. It's an agenda of survival. What good is a pavilion the size of Buckingham Palace to an office worker or a *rickshawalla*? The sumptuous palaces and mansions of the Raj have been shed, like a great slough. Like snake-skins, they lie discarded: an empty reminder of the departed serpent.

*   *   *   *

At eleven-thirty I hailed a rickshaw. Calcutta is one of the few cities in the world where traditional hand-pulled rickshaws still exist. The first ones were brought to the city by the Chinese, around the turn of the century. At the time, the method of transport was considered far more humane than the palanquin, an enclosed litter suspended on poles and carried by bearers. Calcutta's authorities – who realise that rickshaws add to their city's negative image – are phasing them out. But although humanely motivated, their abolition will put more than thirty thousand *rickshawallas* out of a job.

'Happy Christmas, *Sahib*!' said the *rickshawalla*.

I looked at the calendar on my watch. He was right, it was Christmas Day. I thanked God I was in a Hindu nation – Christmas and I detest each other.

I read out Feroze's address.

'*Haa, jadoowalla*,' the *rickshawalla* sniffed. 'Want magician house?'

I was surprised he knew of Feroze, and that he spoke some English.

'How do you know this man?'

'Everybody know *jadoowalla*!'

'Mr Feroze?'

'Yes, Mister Magician!'

Later, I realised that, although few people knew Hakim Feroze by name, virtually every *rickshawalla* knew him as *jadoowalla*, the magician.

The *rickshawalla* reeked of *chullu*, bootleg alcohol made from distilled grain. He was sleek, fine-boned, without an ounce of fat. His legs were slender as sunflower stalks, his hands rippled with muscle, and his back gleamed like a burnished sheet of newly hammered copper. Despite his inebriated condition, the *rickshawalla* moved through the traffic with hushed concentration, covering the distance of about three miles in under thirty minutes. He pulled up outside a large, traditional Calcutta home in the Alipore district, just south of the Zoological Gardens.

Before he left, I asked him how he had learnt English.

'*Sahib*,' he said, tucking the ten-rupee note into his *lungi*, 'was runner – Purulia post office, West Bengal.'

At first the explanation meant nothing. Then I understood. A throwback to colonial times, West Bengal is the only state in India which still employs a relay of postal runners. They carry cumbersome sacks of mail through the jungles and wilds of outlying areas. Over their left shoulder hangs a rounded axe – traditionally a defence against dacoits and wild animals. Across the right shoulder is slung a sack of letters. As with so many Indian professions, runners' routes tend to be hereditary. But in recent times, the younger generation have preferred to leave the forests for work in Calcutta, where they become *rickshawallas*.

Before ringing the bell of Feroze's home, I checked the time. It was exactly noon.

An elderly servant staggered to the front gate. Apologising that Mr Feroze was not yet home from his late-morning stroll, he invited me in to wait.

The manservant led me on a short cut to the house: past the kitchen, which was located in a vine-covered outbuilding, through its vegetable patch, and across the central courtyard to the veranda. The main house was a cross between a Mediterranean villa and a Regency mansion. It was square with two storeys, a flat roof, and imposing lichened walls. The veranda, which spread out like a grand stone doily, was shaded by a simple tiled portico. On the upper floor, set back above the veranda, was a wide balcony, replete with a moulded balustrade. Either side, twin sets of French windows, fitted with wooden jalousie shutters, looked out across the courtyard. Below them were more windows, their glass mottled and sagging like distorted funfair mirrors. A century or so of Calcuttan wear and tear had exacted a heavy toll on the mansion. Random lumps of plasterwork had fallen away, revealing ketchup-coloured bricks. The pronounced cornicing of the window-ledges had crumbled; and the granite lintel above the front door was split at one side.

Once in the main building, the bearer led the way through the vestibule and down a long, book-lined corridor. At the far end of the passage, I was forced to negotiate an overwhelming accumulation of unneeded odds and ends – a number of men's suits; tennis racquets, a bicycle, three crude wicker chairs, and a gate-legged table. The manservant apologised for the hazard, noting that the bric-à-brac was waiting to be taken away to a charity sale.

Feroze was obviously a man of considerable cultivation. The sitting-room was well-appointed, its walls lined with lacquered shelves; its floor, an exquisite Arenberg parquet, was partially concealed by a Baluchi rug. A revolving bookcase in one corner of the room stored oversized books. A Steinway upright piano stood on the far side, with a folio Chopin waiting to be played. The centre of the reception room was dominated by three bergère chairs, upholstered in off-white leather and complete with lace antimacassars.

The servant shuffled ahead methodically in a pair of worn out mule slippers. Ancient and asthmatic, he was bent like a billhook, his expression benumbed with age.

We arrived at Feroze's private study. The orderly escorted me to a cabriole chair. Closing the door behind him with a bang, he left. The room was dark, the windows shielded by wooden venetian blinds. It was filled with an unnerving chill, as if someone was watching me. The chair on which I sat was adjacent to a walnut writing bureau. Three precise piles of correspondence lay upon it. A cylindrical brass box held down one of the piles. Damascened in silver, with Islamic lettering, it had been crafted from part of an artillery shell. The base was inscribed, *Berndorf, 1917.*

There were books everywhere. Not novels, but volumes of substance, in many languages. Many were bound in quarter Moroccan leather, and numbered on the spine. About half were concerned with illusion, conjuring and magic. One complete shelf was devoted to the work and life of the eminent American illusionist, Harry Houdini. Another was concerned with the feats of India's religious ascetics and godmen. A third held the teacher's numerous stamp albums.

Opposite the Houdini books, adjacent to the study's main door, a two-foot section of Kiswah hung framed on the wall. The Kiswah, an immense black cloth mantle, embroidered with gold calligraphy, is crafted each year for the Kaaba at Mecca. Weighing more than two tons, it takes a hundred craftsmen a whole year to weave. That a strip of the revered cloth hung in the study suggested that Feroze was a pious Muslim, a Haji, who had attended the Pilgrimage at Mecca.

Leading off from the study was a storeroom, filled floor to ceiling with papers, journals, and more books. Beside this was a second door. I rotated the cool brass handle. It appeared to be locked.

As I turned my attentions back to the papers on the writing desk, I heard the soles of leather shoes scuffing across the parquet of the sitting-room. The study door flew open. I spun round. Standing to attention in the door's frame was Feroze.

He was dressed in a black astrakhan hat and a spinach-green Ulster coat of Irish frieze. And on his feet were brown suede *chukka* boots. Curious attire as it was seventy-five degrees outside.

'I see that you're having a good poke around . . .'

'Excuse me,' I replied. 'I'm inquisitive by nature.'

'What else are you *by nature*?'

'I am modest,' I said, immodestly.

Assuming my place again on the cabriole chair, I waited for Feroze to take the lead. He hung his astrakhan cap and coat behind the door. Then, without looking at me, he sat at the great leather-topped writing desk. He collected the papers from the surface of the desk, shuffled them into a single wad, and locked them away in a cupboard beside the desk.

'Why do you want to learn illusion?' he asked.

'I've always been interested.'

'Are you only "interested", or are you passionate?' Feroze's teeth chewed on his words.

'I'm *passionate*,' I said, 'but I realise that to be superlative, one needs an extraordinary teacher; and,' I said, hoping to make an impact, 'I understand you are an *extraordinary* teacher.'

Feroze was not interested in whimsical flattery.

'Tell me,' he growled, 'do you do as you're told? Are you obedient?'

'Yes . . . I think I am.'

'If I became your teacher,' he said, 'would you ever question me?'

'Would you want me to?'

'Answer my question.'

'I would question you if, by questioning, I could advance my understanding.'

The Master nodded.

'If I told you to do something,' he went on, 'would you do it, even if it were painful?'

What tortuous designs had he in store? I sensed Hafiz Jan watching from afar, chewing on his fingers. Then I answered with circumspection.

'Sir,' I said, 'if you asked me to do something, I'd make every effort to fulfil the command.'

Getting to his feet, Hakim Feroze picked a pair of navigational callipers from his desk and fingered them as he contemplated. Gazing out of the window to the central courtyard, with its mature mango tree, he forced the ends of the callipers together.

'Hafiz Jan was, as I told you, one of my best pupils,' he said. 'He had passion; he loved illusion. It's always saddened me he had an ancestral position to fulfil.'

Feroze broke off and stared at me. While he stared, I could feel him scrutinising not myself, but my own ancestors.

'I know Hafiz Jan would not have sent you,' Feroze continued, 'unless you meant a great deal to him. For this reason,' he said, again glancing into the courtyard, 'I will give you one chance.'

I smiled, rearranging myself on the confined seat. Outside I could make out the shrill voices of carol singers at the property's gates. The servant was calling for them to go home.

'I am not a patient man,' quipped Feroze. 'If you fail *any* order, *any* task, I will ask you to leave.'

'Thank you for having faith in me.'

'My friend,' said Feroze derisively, 'please note that I have no faith in anyone at all! Tell me, where are you staying?'

'Near Park Street, in a guest house.'

'Go and get your things. You are moving in here where I can keep an eye on you. This house is run along precise lines. Do you understand that?'

I gave a thumbs-up. Hakim Feroze glowered disapprovingly at my gesture. Toying with the callipers, he crossed the room. I noticed he was now wearing a pair of sturdy Oxfords. Odd, as I hadn't actually seen him remove the stylish boots he'd arrived in.

'Once you're within the walls of this house, you do as I say. You get up when I tell you to; eat what I tell you to; and follow my exact orders.'

'How am I to address you, Mr Feroze?'

The magician ran a fingertip across the top edge of a picture frame, checking for dust.

'People like to call me "Master",' he replied.

'When am I to begin lessons?'

Feroze snipped the callipers like castanets. Then, scowling across at me, his green eyes shimmering like fire-opals, he shouted:

'Immediately . . . We start immediately!'

PART TWO

The public see only the accomplished trick;
they have no conception of the tortuous
preliminary self-training that was necessary
to conquer that fear.

J.C. Cannell, The Secrets of Houdini

7

Calcutta Torture

At the centre of Feroze's courtyard, beneath the boughs of the mango tree, I stood to attention like a sentry. Chest out, heels clicked together; spine straight as a ship's mast: frozen to the spot, like a hare before a car's headlights. This was a proud moment. It was the moment for which I had longed. I felt accepted: secure in the knowledge that my apprenticeship with a famous tutor had finally begun.

Arms outstretched like those of a crucified convict, I awaited further instructions. Despite initial confusion at the odd training, I complied with unflagging respect: anxious to make a good impression on my first full day.

Lesson One: stand in the yard with arms extended sideways; palms turned upwards; fingers splayed outwards like a starfish; ten grains of rice on the left palm; a single peeled grape on the right. The drill's relevance eluded me. But with one misplaced foot or questioning glance enough to merit expulsion, I obeyed in what soon became silent agony.

Every quarter of an hour I was permitted to rest both clenched fists on my head for a single minute. Each bout would be timed by Feroze's precious silver pocket-watch; a possession which was never far from his hand. The respite's end was signalled by three clinks of a teaspoon on an enamelled mess mug. The cup hung from the Master's belt like a rabbit-foot talisman. Every so often he left the shade of the mansion's impressive veranda. Haughty as a llama, he would step over to ensure the grape was dust-free, and that the ten grains remained as he had placed them.

The weather was unusually hot for late December. The heat of the winter sun seared down through the branches of the mango tree. I bore what I believed was unbearable. Twinging with electric spasms of pain, my arms quivered as if about to snap. Little did I know that, as the austere initiation into the magician's world progressed, I would soon be craving the grape and rice ordeal.

The drill came to an abrupt end. With talons slashing like bayonets, a buzzard swooped down from the mango tree and seized the grape. As the colossal wings flapped around me, I tumbled to the ground. Feroze dropped his newspaper and marched over. I exhibited the gashes on my forearms, moaning loudly, hoping for pity. But the magician was not the sort of man concerned with trifling flesh wounds. He preferred broken bones.

'Did you see that?' he said.

'*See* it? Didn't you notice me wrestling with it? Look at my wounds.' I held out my arms once again.

'*Butastur teesa*, the white-eyed buzzard . . . don't see those in Calcutta very often . . .' sniffed Feroze. 'I think he might be making a nest up there. Better start keeping an eye on it.'

Yanking the mess mug up from his belt, he struck it thrice with the teaspoon. On to the next task.

Lesson Two: strip down to your underpants and crawl around the courtyard on your stomach, picking up fragments of sea-shell. Stop only when you have found two hundred fragments of shell.

There is nothing quite as unpleasant as wearing a pair of briefs which have been trailed through a Calcutta courtyard. Nothing, that is, except having one's elbows and knees lacerated by unseen slivers of glass and discarded razor blades. As I fumbled forward, whimpering, shards of broken bottles pierced my skin, and I struggled to think righteous thoughts.

Scholarship, my conscience cautioned me, is about making sacrifices. Success in any field always depends on forfeiture. Although unorthodox, the trials must be preparation for my studies in illusion. Without these basics, I told myself, I'll never get through the course.

After three hours of crawling in zigzags like a maggot, I had managed to locate only three pieces of shell. One of them was questionable.

Feroze came over to inspect my work.

'Put them in this,' he said, dropping a rusty tobacco tin next to my bloodied elbow.

The sound of shells falling into the box displeased the teacher. Instead of a hailstorm, there was a dismal *ting, ting, ting.*

'Oh, dear,' Feroze said gruffly, 'that won't do. That won't do at all. Better keep on at it.'

'There aren't very many shells round about here,' I lamented, my nose pressed into the dirt.

But Hakim Feroze did not hear me. He had already marched back to the shade.

Three hours later, I had located another seven pieces of sea-shell. As I probed about haphazardly, I wondered how many other poor neophytes had been subjected to the same ordeal. The lack of shells implied that I was not the first. Had Hafiz Jan been forced to do this, too? I felt sure he had. Was this the terrific baptism by ordeal of which he had so persistently warned me? The more I thought about the regime, the more questions remained unanswered. Was the shell-picking a ritual to which all initiates of magic are subjected? I suspected not.

When afternoon had turned to evening, the magician returned from taking a nap. He was clean-shaven, dressed in a crisp gabardine shirt, herring-bone breeches and honey-yellow brogues. He looked down at me slithering around on my stomach, like an alligator. The front part of my underpants had virtually disintegrated. Like a newly evolved chameleon-mole hybrid, my weary and injured body attempted to adapt.

Feroze pulled out his pocket-watch, studied it for a moment, and put it away. I gaped down at the muck and then back at the Master. A second before he had been standing tall, inspecting me like a drill sergeant on parade. Now he was reclining in a deckchair. I hadn't seen him sit down, or even set up the seat.

'You're pretty filthy!' he sneered as if surprised at my condition. 'It's almost eight o'clock. You better go and wash. Ask Gokul to give you something to eat and get you a mattress. We'll begin early in the morning. Make sure you sleep well.'

'Thank you,' I said meekly, unsure of what exactly I was giving thanks for.

Gokul, the frail manservant, appeared from nowhere and helped me to my feet. After spending much of the afternoon on my belly, the abrupt transition from slithering reptile to *Homo erectus* was not an easy one to make. Sensing the problem of readjustment, Gokul instructed me to lie on the veranda. He removed his sandals, and climbed on to my back. Prancing up and down my spine like a gymnast on a beam, he nudged his toes into the dips between the vertebrae. Then, after I'd had a steaming bath in the servants' antique cast-iron tub, he applied tincture of iodine to the raw wounds on my underside.

After this, he led me to the kitchen.

'Hot all day on stomach,' he said, cheerily.

'Yes, it was quite hard. Quite dusty.'

He opened a steaming pot and served me a bowl of *daal* and *sukto* – fried, diced vegetables.

'Tomorrow will be a nice day,' he said, as if hoping to elevate my spirits.

'Yes? Do you know what Mr Feroze has planned for me tomorrow?'

A nervous expression crept across the manservant's face.

'Eat more *daal*,' he said. 'It make you strong.'

*   *   *   *

The first phase of the initiation continued for seven days. Each evening Gokul would straighten out my back with his rubbery feet, apply iodine to my lacerations, and darn my underpants. When Feroze's piercing gaze was not upon me, the good-natured servant would throw over a chunk of coconut, or slip me a mug of bracing tamarind juice.

Each day seemed to bring a new and more horrible trial.

Lesson Three: dig a hole in the courtyard – two feet square, two feet deep – using a dessert spoon. The spoon may only be held in the left hand.

Lesson Four: jog round the courtyard backwards, holding a five-kilogram block of sackcloth-covered ice. Stop only when the ice has melted.

Lesson Five: blindfolded, sort a jar of dried rice and lentils.

Lesson Six: catch twelve live cockroaches in a tin mug. No props permitted.

After a full week of the torture I could endure little more. The drills were exacting a heavy toll. My legs were afflicted with housemaid's knee and my spine seemed permanently distorted. My hands had been badly slashed; my elbows were ridged with welts; my stomach was bruised like a plum fallen from the highest branches of a tree. My face had blistered, and my eyes were bloodshot and bulging after so many hours in the dazzling sunlight. The wounds were made worse by the lack of healing time, and the constant reapplication of dirt.

Feroze no longer signified a man of great skill and refinement. I had begun to despise everything he stood for. Always immaculate in tailored finery, with his hair slicked back like the barbs of a moist feather, his face scented with aftershave, he was the diametric opposite of what I had become. Even when blindfolded, fumbling for rice grains, I could sense him bending over me. A whiff of lavender *eau de toilette* preceded him, alerting one to the random inspection.

Perhaps the magician really had a deep-seated hatred of Hafiz Jan.

Was torturing me the most pleasurable route to revenge? But then again, the Pashtun had warned me constantly of Feroze's merciless methods.

A cross between a foreign legion boot-camp and a secret-society initiation ritual, the ordeals were grounded in pain. One thing was obvious: the agenda, which was dedicated to grave discomfort, had been drawn up by a passionate sadist.

Feroze relished the ever-expanding curriculum of tribulation. The more pain that was inflicted, the more successful the lesson had been. I was kept going by the idea that all the hardship might be leading somewhere.

The unconventional assignments were graded by an equally off-hand system. The few times I had managed to comply with the instructions, I was condemned more vigorously than if I had failed. The whole thing left me confused and further enfeebled.

As if the courtyard ordeals weren't enough, additional chores were added to the schedule. In the middle of the night, Feroze would appear in my dingy, roach-infested room in the servants' quarters. How he got in, I don't know. After the first nocturnal intrusion, I kept the door bolted from the inside and a chair pressed up under the handle. I would have queried how he had traversed the barricades without disturbing them, but he was not the kind of man who took kindly to his movements being questioned. He would chime three times on the mess mug. The signal for my attendance.

'Yes?' I would wheeze, still half asleep.

'I want you to learn this Bengali poem. I will test you on it later.'

Four printed sheets would be dropped on the floor.

'But I don't read Bengali.' I would murmur, knowing well such an excuse was not satisfactory.

'Then,' Feroze would say, 'you had better find someone who does.'

Long before dawn, I would rouse Gokul from his slumber and beg him to read me the poem. Without an uncivil word, he would go through the stanzas.

At dawn, which was commencement time for lessons, I would ask the magician to test me on the poem. Sometimes he would do so. But on other occasions he would ask:

'Have you learnt it?'

'Yes, I have,' I would reply.

'Then what point is there in testing you? We aren't in kindergarten now, you know.'

*   *   *   *

At six p.m. on 31 December, Feroze came over to where I was lying face down like a fallen soldier. For most of the day I had been crawling on my knees, ferrying teaspoons of dirt from a bucket at one end of the courtyard to another at the other end.

I was close to tears. Until then I had maintained some sort of composure. During the first week there had been no mention of magic. For all I knew I had joined the wrong course.

Feroze's ruthless regime had finally broken me. Dirt was still finding its way into the rent skin of my elbows and shins. My right knee, now copiously bandaged with strips of rag torn from an old sheet, was despicably damaged.

As always, Feroze was oblivious to the distress he had caused. Bending over me, he ruffled his shoulders like a cockerel marking its displeasure. He handed me a fluffy handkerchief with which to wipe my nose. I buried my sunburnt face in the cool folds of silk and blew very hard. Plugs of compacted Calcutta dirt were discharged at high speed, like darts fired from a blow-pipe. It was a satisfying feeling. Unable to stand up unaided, I stretched up in the hope of returning the handkerchief to the magician. With a horrified grimace, he waved the cloth aside.

Rapping once on his tin cup, Feroze signalled for Gokul. The faithful valet pottered out from the kitchen. The staff of four servants had been trained to recognise their own individual signal, all of which were tapped out in Feroze's own form of Morse.

'Gokul,' he instructed, 'please help Mr Shah to his feet. See that he's bathed. Make sure his ears are very clean.'

'Yes, *Sahib!*'

'You won't be staying here tonight,' Feroze said, peering down at me.

'Oh?'

'You will be spending the night on Park Street.'

Images of a whirlpool jacuzzi and a double bed with crisp linen sheets overwhelmed me.

'Should I go and stay in a hotel?'

'That won't be necessary,' replied the magician dryly. 'I have arranged something *special* for you. Gokul knows the details. He'll escort you.'

As I extracted the grime from the inner reaches of my nostrils and ears, I found myself filled with new energy. Park Street: Calcutta's answer to Piccadilly . . . what could be a more capricious contrast to the teacher's compound?

The manservant led me out into the street. It was already dark. Under his right arm was a brown paper package, tied up with string.

'Where are we going, Gokul?'

The servant chose not to respond verbally. Instead, with a solicitous expression, he looked me in the face sombrely. Then he gazed down at the mysterious package.

'Are we going to a New Year's party? Will there be fireworks?'

Gokul was silent.

'Is that a gift you're holding?'

Still Gokul said nothing.

When the taxi ground to a halt at the quiet end of Park Street, I began to question exactly what was going on.

'All the fancy hotels are the other end of Park Street,' I said.

'Yes, all at other end,' replied Gokul.

'There's nothing down this end except for some *paan* stalls, petrol stations and . . .' Remembering the third thing which Park Street was well known for, I fell silent with mounting distress. '*Paan*, garages,' I recapped, 'and the South Park Street Cemetery!'

Gokul ducked his head in confirmation. He was not taking me to a lavish fun-filled New Year's bash, but to the cemetery – where I was to spend the night. Alone.

'Gokul,' I whispered as he pushed open the wrought-iron gates of the British burial grounds, 'is there any chance we can come to an arrangement?'

The servant made it known that corruption was not a possibility.

'Master may be checking up on you,' he replied sternly. 'Cannot cheat.'

We passed the gatehouse, making our way down one of the main paths to the end of the expansive graveyard. Without warning, Gokul froze in his tracks, placed the packet on a mid-sized tomb, and wished me luck. He would be back for me in the morning.

Turning on his heel, he walked through the blue-tinged darkness back to the gates. I sensed his fear of the cemetery; but despite it, he marched away with reserved dignity.

When he had gone, I opened up the parcel, fumbling its contents in the darkness. Inside were a candle, a box of matches, a nylon blanket, a handful of dates, six deep-fried samosas, and a low-quality pamphlet about the cemetery.

Park Street Cemetery is a fascinating place. Were it not for the abominable circumstances of my visit, I might now be publicising it more enthusiastically. Built on what were once the furthest boundaries of the city, the cemetery is almost in the centre of the modern Calcutta.

Deserted by everyone, even Gokul, whom I had begun to consider as a true confidant, I pondered what to do next. Within minutes my eyes adjusted to the unrelenting darkness. A high mildewed wall surrounded the entire graveyard, shrouding the disconcerting world within. Beyond it, I could hear the clash of evening traffic, enlivened by the prospect of ushering in the New Year. The wall was like a barrier between two worlds. Unfortunately for me, I had crossed the River Styx, into Hades.

Anxious to preserve morale, I decided to treat the night as a military reconnaissance exercise. This approach would keep me focused and might dispel any trepidation at enduring a night with the dead.

First I repeated my grandfather's trusted maxim: *Time spent on reconnaissance is seldom wasted*. Then I tightened the muscles of my back, like a hunter stalking his prey. I was ready for a preliminary exploration.

With the candle burning brightly, I slunk forward, inching down overgrown paths, taking in the assortment of tombs. Pyramids – no doubt inspired by those at Giza – rose up into the night sky. Roman cupolas were dotted about like bandstands at Brighton. Wherever I stepped, there stood imposing monuments of stone – mausolea the size of country cottages; faced with Carrara marble, topped by imposing granite urns.

Flicking through the pamphlet in the candlelight, I read the history. Founded in 1769, the cemetery was closed twenty-three years later, bursting at the seams with Englishmen. Some of the most illustrious children of the Empire are buried there. The Calcutta they knew was very different from the modern city. Then it was a place of fearful illness, where the feeble expired in agonising deaths. Struck down by cholera, rabies, smallpox, malaria and tuberculosis, the tender European constitution had little chance. Many more were slain by mysterious diseases of unknown name. The tomb of Jane Eliza Maclean – who died in 1826, five months after reaching Calcutta – records that her death was due to 'one of the fatal diseases incident to the climate of India'.

As some perished at the hand of exotic disease, others met their end through lifestyle. Drink was the most notable executioner. But others died by more startling methods. Sir John D'Oyly, the sixth baronet and former MP for Ipswich, was buried at Park Street after expiring from 'a nervous complaint due to an inordinate use of the hookah'. Another, Rose Aylmer, a girl of seventeen, was buried beneath a glorious twisted cenotaph, having expired from 'eating too many pineapples'.

The largest of the pyramids was Elizabeth Jane Barwell's mausoleum. It served as a landmark in my night wanderings. As I stumbled through the low undergrowth I came across many extraordinary graves: a great-granddaughter of King Charles II; a great-grandfather of William Makepeace Thackeray, and a son of Charles Dickens. They rest in the tranquillity of their garden at the centre of one of Asia's most unwieldy cities.

Overshadowed by sprawling *pongamia* trees, planted by the British, the cemetery was more like an enchanted druid grove than an antique burial ground. Strangely, I felt no misgivings walking there at night. This sense of ease was perhaps because, in India, one can never be truly alone.

At its south-east corner the brick wall had been breached by a great hole, the kind which an iron cannonball makes. Through the opening I could easily make out the tail-lights of Ambassador taxis. They beckoned me like a mirage. Why not make an escape? Sneak into town for a gourmet meal . . . a night on the town . . . then skulk back to the cemetery before dawn. It was a fine plan. Lowering my head, I glanced left and right. Silence.

I made my way to the huge aperture. But someone was following me. I heard footsteps approaching from behind. I swung round, terrified. No one was there.

'Who is it?' I called.

'Where are you going?' said a voice, in fluent English.

'Nowhere,' I spluttered. 'Just going to have a look at the hole.'

'You mustn't leave the cemetery!'

'Oh,' I replied apprehensively. 'Who are *you*?'

A figure slipped out from behind a crumbling tombstone. I squinted to get a better look at him. It was a boy, aged about fifteen. He was barefoot, dressed in a light-coloured shirt and a chequered *lungi*. His back was long as an archer's bow, his movements spry and over-accentuated.

'You're supposed to stay here!' he shouted.

'Yes, I know. But how did *you* know?'

'It's my business to know,' he said. 'Come and sit with us.'

'*Us?*'

The cemetery's brochure had said that brigands once lived in the tombs. It said they buried their treasure in pits between the mausolea. Was this a juvenile brigand? How did he know about my latest hardship?

'Come and sit with us,' repeated the young man.

'Who *are* you?' I asked again.

'My name's Topu. I live here with the others,' he said, motioning me to follow him.

We came to a crude home-made tent. Located well away from the gatekeeper's lodge, it was concealed from the main graveyard by a low earth bulwark. Outside it, three others – about the same age as the first – were hunched around a fire. They showed no surprise at seeing a foreigner.

'They don't speak English,' said Topu.

'Are they your brothers?'

'No, we're friends.'

'What are you doing here?'

'I told you already, this is where we live.'

'You live in the graveyard?'

'What's wrong with that?'

'Nothing, I suppose.'

The boy clicked his knuckles.

'Of course we get thrown out quite often,' he said. 'The workmen rip down our tents and burn them. But we always come back. Just outside the wall, a free soup stall is set up every morning. We're usually first in line.'

'How did you know I was meant to spend the night here?'

'A man came and told us to watch out for you.'

'A man . . . ? Was he an old, well-dressed man with a moustache?'

'Yes, he *was* old and very well dressed. He gave us a hundred rupees.'

'Feroze!' I choked. 'He hired spies to make sure I didn't cheat.'

'The man asked us to watch out for you,' said the child.

I had endured enough of Feroze's barbaric treatment. Even when stripped of all dignity, abused like a convict in a Siberian gulag, I had put a brave face on things. But this time the magician had surpassed even his own despicable record. Beside me, the four boys stared into the flames – their faces illuminated like those of choirboys at a midnight Mass. For me, this, the year's final night, was its most unconventional; for them, it was another night in a life spent under the open sky.

I had come in search of stage magic, and was spending New Year's Eve in an abandoned cemetery. India has a way of perceiving what one lacks, before surreptitiously prescribing its own antidote. Rather than a grounding in conjuring, was I getting what I really needed instead?

One of the boys held out a piece of burnt *chapati*. It tasted surprisingly good. Remembering that I, too, had a little food, I brought out the dates and samosas, and passed them round.

'This is a big graveyard,' I said, breaking the silence. 'Why don't more people live here?'

'Hundreds of people used to,' replied Topu, biting into a samosa, 'but then they were thrown out when the cemetery was cleaned up. A lot of criminals lived here till recently.'

'Yes, I read that.'

'It's true,' continued the boy. 'Some of them hid their loot in the ground. There's lots of treasure here. They even stole the skeletons to sell to the *konkalwallas*.'

'Who are they?'

The boy raised both his eyebrows at once. Lowering his voice, and leaning towards me, his face bathed in marigold light, he explained:

'The *konkalwallas* buy bodies dug up from cemeteries and from the unclaimed body dump. They dip them in an acid bath and then ship the bones abroad.'

'Who wants skeletons?'

'Schools that teach doctors, of course . . .' Topu paused to stuff another samosa into his mouth. 'But now it's illegal to export skeletons.'

'So has the business died out?'

'No, it's just much quieter now. It's gone undercover.'

Topu knew so much about the used-skeleton business that I suspected he was himself somehow involved in the illicit trade.

'How did you learn such good English?' I asked, changing the subject.

'I used to help at my friend's bookstall at College Street. It sold medical textbooks. My friend taught me to read and speak English.'

'What do you do now?'

'Well,' said Topu, 'we do odd jobs.'

'Why don't you look for the cemetery's buried treasures?'

Without saying a word, Topu looked across at me, and smiled.

The sound of Calcutta's rooks woke me to the first sunrise of the year. Flapping their immense wings like pterodactyls, the great black birds soared round the graveyard, swooping down between the monuments. I looked at my wristwatch. It was already seven o'clock. I glanced round. The boys had fallen asleep, curled up beside the smouldering fire outside the tent.

Anxious that Feroze, or even Gokul, didn't realise I had met the boys, I prepared to creep back to where I had left the manservant.

Topu heard me clambering to my feet. He opened his eyes and sat up.

'See you again,' he said.

'Yes, I hope so.'

'If you need anything in Calcutta, you know where to find us.'

'Thanks, Topu, I'll remember that.'

The cemetery was as serene in day as it had been at night. Its tombs seemed distinctly out of place, like the remnants of a lost world. I could imagine with ease the solemn colonial cortèges lowering their loved ones by torchlight. Brothers of the Raj, who had lived and died here – they were of another time. Like the opulent imperial buildings they had constructed, the mausolea at South Park Street were no longer on Calcutta's agenda.

At eight o'clock Gokul found me, propped against Elizabeth Barwell's pyramid, wrapped in the pink nylon blanket.

'Did you sleep?'

'Like the dead.'

'Good, *Sahib*,' he brooded, 'because Master waiting for you.'

As the taxi pulled to a halt outside the Alipore mansion, I found myself yearning for the cemetery. At least I could do what I liked there. For someone who had come to India in search of magical tuition, I was accomplishing very little. Hafiz Jan had taught me more in my attic bedroom twenty years before. I rebuked myself for not persuading the Pashtun to take me on at Burhana. As I contemplated the situation, Feroze strolled over from the veranda.

'Happy New Year! How was your evening?' he asked.

'Quite interesting. I've learnt all about Park Street.'

'Meet anyone out of the ordinary?'

'Not especially.'

As usual, Feroze wasn't listening.

'Tahir, please follow me,' he said in a loud, exultant tone.

The Master had used my first name. I hadn't realised he even knew it.

'Where are we going?'

Feroze led me into the mansion: a place which, until then, had been out of bounds. We ascended the winding teak staircase with its exquisite carved banister. Once on the first-floor landing, the magician slipped a brass key into the lock of a solid white panelled door. A click to the left, and the door swung open.

I entered an ample lavender-walled chamber. The room was dominated by a spectacular mahogany four-poster bedstead, with plumped-up pillows, scatter cushions, and an embroidered eiderdown. For a man who had spent the night in a cemetery, it was a sight for sore eyes.

Opposite the bed stood a pine commode; its front panel hinging down to reveal a washbasin and miniature shaving mirror. Standing in the far corner was a rosewood davenport, inlaid with ivory marquetry and geometric lines. The room smelt of naphthalene mothballs.

'As a New Year's gift you can stay in here,' exclaimed Feroze.

'I'm fine out there in the servants' quarters,' I replied meekly.

'Are you *really* sure?' rejoined the Master.

'Well, if you're pressuring me to stay here,' I said, bouncing my hand on the bed, 'I don't want to disappoint you.'

Feroze scoffed:

'As far as I'm concerned, you're welcome to stay out there with Gokul!'

Without another word, I grabbed the key and followed the teacher downstairs. Had the reign of tyranny now come to an end? Would I at last be getting on with serious work?

I would have to wait and see.

'Show me your hands,' Feroze snapped once we had reached the study.

When my fists were presented before him, he observed them carefully, inspecting the skin between each finger. His piercing scrutiny took in the torn nails, the lacerated digits and bruised palms.

Sighing with a veiled hint of pleasure, he began to speak:

'It's essential that when I tell you to do something, you do it – perfectly,' he said. 'Only then can you progress as a student in the field of conjuring. Now,' he continued, 'you have proved to me that you can obey . . . that you can be obedient.'

Feroze stood up and peered out the window in meditation, composing his thoughts. Rather than trying to drive me away, the trials of submission – as they were now being advertised – seemed similar to those employed by the SAS. The British élite fighting forces adopt a regime of reduced severity. They begin training with the hardest exercises and work backwards. The approach serves to purge the stragglers at the first hurdle – hacking away the dead wood. Although damaged, perhaps beyond repair, I could rest assured. Like a sprightly young sapling, I was free from dead wood.

'Now that they're over, can you tell me what relationship the ordeals bore to stage magic?' I enquired.

'You mean holding out the grape; digging with the teaspoon . . . crawling around for shells . . . all that?'

'Yes, *all that* . . . What relation did it have to the studies?'

The Master clicked his heels together and coughed.

'All that,' he quipped, 'had nothing whatsoever to do with illusion or magic!'

'Then why did I have to go through it?'

Feroze's face clenched tight with anger.

'Are you contesting my judgement?'

'Certainly not.'

'You say you want to learn about illusion and conjuring,' he blustered, regarding me straight on. 'Before you learn anything . . . before we start work . . . there are some things that you should understand.'

'Of course.'

'You must remember that this is India. And in India, illusion is different from the version you find in the West.' Feroze paused to take a deep breath. 'In India, illusion, magic, conjuring, sorcery – whatever you call it – is not a frivolous, whimsical thing. It's an extremely serious matter. It's a tool of incomparable capacity.

'Every day across this country,' the Master persisted, launching into a harangue, 'people use illusory techniques for different reasons. *Sadhus*, healers and mendicants, mystics and astrologers, so-called "godmen", and street entertainers: they all use stage magic. Some perform tricks to make an honest or a dishonest living. Yet through illusion, ordinary people realise their dreams of amassing astounding wealth and magnificent power.

'Remember what Europe was like two or three hundred years ago.' Feroze paused to unfasten his cuff-links. 'People were superstitious. They believed in witchcraft, in magic, in miracles, and in all kinds of supernatural powers. Look throughout India today and you'll find people with precisely the same beliefs. Pick anyone at random out there,' the magician motioned to the street, 'pull a gold watch from thin air, and they'll believe it's *real* magic.'

Feroze was right. In the West we dismiss conjuring as mere sleight-of-hand. Everyone knows that a magician's card trick is exactly that – a trick. But in India, simple feats of deception are enough to draw a following of thousands.

'I have spent my life studying illusion,' said Feroze pointedly. 'I have studied the effect of conjury on a man's psyche; the intensity of a "miracle" used in an Orissan village; and the power of the simplest trick seen by the pious in Varanasi.

'I have travelled through India's most remote regions and its greatest cities: always searching for one thing.' Feroze stopped talking. He wiped a hand across his mouth. 'I'm searching for those whose lives depend on deception: for those who conjure miracles for the masses!'

I leant back in my chair, watching as the sorcerer crossed the study. First he locked the door. Then he marched over to the bookshelf dedicated to Houdini. The shelf had been positioned at eye level. Or, rather, at nose level. Pressing his nostrils to the spine of the left-most volume, Feroze moved to the right, smelling each book in turn. As he sniffed, he tensed the muscles of his back, clenching his fists. He appeared to gain strength from the exercise. Only when he had smelt each book did he continue with his lecture.

'Now you have shown that you can follow orders,' he went on, 'I am willing to go on to the next step. In due course I will teach you some of my techniques. It's up to you to do with this knowledge what you will. When you have learnt from me, you may decide the material's too powerful a tool ever to use. Only you can make that decision.'

My attention was distracted by the sound of two vehicles smashing together on the street outside. I peered out to have a good look, hoping that I might spy the carnage through the back hedge. Realising that the blood and gore was out of sight, I swivelled round to face Feroze. But he had vanished.

The study's door was locked from the inside. Its key was still in place. The two other doors leading from the room were also locked, as were the windows. I searched for a trapdoor, a secret lever . . . but with no success. The only possible clue lay beneath the Houdini bookshelf. Inky black and as thick as treacle, I found a pool of high-viscosity engine oil.

8

Sorcerer's Apprentice

'To be a great illusionist,' said Feroze defiantly, when we had convened for work at six the next morning, 'you must study the experts.'

'Which experts?'

'First, you must immerse yourself in Robert-Houdin and Houdini, Cagliostro and Kellar. Then there are the illusions of godmen, sages and *sadhus* – India's own sublime conjurors – to be examined.'

Dressed in equestrian costume, replete with jodhpurs, knee-length riding boots, and a hound's-tooth jacket, Feroze motioned with a bull's pizzle riding crop to a set of shelves.

'Those are the classic texts,' he said. 'You must read them all and learn them. But before that, there's much preparation to do. Preparation is what it's all about!'

The Master had taken down a biography of Alessandro Cagliostro, the eighteenth-century Italian illusionist and mountebank. He held the leather-bound volume in his hands, caressing the tooled spine with his fingers as if it were a bejewelled reliquary.

'Before Cagliostro can become your confidant,' he hissed, 'there are other studies to attend to . . . Before Cagliostro's wickedness comes Houdini's genius.'

The monologue was interrupted as Gokul knocked at the door with a tray of tea. Feroze pointed the riding crop like a sabre at the manservant's chest, and then at the coffee table. Shuffling to the table, like a child in its mother's shoes, Gokul dispatched his load.

'During your studies,' said the Master in a calculating tone, 'I'll disclose shocking things. You may scream when I reveal the truth. But to discern any of the course, you must grasp a single key point.'

'I will try to understand it,' I said willingly. 'What is it?'

'One central element links all the greatest masters of stage magic and conjuring.' Feroze poured himself a cup of tea and breathed in the steam as if it were perfume. 'Each of them recognised the crux of all magic.'

'What's the crux?'

One had to wait for answers. Feroze controlled his material, rationing it at will.

'Nothing in illusion,' he went on, 'is so important as the cross-fertilisation of information.'

'What do you mean?'

Feroze swished an 'F' with his riding crop.

'Harry Houdini's maxim . . .' he roared. '*Polymathic proficiency makes a magician*!'

'Your studies must include multiple areas – both theoretical and tangible. Mathematics, chemistry, the arts, and psychology.' Feroze paused to gulp his tea. 'Then you have to grasp everything from bee-keeping to doxology!'

'*Doxology?*' I replied, limply.

The magician rubbed his chin, troubled at my lack of rudimentary knowledge.

'Doxology,' he elucidated, 'the study of hymns.'

Leaving no time to consider the importance of such an under-patronised area, Feroze continued with his discourse:

'It's upon these foundations that a magician builds,' he said. 'There's no point in learning a trick if your mind isn't sufficiently exercised and developed. Preparation forms the first part of your curriculum. Complete the groundwork and you can move on. The illusions themselves are the next section. Then . . .' Feroze said, stretching, 'then comes "insider information".'

'Insider information? What's that got to do with magic?'

'Excelling in illusion,' explained the Master, 'is all about learning secrets and applying them. Find out a man's trade secret: first, you have unlocked his puzzle; and second, you have a chip of information which – somewhere down the line – you may be able to apply yourself.'

Feroze's course seemed comprehensive, but I was startled at the lack of hands-on training. Wouldn't it have been better to cut to the chase and get on with the tricks themselves? I had so many questions, but when I expressed them, the magician would simply scrunch up his eyes and answer with another question:

'How long is the course to be?'

– 'How fast do you learn?'

'How much do you charge for the tuition?'

– 'Did you pay your father for teaching you to swim?'

'Why do you always answer one question with another question?'
– 'Do I?'

*   *   *   *

Work began at six each morning, with four hours of private study, mostly from terse scientific textbooks. As with the grim trials of the courtyard, much of the academic tuition appeared pointless. What illusionist needed to know the full Periodic Table, Linnaean terms for cacti, or Boltzmann's Constant?

As the schedule developed, I started to learn more of Feroze's abnormal nature. Never before had I met a man so preoccupied with time and detail.

Considering meals as an absolute waste of time, he permitted exactly twelve minutes for each one. Even then, he only picked at Gokul's offerings, rarely eating more than a mouthful or two. Lunch was taken at five past ten. A period of four hours followed, in which I was instructed on a wide range of sciences and unrelated areas. These ranged from coin collecting to the monastic architecture of thirteenth-century France. Dinner was consumed at five past two in the afternoon. After dinner, I was left to tackle the ever-expanding list of assignments and readings.

The odd timings of Feroze's life, and his senseless concern for minutiae, suggested he was a man haunted by an extreme condition of obsessive-compulsive disorder. Only a true obsessive would go as far as timing every feature of his day. A pocket-watch was always within easy reach of the magician's hand. Sometimes I would catch him noting down times: how long it had taken him to drink his tea; to walk from the kitchen to the study; to read a chapter of text; or to peruse his post.

The rigid agenda for everything began to drive me mad. But what I was subjected to was nothing in comparison to the magician's private regime.

Gokul, a devoted servant of many years, knew each of his master's eccentricities. Laughing them off, he listed a handful of the many obsessions one morning.

'He likes everything just so. His bath always at forty-five degrees; always shaves with seven sweeps of blade; shirt buttons fastened with the left hand; shoes must be relaced each day; his toenails clipped on Wednesday nights; the clothes in cupboard are hung facing west; he stirs tea clockwise, and coffee anticlockwise; he never enters or leaves a room without pressing his thumb to the doorknob twice; and,' said the servant, smiling, 'he cannot sleep unless window is left open exactly three inches.'

'Tell me, Gokul, what happens if any of these compulsions are forgotten?'

The servant jumped to his feet in a rare display of verve. Gaping at me, his face rigid with terror, he spluttered:

'No! No! Nothing *ever* is forgotten!'

* * * *

At first I was rather lackadaisical about my studies. Although challenging, the curriculum was a far cry from the misery of the courtyard ordeals. The cockroach-free room, with its soft bed and exquisite furniture, was a great improvement on the servants' quarters. But self-assurance soon turned to consternation, as the monumental workload began to take its toll. Feroze appeared to have no idea of the limits of a human's capacity for study.

Each day he piled dozens of treatises, books and heavy calfskin volumes before me. 'Another one or two for your pile,' he would smirk, loading five more editions atop the great ruck of books. As I stacked up the publications, I perceived the awesome artistry of the magician. His was a plan of unscrupulous cunning: first lull the student into a false sense of security; then bury him in work. Not content with damaging my body, he was now preparing to injure my mind.

The days began to pass, and I found myself exploring new thresholds of knowledge. I was learning about all kinds of things. All kinds of things, that is, except for stage magic. When Feroze caught me secretly reading one of Houdini's books, he vented his rage.

'Finished with your other studies, have you?' he said, snorting like a charging warthog. 'Well, you'd better plough on with these!' Half a dozen volumes on environmental pollution were thrown at me.

'Why do I have to study all this rubbish?' I protested.

'Learn to prepare your mind,' said Feroze with placid reflection. 'Without a foundation, even the mightiest building will collapse.'

'But I just want to learn something about conjuring! That's what I came for . . . to learn about magic!'

The Master gazed at his pocket-watch. He remained silent as the second hand wound round in miniature increments. Two minutes went by. I waited for the order of expulsion, recompense for my outburst. But it didn't come.

Instead of exile, Feroze doubled the workload. Every hour, the routine became more Draconian. Anything but full marks were unacceptable. Work graded below this – considered by him as sub-standard – was ripped up in a new orgy of humiliation. In the few instances praise was meted out, it was so brusque that most people would have regarded it as a mild rebuke. 'Life,' the teacher would say, inspecting his knuckles, 'doesn't recognise good and bad – just excellence.'

Only after three nights in the four-poster bed did I genuinely understand the true genius of Hakim Feroze.

Rather than a soothing berth for a weary head and dislocated spine, the bedstead was a foul accessory of persecution. On Alcatraz, penal offenders were afforded one luxury: each morning they would be given a piping-hot shower. But instead of being a gesture of compassion, the scorching showers had a more devious purpose. Had the convicts grown used to icy water, they would easily have been able to survive in the surrounding waters of San Francisco Bay. In the same way, the lavish splendour of the new bedroom was designed to weaken me. After the third night I resolved that, henceforth, I would sleep on the floor.

The disconcerting sleeping arrangements were only one of many peculiarities a pupil resident at the mansion was required to withstand. The ceaseless workload and stringent system of trials and exams, the strange meal timings, studies of fringe fields and dawn sessions . . . none was easy to get used to. But no idiosyncrasy of the household unsettled one as much as Hakim Feroze's inexplicable feats. By 'feats', I don't refer to conjury. I had enrolled to become proficient in that art, and was fascinated by it. Rather, I allude to the Master's other abilities – some of which seemed to have a grounding in what can only be called the occult.

How else could he change his shoes at will; or, in the dead of night, gain entry into a bedroom bolted from the inside? What explanation is there for popping up in different parts of the house without moving a step? How could he know the most recent details of people who had lost touch with him years before? Or, for that matter, how could he absorb information, 'reading' by holding a closed book in his hands?

When I turned to Gokul for answers to the constant stream of inexplicable behaviour, he avoided eye contact. Gazing at the ball of dough he was kneading in the kitchen, he said with ominous and uncharacteristic fluency:

'Do not ask these questions . . . dangerous questions make for dangerous answers.'

*

My interest in sleight-of-hand was built upon a foundation of scepticism. But the longer I spent at Alipore, the more unnerved I became at the prospect of bona fide necromancy. For the first time in my life I found myself doubting the foundation of cynicism that had always been my bedrock. On the one occasion that I confronted the Master directly, he exclaimed I was imagining his feats to be occult. 'True magic', he contended, was nothing but successful illusion.

But my thoughts had already begun to churn . . . Was there such a thing as legitimate witchcraft? If there was, could Feroze be a real sorcerer, capable of genuine magic? Whereas godmen claim their conjury is 'real magic', was Feroze maintaining the opposite – that his real magic was an illusion?

As time passed, I found myself scrutinising Feroze as closely as he was observing me. Like a pair of goldfish in bowls, placed opposite each other, we watched and watched . . . desperately hoping to catch the other out. I yearned to witness Feroze perform a feat of real magic. And he longed to discover gaps in my studies – which were to him a *carte blanche* to inflict chastisement.

*   *   *   *

The low point of each day was the ritual of examination. With no advanced warning, I would be commanded to enter 'examination stance'. The posture, which must have been borrowed from an elaborate Masonic ritual, was truly bizarre. Feroze insisted that the pose helped one concentrate. By this, I think he meant it helped *him* concentrate. I would position two chairs two feet apart in the centre of the study. An indigo-coloured velvet blindfold would be passed to me. Fastening it tightly about my eyes, as if readying myself for a firing squad, I would ascend. When in place, with my left foot on one chair, and my right on the other, the unrelenting inquisition would begin.

The exam took the form of five random questions. Any mistakes and I was expected to endure a further five questions. Feroze delighted in the fact that I had never managed to answer all five correctly. The examinations provided him with hours of entertainment.

A last-minute check that the blindfold was tight, and the test would begin:

'Tell me, what's Coulomb's Law?'

'It's the fundamental law . . .' I would murmur uneasily.

'Louder! Louder! I can't hear you, boy!'

'It's the fundamental law which states that the electric force of attraction or repulsion between two point charges is proportional to the product of the charges and inversely proportional to the square of the distance between them.'

In any other examination one might have expected applause. But Feroze was not concerned with what I knew – he was searching for pockets of ignorance.

'Next question . . . What is the Joosten Process?'

'Um, er,' I would stutter. 'But I studied that ages ago.'

'Again: what is the Joosten Process?'

'The Joosten Process is . . .' I would hold my head in my hands, taking care to keep balance astride the two chairs. 'It's the use of a chemical reaction between solutions of calcium chloride and sodium silicate to consolidate running soils or gravels when tunnelling.'

'Third question . . . on the *Mahabharata* . . .'

An excruciating pain shot down my right side as I heard the title of the Indian epic. The tale, consisting of 220,000 lines, was a subject which obsessed the magician. Claiming to have committed most of the incredible narrative to memory, he said it was fine preparation for any student. Without doubt the greatest narrative poem ever recorded, it's a feat to understand the convoluted plot of the Mahabharata, let alone to remember it.

'To start with,' he crowed, 'tell me what happened after Dhritirastra captured the Kuru throne?'

'Well, as Dhritirastra was blind, his brother – Pandu – assumed the responsibility of governing. But a curse led his brother to relinquish his position. Dhritirastra took control again, as Pandu went off with his two wives to live a life as a hermit in the Himalayas. Now, Pandu's five sons . . .'

'Enough! Tell me who wrote the poem.'

'No one knows for sure,' I replied, 'but legend has it that the complete tale was dictated by Vyasa to Ganesha, the elephant god. Supposedly, Ganesha agreed only to undertake the job on the grounds that Vyasa didn't stop for even a single break. The pace was furious, with Ganesha struggling to keep up. At one point he broke off a tusk to use as a pen after his stylus seized up.'

'All right!' barked Feroze. 'Enough of that. Tell me, what is occipitalla?'

The sudden switch from Hindu mythology to cranial osteology was not an easy change to make.

'It's the set of cartilage bones forming the posterior part of the brain-casing in the vertebrate skull.'

'Last question . . . a bonus one. Tell me, what is . . .' The Master would rub his fingertips together as if counting a bundle of banknotes. 'What's the chemical formula for monosodium glutamate?'

'Impossible!' I would exclaim. 'No one could remember that formula.'

Feroze would smile wryly.

'You know the rule,' he would say. 'Tell it to me loud and clear!'

Like a law of physics, I would run it off:

'Any error on the part of the student, however insignificant, permits the tutor to extend his examination with a further five questions.'

'Quite so!' the Master would shout. 'Now, give me a minute while I think of some more.'

Feroze's strict emphasis on subjects entirely unrelated to conjury became a bone of contention between us. The courtyard exercises, even the obscure mathematical formulae, may have had some bearing on the core subject. But surely, I pondered, before turning over to sleep, surely there was no need to study areas as esoteric as barbed-wire collecting and bagpipe infections.

Since I had come in from the cold of the cemetery, sleep had begun to elude me. Each night it seemed to take longer to drift off. My thoughts bounded from one recently studied subject to the next, as I struggled to get comfortable on the floor. First, it was the theory of quantum mechanics. Next, Russian espionage terms; followed by Indian cookery. After that came the ubiquitous heroes of the Mahabharata. As if highlighted by eerie cosmic search-lights, the stage of my subconscious mind ran wild. Krishna slipped a secret KGB code to a quantum physicist, while cooking up a dish of *murgh mussallam*.

As I thrashed about to rid myself of the vision, there came a scratch at the door. I sat bolt upright. The scraping came again. High-pitched and unwelcome, like a baby's scream at dawn, it was repeated for a third time. As usual, the door was bolted from inside. There was no way he could get in. But as usual, he was already inside the bedroom. Sensing my insomnia, Feroze had arrived to offer his most effective soporific: an impromptu examination.

*   *   *   *

Obsessive-compulsives often suffer from deeply entrenched fears. If you're obsessive, there's nothing quite so satisfying as being obsessive about a phobia. For years I've been keeping notes on phobics and obsessives. My note-taking is, in itself, bordering on the obsessive. Casting an eye through my notebooks, the correlation between obsessive-compulsive disorder and phobias becomes obvious. I've noticed that, the more extreme the obsessive, the more ludicrous the phobia. A friend of mine who's extremely obsessive, has *pognophobia*, a fear of facial hair. Show her a man with mustachios and she flips out.

With the Master's disorder so pronounced, I felt certain that in the darkest reaches of his mind there was a choice, ripe phobia waiting to be exploited. It was just a matter of isolating this Achilles' heel.

Nothing is so enjoyable as poking about someone else's belongings. Abandoned by the magician, who had gone to meet his old friend Rublu, I laid down the treatise on phonetics, slipped into the study, and pressed the door firmly shut. Then, closing the blinds, I got down to business. Just a little poke about, a riffle through Feroze's stuff . . . in search of his Achilles' heel.

Although confined, the room was a cloister dedicated to illusion and the unusual. For the Master, the magical arts could only be conquered by his true infatuation – polymathic study. His office was testament to this curious fixation. Its walls were lined with lacquered oak book-cases, their numbered volumes arranged by subject. The shelves pointed to a man with a staggering range of interests. The titles included gems like: *Selected Cuisine of Papua New Guinea*; *Advanced Volcanology*; *Cannibalism: A Question of Morality*; and *Elementary Techniques of Cosmetic Surgery*.

The space between the bookshelves was a mosaic of medals, framed diplomas, photographs and awards. At the centre of the arrangement, in a deep glass frame, was a golden twelve-pointed star, mounted on pink silk – a breast badge of the Sudanese Order of Distinction. Beside that, in another display frame, was hung an enamelled neck badge, suspended on tricolour silk – the Order of the Niger, Third Class. Under it, between a Fijian military medal and the Gallantry Cross of Malawi, shone a silver and gold medallion, The Star of the Solomon Islands. Below the medals was a simple framed letter of thanks from Juan Perón of Argentina. Beside it hung a diploma from the École Le Cordon Bleu de Paris. Lower down, below a pair of inscribed ceremonial *jambiyas*, curved Arabian daggers, was a studio photograph of an elderly black man with a trumpet at his lips. The picture was inscribed with the words 'To my dear friend Feroze, all the best, Louis.'

A glass-fronted cabinet, tucked away behind the chesterfield sofa, provided yet more clues to the Master's varied past. More than a dozen assorted silver trophies recorded his excellence in sports as eclectic as archery, rowing and épée. Beside the cabinet, a mahogany Prescot long-case clock recorded Feroze's obsession with time.

The drawers of the walnut writing bureau contained correspondence with well known writers, politicians and scientists. I scanned several of the letters. Most seemed to be thanking the Master for his judicious advice.

My being taken on as a student of such an unlikely man was astounding. Feroze was renowned as a magician, but his skills extended far beyond the realm of illusion. He was a polymath of prodigious scope. His skills, it seemed, were unlimited. Cordon Bleu chef, expert cartographer, linguist and scientist; authority on encryption and theoretical physics; arbiter on the stage of international relations; accomplished musician; connoisseur of ballet, opera and cinema; aficionado of philately – this was a man of unrestrained capacity. He was many things to many people. To me he was a slave-driver thirsting for blood. But, I counselled myself to remember, beyond that, he was my teacher.

Respect was one thing. Survival was another. It was important that I kept my priorities in the right order.

After an hour of rummaging around, I gave up. Not a hint of a phobia anywhere. Then I had an idea. If Feroze had an Achilles' heel, there was one man who would be sure to know it – Gokul.

I hurried out to the kitchen. The frail manservant was chopping up vegetables.

'Gokul, I've been playing a hilarious game!'

The servant looked up and grinned.

'What game?'

'Well, you have to reveal what makes you more frightened than anything else. For example, I detest cockroaches . . . can't stand them for a second.'

'Oh, and I hate a snake,' beamed Gokul, surrendering his own phobia.

'What about the Master?' I laughed. 'What is it that he can't stand?'

Stabbing the chopping knife into the board, Gokul stared at me coldly, his features locked in a fearful expression.

'There is something the Master not liking,' he said.

I leant forward, pretending to smile.

'Tell me what it is and we can carry on with the game!'

The sides of the servant's mouth turned downwards.

'Can't tell you.'

'C'mon, it's only a game.'

After ten minutes of cajoling, Gokul agreed to divulge what he knew. He made clear he was only doing so in the spirit of sportsmanship. Bowing close to me, he whispered:

'Rubber bands. The Master hates rubber bands very very very much.'

Anyone who had not spent years jotting down people's obsessions and phobias might have been surprised by Gokul's information. However, I had heard of the rubber band phobia before. A friend once told me of how, as a child, she was introduced to the late financier Sir James Goldsmith. All was going well. Then, lapsing from her best behaviour, my friend flicked an elastic band across the room. It landed at Sir James' feet. The billionaire, so the story goes, became deeply disturbed.

Thanking Gokul for playing the game so well, I hurried back to the study. I searched the shelves, the desk, its drawers, the table-tops and windowsill. Not a single rubber band to be found. My face distorting maliciously, I returned to the sitting-room and to my studies. Nothing to fear now . . . I had Feroze by his Achilles' heel.

*   *   *   *

The pressures resulting from the Master's reign spiralled out of control. A mysterious and virulent rash developed on my left shoulder. Within three days it had spread down to my elbow. When I exhibited it to the teacher, he explained it was *dhobi*'s itch – an unpleasant eruption of the skin, more commonly found on the inner thighs. In exceptional conditions it had been known to travel. Feroze instructed me to wash the area morning and night in potassium permanganate solution. A few days later it disappeared.

When I was cured, the Master made an announcement. It was almost time to move on to the next stage – to the actual study of illusion. The proclamation seemed long overdue.

'When will we be starting the new phase?'

'When you have passed the final exam!'

Although held in the customary 'examination stance', the final test would take a new form. Instead of fielding a series of specific questions, I would speak on a single subject of my own choice. If my deliberation was unsatisfactory, I would have to retake the complete segment of study. By 'unsatisfactory', the Master meant a single slip or inaccuracy. The test was scheduled for five minutes past five the next morning.

The thought of reliving the rigours of the previous three weeks was enough to turn anyone's blood cold. Before retiring to bed that night, I mugged up the most esoteric topic I could think of. Feroze craved the extraordinary . . . I would give him the cutting-edge in outlandishness. My head was heavy on the pillow that night, my eyes bloodshot and circled by brick-red rings. The next morning would prove my worth.

The aggravated levels of stress revealed themselves before the night was through. Gokul found me crouching beneath the courtyard's mango tree just after two a.m. Inspired by a mysterious dream, I had sleepwalked out of the mansion and into the yard. The tree had been calling to me. It told me to climb up into its branches, saying it would hide me from the tyrannical Master. It had once been a pupil, too, but having failed the final exam, the sorcerer had transformed him into a mango tree. 'There's one hope of escaping and dissolving the spell,' the tree called out in my dream. 'Find a rubber band!'

Taking the fingers of my hand in his as softly as one would a butterfly, Gokul led me back to bed.

Three hours later, I was blindfolded and straddling a pair of cabriole chairs in Feroze's study.

'Had a nice somnambulation?' he asked, rolling the syllables like marbles around his mouth.

'It's the pressure,' I gasped. 'It was beginning to get to me.'

'Are you ready for your little test?'

'Yes.'

'What's your chosen subject?'

'I've selected the strange case of the Man in the Iron Mask.'

Feroze raised his left eyebrow.

'Dumas?'

'No, the other one.'

'What *other* one?'

'Harry Bensley . . . the lesser-known Man in the Iron Mask.'

'All right!' blustered Feroze, placing his pocket-watch on the desk. 'You have four minutes to speak about your Man in the Iron Mask, starting . . . now!'

'In 1907,' I said, loosening the velvet blindfold, 'Lord Lonsdale and John Pierpont Morgan were relaxing after a heavy lunch at their club. The two millionaires discussed matters of national importance before turning their attentions to more trivial concerns – namely, whether a man could walk around the world without showing his face. American financier J.P. Morgan felt sure it was impossible. His associate, sporting peer Lord Lonsdale, was certain it could be done. Without further ado, each placed a bet of $100,000 backing their claim. Now the millionaires needed someone foolish enough to undertake the assignment. Fortunately for them, a young man named Harry Bensley was also present in the smoking-room.

'A playboy by profession, and aged thirty-one, Bensley jumped at the chance. Investments in Russia provided him with a substantial income, permitting him to enjoy a life of leisure. Tired of the tedium of the club, he volunteered his services.

'Lonsdale and Morgan drew up an agenda of strict rules: Bensley would wear an iron mask at all times. He would push a pram on his journey around the world, and would set off with only one pound in his pocket. No luggage was permitted, except for a single change of underwear. Bensley would have to pass through a specified number of towns in Britain, then at least 125 cities in eighteen or more countries. Other stipulations were that he was required to find a wife on his journey, who would agree to marry him without seeing his face. The trip would be financed by Bensley himself, by selling postcards from the pram. An escort was employed by the two millionaires to ensure that the strict rules were not infringed.

'Strapping the four-and-a-half-pound iron helmet to his head Bensley set out from Trafalgar Square on the first of January 1908, pushing a two-hundred-pound iron pram.

'For the next six years he pushed the pram across twelve nations, including the United States, Canada and Australia. More than two hundred women petitioned him for his hand; but he declined them all. Then, in August 1914, Bensley arrived in Genoa with only six more countries to visit. With the onslaught of the First World War, he was forced to call off the remainder of the trek. On his arrival in Britain, Morgan and Lonsdale offered him a consolation prize of £4,000, which he gave to charity. He enlisted soon after. Unfortunately, in 1917, with the Bolshevik Revolution, his Russian investments were nationalised. Harry Bensley died impoverished in 1956, in a bedsit in Brighton.'

When I had finished the tale, Feroze directed me to descend and remove the blindfold. Outside in the courtyard Gokul was peeling potatoes. It was not yet six a.m.

The Master stood up and strode over to the shelves which contained his magical texts. Without pausing, he removed a book from his Houdini collection. It had a torn violet dust jacket.

'This is for you,' he said, passing it over with both hands.

I read the title aloud:

'*Houdini's Magic.*'

Feroze nodded.

'The Magnificent Houdini,' he said, frowning. 'Acquire his eye for detail, develop his sense of timing, perfect his skills, master his tricks and . . .'

The magician fell silent. His nose twitched, the nostrils distending sharply.

'And . . . and what?'

Feroze smoothed a hand over his moustache.

'You will know when you have become it,' he said.

9

Swallowing Stones

The morning light drenched Feroze's study like syrup, illuminating its gilt frames and warming the lacquered bookcases. Outside, a pye dog had found its way into the courtyard and was marking its new territory with a chorus of melancholic howls. Dogs rarely ventured anywhere near the mansion. A man who came to sharpen the knives told me in broken English that, like all animals, they were fearful of the Master's witchcraft. Long ago, he said, Feroze had put a spell on a thief, turning him into a mange-ridden mutt.

Rublu, the hunched acquaintance, had turned up for a cup of tea and a twelve-minute lunch. Only a friend of many years would tolerate bolting down the midday meal at five past ten.

Feroze sat cross-legged on the study floor. He had removed his shoes and had undone the top three buttons of his twill shirt. Rolling up the cuff of his left sleeve, he asked me to take his pulse. I applied my index and middle fingers to his wrist. The rhythm seemed normal.

'Keep your fingers there,' instructed the magician.

I edged closer. Pushing his shoulders back, with his palms upturned, mouth closed, and eyes staring forward like a zombie's, Feroze began to meditate. His body was soon trembling. Within seconds, he had fallen into a trance, a state known to Indian mystics as *dhyaan*, literally 'concentration'. His eyeballs rolled back in their sockets. A trace of foamy saliva oozed from the right corner of his mouth. Crouched only inches from the Master, I watched with awe as something quite astonishing happened. Feroze's pulse grew slower. And slower. Then it stopped altogether.

Concerned that my teacher was about to expire, I called out to the hunchback. His head bobbed up from the newspaper.

'His pulse – it's vanished!' I yelled.

'Relax,' said Rublu, returning to the crossword. 'I wouldn't worry too much.'

'How can you be so unconcerned? I think he's dead!'

'*Really?*' scoffed Rublu from behind his paper. 'Better call an undertaker then.'

A spry Scottish nurse, who had been dressing an Afghan *mujahed's* gangrenous leg, once passed on to me a trick of her trade. To check if someone's dropped dead, tug both their earlobes down twice, as hard as you can. If they're alive, they wake up. Until that moment I had never had a chance to try out the tip. But far more enticing than testing the nurse's information was the prospect of yanking Feroze's ears. On the off-chance he was still alive, a brusque yank of the lobes would pay him back for the suffering he had inflicted upon me.

So, stretching out, I grabbed the Master's earlobes, and as if I were milking a cow I wrenched them twice.

The result was immediate. Feroze's eyes spun back into position. His body ceased quivering, and his pulse was instantly normal again.

'I brought you back to life!' I clamoured, my hands still clamped to his ears. 'Even Rublu thought you were a goner!'

'I thought nothing of the sort,' puffed the hunchback.

'Nonsense,' declared the Master, rubbing his sore earlobes. 'It was nothing more than a simple illusion. And, next time, leave my ears alone!'

'But, your pulse disappeared. You died . . . It was I who brought you back. I'm incredible,' I gasped, staring in disbelief at my miracle-working hands.

'*You* aren't incredible,' corrected Feroze. 'But *it* is . . . What you saw was incredible. First I died. Then returned from limbo. If I were a godman, you might have fallen down and worshipped me. But unfortunately, I'm an illusionist, and I performed a simple trick.

'Anyone can return from the dead – they don't have to be zombies,' said the magician. 'This is the first piece of stage magic that you are to learn.'

Feroze slipped his right hand inside his shirt, and withdrew a miniature object from his armpit.

'This,' he said, holding up a walnut, 'is the secret of returning from the dead.'

I might have asked how a humble walnut had played a part. But I was embarrassed at being taken in by what was now being hailed as a deception. Uplifted that my hands-on magical training had at last begun, I paid close attention.

'The illusion is elementary,' intoned Feroze when he had buttoned up his shirt. 'First, stick the walnut in your armpit, and pretend you're going into a state of *samadhi*. Next, gently press down on the nut. The trembling of meditation masks the contraction of one's shoulder muscles. Soon, as you saw, the nut reduces the pulse, by pressing on the axillary artery.'

The Master instructed me to clear away all the notes I had taken up until then. The trials beneath the mango tree had been a preparation for my body; and the random tutorials had prepared my mind. With the groundwork completed, the stage was set for the real lessons to begin.

It was with trepidation that I entered the new phase of instruction. But the prospect of at last getting down to serious magical scrutiny after the long build-up was thrilling. So appealing was it that I became blinkered to the anguish of the previous sections of the course. In a single, depraved moment I counselled myself to forgive and forget . . . to work towards détente. The regime had changed. I was already learning the magic of godmen.

The Master replaced the tarnished silver cuff-link at his wrist. Its familiar design – a set-square and compasses – confirmed my suspicions: Feroze was a Freemason. I had seen no overt symbols of Masonry in the mansion, but since we first shook hands at the Albert Hall, I had had little doubt. Feroze had pressed his right thumb between the knuckles of my middle and third finger: the cryptic sign of a Master Mason.

'Rublu,' he said dryly, 'please excuse us for a moment.'

Opening the glass-fronted display cabinet, the magician snatched a square-edged key from one of the trophy cups. Then, leading me to the door beside the store-room, he slipped the key into the lock, clicked it anticlockwise, and pressed his thumb to the doorknob twice.

'Come with me,' he whispered, pulling the door towards him. 'From now on this is where you will be studying.'

The chamber beyond was a scientist's laboratory. Stinking of astringents and gamy meat, it was stone-floored and windowless, with pastel-blue walls. A broad workbench filled much of the space. Upon it lay an array of alembics: distillation retorts, test-tubes, beakers, Bunsen burners, a Van de Graaff generator, and an assortment of chemicals. A thick layer of oily olive-black dust covered everything. Cobwebs dangled from the ceiling like silken parachutes; and rat droppings were scattered everywhere like hail. I showed surprise that a workplace should have fallen into such a state of disuse.

'Well,' Feroze snapped curtly, 'I told you I'd retired!'

Gokul was called. With a brush in one hand, and a rag mop in the other, he set to work spring-cleaning the laboratory. The magician led me back to the study. We would start lessons in the lab in due course. He launched into one of his many passionate orations on the theory of magical science. This time would I be given an opportunity to practise tricks?

'First,' said Feroze, as the crash of a glass flask echoed next door, 'think of the word "illusion". Ask yourself what it really means.'

I mulled over the question.

'It means "the effect of . . ."'

Feroze interjected:

'It means something that deceives by producing a false or misleading impression of reality.'

I repeated the magician's definition; but he had already moved on.

'As I told you before,' he expounded, 'you have to study all the great masters of illusion. Watch for what they find important . . . learn their techniques of sleight-of-hand . . . see how they manipulate a crowd . . . question everything that the audience does not. Then,' commanded the Master, 'Practise, Practise, Practise!'

Gokul shuffled through the study in his mule slippers, ferrying a dustpan of rat droppings outside.

'But beyond all else,' grunted Feroze, his concentration unbroken, 'you must pay attention to detail. From now on, detail – any detail – is of prime importance. Become a connoisseur of detail, and you will excel as an illusionist.'

'Is detail more important than the tricks themselves?'

'Of course the illusions are key,' replied the Master, 'but you can go away and devise your own deceptions. I won't be standing beside you forever. Before you leave me, your eyes have to be looking in the correct places; your ears must be tuned to pick up the right frequencies.'

The long-case clock chimed noon.

As if signalled to move by a clarion call, Rublu sprawled out on the chesterfield and promptly fell asleep. He must have had a hard life. His clothing was dishevelled and reeked of stale tobacco; his shoes were scuffed, and his spine hopelessly contorted – most probably from years slouching in a stifling Calcutta office.

Feroze noticed me glance over at his friend.

'Close your eyes,' he ordered. 'Now, tell me: what's Rublu wearing? Describe his clothes in as great detail as you can remember.'

The disorderly figure slipped into my mind.

'He's wearing brown lace-up shoes,' I reported. 'His shirt is white; his cardigan is a sort of dusty green; and his trousers are a blotchy shade of blue, I think.'

The magician was unimpressed at my description.

'Where was the detail?' he contested.

Closing his eyes, Feroze began to speak:

'Rublu is wearing one of my old cotton shirts. I believe the tailor called the shade of cloth "cornhusk". It has a spread collar, an accentuated yoke, single cuffs, two gusseted breast pockets, in-box pleat and mother-of-pearl buttons. Over the shirt, he's wearing a fern-green V-neck cardigan, knitted in moss stitch, with a single welt pocket on the left side, and with light ribbing on the cuffs. The cardigan is fastened by six elm-green shank buttons. His trousers are tailored from a lightweight polyester-rayon blend.' Feroze paused for several seconds, his eyes twitching surreptitiously beneath their lids. 'I recall that they have turn-ups,' he continued, 'and button flies, a knife pleat and, as for the colour . . . it's Dresden blue.'

'Very good,' I sniffed. But Feroze had not yet finished.

'His shoes,' he went on, 'are rather inferior Calcutta-made buffalo half-brogues. If I'm not mistaken, they were made in the Chinese district of Tangra. The leather has been dyed a rather uneven tint of iris leaf grey. The shoes' back cuffs have been trodden down; the lace-tags are severely frayed; and the vamps are badly creased – a result of poor Rublu's posture. I think that's about it . . .' The sorcerer opened his eyes and smiled. 'Oh no,' he remembered, 'I quite forgot his wristwatch: it's a Titan chronometer with a steel casing and a vinyl strap. It loses between three and six minutes a day.'

Feroze set an example which was hard – if not impossible – to emulate. He considered the observation of detail to be the most important factor in the course. 'Learn to perceive the smallest insignificance,' he would say, 'and the rest will follow.' This approach, I soon learnt, had been preached by the century's most famous illusionist, Harry Houdini.

As I studied more of Houdini's methods, I began to realise the similarity between his character and that of Feroze.

Both men understood the unlimited strength of conjuring and illusion – especially when used in the developing world. Both were arrogant beyond the point of reason; both accepted nothing short of miracles from their students; both were masters of crowd manipulation and showmanship, and were preoccupied with observing minutiae. Yet most significant of all, both were tormented by obsessive-compulsive behaviour.

Now he had reached the main body of his course, Feroze moved speedily from one illusion to the next. After an initial demonstration, I was expected to explain how each trick was accomplished, before repeating it myself. Many of the simplest illusions involved sleight-of-hand. Although easy to grasp, sleights require hours of frustrating practice to perfect.

In India, one deception is performed by godmen and religious *pandits* more frequently than any other. It involves the sprinkling of silvery-white holy ash, known as *vibhuti*. The chalky dust is materialised from nowhere by spiritual leaders and shaken on to the palms of their devotees. The faithful generally lap at the ash with their tongues. Anyone with the ability to produce *vibhuti* is considered to have supernatural powers.

I protested that the exercise would be of little use to me, for I had no intention of becoming a godman. Feroze insisted that mastering *vibhuti* would develop my sleight-of-hand abilities. Adept conjurors, he said, can eat, drink tea, and write with one or two of the pellets hidden in position – lodged in the web of skin between the thumb and forefinger. With a single circling movement of the hand, they can withdraw the pellet and crush it with the fingertips.

Feroze demonstrated how to make the tiny pellets. A quantity of perfume and ash is mixed in a pan with a few drops of *kanji*, a starchy water in which rice has been washed. Stir in enough ash and one gets a form of dough. Pea-sized beads of the preparation are dried, ready for use.

As I had suspected, the practice schedule of the routines was relentless. Feroze introduced ten new illusions a day. He expected me to master each one before the next morning. My demonstration of the previous day's tricks was followed by a random quiz on the life and work of famous illusionists. After that, I was ordered to describe an object of his choice in infinite detail.

Despite the concentration-camp style of Feroze's tutelage, the study of illusions was supremely satisfying. The rules and regulations which surrounded every aspect of life at the house were still unbearable. The only consolation was that, for the first time, my concentration was applied to studies, rather than survival. Finally, I was learning what I had come to learn.

As I practised the experiments in the hush of Feroze's laboratory, it was as if I had travelled back two decades in time. I could almost sense Hafiz Jan breathing down my neck as he leant over the desk in my attic. To be learning from the man who had taught the Pashtun gave me a rush of joy. I was certain Hafiz Jan would feel proud that his own teacher had accepted me.

*   *   *   *

One morning, Feroze came to the laboratory carrying a faded shoebox. A series of holes had been poked through the top with a ball-point pen. Placing the carton at the far end of the desk, the magician tested me on the illusions studied the previous day.

First, I demonstrated the 'smoking fingers' routine. A mixture of yellow phosphorous and carbon disulphide is prepared, with a ratio of 1:6. Two drops of this are applied to the thumb and forefinger. When the two fingertips are rubbed together, a plume of smoke rises upwards from the hand.

Next, Feroze commanded me to sip a cup of tea and take dictation with two pellets of *vibhuti* concealed between my fingers. I complied with reasonable success. After that, he directed me to burn a cube of camphor and place it on my tongue. Despite regular practice sessions, the experiment is always distressing. A piece of camphor a little smaller than a sugar lump is set alight. As the flames lick upward, it's quickly thrown on to the tongue, and the mouth is snapped shut. The cheeks glow for two or three seconds as the fire burns inside. Many Indians believe that camphor will only burn when offered in front of an idol. Although impressive to an audience, the trick is not overly dangerous. Even when the camphor is burning, the bottom of the cube – resting on the tongue – stays relatively cool. Before the fire has a chance to burn the saliva-coated tongue, carbon dioxide exhaled from the lungs extinguishes the flame.

Other illusions followed. Feroze awarded points for performance and general style. As one might expect, he was parsimonious when it came to awarding high grades. I never received more than three out of ten for any illusion.

When I asked what was in the shoebox, the magician called for me to describe the piano in the sitting-room. He disliked others steering the agenda. For the first time I could relax: the piano was my trump card.

'It's a Steinway upright piano,' I asserted, 'manufactured in Hamburg, with a standard eighty-eight-note keyboard. The keys, which are elephant ivory, have yellowed with age. Those most frequently played have worn down slightly at the ends. The middle-C key is cracked, filled at some point in the past with window putty. The casing is veneered in seasoned walnut, with a mahogany base frame. Its top flap has a circular scuff, where a jardinière may have stood. The brass pedals are well-polished; but the fronting-board, into which they slot, is stained where the polish has spilt over on to it. One of the casters has broken off and has been replaced by a single book. I believe it's a 1913 edition of *The Land of the Peaks and the Pampas*, by Jesse Page, bound in geranium-red cloth.'

When I had finished, Feroze twisted the knurled crown of his pocket-watch.

'Is that all you can tell me?'

I nodded meekly.

'What about its sounds . . . its smell . . . or the way it feels to touch? What about its inner workings? How could you leave out all the most important details?'

The teaching profession, I recalled, attracts two types of sadist. The first, although ruthless, secretly hopes his students will improve. The second, who employs fierce, malignant methods for their own sake, couldn't care less about the wretched pupils. Feroze was quite obviously that type.

'Enough of the piano,' he said with sinister delight. 'Time for something rather special.'

Moving over to the far end of the table, he dislodged the lid of the shoebox and, with some care, lifted out a curled viper. With the snake's head in his left hand, and its tail clasped between the fingers of his right, Feroze stretched the reptile straight.

'This morning,' he intoned, 'I am to teach you one of the oldest and most important of all magical tricks. We are to turn a rod into a serpent. This illusion has beguiled both kings and peasants for over three thousand years. It's shrouded in mystery, and is as significant in magical lore as the rope trick, the bed of nails, or even levitation. Master this, and you will be performing a trick that was key to the development of all magical illusion.'

'When was the trick first done?'

The magician examined the serpent's head.

'Aaron is recorded as having performed this "miracle" in the bible. You can read the account in Exodus, chapter seven, verse ten. But,' continued Feroze, 'this illusion even pre-dates Aaron. The ancient Egyptian texts also chronicle the marvel of transforming a rod into a serpent. Dervishes of Central Asia and *avatars* throughout the East have used the feat to demonstrate what, to the audience, is genuine magic.'

'If this is the snake, then where's the rod?'

'That's it,' said Feroze. 'There is no rod. This is illusion in its purest form. We're going to use the instinct of the reptile to create an illusion.'

'Where does a snake's instinct come into it?'

'Firstly, I should tell you that the serpent has been chilled for three hours. So it's a bit more sluggish than usual. Now, notice how I'm pressing my thumb down firmly at the centre of its head. My index finger is on the other side of the jaw, countering the pressure.'

The Master held the viper's head to my face for inspection.

'The conjuror,' he went on, 'keeps up the pressure for several minutes. Its effect is to stun the snake – which assumes that a predator of gigantic size is attacking it. Unable to defend itself, it's gone into shock. Even if I lower its tail to the floor, it still can't move.'

Feroze demonstrated. He was right. The snake was utterly paralysed.

'Now, watch what happens when the viper is thrown to the floor.'

Taking care not to damage the delicate serpent, Feroze dropped it on the laboratory's stone floor. Two or three minutes passed before it started slithering about.

'*We* know that – realising it's free – the snake jolts out of shock. But,' said Feroze, picking the viper up once again, 'with correct lighting and so forth, the audience is certain they've seen a miracle!'

That afternoon, when Feroze had tested me on the life of Harry Kellar – American conjuror and close friend of Houdini – he pulled a large glass carafe from one of the teak cabinets mounted high on the laboratory's back wall. The jar was about the size of an old-fashioned sweet jar. It was full of pebbles.

Feroze unscrewed the plastic lid and fished out seven pebbles, each the size of a quail's egg. Having wiped the dirt off them with a rag, he gulped down a mug of water and then, one by one, he swallowed the stones. They went down as smoothly as vanilla ice cream.

'Now it's your turn,' he announced, when he had finished off the seventh pebble.

'I'm not going to swallow stones!' I protested. 'They won't go through my system. I've just had my supper – I'm not hungry.'

'They aren't dessert,' rejoined the Master facetiously. 'In any case, the stones don't go *through* your system.'

He spun round to face the door. Two minutes later, his eyes bloodshot and blinking, he slammed the seven nuggets of stone on the bench.

'There!' he shouted. 'They didn't go anywhere near my system!'

Some of the Master's illusions had been distinctly unpleasant. But until this point, none had been truly life-threatening.

'I'm not going to swallow stones,' I repeated. 'I'm sorry, but I draw the line at this. Call me a sissy, but I simply have to draw the line somewhere.'

Feroze said nothing. He washed his cherished pebbles under the tap and returned them to the jar. Then, rubbing a hand across his chin, he looked at me quizzically.

'Stones too big for you then, eh?'

'Very much too big,' I stammered.

'Then we'll start you off with something a bit smaller.'

Feroze pulled a teaspoon from his left pocket and struck the tin mug which always hung from his belt. A second later Gokul appeared. Wherever the servant was, he never failed to be summoned by the Master's gong.

'Gokul,' he roared, 'go and fetch some new potatoes.'

'Yes, *Sahib*, how many to bring?'

'Oh,' said the Master, 'about a dozen will do.'

Twenty minutes later I had swallowed my first raw potato. Admittedly, it was not a King Edward, but a baby one grown in the compound. Although modest, the stunt filled me with satisfaction. As I drew in a deep breath, and waited for my eyes to slope back into their sockets, Feroze tossed another potato over.

'Come on,' he said energetically, 'there're lots left!'

'I don't want to hog them all. You have some, please, I feel so greedy.'

But the magician would have none of it. One after another, the miniature potatoes rattled down my oesophagus like balls down a bowling alley.

'How many's that now?' he prompted, delighted with the experiment.

'Five,' I choked. 'I may be a killjoy, but I really don't think my belly can take any more. You can quite clearly hear it churning.'

The sorcerer poured a mug of water. I gulped it down. It trickled towards the potatoes, soothing my gullet. But my stomach was in disarray. It was informing my nervous system I had coughed down a box of billiard balls. My brain warned my oesophagus to reject any more of the unwelcome vegetables.

Feroze examined his right thumb from a distance, picked at a cuticle; then poured a cup of water from another jug.

'I don't think I can take any more,' I stuttered. 'My stomach is shutting down – you have it.'

'You *must* drink this.'

Unfit to argue, I complied with the demand. In mid-flow – as my mouth was awash with the fluid – I grasped that this was not water. There was none of the cool, soothing delectation which accompanies the liquid. Instead, my mouth, gullet, and then what was left of my stomach reeled in horror at what it had just consumed.

Within the blink of an eye, my whole abdomen became involved in a fit of unprecedented vomiting. A mass of half-digested *daal* and rice, puréed mango and *mattar-paneer*, coconut and yoghurt was propelled at momentous velocity from the innermost depths of my thorax. Like the wad which precedes a cannon's grapeshot, the concoction heralded the ensuing barrage of vegetable missiles.

As the one who had fed me the powerful emetic, Feroze deserved the drenching he got. All thoughts of reaching an entente cordial evaporated. The elixir, syrup of *ipecac*, made from the root of Brazil's *ipecacuanha* shrub, is preferred by hospital casualty departments for treating overdose patients.

The sight of the omnipotent magician, dripping with curry-based vomit was ample pay-back. As the spew oozed down his face and shirt-front, I castigated myself. How could I have been so myopic? After what I had been through, how could I have put my trust in his fiendish hands again?

Although he knew my digestive tract had responded with reflex action, Feroze was not the kind of man to disregard involuntary behaviour.

A series of harsh recriminations followed.

Directed at my subconscious mind, the retaliations were designed to discipline my stomach. In future, when practising regurgitation routines, the organ was to accept the *ipecac* syrup in silence.

Over a period of six days, the Master introduced a regime of vile and barbaric magnitude. First, he cancelled the twelve-minute lunch, claiming that it obstructed lessons. Next, he stepped up the regurgitation exercises to three sessions a day. Additional illusions were still woven into the curriculum. But now they were of the most repugnant variety. Extra sessions were devoted to lectures, sometimes held in the middle of the night, on conjuring and the great masters. Immediately after each discourse, I was expected to write an essay deliberating on the chosen subject. Like a half-price sale gone wrong, my grades were slashed with reckless abandon.

By the third day, my stomach was sore beyond belief. Like that of a new-born baby, it was no longer able to deal with solid food. As if dispatching desperate smoke signals, the organ made known that it had begun the countdown to ulceration. I drew its deteriorating condition to Feroze's attention. Still recovering from the discomposure he had suffered – or which he thought he had suffered – he waved my petitions aside.

'You must learn to control your stomach,' he asserted. 'Houdini taught himself to move every voluntary muscle independently. You must do the same. I can't help it if you're feeling a *little* discomfort!'

Feroze didn't realise it, but he had tipped me over the edge. I revived my scheme for all-out revenge. Only one form of requital had the capacity to pierce the magician's defences. I would have to strike without delay at his phobia. But first, the ammunition . . . I needed a supply of rubber bands.

I scoured the mansion from top to bottom. Not an elastic band in sight. Worse still, I rarely had the chance to leave the compound. If he had found me sneaking out to buy rubber bands in the middle of the night, Feroze would have been rabid with fury. Gokul and Rublu frequently came and went. But I could trust neither. Only after considerable meditation did I come up with a secure method of smuggling in a supply. I asked Gokul if, on his next trip to the market, he could pick me up a bundle of *neem* sticks with which to clean my teeth. Everyone knows that bundles of *neem* sticks are always kept together with coloured elastic bands. Pleased that I was forsaking my toothbrush for a more natural cleaning method, the elderly servant agreed to fetch me the twigs. Before he hurried off, he swore not to tell the Master, who was keen to control all matters relating to personal hygiene.

Meanwhile, the drills continued.

On the fourth day, I brought up my first pebble. The feat was all the more astounding for I had used no emetic. As if reaching a tacit understanding with my belly, I found that I was able to regurgitate merely by controlling internal muscles. The mouth, oesophagus and stomach were willing to do all they could to help: so long as no *ipecac* syrup was administered.

Of course, Feroze took all the credit for my achievement. Motioning for me to replace the stone in the jar, he declared that we would return to regurgitation later. Instead of putting the pebble back, I wrapped it in my handkerchief. Like a first-born child, this one was special. I would keep it as a lucky charm.

Without wasting any time, the magician rapped once on his chipped enamel mess mug. Gokul emerged like a phantom from nowhere. He was shuffling even slower than usual, his upper body bent over his trembling arms. When he turned around, I realised he was carrying a pot. The vessel seemed to contain something of enormous weight.

'Put it down here,' instructed Feroze, pointing to a large iron tripod.

'Yes, *Sahib*,' gasped the valet, straining to do as he was told. I slipped him a glance as he exited the room. He shook his head evasively. No *neem* sticks yet.

When the pot was in place on the tripod, the Master lit a Bunsen burner beneath it. I peered in. No wonder Gokul had been so burdened. The container was full of molten lead.

'Now,' said Feroze, talking above the roar of the Bunsen burner, 'you have to be careful with this stuff. Molten lead can be quite dangerous if not handled with care.'

'I understand,' I remarked, with mounting anxiety at what part a vat of boiling lead was to play in the lesson.

The Master brought down a Fortnum & Mason biscuit tin from the wall cabinet and pulled away the lid. It was filled with ordinary sand.

'I'm going to teach you how to put your hand into a pan of boiling lead,' explained Feroze. 'Before we do the trick, you have to prepare. Without adequate preparation mistakes are made: then people get injured.'

'I see,' I grunted. 'We don't want any more injuries. Or at least *I* don't.'

'Before plunging your hand in the lead,' the magician instructed, 'you have to "wash" your hands in dry sand. This soaks up all the moisture. You must attempt this trick *immediately* after rubbing the hands with sand. Wait a second longer and the hands perspire. Sweaty hands and molten lead don't go well together. Understand?'

'Yes, I understand.'

'Good, now watch this.'

Feroze scraped away the thin film of residue from the surface of the lead. An alluring silvery sheen lay beneath. In a single expert movement, the teacher plunged the fingers of his right hand into the molten metal. He counted to three as hastily as possible; glanced me in the eye, and removed the digits.

'Now you do it,' he said.

When my hands were washed in the fine pheasant-brown sand, I positioned myself carefully over the pot of smoking lead.

'I'll do a countdown,' said Feroze, loosening his cravat. He loved doing countdowns.

'Wait . . . let me prepare.'

'The time for preparation is over!' snapped the Master. 'Your fingers will start to sweat. One . . . two . . . three . . . now!'

'Aaaah!' I screeched, as my left hand plunged up to the knuckles into the silvery metal. A fraction of a second later, I withdrew.

'What's all that fuss you're making?' said Feroze. 'Anyone would think you've just pulled off a miracle.'

Raising his tin mug, Feroze summoned Gokul. But even before he had struck the bowl of the spoon on the enamel, the servant appeared. He turned off the Bunsen burner's tap and shambled away with his pot of lead.

'Now,' said Feroze, grandly, 'I want to tell you about Houdini.'

'But we're always learning about Houdini.'

The Master countered my complaint with a wrathful glare. His eyes twitched three times. I deciphered the code. Three twitches threatened a recriminating bout of stone-swallowing. My stomach knotted in anticipation.

'Sorry for bursting out.'

Feroze smiled on the left side of his mouth.

'So,' he said, leading me out into the study. 'Let's consider the genius of Harry Houdini.'

Mindful that I would soon be writing a detailed essay on the lecture, I paid attention.

'Harry Houdini,' began Feroze, running the name across his tongue with grandiloquence, 'was born Erich Weiss in 1874. He chose "Houdini" as a stage name in honour of the great nineteenth-century illusionist Robert-Houdin. "Harry" was adopted for the alliteration. This reverence for Houdin evaporated in later years. It culminated in Houdini's tireless efforts to discredit his former idol.'

The magician paused and caught me with a crushing glance. Was he musing that I would, one day, turn against him? I returned Feroze's gaze with a servile grin.

'Whatever his motives for slurring his hero,' he continued, 'Houdini was an extraordinary illusionist. He was unusual in that he had the gifts and talents of many magicians all rolled into one. He was brilliant at sleights and complex tricks; a master of delivery, an actor; as well as being brave, fast-thinking, pugnacious, a maestro of the esoteric, and a connoisseur of detail. And we have seen the importance of detail.'

I nodded twice. Then again.

'Yes, detail is very important.' I confirmed.

'Houdini,' continued Feroze, satisfied with my alertness, 'understood that without mystery there was no magic. He knew also that without publicity, word of one's skill would not travel. Houdini built up the sense of mystery. He would keep the audience waiting. By the time he came on, they were already at fever pitch. His illusions would be peppered with red herrings . . . designed to distract the crowd's attention. Of course it was Houdini's ability as an escapologist which made him a legend. We're not so concerned with escapology, but we can learn from his methods.

'When touring, he would challenge local safe-makers to deliver their strongest safe to his encampment a day before the show. During the performance, he would be locked inside the safe, trussed up in a straitjacket. A curtain would be drawn around the coffer. An hour of so later, Houdini would emerge from behind the curtain. The audience would be thrilled. But Houdini was always cautious not to be too good.'

'What do you mean? There's no such thing as being *too* good!'

'Of course there is,' riposted Feroze. 'Houdini could get out of the safe within five minutes. He'd spend the rest of the time reading a novel, or practising another routine. If he had emerged after five minutes everyone would think the trick was rigged.'

'Was it rigged?'

Feroze glowered across the room.

'Of course it was rigged! When the safe was delivered, Houdini and his crew would remove its workings and replace them with locks from their own stores. Sometimes the task would take all night. Yet no one would suspect they'd go to such trouble. Before the safe was returned, all the original locks and hasps were replaced.'

'Did Houdini often rig his tricks?'

'What are you saying?' cried Feroze, clasping his cheeks in his hands. 'Haven't you learnt anything? Of course he rigged his tricks! He was an *illusionist*. They were illusions!'

Feroze went to the bookshelf and pulled down a worn hardback volume.

'*The Secrets of Houdini*,' I read aloud. 'By J. C. Cannell.'

'You had better read it right now.' quipped Feroze, pulling out his pocket-watch. 'I'll give you an hour.'

Cannell's book described many of Houdini's devilish schemes. Anyone who has fond images of 'Houdini the incorruptible champion of magic' should not read the book. Houdini might, I brooded, have been strong, dextrous and quick-thinking, but he resorted to the most base deceptions ever devised. He used bogus handcuffs. His stooges would pose as bona fide members of the audience. The trunks from which he escaped had sliding panels; the armoured vans had false floors; and the giant water-filled milk-churns even had sham rivets. But then, as Feroze had so correctly reminded me, Harry Houdini was a master of illusion.

'Remember,' the Master reminded me the next morning, as he examined my essay on Houdini, 'half the secret of any illusion can be put down to building up the spectacle. The more incredible the feats, then the more the audience's tongues will wag when they leave. The greater the mystery, the faster word of the skill will spread. People are the same here in India. If a godman thrills them, they hurry away to tell others.

'Houdini was a great conjuror,' continued Feroze. 'Of that there's no doubt. But he was a far greater showman. He charmed the crowds. He encouraged them to inspect his props and equipment. And he baited them, until they were feeding on the infectious suspense he conjured.'

The Master halted to pull a ruffle from the carpet.

'It's a beautiful morning,' he said abruptly.

'Yes, it is. The first cool, sunny morning in more than a week. Are we going to start with regurgitation this morning?'

'Another time,' he said restlessly. 'Today is such a fine day. So fine it merits something a little special.'

'What, more special than swallowing stones?'

'Oh, yes,' recoiled Feroze, '*much* more special than that.'

At nine-thirty Rublu arrived, anticipating a swift lunch. He was, I noticed, wearing new clothes. They were rather familiar. The cotton trousers were a murky shade of olive green; the shirt, also cotton, was peach. Although peculiar, the combination wasn't original. Feroze himself had worn identical colours five days before. Then I understood. These were the clothes over which I had spewed the contents of my stomach earlier that week. Appalled by the thought of ever wearing them again, the Master had passed them on.

'Let me know when you're ready to eat,' mumbled Rublu as he picked up the newspaper.

'Oh, *we* have no time to eat today, Rublu,' replied Feroze airily, 'but I'm sure Gokul has prepared something for you.'

The punishment for my indiscretion with the emetic still hung over the house like a storm-cloud.

'We'll just have a cup of Darjeeling,' said Feroze wistfully, as he led me into the laboratory. As if by magic, Gokul appeared with a tray. He shared Feroze's uncanny ability of materialising from nowhere. Was the ancient valet under the magician's spell, I wondered, or was he a sorcerer as well?

Pouring my tea, Gokul looked me in the eye, and winked. It was a sign . . . a secret signal which could have alluded only to one thing. The *neem* sticks had arrived.

'Now . . . for that special little something,' sung Feroze in a sinister staccato.

Exercises which he billed as 'special' tended to be distinctly unpleasant.

'First, for a warm-up,' he said, rolling up his sleeves. 'This is one of the Israeli-born spoon-bender's favourites.'

'You don't mean Uri Geller?'

'Of course I do . . . Uri Geller – the Western world's foremost illusionist, and,' Feroze went on, 'the most famous conjuror to claim that his illusions are *real* magic.'

'Maybe he *is* gifted,' I said.

'I don't doubt he has a gift,' retorted Feroze, 'but it isn't magical. Remember . . . all Geller's feats have been explained: from the spoon-bending to the reading of sealed documents. We can speak about that later. But now there's work to do!'

Feroze turned his back, then presented me with a crumpled ball of aluminium baking foil.

'I want you to hold this in your fist,' he directed. 'When I say so, and only when *I* say so, the foil will become warmer. Are you ready?'

'Yes,' I responded, clasping the glittering metal tightly in my fist.

'All right,' said Feroze, clearing his throat. 'I'll concentrate very hard on the ball of foil.'

Applying his fingertips to his temples, the magician began to focus.

'Tell me when you begin to feel the metal heating up.'

A minute passed. Then another. Nothing. The metal was room temperature. But then, as I stared at the stone floor, it began to grow warm.

'I can feel the metal getting hotter!' I burst out. 'Yes, it's getting much warmer now.'

'Good,' said Feroze softly, still with his fingertips pressed against his temples. 'Now, when I tell you, the metal will begin to heat up so much that you will have to drop it.'

Rublu broke my concentration, as he called us to eat from the study.

'Rublu!' cried the Master sharply, 'I told you – we're not eating lunch. Far too much work to be done. You go ahead!'

Footsteps could be heard pacing out to the dining-room.

'Where was I?' mumbled Feroze. 'Oh, yes, when I count to three, you will find the metal almost too hot to handle . . . One! Two! Three!'

The aluminium was already exceedingly warm. Then, as I thought about it, the ball of crumpled metal foil became too hot to hold in my fist. I threw it on to the work-bench.

'Excellent!' announced Feroze. 'My powers of concentration paid off!'

'What do you mean? Were *real* psychic powers used?'

'You should know better than that,' he quipped. 'It was magic, but stage magic!'

'How's it done?'

'This is the Hot Foil Trick,' remarked the Master. 'You may have seen that, before passing you the foil ball, I turned my back to you.'

'Yes, I did notice.'

'Well, that was to cover one surface of the aluminium with a solution of mercuric nitrate. I painted it on with the back of a spoon, before rubbing the solution into the metal with a cloth.'

'Mercuric nitrate?' I said. 'Isn't that incredibly poisonous?'

'Yes, as a matter of fact it is,' said Feroze coldly. 'It's lethal. The toxicity is the drawback of the trick. But that's irrelevant for now. The key point,' he continued, 'is that the chemical causes the metal to oxidise very rapidly. The exothermic reaction creates the heat – not mind power!'

'And this is one of Geller's tricks?'

'He loves this one. It's great for modest audiences or for television demonstrations. But,' said Feroze, 'it's also been widely used by godmen. They take the trick a stage further. Insert an amulet or, say, a ring in the foil ball . . . When the devotee finds the charm in the ball of metal, he thinks that real magic's been at work.'

As I washed all traces of the deadly mercuric nitrate from my fingers, Feroze clapped his hands together.

'Now we've dispensed with the warm-up,' he exclaimed, 'on with the *pièce de résistance*!'

'What is it to be?'

Feroze's enthusiasm was always fuelled by one thing – pain . . . someone else's pain.

'This is a very antique piece of conjury. You find it in many forms across Asia, but the basic gist is always the same.'

'What is it?'

'I'm going to teach you how to raise your body temperature very dramatically.'

'What good's that?'

Feroze seemed surprised that I had not grasped the immediate use of such a feat.

'The power to raise one's temperature at will to 104 degrees Fahrenheit,' he said, 'is enough to prove superhuman ability.'

'Tibetan lamas can raise their body temperature, can't they?' I asked, remembering seeing a photo of naked lamas in the snow.

'Lamas can maintain their body warmth even in freezing conditions,' the sorcerer replied, 'but they achieve it by anointing themselves with yak fat.'

His response was comforting: it implied we would not be rubbing yak fat across our naked bodies.

'If we're not using yak fat,' I asked, 'then how do we achieve a temperature increase?'

Ever serious when divulging a significant feat, the Master went over to the laboratory door to ensure that it was firmly closed.

'Today,' said Feroze, 'you're going to demonstrate the temperature raise. I will guide you through the procedure.'

Previous experience had taught me that the teacher only side-stepped the harshest, most exacting exercises.

'This isn't going to be horribly upsetting for me, is it?'

'No, no,' replied Feroze frivolously, 'I wouldn't say that. No, I wouldn't say that at all.'

'All right. Let's get it over with. What do I do?'

'Well,' he continued, 'first eat this. Make sure you chew it very well.'

He handed me a chalky white lump, about twice the size of a school-child's eraser. It felt soft, yet firm, like soap. I placed it on the tip of my tongue and chewed. My initial reservations were confirmed. It was soap . . . of the coal-tar variety.

'How could you make me eat soap?'

'What? Don't you like it?'

'It's disgusting. Have you ever eaten soap?' I asked, my mouth spuming like shaving foam.

'Oh yes,' murmured the Master dreamily, 'I've eaten soap many many times.'

When the chewing was at an end, I swallowed hard. The soap slid down my oesophagus like a scallop. My stomach, still suspicious and inflamed, squirmed with hostility as it began work digesting the detergent.

'Well done,' the Master said, when I had done as he had told me. 'Now you can have your cup of tea.'

He poured a cup of Darjeeling to the brim, and slid it over to me.

'Make sure you drink the whole thing. Mustn't leave a drop.'

The tea was boiling, but soothed my mouth. Only when it reached my stomach did I sense the familiar urge to retch. My eyes bulged with tears.

'Is this an emetic?' I asked gagging. 'Am I going to be sick again?'

'No . . .' instructed Feroze, launching himself to the far end of the room. 'Be sure not to throw up!'

My stomach was churning like a dishwasher loaded with too much soap powder. Stray bubbles were refluxing up into the back of my throat.

'What's this got to do with body temperature?'

Feroze glanced at his pocket-watch and tapped it twice.

'Give it five or ten more minutes and you'll have your answer,' he said.

Three minutes later the soap, tea, and the acid of my stomach had moved on into my intestines. My head spun as the virulent concoction began to be absorbed into my blood-stream. My mouth was dry, my back was burning, my vision became clouded. The skin of my neck and face began to drip with sweat like never before.

'Feeling warm, are you?' asked Feroze a few minutes later.

'Yes, warm . . . feeling warm,' I panted.

'Toasty,' he chortled, 'you'll start feeling toasty!'

'Why's this happening? What's happening to me . . .'

Before I could finish I found myself choking. A chunk of undigested soap found its way back to my mouth.

'You ate a piece of fine Crabtree and Evelyn coal-tar soap,' explained Feroze as he fetched me a blanket from the study. 'The soap – an alkaline – mixed with the tea, which contains tannic acid, causes a curious reaction when it reaches the stomach.'

'Curious?' I frothed.

'Stay still for a minute,' commanded Feroze, as he stuck a thermometer under my tongue.

'Excellent! You're already up to one hundred and one.'

'How much higher?'

'Well, let's give it five more minutes, shall we?'

Five minutes slipped by as I glided in and out of consciousness. The Master probed beneath my tongue with the glass thermometer, like a stoker attending to the firehole.

'Bingo! You're almost up to a hundred and four. Well done! This *is* impressive.'

Wrapped in the black, red and green blanket – a tribal shawl of the Angami Nagas – I was shaking uncontrollably.

Feroze appeared more stirred now than at any other time during my tutelage. But then again, he had never demonstrated admiration of any kind before.

'Rublu! Come in here and have a look at this!' he bellowed. 'Gokul – you come and have a look as well. This is too good to miss!'

My body, now in spasm, was ignited to a temperature of inhuman severity. Shivering like a heroin addict without a fix, I tried to focus on the Master, Rublu and the line of servants who had turned up for the unexpected treat. My mind might have entertained thoughts of revenge – but it was too preoccupied in the desperate business of maintaining homeostasis.

'Feroze,' said Rublu, 'I hope you haven't been mistreating your pupils again. You should know better.'

The Master raised one finger in the air, preparing to defend the accusation.

'Well,' he said stolidly, 'perhaps I did prescribe a little more soap than I should have. But then how are we to breach the boundaries of science if we do not test them?'

10

Insider Information

Irritated by pebbles, potent emetics and coal-tar soap, the delicate lining of my stomach finally began to give. The magician's latest wheeze had played havoc with my body's finely-tuned homeostatic system. Mine was a case in which the scientist had lost control of his experiment. Decreasing the temperature of 104 degrees Fahrenheit had called for drastic action. Gokul had been instructed to find a *barafwalla*, an ice-seller. He ran out into the tree-lined streets of Alipore and commandeered two blocks of ice which were being lugged on the back of a cart to the nearby Zoological Gardens. Taking charge, Feroze pointed his bull's pizzle riding crop at the servant's bathtub; then at the ice and, lastly, at me. The *barafwallas* heaved their load into the bath and threw me on top.

Solace, at last.

The *barafwallas*, the Master, Rublu, and a gaggle of snorting servants gathered round to enjoy the spectacle. Each watched transfixed as I shuddered with cold and heat at the same time. First they observed the sea of soapy sweat surging like tainted spring-water from my pores. Then they gawked as my steaming perspiration melted the ice – revealing an entombed frozen sewer rat.

Like an amateur mammoth hunter, Gokul chipped away at the ice with the end of a spoon to excavate the rodent.

'Good work, Gokul,' said Feroze, who was having a whale of a time at my expense. 'It's a big one, even for Calcutta. When you've extracted it, put it in the fridge . . . we'll do a dissection later.'

Three days passed before I could ingest any soft foods. Even then I limited myself to a diet of soupy *daal* and mashed bananas, washed down with warm water. Ever courteous, Gokul attempted to nurse my digestive tract back to its original condition. But the damage had been done. Abdominal pain, loss of appetite and severe vomiting followed: classic symptoms of a peptic ulcer. My malady would have alarmed the most hardened of surgeons.

Fortunately, despite the grave nature of my condition, I had an incentive to recover – the prospect of revenge.

On the afternoon of the third day after the trial by temperature, Gokul stuck a hand down his *lungi* and fished something out. It was a neat bunch of *neem* sticks. He blew on them lightly, apologising that they had become dampened by his private parts. But his loins were the only place hidden from the magician's continual scrutiny. I snatched the bundle to my chest and examined it. The *neem* sticks were fastened together with three turquoise elastic bands. I hurried the contraband to my room, and hid it beneath the inner sole of my left shoe. Ready for action . . . All I needed now was the right moment to attack.

When I informed him of my deteriorating gastric condition, Feroze regarded the office calendar on the wall.

'It's the middle of February, fancy that . . .' he said dryly. 'Suppose it's about time you got out of the house . . . can't keep you cooped up here forever.'

'I don't know if you understand,' I said, retching. 'I think I've got a peptic ulcer. It has to be treated without delay.'

Feroze removed a doctor's notelet from a drawer in the writing bureau. Then, twisting the lid from his mandarin-coloured Parker Duofold, he scribbled a prescription.

'Go to the Swastika Chemist on Shakespeare Sarani,' he said, peering up from the paper. 'Give them this prescription and take the pills they give you . . . three times a day.'

As with eating, Feroze considered illness to be a waste of time. He disliked anyone associated with him to fall victim to the weaknesses of the human constitution.

'When you've got the medicine,' he went on, 'you are to go out and find your first example of insider information – the third element of your course.'

I clutched my belly like an expectant mother.

'Shouldn't I take a few days off?'

'For what?' he hissed viperously.

'Recovery,' I said. 'I once read a novel called *Broken Spirit* . . . the hero died an agonising death from an ulcer much like mine.'

The Master swished his riding crop like a camel's tail.

'Sounds like a good read,' he gloated. 'I'll have to remember it.'

'What sort of "insider information" do you want me to find?'

'You'll know it when you find it,' replied Feroze. 'Now leave me . . . I have a rat to dissect!'

*   *   *   *

With one hand on my stomach, and the other wiping the stream of sweat from my brow, I set out into Calcutta.

Through disorientation, I headed south by mistake, instead of northeast into the heart of town. Before I knew it, I was inching my way down the macadamised surface of Judge's Court Road. Famed as a haven of the sophisticated in days gone by, Judge's Court is one of Alipore's old imposing roads. Now a place of faded grandeur, it's home to a ragtag assortment of used furniture shops. Packed from floor to ceiling with roll-top desks, chandeliers, organs, and wall cabinets, bracket clocks and card tables, the shops are testament to changed taste. No longer do Calcuttans cherish the Indo-Baroque masterpieces of the past. Who wants a classical rosewood throne when they can recline in the comfort of a fluffy nylon easy-chair?

As I wandered through the wide avenues of Alipore in search of a rickshaw, I considered the magician's medical prescription. How could I be taking medical advice from the person responsible for my condition?

'Bebtic ulcer very bainful,' mused the pharmacist at the Swastika Chemist.

'Yes,' I confirmed, 'it's desperately *baneful*.'

'Take six tablets every day for a week,' explained the professional.

'Shouldn't I be taking three tablets a day?'

The chemist shook his head.

'Oh, no, no, no,' he said, 'sbecial offer . . . double dosage, same brice!'

I made a note of the Swastika's address. Mustn't forget about this place, I thought. This is a hypochondriac's fantasy.

'What about the pain?' I croaked. 'Will these red and white ones take away the pain?'

'Bain . . .?' said the pharmacist. 'Is the bain unbearable?'

'Yes, yes, yes!' I bellowed. 'That's just what it is . . . it's unbearable!'

The chemist screwed up his eyes like balls of paper. Then, sliding open an ankle-level drawer, he took out a brown glass bottle of lozenges.

'These relieve all bossible bain,' he crowed, slapping them down squarely before me.

'How much do I owe you for them?'

'*Bain-blockers*,' said the chemist grandly, tilting his head backwards, 'bain-blockers, no charge . . . exberimental.'

Sliding a wrinkled index finger to his lips, he winked.

Before choking down a bain-blocker, something crossed my mind. A dangerous misunderstanding may have been about to claim a fresh victim. From the abyss of my unconscious mind a timid, lipless woman was signalling furiously. Had the chemist meant 'brain-blocker', rather than 'pain-blocker'? Was I about to induce a self-inflicted lobotomy? Prepared to try anything to dispel the gastric distress, I knocked a couple of the oversized chalky lozenges to the back of my throat and gulped. The experience was not unlike that of swallowing pebbles.

I counted to ten. Then to twenty. My brain still seemed to be intact. But, as I wandered down Shakespeare Sarani, I found myself floating like a ball of fluff in the wind. It was as if there were no gravity. The chemist's experimental pain-killers obviously needed a little more work. But as I glided towards the Maidan – Calcutta's immense central parkland – I reflected that, for the moment, the pills would be just fine.

Without faltering, I listed sloth-like and bewildered into the seething traffic of Chowringhee. In a country where sedate driving is unknown, Calcutta's frenzied thoroughfare is the zenith of all motorway madness. Uncontrolled and maniacal, wild as a nine-headed Hydra, ferocious as ten thousand vampire bats, Calcutta's main street is more tempestuous than any act of God.

Bullock carts and Ambassador cabs; buses, their sides gashed like armour-plating peppered with anti-tank shells; herds of goats charging like migrating wildebeest, and traction engines on suicide runs: fording the commotion is to play Space Invaders for one's life. Dodge the heavy guns, and the stealthy cycle rickshaws creep up like assassins – laden high with sea trunks, and schoolchildren, *hilsa* fish and urinals, balloons and computer monitors. Miraculously, the press of wheels, spokes and tramping hooves parted, like a great sea, allowing me to cross.

In the Maidan, I wafted over to the Ochterlony Monument. A towering fluted minaret, staring out like an alabaster lighthouse, it was a beacon for street performers. Arriving in their droves, they entertained in the long shadows of Sunday afternoon.

Staggering somewhat, searching for insider information, I made my way from one performance to the next. At one, a girl of about twelve was demonstrating her ability to write with a pen held in her toes. For one rupee she would scrawl out a love poem or a secret astrological message. Opposite sat a young *swami* on crossed legs. His face was pasty, his hands tinged with orange specks. A single charred pot stood before him, positioned on a chequered handkerchief. The vessel contained crocodile fat, apparently a cure for arthritis, impotency and abdominal disorders. Beside it was a pile of 'miracle' shells from the Andaman Islands. An hour earlier, I might have solicited the luminary's advice and purchased a square of crocodile blubber. But now the pain of my peptic ulcer was nothing but a distant memory.

Further on, past a skinny boy and his tightrope-walking pye dog, was another chap with wire-walking rats. Beyond him stood yet another lad. Like the others, he was in his early teens. But he was different. He had an engaging Charlie Chaplin smile, blinding teeth, and dimples as deep as sugar-lumps. Although tattered, his clothes were well kept. Yet it wasn't his dress which caught my attention. It was his demeanour. This boy may have been operating in Calcutta's Maidan, but he was haughty beyond belief.

His pitch was being mobbed by enthusiastic punters, all eager to get his attention. Inquisitive at the source of the commotion, I floated over. Once I had pushed my way to the front, I watched the routine.

A member of the crowd would hand the lad a hundred-rupee (£2) note, itself a tidy sum of money in India. The bill would be folded in half; and then folded in half again. Then it would be slipped into a miniature manila envelope which was placed on a brick, before a green parakeet. The bird would grip the sachet in its bill, ripping the corner. Next, the boy would throw the marked envelope into a box containing other identical, yet unmarked envelopes. He would shake the box roughly. Only then would he invite the owner of the money to search for the envelope containing his banknote.

Invariably, the marked envelope had disappeared.

Despite swaying from the bain-blocker, I felt certain I could catch the boy out. What's all my training been for, I asked myself, if I can't trip up an under-age hoaxer?

So when the boy challenged me, I accepted. My hundred-rupee bill was folded in half, then in half again; before being inserted into a crisp manila pouch. The parrot did its duty, and the torn envelope was thrust into the box. When the carton's lid was removed, the child – who was minting money – urged me to search for my note.

I waved the box aside. The crowd stared at me quizzically. The young magician frowned. Swaggering with all the pomposity I could muster, I ripped the stall's tablecloth away.

'This is where you hid my money!' I cried, sweeping the cloth back.

But the table was bare.

The crowd seethed with delight. Obviously expecting trouble from the foreigner, the entertainer slipped me his Charlie Chaplin smile, grabbed his parrot and props, and made off.

Back at the Alipore mansion, Feroze was pacing up and down the courtyard like a stallion before a race.

'Ah, back at last?' he puffed.

Without his captive, the magician had obviously been distraught with boredom.

'How was the rat?' I enquired, crossing the yard.

'Very interesting, actually,' replied Feroze. 'It had a tumour in its intestines. If it hadn't been frozen solid, it would have had an early death.' The Master groomed back his hair with his hands. 'That reminds me, did you get your pills?'

'Yes. Got some incredible pain-killers, too. They're strong as a knockout punch.'

'Oh, can I see?'

Feroze examined the labelless bottle; then, removing the lid, he took a hesitant sniff. He raised one eyebrow, glanced at his pocket-watch, and then coughed.

'Do you mind if I take one away?' he asked.

'Help yourself. In pain, are you?'

The sorcerer chose not to answer. Instead, he enquired what example of insider information I had brought for him. When I retorted that I had come empty-handed – on account of medical reasons – he flew into a rage.

'Never . . .' he roared, 'never return here without completing the assignment I have set!'

Only as I apologised did I conceive the true extent of the Master's anger. By failing to bring him some nugget from my trip into town, I was in some way depriving him.

That night, in the dim light of my bedroom, I reflected on Feroze's unfounded animosity. Brooding, I tugged the inner sole from my shoe and inspected the rubber bands. Revenge, when it came, would be sweet.

*   *   *   *

Next morning Feroze met me as I descended the antique staircase. It was still not light outside.

'Good morning,' I said, inquisitive as to why the magician should be hovering at the foot of the stairs.

'Tahir,' he replied in an unusually sensitive tone, 'do you remember those pills you brought back yesterday?'

'Yes, of course,' I replied, 'the bain-blockers.'

'I've tested the one you gave me,' Feroze explained. 'It contained mercuric chloride. Take two or three more and you'll be dead.'

'Are you sure?'

'If you don't believe me,' Feroze responded coldly, 'keep taking them and see. Don't forget, this is India – when a quack tells you a potion is "experimental", take the hint and run off!'

For a few seconds I was touched by the magician's compassionate veneer. But, as I set out in search of insider information, I remembered the past. I had endured far too much to forgive and forget.

Where does one go in a tremendous city like Calcutta to find insider information? I recalled India's golden rule: do the opposite of what would be normal anywhere else.

The sub-continent is a fine-tuned and well-practised place. To the outsider it may appear random, or directionless. But in India, what seems haphazard is the product of five thousand years of exertion. Go with the flow, I reminded myself – never strain against the nation's natural forces . . . and success must soon follow.

If ordered to scour a Western metropolis for trade secrets, I would have headed straight to the heart of the city. This being India, I turned my back on central Calcutta, and strolled towards the serene banks of Tolly's Nullah canal.

I sat beneath a banyan tree to eat a packed lunch prepared by Gokul. It was five past ten, but my constitution had grown used to the Master's timetable. A group of men were gathering cress with sickles at the water's edge. Others were fishing with wiry concertina keep-nets, wading up to their chests like gazelle fording a river. Behind them, a family were flipping cow dung fuel bricks in the winter sun. Four young boys were diving into the canal in turns, clouding the water, splashing carefree; shrieking like jackals under a full moon.

In Europe, the last person I would turn to for help would be someone with whom I did not share a common language. When applying the golden rule of India, such a person becomes the obvious guide.

Sidling over to a bearded man of about my age, who was flipping dung bricks like dinosaur eggs, I struck up a conversation.

'Do you know where I'd find some insider information?' I asked.

The man looked at me with blank, swollen eyes.

'In-sid-er know-ledge,' I repeated, motioning obscure gestures like a psychotic mime.

Frowning, as he strove to decipher my sign language, the brick-flipping man shook his head.

'*Haa*,' he murmured, as if he had understood my enquiry.

With a dung-clad finger he pointed at a distant building surrounded by a wall.

When I pointed to the same building, he nodded vigorously.

Excellent, I thought, I'm on to something here.

Ten minutes later and the building's details were coming into focus. Rust-red crenellated walls with creamy cornerstones, barred windows, a pair of flat-footed sentries standing outside. Black marias heaved back and forth like overheated water buffalo.

'Alipore Jail,' spluttered a boss-eyed *paan*-seller, crouched outside the gate.

'Oh,' I said, sheepishly. 'That looks like a strange place to go searching for insider information, doesn't it?'

The *paan*-seller clipped a pile of *sopaari*, areca nuts. 'Looking for Bhola Das?' he asked.

'Um, I'm looking for insider information,' I replied. 'Who's Bhola Das?'

The *paan*-seller winked his good eye twice.

'Bhola Das . . . famous hangman of West Bengal!'

'Ah, yes . . . that's who I'm looking for. Yes, that's right. I'm looking for the hangman!'

Who could have better trade secrets than a hangman?

'Where do I go?'

The *paan*-seller motioned to a low hatch within the main studded portal.

Pausing for a moment to get my story straight, I knocked twice on the door. There was no reply. I knocked again. Only then did a guard put his face to the door's grill.

'Bhola Das!' I shouted. 'I have come to see Bhola Das – the famous hangman of West Bengal.'

The guard slid the visor back across the grill. A bunch of keys rattled inside. The door within a door creaked inwards.

One guard ferried me to the next. To each I whispered the cryptic password . . . the name of the hangman.

After a long wait I found myself sitting before the warden.

'I have come to see Bhola Das,' I explained. 'I think you will find that he's expecting me.'

'Very good, sir,' said the warden, signing the necessary paperwork to authorise my visit.

He pressed a button beside his desk. Before I could turn my head, a watchman stepped from the shadows and led me through the fabled jail of Alipore.

Up and down stairs, around corridors and along straight passageways. The soles of my shoes rasped on the flagstones as we proceeded through the maze. The liveried guard halted before a robust steel door.

'Bhola Das?' he confirmed.

'Yes, it's the hangman I've come to see.'

'Very good, sir,' squirmed the watchman, as he knocked on the door. The door opened inwards.

Inside was a square, stone-walled chamber, illuminated by natural light. A solid wood table stood in one corner. On it was a noose, crafted from coarse hemp rope. Adjacent to the table a man was sitting on a three-legged stool. His hair was snowdrop-white; his cheeks were obscured by a rough grey beard, his steely eyes hidden behind scratched lenses, and his shirt and *lungi* were old, yet neat.

'Bhola Das?' I asked.

'Yes,' said the man. 'I am Bhola Das.'

'I would like to speak with you for a few minutes.'

The hangman glanced at a clock mounted high on the wall.

'Do you have an execution to administer?'

'No,' said Das dolefully, 'I have no work today.'

Whereas other states in India elect their executioners on their own merit, West Bengal employs hangmen from a single hereditary line.

'My father and his father and his father before him were all hangmen,' exclaimed Das, stretching his spindly arms behind him like locust wings. 'My father killed more than six hundred convicts; but that was in the time of the Britishers, and there were far many more to execute then. My father was sent to Glasgow during the Raj. He hanged Indians at the prison there. I suppose,' said Das solemnly, 'you could say that hanging is in my blood.'

'What's it like to hang a man?'

The hangman stared at the floor, then with eyes cold as sleet, he gazed at me, taking in the features of my face.

'To kill a man,' he said softly, 'is a dreadful thing. To bring a man's life to an end is almost too much to bear. I am a hereditary executioner. This is the work of my forefathers. I do not judge the profession which they have chosen for my line. But I ensure each man I kill dies with dignity and without pain. I believe I am the finest executioner in India. I do not claim that for an idle boast. Before killing a convict I cannot sleep for three days. I cannot eat either. I spend time alone, thinking about the life which I am about to end. Then, before I place the noose in position, I ask the criminal's forgiveness. I tell him I am only doing what the government and the court has asked me to do.

'When I hang a man,' declared Bhola Das, pressing his thick glasses to his nose, 'the victim remains intact. Blood doesn't ooze from his nostrils, from his ears or from his mouth. That's the mark of the professional.'

'Tell me,' I intoned in a hushed voice, as the footsteps of a guard tramped past outside, 'are there any secrets of the profession which have been passed on to you by your ancestors?'

Das nodded sagaciously, staring out at a pair of pigeons which were squatting on the window-ledge.

'Yes,' he replied. 'There are family secrets . . .'

'Could you tell me what they are?'

The hangman squinted.

'The secrets of which I speak are,' he said, 'known only to me and to the man I execute.'

'Ah,' I winced, loosening my collar, 'I understand. But isn't there some meagre tip you could give, to prove the care you take in your craft?'

Bhola Das rubbed his palms together.

'First,' he whispered, looking from right to left, 'I lubricate the noose with a bar of soap. I make sure it gets into all the creases. This reduces friction. Then I rub it a second time, with a banana. Only after that can I be certain that the knot will slide easily. But,' continued the executioner in a low voice, 'the most important thing is to weave a brass nut into the noose. While slipping the noose over the inmate's head, I position the heavy nut at the side of the neck. As soon as the trap door opens, the nut swings round to the spinal cord and snaps it cleanly.

'Half an hour later,' the hangman went on, 'when I release the rope, there's sometimes an eerie scream from the convict's mouth – it's just air escaping from the prisoner's lungs.'

'Is hanging the only method of execution in West Bengal?'

'Unfortunately, it is. Four men were recently convicted of raping a nine-year-old girl,' continued Das. 'I was told to hang them. They ought to have been thrown into a cage of lions. The noose was too good for them!'

Bhola Das removed his glasses and rubbed his eyes. He was an honourable man, maintaining the work of his forefathers.

'Do your children want to carry on the tradition?'

'Yes,' said Bhola Das. 'My elder son wants to join the business. I have taught him how to twine a rope and craft a noose. He has helped me on some occasions. But,' imparted the hangman wearily, 'he wants the position to pay more and to have better job security. Without that,' he whispered, 'he says there's no future for the profession.'

Armed with the valuable insider information, I thanked the ageing executioner and summoned the guard to escort me from the prison. Bhola Das clasped his callused hands around mine and pressed his lips to my ear.

'If you ever require my services,' he murmured darkly, as I left, 'please don't hesitate to call upon me.'

That was an honest man, I reflected, as I trekked north up Baker Road towards the magician's compound. He had inner strength, and was compassionate under testing circumstances. As for Bhola Das's offer – it was hard to say whether I would ever need to avail myself of the private services of an executioner. But the offer, I pondered, would be good to keep in reserve . . . for a rainy day.

* * * *

It was with elation that I entered the Master's mansion. I was eager to share my new-found insider information. But before making my report, I slipped up to my room to shower and change. Gokul's assistant was polishing the brass carpet rods on the stairs. Climbing over him, I made my way up to the first-floor corridor. My bedroom was situated at its far end. Several other rooms led off the passageway. These were usually kept locked. Feroze was obsessed that they remain so. Noticing that the second door on the right was ajar, I was suspicious. Pushing it inward, I poked my head around the door.

The casual nature of my intrusion added to the surprise.

It was a young boy's bedroom. A home-made model aeroplane was suspended from the ceiling; below it, a clutch of toy animals sat on the bed. A leather satchel was propped up against a chair, its buckles unfastened. A child's sketches were pinned to one wall. The low desk was strewn with the elements of childhood. A catapult, a nest of marbles, cotton reels and a dismembered doll's head. It might have been like any other boy's bedroom. But it was not. The chamber was lit by a single bare red bulb. Its shutters had been closed like an iron visor, preventing daylight from penetrating in. A ghastly scarlet light filled the place.

Rattled by the sight, I stepped back to shut the door. But as I did so, I noticed a hunched figure sitting on a low stool with his eyes closed. It was Feroze. Surprisingly, he had not heard me. I tiptoed away.

When I had changed, I went out to the kitchen to find Gokul. Surely the Master's veteran servant would explain the room's mystery.

Gokul was busy roasting a ladle of spices over a gas flame.

'Hello, *Sahib*!' he said, without turning round.

'How did you know it was me?'

'Very noisy walker,' he snorted.

'Gokul . . . I've just seen something rather strange.'

'What strange?'

'There's a bedroom upstairs with a red light in it. The Master is sitting there with his eyes closed.'

The manservant raised the ladle from the heat. He turned to face me.

'Long time ago,' he said tensely, 'Master's son and wife were killed.'

'How? How did it happen?'

Gokul rubbed both eyes with his left hand, and sniffed.

'They taking cycle rickshaw in Calcutta,' he said. 'Rickshaw hit by petrol tanker . . . Master *Sahib* has kept son bedroom same way. Today,' mumbled the servant, 'anniversary of death.'

Leaving Gokul to his spices, I returned to the main house, my head hung low. The magician may have been my tormentor, but I was willing to agree a temporary truce. Was his venomous attitude to his pupils connected to the death of his wife and child?

An hour later, Feroze found me in the study, where I was combing a copy of *Hobson-Jobson* for magical feats. He was less vitalised than usual. His eyes were circled by heavy rings; his face was drawn and pale, and his clothes quite dishevelled.

'How did you get on?' he asked, through gritted teeth.

'Well . . .' I began, snapping the book closed euphorically.

'Did you find me any insider information?'

I reflected on Alipore Jail and upon the secrets of Bhola Das – hereditary hangman of West Bengal. Should I explain first about the soap, the banana, or the brass nut which snaps the spine? I glanced at Feroze. He wasn't his usual self. How could I discuss an executioner's tips with a man whose family had themselves met such a terrible end?

'I'm so sorry,' I said, 'but my stomach has been troubling me again. I'll make sure to bring back a double dose of insider information tomorrow.'

* * * *

Next day, well before Gokul had shuffled up the passageway with a pot of milky tea, I had slunk out of the house. Today, I told myself, I am going to restore my reputation.

Early morning in Calcutta is a bewitching time. Like the back lot of a Hollywood film studio, it's either teeming with people, or silent as a ghost ship. Calcutta is either off or on. It's the only city on Earth with no half-way setting.

At six a.m. – like scene shifters and extras in a film – the first people saunter on to the set. They are well rested and prepared for another day of furious activity. Some scrape out the gutters, or scrub down the cobblestones, like studio janitors making ready for the arrival of the cast. Others set out dog-eared copies of *Time* and *National Geographic* on makeshift wooden stalls. Nearby, beggars hobble into position, bracing themselves for the crowds. Street-side astrologers prop up their hand-painted boards depicting the constellations; perfume-sellers dust down their carved glass bottles; toothpick vendors arrange their stock; pickpockets step stealthily into doorways. Fruit-sellers divide sour green oranges into clusters of six. Traffic policemen tighten their white steel helmets and climb up on to their rostra. Then – and only then – as if an invisible director has ordered filming to begin, Calcutta is switched on.

Within moments, the streets are choked with vehicles. The air boils with exhaust fumes. And the pavements are packed with shoals of people, jammed shoulder to shoulder like lambs in a wagon.

Nothing in Calcutta is so important as the pavement. Far more than mere conduits for pedestrians, the walkways are dormitories, typing bureaux, markets, cafés, doctors' surgeries and umbrella repair shops, rolled into an endless profusion of activity. Calcutta's pavements are wider than in most other cities, constructed by the British for a grand imperial capital. Twenty yards of Calcutta pavement has more on offer than entire countries. Plastic combs and squashy toys, showers caps in camellia pink, hard-boiled eggs in trays, reconditioned engine-blocks, Bakelite telephones, mothballs in sackcloth pouches, beetroot and jackfruit, dental floss and wooden legs, Zimmer frames and pogo sticks, turbines and theodolites.

*

As I recoiled from the force of the morning invasion, I noticed a man squatting outside the Writer's Building. He had no hands or feet. His stumps were well healed, their skin tight and smooth. Dozens of unfortunates beg on Lal Bazaar Street. But this man was wearing a pair of alien antennae – popular with party-goers about twenty years before. As I bent over him, he twanged one of the springs with his stump. The bloodshot eyeball at the end jangled about, revolving wildly.

'Yes, *Sahib* . . .' he exclaimed eagerly, realising that, as a customer from out of town, I was sure to buy the latest sensation. '*Panch rupia*, five rupees!'

'What would I use the apparatus for?'

'Very good-quality,' he stressed, 'good price. I am cripple. No family. No money.'

I handed over the note and took the alien antennae. They might come in useful down the line, I thought. After all, this was Calcutta.

I tried on the tentacles for the first time. No one even looked round as I pushed through the crowds, the pair of demonic eyeballs jolting about above my head. Then I noticed a man waving at me from the far end of Lal Bazaar. Suspecting it to be another mendicant, impatient to make an easy sale, I turned and hurried off. But a grinding of wheels indicated that the man was in pursuit. Without looking round, I slipped down a side alley, my alien eyeballs flapping about like teasels in the wind. The wheels followed.

'All right,' I snarled, facing the pursuer. 'What do you want?'

It was then I noticed that this was no cart-bound invalid, but a *rickshawalla*.

'*Jadoowalla!*' he shouted. 'Remembering? Mister magician . . .?'

The man spoke gibberish.

He was sleek as a gondola, barefoot and extremely lean. His torn saffron-coloured vest revealed a scrawny back, pocked with dried sores, and with muscles as taut as a drum-skin. When standing still, his body swayed back and forth. He was very drunk indeed.

'What do you want?'

The man pointed at me, then the rickshaw, and then acted out a little sketch.

He was beginning to seem familiar.

'Aren't you the *rickshawalla* who took me to Feroze's house on that first day – you were the runner in Purulia, right?'

The *rickshawalla* tilted his head from one side to the other. '*Haa, Sahib*,' he said. 'Runner. I am runner. Name . . . Venky.'

The *rickshawalla* cracked his knuckle joints, as if demonstrating his enduring strength.

'Where you want to go?' he asked, squinting.

'Well,' I said, 'maybe you can help me.'

He shuffled forwards in concentration.

'I am looking for a special thing,' I explained. 'I am searching for *insider information*.'

Venky the *rickshawalla* raised his eyebrows as high as he could, and swayed his head from left to right. It smelt as if he had taken a bath in *chullu*.

'Do you understand? I want to be taken to someone with insider information.'

The man patted the rickshaw's seat with his leathery palm. I climbed up and we set off. He seemed to know where he was going.

Dodging the onslaught of taxis, juggernauts, and a great caravan of marching bandsmen, who were out drumming up business, the *rickshawalla* scuttled towards the Bow Bazaar. The market is famous for selling fine jewellery, produced in cramped back work-rooms behind each shop. The larger emporia have resident astrologers, advising on the appropriate design of jewellery.

Without warning, Venky dug his heels into the dirt and pointed to a cow. The animal, which had a wreath of flowers around its neck, was tied to a post. Beside it was a middle-aged woman, dressed in a simple white *sari*, tied in the Bengali way.

'How can an animal have insider information?'

The *rickshawalla* hesitated.

'No understand,' he said.

'Then why did you bring me to this cow?'

Venky stuck out his lower lip, revealing his gums. We had only just met, but somehow it was as if I had known him all my life.

'Well, since we're here, can you ask the woman what she uses her cow for?'

Promoted from *rickshawalla* to translator, Venky struck up a conversation with the woman. She held up a bunch of rough grass stems and he slurred a number of disjointed questions.

'She say,' began Venky in his best English, 'people paying little bit money feed cow.'

'Why do people want to pay to feed the cow?'

'Feed cow lucky,' responded the *rickshawalla*.

'Does the woman own the cow?'

Again, Venky chattered away in animated conversation.

'*Haa*,' he said after some time, 'she not own cow. Milking man own cow. She paying milking man for cow in day.'

'You mean that the woman hires the cow each day, once the milkman's finished with it, and she lets strangers pay her money to feed it?'

Venky thought for a moment. Then he smiled.

'Yes, *Sahib* . . . very good!'

The genius of the arrangement bore the unrivalled hallmark of Calcutta. Where else could you find such an ingenious system? The milkman milks the cow and then, instead of looking after it all day, gives it to a woman who pays *him* for the privilege of looking after the animal. Far from being left out of pocket, the woman charges people to feed the creature a few strands of grass. In turn, the cow's devotees attain a sense of inner calm from their charity. The woman sells the dung to fuel-brick makers as a profitable side-line. This was even better than the baby rental.

'Venky,' I said, as Mehboob's Marching Band engulfed us like a sea of crude oil, 'you're a genius!'

Buoyed by the early success of Bow Bazaar, I set my sights on the street's other professionals. If a humble cow could reveal such hidden wonders, then what could be waiting for me further along the street?

But even before I had a chance to put away my notebook, Venky pointed at a group of men cleaning out the gutters beside his rickshaw's wheel.

'*Ghamelawalla*!' he cried.

'What are you saying? What's a *ghamelawalla*?'

The rickshaw-puller was perplexed that I should not understand the term.

'*Ghamelawalla*,' he repeated, 'gold-sweeper!'

'Venky,' I said, 'you're obviously wrong. These men are gutter cleaners. Look – they're sweeping up all the dirt and heaving it on to a metal cart.'

The *rickshawalla* wagged a finger.

'*Ghamelawalla*, looking for gold,' he said.

With Venky translating, I resigned myself to the fact that seeking out the truth might be a slow, uphill task. His English was limited. It was like deciphering a garbled tape-recording made under water. I put his wavering linguistic ability down to the flask of opaque liquid stored in the pouch around his neck.

Bow Bazaar is a street of astounding financial wealth. Bearing this in mind, it wasn't unreasonable that people should be dredging the gutters for gold. Renewing my faith in the man who had brought me the cow-keeper's secret, I licked my pencil.

Gold dealers in the West value the dirt swept from workshop floors. An old Hasid jeweller in Manhattan once told me he had sold the antique floorboards from his factory. Their purchaser incinerated the planks to extract the gold dust which had worked its way into the crevices over the years. But as I came to realise, the clan of the *ghamelawallas*, Calcutta's unofficial army of gold-scroungers, put even the great recyclers of New York to shame.

Taking their name from their *ghamela*, heavy iron pans, the city's *ghamelawallas* begin work in the middle of the night. Long before the bazaar's jewellers are open for business, they turn up to sweep out the workshops. Like the tiny birds which peck the teeth inside crocodile mouths, *ghamelawallas* perform a vital, if not uncelebrated, service. Every grain of dust is meticulously collected. Handing the business' owner a few rupees, the precious dirt is taken away to be treated.

Many *ghamelawallas* make their homes on the streets of Calcutta. Nearly all are migrant workers, with wives and children who they see once a year. Most begin their careers as apprentice *ghamelawallas*, arriving to work alongside their fathers at the age of six or seven. They sleep on *charpoys*, rope beds, in alleyways, and wash at hand-pumps. Wander the back-streets near the Bow Bazaar and you'll see them sitting on the pavements, toiling over the jewellers' dirt. Mixed amid the jumble of pavement life, one could easily dismiss the huddle of squatting figures without a second glance. But like so many in Calcutta, the *ghamelawallas* are masters of creating a living from almost nothing. The tattered sweepers, squatting at shin-level perform an intricate scientific procedure.

First, the scraps of paper and straw and larger pieces of rubbish are removed. These will be sold later to *ruddiwallas*, 'rag-pickers'. Then the actual dirt is washed in clean water. When it has been swilled about, a few drops of nitric acid are added. This dissolves all the metals except for the gold. The residue is then treated with a solution of barium, which amalgamates the gold particles. After this, the remaining compound is burned in a crucible, on a *choolah*, a small stove. As miniature hand-driven bellows blast air into the embers, a tiny nugget of gold is formed at the base of the crucible.

Some other Indian cities have *ghamelawallas* as well. But those in Calcutta dismiss their rivals as impostors. For nowhere on Earth has recycling been taken to such exalted levels as in Calcutta. Whereas *ghamelawallas* working in, say, Bombay, treat the salvaged dirt once, their fellow gold-seekers in Calcutta are far more ingenious. When the initial burning is over, the first group of *ghamelawallas* sell the dirt from which they have extracted gold to another group of *ghamelawallas*. More impoverished than the first, the second group repeat the process, removing even more minute traces of the precious metal. These *ghamelawallas* sell the dust on to yet another team of washers, who pan it on the banks of the Hoogly. When they are finished with the dust, they peddle it to builders, who turn it into bricks.

By late morning, when the first set of *ghamelawallas* have done their round of the workshops, they turn their attentions to the gutters of the inimitable Bow Bazaar. Armed with hard brushes, they scrub the dirt from the streets and cart it away to process. Before they leave to rest in the scorching afternoons, the *ghamelawallas* set up a complex network of miniature dams to prevent any of the valuable dirt from seeping down into the sewers. But, this being Calcutta, another regiment of *ghamelawallas* are on hand to trawl the sewers at night. If too much rubbish piles up for them to treat, they simply sub-contract the work.

Straining to translate the intricate lore of the *ghamelawallas*, Venky muttered that one *lakh*, a hundred thousand, people work as freelance *ghamelawallas* in Calcutta. If each is making, say, twenty rupees a day – and works eleven months out of twelve – then between them, Calcutta's gold-sweepers alone must be bringing in more than thirteen million pounds a year. Not bad for making money from nothing. As they say in Calcutta, '*Ak janar chai, annyar sona*' – 'One man's waste, another man's gold.'

Metro Marriage

The Master sat motionless in his study as I delivered my report next morning. He had placed his pocket-watch on the desk and was timing my narration. When I had spoken of discovered treasure and sub-let bovine deities, he clicked the heels of his brown suede brogues together.

'Tell me,' he said after several minutes of silence, 'did you find the cow and the *ghamelawallas* by yourself?'

I mulled his question over. Was there any way that he could have followed me? Could he have seen Venky? Had he dispatched a cohort of spies to track my movements?

'Yes, I did it all on my own,' I said anxiously. 'You know . . . like a bloodhound sniffing out its quarry . . . it's all part of the job.'

Feroze rose from his chair and stood still for a moment in classic Masonic stance: feet at right angles to one another. Then stalking across the room's fine Herizi rug like a tiger moving in for the kill, he drew near. When within six inches of my face, he withdrew a pair of *demi-lune* spectacles from his shirt pocket, and slipped them on. With great care, he examined the beads of perspiration on my hairline.

'Feeling a little bit warm, are you?' he prompted.

'No, not really.'

'Then please explain,' said the Master, returning to his chair, 'how did you communicate with these people? My instructions forbid you from taking a translator on board.'

Nothing would have given me greater pleasure than to run Hakim Feroze through with a blunt broadsword. Then I remembered the rubber bands. The truce was over. Turning my back to the teacher, I pretended to tie my laces. My fingers fumbled for the elastic bands under the inner sole of my left shoe.

'Come on,' Feroze taunted, 'how did they relate such detailed

information? Did they speak Oxford English? Or have you mastered
Bengali since yesterday?'

Determined not to reveal Venky, my secret weapon, I stashed the
elastic bands in my shirt pocket and fought on. It was now just a matter
of deployment.

'Well,' I proclaimed obstinately, 'there was only one way I was going
to understand such complex detail . . .'

'All right, what is it?'

'I used . . .'

'Yes, out with it!'

'I used sign language!'

Feroze moistened a fingertip with his tongue and groomed back an
eyebrow. I waited for him to look away. All I needed was a split second
to flick the bands on to the desk.

The magician stared into my eyes like a telepath. We both knew he
was reading my mind. I swear I could sense him trawling through my
library of memories. Gazing deeper and deeper, he drained the past from
me until I was physically weak.

There was no choice but to abort the attack. As I drew a deep breath
into my lungs, Feroze swivelled around to pick his tea-cup from the
window-sill. I rubbed my eyes. Then I took my chance. With
haphazard precision, I tossed the three turquoise elastic bands on to
the desk. They seemed to fly across the room in slow motion, before
landing beside the precious pocket-watch. My stomach turned
fearfully. The Master sipped his tea. Then he glanced over at the
watch. Time stood still. Was there a gush of phobic anguish as he
scrutinised his nemesis? Alas, there was not. Had he sapped the truth
from the deepest recesses of my mind? His lack of stupefaction led me
to believe that he had.

Without a word, Feroze cast a silk polka-dot handkerchief over the
elastic bands like a miniature fishing net. He crossed the room, locked
in thought. Then he dropped the projectiles and the contaminated
handkerchief in the waste-paper bin.

'You go out today,' he said after a long pause, 'and do some more of
your "sign language". I want two fine examples by this afternoon.
When you get back: a dozen more illusions to cover and a test on
everything you've learnt so far. We'll be working late tonight! You may
go now.'

I rose from my seat and made for the door in silence. As I leant
forward to grasp the knob, the Master called to me.

'Oh, by the way,' he growled, 'I beat all my aversions years ago. I take a dim view of humour at another's expense. But don't worry about that, it's Gokul who's to be punished.'

*   *   *   *

Deep down I had known that, however high my hopes, the magician wouldn't be conquered by low-quality stationery. I had known, too, that my best efforts the day before would be judged inadequate. The hunch had spurred me to arrange in advance another meeting with Venky. Hiring the *rickshawalla* may have been against the Master's will. But then, as I rationalised it, communicating with Venky was no easy task in itself.

Venky was quaffing a bottle of murky bootleg liquid at the place of rendezvous. Without discussing the day's plan at all, he knurled his face as the hooch corroded his insides like battery acid on a sheet of zinc; tapped the seat for me to ascend, and set off at a furious pace.

Stopping once, to pull a shard of glass from his foot, Venky headed east to Bhawanipur Metro Station. He covered the short distance in a few minutes. Even when drunk, he was a man of startling physical endurance. The years of postal running through the wilds of Purulia had been good training. When he had recovered his breath, Venky stared directly at the sun.

'Early,' he said.

I looked at my wristwatch.

'It's nine-forty . . . Early for what?'

Venky leant over and peered at the dial.

'Clock no good,' he said firmly. 'Sun good . . . sun no breaking down!'

'Venky, what are we waiting for?'

'Wedding-man.'

'What do you mean?'

The *rickshawalla* splayed the fingers of his right hand and pushed them back and forth like a lunatic trying to wave. Look at this, Feroze – I thought – here's sign language in action.

As we waited for the wedding-man to arrive, Venky told me about himself.

'Name Venkatraman . . . Born in Tamil Nadu. Father moving to Bihar,' he said. 'My wife in Gomoh, near Dhanbad.'

'Do you have children?'

'Four son,' replied the *rickshawalla* proudly. 'Go home one time in year. Seeing children . . . seeing wife. Very nice.'

'When do you go back to Bihar next?'

'Easter.'

'Easter? You're a Christian?'

Venky, who had turned his attentions to another sliver of glass in his foot, concurred that he was indeed a Christian.

'What about your life here? What's it like working in Calcutta?'

'Hard work,' said Venky, tensing the muscles of his face until his cheeks shone like mirrors. 'Calcutta hard city. Paying fifteen *rupia* for rickshaw renting . . . working all day making forty-five *rupia*. Sending money to wife.'

'Do your family friends come and visit you from Bihar?'

Venky rubbed at a callus on his right hand.

'Friend come here,' he said softly. 'But friend see me . . . make me sad . . . Friend laughing at me . . . me *rickshawalla* only.'

Calcutta can be a lonely place. Venky had found one true friend in the city. It was called *chullu*.

'Liking drinking *fenny*,' he remarked shyly. '*Fenny* good . . . you liking *fenny*?'

'Well, actually, I don't drink. And you should take care – *fenny*'s very strong stuff,' I said. 'Besides, my stomach isn't in very good shape . . . too many emetics – it got ruptured when I was swallowing stones.'

The *rickshawalla*'s brow furrowed as he translated the words 'swallow' and 'stone' into Bengali. He gave me a stern sideways glance.

'You eat stone?' he enquired apprehensively.

'Only on special occasions,' I said. 'I don't eat them every day.'

Venky smiled. He stared at the sun again.

'Is time now,' he said. 'We go in.'

We crossed the street to the Bhawanipur Station. Leaving his rickshaw with a stall-keeper, Venky led me down into the Metro. He descended the marble stairs with unsure footsteps. I sensed he had not been in India's only underground railway before. I purchased two tickets at three rupees each and we strolled down a staircase on to the platform. Deep in the bowels of Calcutta, with the city's traffic raging above, the underground was like an urban Garden of Eden.

Calcutta's single-line Metro was constructed in 1984 against all the odds. The cost is said to have been an estimated £300 million. In a land where three hundred pounds – let alone a million times that – is a monstrous sum, it's hard to imagine why so much cash was required. But cast an eye around this, the pride of West Bengal, and you can't deny that money has been spent.

The Metro is everything one would expect it not to be. It's cool, spotlessly clean, silent as a grave, soothing on the senses, and it smells of lavender oil. The platforms, with their fresh, chilled air, boast satellite television and piped muzak. The train carriages, which are free from chewing gum and graffiti, exhibit original paintings of local artists.

Most unexpected of all is that the Metro is desperately underused. Whenever I asked Calcuttans why the pride of their city is so empty, they grinned tensely. Some put it down to the fact that Bengalis like to have their feet firmly planted on the ground. Others said the Metro was too cold; or that people were terrified that it would collapse. Judging by Venky's response, it may have been a mixture of the three reasons. Even standing on the platform made him restless.

After waiting on the south-bound platform for twenty minutes, I started to wonder what was going on. Trains came and went. But Venky made it clear we had not come to ride the tracks.

Instead, he held up his hand, motioning for me to be patient.

'No travelling,' he explained. 'Waiting for wedding-man.'

'You still haven't told me who the wedding-man is . . .'

At that moment, a rotund figure with eyes like peeled green grapes sidled up. He was dressed in a tailored bran-coloured suit, with wide lapels and six buttons on each cuff.

'Hello,' he said in faultless English. 'I was delayed. Been arranging the wedding.'

When I had introduced myself, I explained that Venky had not told me why we were meeting.

'I organise weddings,' said the man casually. 'Finding the right spot is getting very difficult, especially right now, in the marriage season. Families get very desperate. They want somewhere cool and relaxing away from the noise, the pollution, where there aren't too many people. The place has to be easy to get to, clean, and large enough to take the full wedding party. So,' said the man blithely, 'that's why I hire out Metro platforms.'

'I'm not sure if I understand.'

His grape-like eyes scanning from right to left like an iguana's, the broker continued:

'Where better for a wedding than a Metro platform? It's clean, cool and convenient to get to. It has toilets, televisions and speakers all around. What place could be more suitable?'

'But do *you* work for the Calcutta Metro?'

The man rubbed his belly, and laughed.

'Oh course not!' he said. 'I tip the station manager something, and that's all taken care of.

'We have a wedding here this evening,' he said. 'I'm here making a few arrangements. The wedding party will come in from here . . .' He pointed to a turnstile. 'The wedding ceremony will take place here . . .'

Puzzled that the *rickshawalla* had managed to line up such an impressive entrepreneur, I had one final question to put to him.

'Is there one secret that has made all this possible?' I asked.

The man shuffled his feet on the marble flooring. Then, grooming his spiv's moustache, he leant over the tracks to peek down the tunnel.

'Yes,' he said plainly, 'there is one thing that ensures I don't have any problems.'

'What is it?'

His wily features reflecting the neon lights, he whispered:

'I always make certain the wedding party have valid Metro tickets.'

*   *   *   *

The best thing about the search for insider information was that I could roam wild far from the magician's compound. The emphasis might have lapsed from illusory science, but at least I could eat what I liked, when I liked.

Venky became agitated when I offered to treat him to a slap-up lunch.

'We'll go to eat at a place on Park Street,' I said. 'It serves quite good *tandoori*.'

The *rickshawalla* wiped his mouth with the corner of his shirt. Then he wiped the festering wound on his barefoot.

'Good eat Sealdah Station!' he replied.

Park Street's snobbish set may have put Venky in an awkward position.

'To Sealdah Station we go,' I said.

Venky raised the twin poles of his rickshaw and lurched into the traffic of A. J. Chandra Bose Road. The prospect of eating at his favourite café seemed to put a bounce into his stride. As we jostled along – with Venky dinging the *ghanti*, a small bell, against the pole – I took a deep breath. Calcutta's vintage blend of monoxides, mercurics and toxic trace elements swelled my lungs. My thoracic cavity tightened as I strained to exhale the cocktail of poison gas. For the first time in my life, I found myself falling victim to asthma.

By the time we reached the outlying railway station at Sealdah, I could hardly breathe. Observing my distress, Venky pressed his burly fingertips into the soft flesh at either side of my lower jaw. As I concentrated on the pulse above my left eye, my breathing slowed to a more regular pace.

'How did you know to do that?' I gasped, as my breath returned.

Venky grinned.

'*Rickshawalla* trick,' he said.

The café at Sealdah Station was unlike any restaurant I had visited before. Leaving his vehicle with another *rickshawalla* outside the station's reservation office, Venky escorted me over the criss-crossing railway tracks to the diner. As we grew closer, his titillation mirrored my apprehension.

The eating house was located next to an overgrown points signal. It was already brimming with regulars. About thirty mendicants lolled about waiting to be fed. Shunned by society, scorned for their handicaps and afflictions, they were the destitute whose name is synonymous with that of Calcutta.

A large, boisterous woman in a fluorescent fuchsia-pink *sari* was in charge. She barked directions at half a dozen young helpers. One was busy chopping vegetables; another was stirring a bubbling pot with a spade-like spoon; a third was fanning the charcoal beneath the vessel. Venky murmured that the raucous woman was the owner. Her name was Sharmila Roy.

We sat on the grass-covered island beside the railway points, and Venky told me about this, his favourite eating place. Regrettably, the highlights dulled my appetite. Every morning, he told me, Sharmila Roy sends her children out to scavenge for food in the refuse heaps around the city. They gather as many unwanted and partially rotting ingredients as they can, hauling them back to the open-air railway diner. Using her considerable culinary skill, Sharmila Roy brews up a buffet of delectable dishes. Beggars and *rickshawallas* come from miles around to sample the food.

I had once seen a television report on a similar kind of café in Washington DC. An entrepreneur sent scouts to forage through the dustbins of the wealthy. The result was a menu which boasted a smorgasbord of epicurean delights – the finest caviar from the Caspian Sea, tournedos of beef with goat's cheese and grilled pine nuts, a terrine of langoustines, roasted quails – all washed down with Japanese plum wine.

Although enthused by such tales of garbage banquets, I found myself growing increasingly uneasy. I sensed that a refuse meal in Calcutta may lack the elevated standards of the American capital. In the United

States, a product is deemed dangerous thirty seconds beyond its sell-by date. But in Calcutta, a little surface mould or ingrained pestilence is considered to add to the taste.

Scrounged ingredients were only half the secret of Sharmila Roy's diner. Most restaurateurs focus on feeding those with money to spend. But the Sealdah Station café had overcome the hurdle of destitution. The answer was simple. Clients were encouraged to pay in kind, rather than cash. Even for Calcutta – home to baby rental and gold-sweepers – the system deserved applause. If you can't scrape together three rupees for a heavy lunch, no problem. Bring a knot of rags, a crumpled ball of telephone wire, an old shoe, a jam-jar, a used toothbrush, a light-bulb stolen from a commuter train, or a handful of rusty razor blades . . . and a lavish helping of fish-head curry will be placed ceremoniously before you.

Obviously one of the diner's regulars, Venky was greeted tenderly by Sharmila Roy. As she welcomed us, some of the other clients voiced concern that a foreigner was amongst them. The *rickshawalla* passed me a mound of rags, a makeshift cushion on which to sit. One of Sharmila Roy's daughters – a girl no older than about six – scurried over to us with three banana-leaf plates. As the tattered banana leaves were brought, I caught my first waft of the curry.

Venky's eyes lit up like candles burning on a dark night.

'Good eating,' he said loudly, demonstrating his command of English.

Before I could say a word, a heap of fish-heads, stewed chicken bones and mixed vegetable was slapped down on the banana leaf. The food smelled highly spiced. I realised later that this was a precaution to mask the flavour of decay. Despite the strong aroma of chilli, the pungent odour of rotting fish rose to the surface like oil in water. When my leaf was piled high with tempting morsels, Venky thrust his hand into his own food, stirred it around, and began to feast.

Vagabonds of all descriptions were in attendance. Those who could walk had formed a circle around us. On one side were half a dozen lepers. Beside them were squatting survivors of road accidents – two men with no legs between them, two more crippled by polio, and another, a victim of acute elephantiasis. In contrast to the lame were the dozen or so *rickshawallas*. Like Venky, they were hale almost beyond words.

My eyes streamed at the thought of eating a meal concocted from ingredients pilfered from a Calcutta dustbin. I am squeamish about food at the best of times. Yet I had to eat, for fear of offending the *rickshawalla* and his colleagues. How would Venky ever hold his head up high here again if I – his guest – did not dig in?

Nudging the thumb and index finger of my right hand into the food, I wondered how I would get through the meal. Sharmila Roy tottered over to see I was getting plenty to eat. At first I hoped I would have enough time to stall, or to think of something. Then it struck me that the entire clientele were glancing back and forth at my fingers and my mouth, waiting for the first bite.

Selecting a mass of fetid fish intestines, I squeezed out the juices with my fist and drew them up to my face. Sixty eyes scrutinised my movements. In a second it would all be over. My fingers trembled with alarm. My mouth twitched in anticipation. Then, as the first globule of fish entrails was about to pass between my lips, I had an idea. It was not one of unknown profundity, but, for a skin-of-the-teeth reaction, it would do. Rather than inserting the rotting fish guts into my mouth, I did a conjuror's sleight-of-hand. The intestines never reached my terror-stricken digestive tract; they were slipped down my shirt instead.

'Delicious!' I exclaimed, after stashing several handfuls of food in the same way. 'I must come here again. Venky, this is a wonderful place.'

The *rickshawalla* translated my applause, to the delight of Sharmila Roy. She was pleased with my ebullient appetite.

In my enthusiasm, I had stuffed two complete *pabda* fish-heads, a pair of chicken's feet, some mushy vegetables and a selection of entrails down my brown corduroy shirt. By the sixth or seventh fraudulent mouthful, my shirt was dark with grease. But, I reasoned pensively, I was no greasier than any of the other patrons. Indeed, the stinking fish oil had helped me blend in with everyone else.

When the meal was finally at an end, I stood up to leave. As my lower abdomen became perpendicular once again, I sensed the fusion of fish-heads, intestines and chicken's feet slithering down into my boxer shorts. Venky led me back across the railway tracks. The forces of gravity drew the comestibles down further. Before I knew it, the *rickshawalla* was giving me unnerving glances . . . fish-heads had slimed down on to my shoes.

The worst possible reception was awaiting me at the mansion. A leading Far Eastern diplomat had dropped in on a flying visit to Calcutta. He was escorted by a military colleague, and by a uniformed factotum. Feroze was entertaining the guests on the veranda. Observing me entering the courtyard, he waved for me to join them. After a lunch at the down-and-outs' café, I was in no condition to meet Feroze, or his foreign dignitaries.

Drenched in putrid curry sauce, with rotting fish intestines trailing from my turn-ups, I was not a good advertisement for the Master's tutelage.

With desperate fumbling movements, I straightened my shirt-front and buttoned up the cuffs.

'You'll never guess what I've been through!' I chortled whimsically, as I approached the veranda.

Unfortunately, before my remark had reached the group of immaculately coutured gentlemen, the odour of putrefaction hit them. The subordinate officer gagged as the stench overpowered him. The diplomat whipped out a handkerchief and stuck its corners up his nostrils like home-made corks. The Master, who was inky blue with rage and trembling visibly, beckoned me forward with his index finger. I edged over to his wicker chair.

'Laboratory . . . now . . .' he whispered, smarting for revenge. 'You look hungry. Have a meal on me . . . ten pebbles!'

*   *   *   *

Two days passed. Feroze had been angered beyond all reason by my gaucherie. He slammed the shutters and roved about the darkened mansion, snarling. Outside trips were suspended. I was to practise elementary illusions until I could conduct myself better.

When I implored Feroze to understand the life-threatening circumstances of my meal, he dismissed all excuses. Neither would he listen to my report – a veritable orgy of insider information and obscure detail. I had failed the course and that was that.

'Please listen to me!' I urged him on the third day. 'Please realise – I only got into such a messy state by a sly sleight-of-hand!'

The Master sniffed haughtily.

'I have practised illusion for many years,' he said acrimoniously, 'and I've never had cause to stick rotting fish down my trousers.'

'All right . . . if you won't listen to my rendezvous with the Metro rental man, or to the meal at the Sealdah Station, would you give me one more chance to study insider information?'

Snatching at a bluebottle with his hand, the Master turned to face me.

'Never say that I am not lenient,' he said coldly. 'You have one chance to prove yourself. One slip up and the jar of stones will be your reward.'

Feroze was more like a villainous vizier from *A Thousand and One Nights* than a prominent conjuror. In times past such a person might have controlled an empire. Hafiz Jan had been right about the Master's tyrannical course – it wasn't a 'course' at all. Rather, it was a tortuous regime run by a confirmed sadist. Although avid for revenge, I still wanted to impress Hakim Feroze. A single word of applause would have been remuneration for the suffering.

Looking back, I must have been deranged to consider infiltrating Calcutta's most arcane profession. But as I reasoned it, the magician wanted insider information: and I would provide him with just that.

There would be no need for the services of Venky, at least not until I had done the reconnaissance myself.

During the six and a half weeks I had spent under the supervision of Feroze, a mysterious theme had distracted me. With my daily routine mapped out with illusory training and dead-end studies, I had not had time to explore the subject fully. Not, that is, until now.

Rather than searching for conventional fodder to requite the Master's craving, I took a rickshaw to South Park Street Cemetery. The time had come to penetrate Calcutta's most sinister realm – the world of the skeleton dealers.

Instead of entering the graveyard through the main gates, I climbed through the hole in the east wall. I could not chance being noticed.

As if enveloped by a spider's web, everything in Calcutta is connected to everything else. To locate his prey, a hunter must navigate a course across the delicate gossamer of threads. Given enough time, everything in Calcutta would lead one to everything else. But with Feroze impatient for results, I had no time to waste.

Within the hour I had tracked down Topu, the youth who lived with his friends in the cemetery. I explained that I required an appointment with the city's *konkalwallas*. Topu showed no surprise. He said that, for a fee, he could arrange such a meeting. I was to return to the cemetery shortly before midnight. It all seemed very easy – almost as if Topu was used to arranging rendezvous with the skeleton dealers. But as I handed over a few rupees to lubricate the wheels of efficiency, I was nagged by doubts. What if the *konkalwallas* thumped me on the head? Before I knew it, I'd be travelling freight class in a crate to Zurich as a medical skeleton.

The risks were high. But I was not going to be beaten by a few niggling doubts. Rather than descending into the Underworld alone, I would take a confidant with me. I pondered the situation. Who could I trust? The Master? No chance. He would have nothing to do with such a scheme. What about Gokul? Too old. Rublu? Too hunched. My shortlist was thin on names. With the others unsuitable, only one name remained. Venky.

I had not known him long, and had not seen his reactions under fire.

But there was no other choice.

Topu had been hesitant in agreeing to let me bring an acquaintance along. A supplementary fee, paid in crisp hundred-rupee notes, quashed his indecision. Venky was worth the expense – he would be my insurance policy against the acid bath.

Next stop after the burial ground was a roadside drinking den frequented by *rickshawallas*, in Chetla, south of Alipore.

Venky, who had been spending all his wages on *fenny*, had told me I could find him there when he was 'off duty'. Unfortunately for his family in Purulia, Venky was off duty and inebriated much of the time. A wooden shack set in bushes off the main road, the bar was haunted by a select breed of cirrhotic alcoholics. In ambience, it was like a contemporary version of a nineteenth-century opium den. Instead of opiates, gritty moonshine was poured from a single jug. An uncomfortable aroma of alcohol-based urine lingered about the room. Seven or eight hardened drinkers lay comatose in the dirt. One of them was Venky. When we were done with the *konkalwallas*, I would have to give him a few days to dry out.

'Venky,' I said in a solicitous tone, 'I'd like you to come with me tonight.'

The *rickshawalla* was too intoxicated for conversation. He was singing in his sleep. I pushed back one of his eyelids. The eyeball was rolled upwards. As I felt for a pulse, the owner of the watering-hole wandered over. A great hulk of a man, his face was obscured by six days of beard. He pointed quizzically to the unconscious *rickshawalla*. I nodded. Seizing Venky by his throat, the manager pulled him to his feet. Venky opened one eye and surveyed the room.

'*Haa, Sahib!*' he choked as his single functioning eye focused on me. The pupil dilated sharply.

'Venky, wake up!' I shouted. 'All this drinking is very bad. You should be ashamed of yourself!'

His neck still imprinted with finger marks, Venky stood to attention as best he could.

'You are to come with me later,' I said. 'I need your services tonight.'

'OK,' he coughed. 'Where to going?'

'First to Park Street,' I said, attempting to conceal the evening's gruesome schedule, 'then we'll be going on to meet some old residents of Calcutta.'

'Very nice,' winced Venky, 'elderly gentlemen?'

'Yes, elderly gentlemen,' I said. 'I suppose you could call them that.'

Curse of the Skeleton Dealers

With the moon high overhead, and a chorus of bats screeching in the mango trees, Venky, Topu and I roved out of Calcutta, towards our nocturnal engagement with the skeleton dealers. The journey was too far to be made by rickshaw, and so we took a battered old Ambassador cab. By his quiet enthusiasm, I suspected this was Venky's first time in a Calcutta taxi. The vehicle rumbled away from the deserted streets of central Calcutta, heading north-west over the Vidyasagar Setu Bridge. Venky chortled that we should have taken his rickshaw. But then, quite suddenly, he passed out. His blood was still pure alcohol.

Twenty minutes after crossing the Hoogly, Topu called for the taxi to pull up. The driver was paid, and we descended into the jungly undergrowth. Venky would not waken from his slumber. I feared he would be more of a liability than a life-saver. Topu bent over him, and pinched a nerve behind his left ear. Although I'm unclear which nerve it was, the reaction was startling. The *rickshawalla* jumped forwards, charged with adrenaline.

We waited in a drainage ditch beside an amber light. Every few seconds it would flash on, bathing us in a glorious surge of saffron. The road disappeared into the darkness about thirty metres ahead. When I asked Topu what we were doing, he told me to be patient.

Skeletons have always appealed to me. My fascination began when, as a child, I was taken to the crypt of a former Cistercian monastery in Sedlec, in what's now the Czech Republic. The thirteenth-century vault had been designed as an ossuary, a bone store. Every so often, when the graveyard was full to capacity, the skeletal remains of the villagers would be dug up and stacked up in the crypt like logs ready for burning. By the 1870s more than forty thousand skeletons had been squirrelled away in Sedlec's ossuary.

Spurred on by eccentric whims, the Schwartzenberg family, who owned the church, commissioned an artist to create something special from the bones. The maestro, Frantisek Rint, yearned to convert the skeletons into magnificent art. He set to work transforming the crypt into his fantasy.

Twin bone urns line the steps which lead down to the vault. The chamber itself is crammed with exquisite cherubs, ships' anchors, candlesticks, skull-and-crossbone bunting, and the formidable coat of arms of the House of Schwartzenberg: all created from human bones. Rint even signed his name in bones. But the masterpiece is the mighty chandelier. With at least one of every bone from a skeleton, it has seven candle-holders, each crafted from a human skull. As a child, the Sedlec crypt had affected me considerably, spawning a macabre curiosity for the used-body business.

A half-hour passed. No sign of our contact. Only dismay as we realised that the gutter was full of cockroaches. Another half-hour slipped by. Venky was sleeping peacefully, unaware of our investigation. Then, just as I was about to quiz Topu for the hundredth time, a slender figure slipped from the undergrowth behind us. At first I couldn't make out his face; just that he was wearing a chequered lumberjack's coat.

Topu exchanged greetings with the man. Venky and I were introduced to him. I tried to sustain an air of solemnity, as if the used-skeleton business was one of high stakes. As my eyes scrutinised the contours of his face, the amber light flashed on, bathing him in apricot light.

This was a man with truly hideous features. His eyes were pea-sized and unfriendly. His right cheek was bisected by a deep scar; and the lower portion of his face was dominated by a distinct lantern-jaw. One would have been hard pressed to imagine a more suitable façade to go along with his profession, of grave-robber.

Well, 'grave-robber' implies one who exhumes buried corpses from the earth. Our contact was more of a straightforward body thief than an all-out grave-robber.

Venky and I had had no idea, but the walled patch of land behind the main road was one of Calcutta's leading body dumps. Moving in single file, we edged our way to the far end of the wall. The lantern-jaw man pulled a home-made ladder from the gutter and propped it against the barrier. One at a time we clambered up, and jumped down into the enclosed field.

His lungs filling with the stench of rotting flesh, Venky turned to me, as if ordering an explanation.

'Old gentlemen,' I whispered.

Dozens of pedestrians are killed in Calcutta's traffic every month. Most of the corpses are claimed by relatives and taken away to be cremated. But a sizeable number are never collected. Some are too mutilated to be accurately identified. Others are not claimed as their families can't afford to have them cremated. With Calcutta so close to Bangladesh, the authorities are fearful of sparking another dispute between Muslims and Hindus. So, instead of automatically being cremated according to Hindu funerary rites, all unclaimed cadavers are abandoned in a secluded field on the outskirts of the city. Intentions are sound: the residents of the dumping ground are intended for burial. But with so many random forces hindering legitimate actions, the body-stealers slip by and spirit away what is, for them, a valuable commodity.

Even by moonlight, the body dump was extremely unpleasant. Dozens of corpses lay strewn about in varying stages of decomposition. Some had been gnawed by pye dogs and were missing their heads, hands, or entire limbs. Others were partially clothed. More still had rubbery Bengali weeds, what looked like liverwort, growing up through them. All were rotting. The odour of fetid flesh is especially unpleasant. Inhaling it is like being hit in the face again and again with a cudgel.

As I trod in the giant footsteps of Lantern Jaw, I chewed on my fist. I wasn't cut out to be a skeleton thief. Staggering behind me was Venky, who had lapsed into a state of deep trauma.

Lantern Jaw poked about with a stick, searching for a corpse of good height, with good teeth. He selected a relatively new cadaver. It was that of a female. By the light of my key-fob torch, I made a swift examination of her face. Death is not a condition which live members of the human species are apt to understand. As I stared at this and other cadavers, so many questions came to me. How had the repulsive blemishes occurred? Why were the hands gnarled and distended like root-ginger? Was I going to look like this one day?

Topu observed me staring into the face of Lantern Jaw's find. He placed a hand on my shoulder-blade and tugged me away. Perhaps he sensed that I was already deeply disturbed. Whereas my agitation was inward, Venky's was loud and overbearing. The *rickshawalla* was praying at the top of his voice. When I tried to hush him, he grew even more distressed.

Fearing we might be given away by Venky's screams, Lantern Jaw wrenched the female cadaver from the soil like a discarded, decomposing mannequin. He hid it beneath branches at one end of the field. He would, I suspected, be back for it later.

Topu had sworn me to secrecy. He said it was he who would be held accountable if I were to reveal the factory's location. In any case, I have no idea how he supposed I would remember details of the convoluted route.

By three a.m. we had reached the plant.

Lantern Jaw slid into the shadows like a cat-burglar, as the main door was pushed open. Topu went in first. Moments later he beckoned for Venky and me to follow. By the way Topu was greeted, it was evident that he was in some way involved. As the dozen or so workers welcomed him, I considered his motives. Had he been peddling antique English skeletons from the Park Street burial ground?

The two hours which Venky and I spent at the skeleton processing factory constituted one of the most unnerving experiences I have ever endured. It's impossible to liken it to anything else. But rather than being repugnant, the business struck me as constructive. Its products – medical skeletons – were fashioned from unwanted raw material . . . rotting corpses.

Located in an abandoned brick-walled warehouse, the plant was formed from a series of small chambers. Lit by three or four low-watt bulbs, each was dedicated to a specific purpose. In the West we tend to think of factories as cavernous halls filled with unwieldy machines and uniformed workers. This misguided perception evaporated as we toured the plant.

The *rickshawalla* and I regrouped in the modest reception area. I whacked Venky on the back, hoping to reassure him. He perked up somewhat. A tattered sofa, a desk and tranquil posters of the Himalayas belied the grisly business of the next room. A manager had arrived to show us around the premises. He was introduced grandly as the 'night operator'. By his fawning mannerisms and obsequious demeanour, it was obvious he was expecting a hefty bribe.

The manager's body, with the proportions of a whisky barrel, was balanced above a pair of child-sized feet. The ratio resulted in awkward, listing movements, like those of a Sumo wrestler in ballet shoes. Buffing his fingernails on his stained teal-green kitchen apron, the night operator filled me in on some of the details of his profession. Topu translated.

He explained that, until the mid-1980s, Calcutta was Asia's largest exporter of human skeletons. At the height, about fifty thousand human skulls, and more than twenty thousand complete skeletons, were shipped from Calcutta to international buyers every year. Most were exported illegally to Europe via Bangladesh.

But this was just the tip of the bone-business iceberg. Impecunious states like Bihar and Orissa have two things in abundance. The first is live people. The second is dead people.

In 1988 at least seventy thousand human skeletons were smuggled abroad. Many were victims of road accidents. Thousands more were the decomposing corpses of the exhumed.

Doms, scavengers, across India snatch bodies from hospital morgues, newly dug graves, and crematoria. One distraught relative went to the newspapers when he saw a suspicious-looking man skinning heads at his local morgue. The thief, who was stuffing the skulls in a rough wooden box, was, no doubt, about to dispatch them to Calcutta for a quick sale.

As he led Venky and me around his factory, the night operator warned us to cover our noses. His sense of smell must have withered years before, scotched by the vicious stench.

The first workshop was the size and shape of an inter-city railway carriage. Its walls were dark with grime and the floor was caked in mud like a pigsty. The room stank of death. Rotting human flesh radiates a rumbustious, chaotic smell. It bombards the full spectrum of the nasal senses like a stink-bomb. Humans interpret the odour as irresistibly unpleasant – an instinctual alarm. Curious as to Venky's reaction to the aroma, I glanced over at him. The muscles of his face had locked, creating a warped, petrified expression.

'Don't worry,' I gagged through my handkerchief. 'Think of it as a scientific exercise.'

The *rickshawalla* blinked once. The shock had made him mute. A single male corpse was being stripped by a pair of deferential assistants in front of him. The ease with which they handled the cadaver suggested they were not novices to the profession.

Weaned on censored television, the Western world has an erroneous idea of what a cadaver is like. We're used to seeing clean, well-turned-out corpses on 'slabs' in low-budget police dramas. The toe-tags are orderly – the corpses lie straight-backed. Five minutes in a West Bengal skeleton factory amends such trim images. Cadavers are bloated with internal gas. Their skin is rotting, falling away from the bone. The limbs are twisted; the fingers gnarled like a bird's talons. The face is swollen and contorted, with the mouth open and the nose knocked off. The skin itself is devoid of that refined, even tint of oyster grey from police dramas. It's black with decay; blotched and haemorrhaged, like a gangrenous, suppurating lump of meat.

*

As he led us through to the next chamber, the night operator lamented how difficult it was to get good-quality corpses.

'We get offered so many,' he said whimsically, 'but the *doms* are very greedy. They don't pay enough attention to the condition of the bones. What good is a corpse which has been mangled in a car crash? How can we export such a thing?'

I grunted once, then again, echoing the manager's despondency.

'We only deal with perfect cadavers,' he continued. 'Before all the restrictions, we would export only the skull if the actual body was damaged. But now we're much more careful. Fewer skeletons are being sold from Calcutta, and so we make sure they're in good condition. The hardest thing to get right is the teeth. What scientist would want a nice white skeleton in his office that's missing its front teeth? Most of the older cadavers have awful teeth; and the young ones tend to have been killed in traffic accidents.'

'So what's the perfect specimen?' I asked, slipping the handkerchief away for a second to splutter out my question.

The night operator, who seemed to have a genuine fondness for his vocation, smiled.

'Well,' he said, with Topu still translating, 'often the best examples are young men who have died of a disease.'

'What kind of disease?' I snapped, fearful of what contagious infections were inhabiting the premises.

'Oh, all types . . .' the manager said casually. 'We get a lot of tuberculosis, smallpox, cholera, and venereal diseases. As long as the illness hasn't corroded or distorted the bones, we consider them. *Doms* get very angry when they have their corpse refused. But if, say, it's got polio, rickets, or elephantiasis, how can we accept it?' The night operator paused to shoo away a rat. 'Sometimes we get in a nice example,' he continued. 'It's a young man of good size, with good teeth. You think it'll look really nice when it's cleaned up. But then, when the flesh has been removed, we see that the bones have been eaten away by syphilis. And it's us who lose out. We pay the *doms* before the corpse has been stripped.'

'Syphilis . . .' intoned Topu sombrely. 'It's the curse of the skeleton dealers.'

'How long have the bodies been dead when you get them?'

'It's often hard to say,' the manager explained. 'Sometimes we get them when they're quite fresh – a week or two old. Other times, they're much older – months, even years. With the restrictions, it takes *doms* longer to bring them from other states, like Orissa.'

The official ushered us into the next chamber. Much wider than the last, but with a lower ceiling, the room was filled with a series of dented grey metal troughs. Each contained a dark, pungent liquid.

'The corpses are placed in the acid for a complete day,' said the night operator. 'The acid dissolves most of the flesh; but it mustn't start to work on the bone. If that happens, then the cadaver's useless. We take care the acid isn't too strong.'

We paced through into another workshop.

The night operator lit a *biri*, a hand-rolled Indian cigarette, and carried on outlining the factory's task.

'After a day in the acid,' he said, 'the corpse is pulled out and the workers clean off any flesh which remains. The vertebrae, feet, toes and joints all need a lot of work. But hardest to prepare is the skull. What's left of the brain is removed, even the smallest traces of flesh and skin are cleared away. Only very skilled workers clean the skull.'

Four men were squatting on the concrete floor. Without glancing up at us, they continued with their work. A jigsaw puzzle of bones was scattered before them. One, clutching a skull in his hands like an orb, cautiously brushed out the eye sockets. Another was scrubbing individual vertebrae with a toothbrush.

'See what care they take with their jobs!' the night operator exclaimed. 'Our workmen like it here very much. Of course, before the ban, we had a much larger staff. We used to export all over the world, bringing a lot of valuable foreign currency into the country.'

Like any other small business executive, wounded by punitive legislation, the manager was bitter.

'After the bones have had the remaining flesh removed,' he said, 'they get dipped in a series of other baths. First, a strong acid, and then a bleach solution.'

'What happens then – after the bleaching?'

'Then comes the most time-consuming and skilled part,' intoned the executive. 'The bones are checked for damage, then they're drilled and pinned. Synthetic cartilage is fitted between the vertebrae and in the ribcage. All that is now done at another factory.'

The night operator broke off, disturbed by a falsetto whining similar to the sound of a doodle-bug careering to earth. He, Topu and I turned in unison. Behind us, trembling in the skull-filled corner, kneeling and rocking back and forth, his hands splayed across his face, was Venky.

* * * *

Back in Alipore, the magician listened with veiled interest to my description of the night's sordid observations. Waving general descriptions of the skeleton factory aside, he searched for intricate details. What colour was the flesh being scrubbed from the vertebrae? Was the metal of the acid baths corroded at the seams? Had I noticed any stray teeth on the floor?

As before, I bit my tongue when grilled about contacts. Feroze would have been displeased to learn that his own former agent had set up the rendezvous. The Master feigned ignorance of the body business, but he obviously knew all about it. A rummage through his desk drawers had revealed a metacarpus, a human finger bone. Before leaving the factory, I had handed the night operator an outrageously large tip. In return, he offered Venky and me souvenirs of our tour . . . finger bones.

'You *have* done well, haven't you?' said Feroze sarcastically when I had finished.

'Thank you.'

The magician glanced at his watch.

'You can have the rest of the morning off,' he sneered.

It was a quarter to twelve. With a full fifteen minutes to squander, I went out to the kitchen to have a chat with Gokul.

The manservant was standing on a chair, hanging a new fly-paper from the ceiling.

'Your chest not sounding good,' he said as I entered.

'It's the city's pollution,' I responded. 'I've never had asthma until now. Calcutta's air should carry a health warning.'

'You know . . .' said Gokul quietly, 'someone told me about special cure for asthma. In Hyderabad . . . Gowd family giving free miracle cure on one day at start of every June.'

'Miracle cure?' I replied. 'What is it exactly?'

Gokul hunched his shoulders.

'Don't know what,' he said. 'But I always wanting to go there. I, too, having this asthma.'

Gokul wheezed severely to prove the advanced state of his condition.

'Sounds interesting . . . I'll drop by if I ever happen to be in Hyderabad in June.'

As the long-case clock in the sorcerer's study struck the last chime of noon, I stood to attention beside it.

Feroze peered up from his writing desk. He pointed to a stack of forty or so books, mostly on illusion.

'Have you read those?'

'Yes, all of them. Shall I put them back on the shelf?'

'Have you practised all the illusions we learned last week?'

'Yes.'

'Did you scrub beneath your nails with bleach after your little foray last night?'

'Yes . . . twice.'

'All right,' replied the Master, standing on tiptoe for a moment. 'Then you're to come with me.'

Feroze led me into the street, where he hailed a taxi. Although he often slunk out of the house to meet Rublu at the Albert Hall, the magician had rarely invited me to accompany him anywhere.

'Are we going for coffee at the Albert Hall?' I asked optimistically.

The Master did not reply. He was concentrating on other matters.

'Are your shoes waterproof?' he asked at some length.

'Well, not very,' I retorted. 'They're suede. But I suppose they're no worse than your loafers.'

'Don't worry about me,' he barked.

The taxi bypassed central Calcutta, heading north-east towards the gridlock traffic of Tangra, the Chinese suburb. Calcutta's suburbia was until recently patched with lakes; some salty, others freshwater. The pressure for new tenement blocks had spurred on the illicit draining of such entrancing pools. Calcutta's climate was changing as a result. I asked Feroze what he thought of the destruction. He told me to hush. Other problems occupied his attention.

With gritted teeth, the taxi driver charged through the swarm of vehicles and incessant road-works. Once beyond Tangra, he turned on to a secluded tow-path and proceeded for half an hour. The trail became increasingly jungly and overgrown. Still deep in thought, the Master stared in concentration at his lap.

Five minutes more and the taxi veered sharply to negotiate an unexpected blind turn. As we recovered from the jolt, Feroze tapped the driver's neck, signalling for him to stop. The brakes were applied with tremendous force, sending the vehicle into a prolonged skid.

'Come with me,' instructed Feroze sternly. 'Welcome to East Calcutta Marshes.'

We marched down to the water, where a ramshackle launch was waiting. The boat's owner helped us into the craft. The magician barked a set of instructions at him. Nodding, the man pushed the boat away from the bank. Very soon we were plying forward into the swampland ahead.

Every day about a third of Calcutta's sewage seeps directly into the wetlands. With a little hard work and a lot of help from nature, the slurry is broken down. When the toxins are no more, fish and vegetables thrive.

The marshes lie due east from the rank-smelling tanneries of China-town and the mountainous refuse heaps of Dhapa. More than twenty-three million litres of sewage and industrial waste flow into them every day. Despite this, they provide hundreds of tonnes of food in return.

Part of the secret lies in the efficiency of the city's rag-pickers. They sift out every morsel of reusable material – from scraps of metal and food to fragments of cloth, glass, and plastic. The rest of the secret lies in the marshes' extraordinary plant life. The water hyacinth filters out the heavy metals, including mercury; while yet more plants strain out the oil, grease, and toxins. Cast an eye across the wetlands, and you see dozens of miniature rice paddies and vegetable plots poking above the reeds and tall grasses.

Politicians are eager to drain the marshes to provide yet more cheap housing for the masses. To them, an ecological recycling plant is of no use. Instead of a twenty-thousand-acre botanical paradise, their vision is of tenements for all the voters.

Feroze had no interest in discussing the marshes' ecological web of life. Something was bothering him. When I quizzed him on where we were going in the leaking craft, he told me to shut up.

Only when I drifted off to sleep did he address me.

'Godmen are having a field day in India!' he shouted.

'But they're nothing new . . . they've been around for thousands of years.'

'That might be true,' the Master responded, 'but they're developing now like never before . . . they're changing. And as they change, they're increasing their power over every hamlet, village, town and city. Soon the whole country will be at their mercy!'

Sensationalism was not something which Feroze generally went in for. I suspected that, about to launch into one of his fearsome diatribes, he had a point to make.

'But you yourself have taught magical feats to godmen,' I said.

The Master looked out across the marshes. He sniffed the air like a spaniel.

'That may be so,' he replied. 'I'm not condemning the rise of the godmen, but merely making an observation. Today in India there are about five thousand leading godmen. That's five thousand deities in human form. The most celebrated attract hundreds of thousands as their followers . . . from peasants in the rice paddies to the Prime Minister.'

'You are against them?'

'Absolutely not,' intoned the Master. 'I've known many of them most of their working careers. I taught illusions to dozens of them. Do you think they came up with those "miracles" all on their own? Miracles are easy . . . *you* know that. But they're not everything.'

'Then what's the key?'

Feroze pressed his hand to his mouth.

'Presentation,' he said. 'Spew out three hours of "woolly" talk – preach about *kundalini*, self-purification, the cosmic soul or karmic forces – and you'll keep your followers. Remember, the illusions are the flame which attracts the moth – the rest is down to the gift of the gab.'

'What about all the Westerners who come here looking for a guru?'

Feroze shook his head.

'All those foreigners,' he said, 'are looking for something quite different than the Indians. Both have contrasting demands on their gurus. Indian people – especially those in villages and small towns – are looking for a cure for illness and increased prosperity. Guru means "dispeller of darkness", but that's not what the Westerners are after. They're looking for someone to praise them – to reinforce their self-confidence.'

The oarsman stood up and started to bail water from the centre of the craft. Although relatively stable, we were sitting in eight inches of water. My suede brogues were ruined. I looked over to see how Feroze's slip-ons were faring. He had somehow managed to change shoes en route. Instead of loafers, he was now kitted out in a sturdy pair of Gore-Tex hiking boots.

'Don't forget,' he said after a minute of thought, 'that illusion and magic are taken far more seriously in India than in the West. I've told you this before. The faddish superstition of Elizabethan Europe is a feature of modern-day India. Conjury is used by godmen, healers, priests, *sadhus*, and many others. All of them are seeking to create an impact. The metaphysical is a key facet to life here . . . Indians explain the natural through the supernatural.'

As Feroze ranted on about illusion, the boat's pilot docked on a sandbank. Stepping out on to the beach, the Master's thoughts returned to the situation at hand.

'Can't you tell me where we're going?' I moaned, as we tramped a mile east over mud flats.

'Wait and see.'

The earth was moist, and thick with a thorny form of reed. They snagged on my trousers as I struggled to keep up. Every shade of green was represented there. I called out to Feroze, asking what he thought of the colours. But as always uninterested in my observations, he ordered me to hurry.

'We don't have much time,' he said, glancing at his pocket-watch. 'The assembly's about to start.'

'What assembly? What's this all about?'

As yet another question went unanswered, we arrived at the outskirts of a sprawling village. Feroze led the way to the central square. He seemed to know the layout of the village well.

About three hundred people were already in attendance at the north end of the square. Bunched up together like sheep in a pen, they formed a crude semi-circle. Most were standing. Mothers and their children, old men and gangling youths. All were concentrating on the figure standing before them.

We took our places on the extreme left of the audience.

I whispered to Feroze:

'Who's that man?'

'That . . .' he replied grandly, 'that is a psychic surgeon.'

'But I didn't think Indian godmen did actual surgery.'

'They don't,' said Feroze.

'But look, he's Indian . . .'

'This is one of the only psychic surgeons on the sub-continent,' declared Feroze. 'He was taught by a Filipino in Madras. He's trying to make a name for himself in Calcutta . . . speaks Bengali quite well.'

Before the magician could disclose further details, the show began.

The surgeon was a tall, balding man with an expansive forehead and a flaccid complexion. His hands were broad as cymbals, his body was cloaked in a lavish aquamarine robe, belted at the waist with a fraying red sash. A distance of about twenty-five feet separated him from the crowd. Before him stood a large dining table, covered by a plastic sheet. In front of that was a rug.

'Pay close attention,' Feroze hissed, as the ritual got under way.

One of the surgeon's assistants scuttled forward carrying a brass incense burner. Copious amounts of gargoyle-grey smoke poured from its latticed top. The burner was positioned at the right-hand corner of the carpet. As the surgeon sat cross-legged at the centre of the rug, the attendant returned with a second, identical burner. This was placed at the rug's top left corner. The physician closed his eyes, lolled his neck back like a loggerhead turtle, and started to chant mantras. A light southerly breeze conveyed the two plumes of dense sandalwood smoke into the audience.

When the prolonged session of chanting was at an end, the surgeon thrust his arms in the air and addressed the villagers.

'He's telling them that God has sent him here,' said Feroze softly. 'He is saying his hands have the power to restore the sick. No illness, he says, is too severe. There's hope for everyone.'

A wave of expectation gripped the audience. An old man cheered; a young boy shouted praise. The three hundred villagers inched forward in anticipation. As they did so, the surgeon commanded them to stay back.

'Now,' said the Master, 'he's saying his powers only work if everyone stands perfectly still. If anyone moves, even an inch, his magic will vanish and no one will be healed.'

The doctor appealed to the crowd. Which of them had an illness? Virtually everyone stuck up their hands.

The first patient selected by the surgeon was an elderly, anaemic-looking woman. She claimed to have an ulcer in her stomach. When she was asked to point to the pain, she motioned to her chest. Nonetheless, she was lifted up on to the doctor's examination table, to the delight of the audience. The table had been placed on a raised bank of ground, with the onlookers standing lower, at the very edge of the square. The table's height – which was obviously intended – made it impossible for the audience to get a good view of the tabletop.

The physician performed a superficial examination on his patient. From where I was standing, it appeared as if he was probing specific lymph nodes at points on her abdomen. He took care to obstruct the view by standing on the outer side of the operating table. With the external scrutiny over, the doctor pressed his palms together and touched them to his mouth. The villagers stretched forward for a better look. Some were straight-faced. Others chattered away, giggling to their friends in anticipation.

They watched in awe as the doctor drew a grubby scalpel from his belt, flailing it to and fro like a cavalry officer signalling the charge. Inhaling all at once, the villagers inched forward. The assistant poured *ghee* on to the incense burners. The operating table was veiled in an impenetrable cloud of greasy smoke.

As the surgeon motioned wild, slicing movements with the scalpel, one of the helpers tapped out a rhythm on a tambourine. The drumming, the asphyxiating smoke, the perfume of sandalwood, and the glint of the blade mesmerized the audience. The beat grew faster. And faster. Another assistant bounded in front of the table and twirled round and around like a ballerina. As the drumming reached a climax, the dancer leapt towards the crowd, emitting a terrible scream. The surgeon thrust a chunk of meat into the air. Caught expertly by the aide, the trophy was exhibited to the villagers. The meat was said to be the woman's ulcer. It was white and bore an uncanny resemblance to a lump of mutton fat. I asked the assistant if I could inspect the ulcer at closer quarters. But as I made my petition, he threw the flesh to a ravenous pye dog. A second later and the evidence had been gobbled up.

The surgeon wiped his bloodied hands on a cloth and helped the woman from the operating table. The villagers watched as he sponged away a patch of blood from her stomach. The wound and all scars had vanished, healed by the psychic surgeon's magical powers. The grand-mother thanked her benefactor and confessed that she felt much better.

When the audience had finished cheering, the surgeon called for a second patient. A boy of about seven was pushed forward by his friends. He conferred with the physician, who made an announcement.

'He says that the child has tonsillitis,' explained Feroze. 'He's going to chop out the tonsils. Again, watch how the smoke and the drumming distract the audience.'

As before, the patient lay still on the operating couch. The scalpel flashed in the sunlight like the eye of a demon as it was lunged towards the boy's mouth. A ladle of *ghee* was poured on each incense burner, creating a riot of billowing smoke. The tambourine's sound echoed like a clap of thunder. The assistant shrieked and the child's tonsils were hurled into the air. The pye dog had another snack. A moment later, the boy stood up, spat out a mouthful of blood, and returned to his friends – miraculously healed.

Psychic surgeons have had an uneasy honeymoon with the Indian public. When they first appeared during the early 1980s, they were discredited largely because of a single foreign 'surgeon-priest'. Profes-sing to have the ability to heal through mind-power, the self-taught surgeon arrived in India and started holding regular sessions. But then he himself fell sick after eating some local food. He called for an ambulance and was rushed to hospital. Rather than being pleased that the mystic was being cared for in hospital, people turned against him. 'If he's a miracle-maker,' they asked, 'why doesn't he cure himself?'

Manila, capital of the Philippines, is the world centre for psychic surgery. As at the village in the marshes, Filipino surgeons generally feign the operation – pretending to excise a morsel of cancerous flesh. In some cases, a 'doctor' performs actual minor operations without anesthetic. The patient's surge of adrenaline as the audience cheers them on, and their natural endorphins, mask the discomfort. In Latin America, genuine cataract surgery and tonsillectomies are often carried out by so-called psychic surgeons. Yet there's very little one could call 'psychic' about their work at all.

Feroze nudged me to pay attention. The next patient was on the table. A woman of about forty, she had been complaining of severe abdominal pains. When the physician pressed his fingers to her appendix area, the lady screeched wildly. The doctor felt certain she had appendicitis. Immediate surgery was necessary to save her life.

This time, the operation was longer and more involved. A blindfold was placed over the women's face to keep her from seeing her own intestines. A fresh scalpel was passed to the surgeon. Its blade was tested on a strand of hair. It was as sharp as a sickle. *Ghee* was applied to the burners. The drum beat out a mysterious rhythm. The pye dog licked its lips expectantly. The villagers stood on tiptoe to get the best view possible.

Pulling me to his own vantage point, Feroze gestured to the surgeon. 'Watch the front fold of his robe,' he whispered. 'Don't be distracted by all the song and dance.'

Locking my eyes on the surgeon's hands, I watched in astonishment as he slipped a large lump of meat from the lining of his garment. The costume's bright colour was well-suited to concealing raw mutton. As one of the surgeon's hands slashed about with the blade, the other squeezed blood from a sponge across the woman's abdomen. None of the villagers queried that a human appendix could so resemble a chunk of meat carved from a sheep's thigh. They were too enthused with the presentation to voice questions.

'All right,' said Feroze as the fourth patient was getting ready to have a tumour excised, 'that's enough. Let's go back to Calcutta.'

We tramped back across the mud flats to where the boatman was waiting. Spreading the fingers of his left hand in a crude salute, he helped us into his waterlogged craft.

Against all the odds, the taxi driver had remembered to fetch us from the embankment. It was good to be on dry land again. Soaked through below the waist, I tugged off my shoes to check for trench foot.

'How did you enjoy the surgeries?' Feroze asked in a clement tone.

'Not bad at all . . . especially the appendectomy.'

'I'm glad the display met with your approval,' mused the magician. 'You'll be able to think about it when you go away . . .'

'Go away?' I said. 'Go away where?'

'Oh,' he exclaimed with a phony blank expression. 'Didn't I tell you?'

'Tell me what?'

'You're going on a journey.'

'*Am I?* What sort of journey?'

The Master wound down the taxi's window and drew in a sharp breath of Chinatown's turbid air.

'A journey of observation!'

'Tell me more . . .' I said, recoiling from the sudden announcement.

'The journey is the next phase in your course,' Feroze declared, picking his teeth with his tongue. 'You're to spend time watching people.'

'People? Only people? What of the scenery? What about landscapes?'

'Rubbish,' said the magician. 'Don't give a damn bit of notice to the scenery. People change, they're changing all the time . . . they're doing things . . . the bloody scenery will be there forever. No – people are the thing you're to observe!'

'What kind of people?'

'All kinds. But I want you to search out godmen, *sadhus*, astrologers, and *anyone* who's out of the ordinary. Remember Houdini's principle: everyone, however unlikely, has something from which one can learn. You are to make notes on all that you observe – they're to be sent back regularly for my attention.'

'But where am I to go, on this journey?'

The Master prodded me in the chest.

'Anywhere you like!'

'How long is the trip supposed to go on?'

'A day . . . a month . . . a year . . . a lifetime: however long it takes!'

The lack of guidelines was galling. Feroze knew how I liked basic, straightforward questions to be answered. He had clearly dreamt up the scheme to harass me. Or, more likely still, to get rid of me.

'If you won't tell me where to go, or how long to go for . . . will you at least tell me when I am to leave?'

Handing a rupee coin to a beggar as the taxi paused at a traffic light, Feroze pivoted to regard me straight on.

'You are to leave at sunrise,' he said.

PART THREE

Much travel is needed before the raw man is ripened

Proverb

Chapter 13

Dick Whittington and the Black Hole

Gokul slipped into my room in the middle of the night and packed my bags, as stealthily as a secret agent on assignment. At five-thirty a.m. he tweaked the little finger of my left hand.

'Time for shower,' he sniffed, as I woke from a nightmare.

'Gokul . . .' I yawned. 'I've been having the most unpleasant dreams.'

'What you dream?' he asked sensitively.

'I dreamt that Feroze was sending me away . . .'

Gokul did not reply. He was too busy stuffing my shaving kit into a side pocket of my case.

'Must waste no time,' he said a few moments later. 'Master say you must go by six. Twenty-five minute time.'

My stomach knotted like a bullwhip. The future was suddenly so uncertain. Where was I to go? How was I to get there? Was I being expelled from the course?

Ordering the elderly valet to unpack my things, I charged downstairs to confront the Master. I was tired of being used as a pawn in his grand scheme. As always he was merely toying with me; abusing my pledge of unequivocal obedience. I searched the study, laboratory, sitting-room, and even the kitchen. The magician was not to be found.

Gokul, who had ignored my instructions, was dragging my case to the foot of the stairs.

'Do you know where the Master is?'

'He gone out,' said the servant. 'He wish you luck and say he see you when you return in few months.'

'A few months?' I swallowed hard. 'Is that how long I'm supposed to be gone?'

Gokul hunched one shoulder. Then the other.

'Yes,' he replied innocently, 'I am thinking so.'

'Didn't he want to see me off himself?'

'Oh, no, he too busy. He having business across town.'

'What, at six in the morning?'

Fumbling, Gokul dislodged a packet from the inner depths of his *lungi*. It was wrapped in green sugar paper.

'Master ask me to give you this. Almost forgot.'

'Ah, excellent!' I said. 'This must have all the directions in it for my trip.'

I tore the sheets of sugar paper apart. Inside was a map and a note written in the magician's hand. I read the message aloud:

'*Have a productive journey. All the best, Feroze.*'

The valet smiled through the right corner of his mouth. He continued to haul my case out into the yard.

'Is that it?'

Gokul nodded.

I unfolded the cloth-backed map, which was rather like unfurling a starched ship's sail. It depicted the entire Indian sub-continent. Scanning it gingerly, I searched for random pencil lines, an arrow, an 'X'. Anything. Despite its great age, the chart – manufactured by Sifton, Praed & Co. of St James's – was unblemished. The only mark was a Chinagraph circle around Hyderabad.

'Hyderabad . . . What's in Hyderabad?'

'Gowd family asthma cure,' said Gokul.

'But . . . that's not until the first week of June.'

I looked at the date on my watch.

'Today's the third of March.'

Gokul warned me that it was one minute to six. The Master, he exhorted, would be incensed if I were there when he returned. We hurried through the courtyard.

'Good journey . . .' exclaimed Gokul abruptly, pulling back the gate for me to leave, 'and watch out!'

'What for?'

The manservant raised his right palm to his brow in a crude salute.

'You will be knowing . . . soon you will be knowing,' he said.

*   *   *   *

With no one else to turn to for advice, I sallied down to the other end of Alipore, in the hope of finding Venky at his usual bar. The *rickshawalla* would probably be passed out on the floor after a wild night of carousing. It was time to rouse my secret weapon.

The sudden proclamation that I was to hasten away on an epic journey of observation worried me deeply. Feroze was an expert at destabilising those around him. He must have noticed that I had begun to actually relish his intolerably sadistic regime. Despite being savaged by the unbearable pressures of the course, I had developed dour masochistic tendencies. Doubtless an instinctual tactic of survival. The very prospect of digging trenches with a teaspoon, memorising formulae, or selected works of Plato, raising my temperature to suicidal levels, even swallowing pebbles now filled me with ominous delight. Suddenly, the magician was swiping all these indulgences away. He was revoking the outlandish lifestyle of the past two months. In doing so he was sentencing me to the most sadistic ordeal so far – an existence without routine oppression. Cast back into the world like an ex-con who had done his time, I had become dependent on incarceration.

I considered the journey. My neck stooped downwards with despondency. What was I going to do? As I stumbled ahead I sensed an invisible force clutching my shoulders. I stopped in my tracks. The sensation was still there. Although forceful, it was warm and pleasing. 'Don't be beaten by this!' growled a familiar voice. 'Remember your ancestor Nawab Jan Fishan . . . Even when his own sons were slaughtered in battle, he continued fighting until victory!' An instant later Hafiz Jan's embrace had disappeared. But his words had stirred me. He was right. Why be conquered by uncertainty? Why not roam about India for a while, searching for godmen and illusions? I hadn't spent much money while staying with Feroze. Living on the cheap I could afford to survive for months.

All right, I mused, I will fulfil the sorcerer's orders. I'll go on a trip – and not some pathetic little jaunt, but a great journey.

Venky was not, as I had expected to find him, unconscious at his Alipore drinking den. Instead, he was dressed in a fine new *lungi* and poly-cotton shirt, with a large *tikka* on his forehead. He was in the street washing his rickshaw.

'Venky . . . is that you?' I asked, aghast he was even fit to stand. 'What's going on? Why *aren't* you drunk?'

The *rickshawalla* probed the spokes of the cartwheel with an oily rag. They had not been cleaned for a very long time. He greeted me with *namaskar*, and offered me his clay cup of cold, milky tea. When I refused it, he gulped it down and dropped the cup in the gutter, breaking it.

Everything in Calcutta – from tea leaves to sticking plasters – is reused. Nothing is ever thrown away after one use . . . nothing, that is, except for *bharh*, the minuscule bisque cups. Little bigger than thimbles, they fill every gutter. Calcuttans laugh hysterically when the mad foreigner suggests reusing them. To me, the cups were dainty objects of art. To Venky, and everyone else, they were the most worthless things around.

'*Sahib*,' the *rickshawalla* said, 'you were sended to me!'

'What are you talking about, Venky? I found you all by myself. No one knows about you . . . you're my secret weapon.'

But the *rickshawalla* had more to say:

'No, *Sahib*, you no understanding! You were sended to me by angels . . . from Heaven!'

Venky *was* obviously drunk.

'I thought you were sober,' I said. 'You should know better than this.'

'But *Sahib*,' he replied earnestly, 'I am no drunk. I will no be drinking again. You were sended to me . . . you are warning from God. I was drinking . . . wasting money. Sending little bit to wife in Purulia only. God sending you to me!'

'Venky,' I replied, 'if you're not drunk, then you've gone mad. How could you possibly think *I* was sent from Heaven?'

He lay out on the ground, as if mimicking a corpse.

'*Konkalwallas*,' he shouted, 'this was sign!'

Venky was eager to explain how the horrors of the skeleton factory had jerked him into a new, unknown life of moral rectitude. He had witnessed a vision . . . not God or angels, but skeleton dealers and their corpses. Somehow, he now saw me as his saviour. But there was no time for the adulation.

'Venky,' I said, 'I'm going on a trip. I need your help.'

'Trip? Oh, very nice. Where you to going?'

'I don't know.'

'When you are going?'

I tapped my watch.

'Immediately,' I said.

The *rickshawalla* gave me an uneasy glance.

'I need some ideas,' I said. 'If you could go anywhere in India to meet a godman . . . where would you go?'

'Holy man . . . *sadhu*?'

'Yes, that's right . . .'

Venky thought long and hard. He masked his face with his spindly fingers. A minute passed. Five more minutes slipped away. The *rickshawalla* seemed to have fallen into a trance. Perhaps the sudden shortage of alcohol had been too much for his addicted system.

'Venky!' I shouted. 'What are you doing?'

'I thinking, *Sahib*.'

'All right, well stop thinking now. What have you come up with?'

Venky raised a finger in the air, as if he were testing the direction of the wind.

'I going to Jamshedpur Mental Hospital,' he said, pointedly.

'Where's that?'

'Bihar.'

'But I'm not mad. At least, I don't think I am.'

'Yes, *Sahib*. You no loony. Famous *sadhu* at Jamshedpur Mental Hospital. Very popular.'

'Is *he* mad?'

'Oh, no, *Sahib*,' came the reply. 'He no loony . . . he just living there.'

'Hmm, an asylum for sane people: sounds like a great idea.'

I pulled the map from my back pocket and hunted for Jamshedpur.

'Well, that's quite close . . . due west,' I said when I had found it. 'I suppose it's a start.'

Venky patted the seat of his rickshaw and widened his eyes.

'Train leaving Howrah Junction,' he said knowingly. 'I take you there.'

Heaving the rickshaw's handles up to his armpits like upturned hockey sticks, Venky padded his way north to the famous Calcutta Strand. I was horrified he should still be working barefoot. On many occasions I had offered to buy him a pair of shoes. But Venky insisted he had never worn footwear – even when he was a postal runner in Purulia. Shoes made his feet itch and sweat, and that made his work impossible. So, it was with bare feet that he dodged the potholes on that bright yet uncertain morning.

India is accustomed to pandemonium on a grand scale. At any one time, it seems as if all nine hundred million people are careering about, guided by their own evolved form of Brownian motion. Like constellations in a distant cosmos, they move according to predestined trajectories. And at the centre of each unending galaxy is India's version of a Black Hole: a central railway terminus.

Amid the structured chaos of the sub-continent, a special and venerated place is reserved for major railway stations. Those who enter them can never be certain of when, or where, they will emerge. Indeed, some never reappear at all. They become trapped in the cycle of polishing shoes, picking pockets and selling frothy mango drinks.

Howrah railway station is the most visually spectacular Black Hole of all. It might not have the architectural appeal of Bombay's Indo-Gothic Victoria Terminus, but it boasts an inexorable blend of life. The floor's rich patchwork stretched out like a grand *kelim*, covering every inch of the station. Knotted together, sealed in position like frozen atoms, there was almost no room to move. Even if they could have moved, no one would have dared. As in a perpetual game of musical chairs – without music or chairs – stand up and you would be out.

Every conceivable type was locked in the human traffic jam. Flower-sellers with bundles of lilies; a dentist with his mobile clinic – a pair of pliers; a company of Jain pilgrims with white cardboard masks; fifty schoolboys searching for cigarette ends; a nest of kittens abandoned by their mother; sixty turbaned porters, each with a bale of hemp at his side; a blind beggar with his crippled monkey; a Kali-following *sadhu* with a clip-on tongue, strap-on arms, a crown, and clutching a sword dipped in red paint . . . to them all I was an untouchable with nowhere to sit.

When the ticket booth opened I purchased a second-class ticket on the Hatia Express to Jamshedpur. It was to leave at 2135 hours. There was exactly thirteen hours to wait.

Venky offered to take me back into town. But I had already fallen victim to the listless indifference of life in the Black Hole. When I explained this, the *rickshawalla* asked me if it was the same sort of Black Hole into which the British prisoners had been crammed in central Calcutta. I replied that, although not entirely dissimilar, there were fundamental differences. Both were dingy, pungent and packed to the point of bursting; both kept prisoner those ensnared within. But, I said, as far as I knew, the Black Hole of Calcutta had no electric fortune-telling machines, no tea stalls or eunuchs soliciting alms.

Bidding farewell to my secret weapon, I ordered him to leave me. I would have to hurry if I was to get prime waiting position on platform nine. Once again, Venky thanked God for sending me to him. He would, he said, never drink *chullu* again. He was a new man.

The first five hours passed very slowly. The platform's newspaper stall had never seen such brisk business. In the first hour alone, I slurped my way through five Frooti mango drinks, flicked through six Bengali film magazines, and began reading a book entitled *How to Breed Reptiles*. When I had learnt all about breeding boxes for expectant iguanas, I mugged up *How to Renovate Dentures* and *How to Draw Cathedrals*. Magazine kiosks on Indian railway platforms always specialise in 'How to' books. Shrewd passengers realise there's no better time for self-help than when waylaid in a railway Black Hole.

By the tenth hour, the Hole had taken total control. All earthly concepts of time and place had been suspended. Sustained by the stream of self-help publications and frothy fruit drinks, I yielded to an infant boot-boy's petitions for employment. My shoes had, somehow, become covered in cow dung. As soon the boy had scampered away to splurge his five rupees, a herd of platform salesmen bustled around. Did I want to buy a set of billiard balls, a lime-green mohair balaclava, an eyelash curler, ten gallons of lubricating oil for a diesel locomotive, a box of live white mice, a green parrot, or a lava-lamp?

I waved them all aside. Another shoe lad stumbled over. This one had a trolley in tow.

'*Sahib*, shoe cleaning?'

'No, thanks, I've just had them done.'

The child screwed up his face. I peered down. My shoes were covered in diluted cow dung. I was about to say 'How did that happen again?' when I noticed a lilac paint tin dangling from the back of the boot boy's trolley. It was full of cow dung mix. The child hurried away, fearful of my vows of retribution. Then I scanned the platform. Far too engrossed in their newly purchased self-help books, the other passengers hadn't noticed the scam. First a boot boy would surreptitiously splatter the potential customer's shoes with excrement, then he would offer to clean them. The perpetual cycle – the Calcutta Special – guaranteed a lifetime of employment.

Two hours before the Hatia Express was to arrive, something curious happened on platform nine: the epicentre of the Black Hole. A young street entertainer set up his stall a few yards away from where I was sitting. He performed various simple sleights-of-hand and feats of conjury. A discreet crowd of porters, white-mice-sellers and browbeaten travellers huddled around. Then the boy – who was aged about thirteen – started a new routine. He coaxed a member of the crowd to hand over a fifty-rupee note. The bill was folded twice and placed in a brown envelope. The owner of the money wrote his initials on the envelope; which was then thrown into a box with similar sachets. When the man dug into the box and searched for his own envelope, it had gone. The trick was executed very skilfully. The crowd clapped each time the child duped another unsuspecting person. As I watched the young conjuror perform his trick, he began to seem familiar. Shooing away a brigade of platform salesmen, I stood up to get a better view. The boy's face . . . that was it. The Charlie Chaplin smile . . . I knew that smile. It was the boy from the Maidan: the one who had tricked a hundred rupees from me.

Wasting no time, I marched over and ordered the boy to hand over my money. I made a series of empty threats: I would tell his parents; I would call the station manager; I would expose him as a fraud. But the lad pulled a face and cackled something to his faithful audience, who turned against me. Handing over her fifty rupees, one woman commanded me to pick on someone my own size. Another shouted that I should go back to my home country. I had not seen an assembly turn so quickly from rapture to anger. With them baying for my blood, I returned to my seat, vowing revenge.

Still an hour to wait. I wolfed down a handful of *paan*-flavoured Polo mints. To take my mind off thoughts of retribution, I pulled out the cloth-backed map of India, and laid it down on the ground.

After the mental hospital, where was it to be? What cities and provinces should a journey of observation take in? Narrowing my eyes, I stared at the multitude of names. First, I circled Calcutta, then Jamshedpur. Why was Hyderabad already marked? Did the Master intend me to go there? After all, this was *his* map. Gokul's miracle asthma cure was a good enough reason to go there. My breathing had become more strained each day, and an asthmatic inhaler had had little effect. I needed a miracle. Another motive to visit the city was to see the Rock Castle Hotel: favoured as a writing haunt by the explorer Sir Wilfred Thesiger.

Although sketchy, Gokul's information was that the Gowd family's miraculous asthma cure took place in early June. That was still three months away. I required another destination before Hyderabad. What about Bangalore? Nowhere had ever seemed more exotic than the city's sixteenth-century Bull Temple. I etched a circle around Bangalore. I would ramble south first, then backtrack to Hyderabad by the start of June.

Enough map work for now, I mused, putting the cloth-backed chart away. A journey of observation must leave as much as possible to chance. Random movement is the best plan for maximum observation.

Twenty minutes ahead of schedule, the Hatia Express gushed into the station. The Black Hole was galvanised into action. A thousand red-shirted bearers scuttled about, swaggering like junior seamen after a night on shore. Each of their heads bore a sinister palm-leaf package.

As waves of passengers clambered over each other to board the train, I again noticed the young ruffian. This time there was no militant crowd supporting him. So, I collared him.

'Give me back my hundred rupees!'

'Oh, there you are,' said the boy, almost as if he were pleased to see me. 'All right, here's your money. I was just looking after it for you.'

The child handed over two fifty-rupee notes. His afternoon's hoaxing must have brought in a considerable sum if he was prepared to reimburse his victims.

'You must need the money more than me,' he said arrogantly, in fluent English. 'You're dressed worse than a beggar! Where are you going . . . to sleep with the sewer rats?'

'How dare you insult me?' I said. 'I've got no time to talk to you, you horrible child . . . I'm off to Jamshedpur on the start of an important journey.'

With that, I scrabbled up the thrashing ladder of passengers into the appropriate carriage. The thought of a window seat all to myself was almost too much to take. I lounged about, flexing my arms like a psychotic whose straitjacket had been untied. The sense of glorious extra space didn't last long. Well before the train pulled out of Howrah, I was squashed up against hundreds of others like a dried date in a box.

On the dot of nine thirty-five the Hatia Express sheered out from Howrah Station and into the unknown.

The man sitting beside me whipped open a reinforced pewter-grey attaché case which was resting on his lap. I told him that I felt like Dick Whittington heading off for fame and fortune; and that all I needed was a cat. The man's face twisted in a confused smile.

'It is a pleasure to meet you, Mr White-ting-don,' he said politely. 'J. P. Kamaraj at your service. Call me J.P.'

'No, no . . . I'm not Whittington. I just feel like him.'

The man adjusted his hairpiece, which was skew-whiff. The crude swath of dark hair resembled a horsehair oven mitt.

'You have a cat?' he asked.

'No, I'm afraid not. I'm on a journey of observation.' I tapped my bag. 'No space for cats,' I said.

With his wig once again realigned, J.P. poked about in his own case. Indian trains are full of bewigged gentlemen with reinforced VIP Luggage attaché cases. Most are salesmen. Those who are not are scientists. Travelling the sub-continent in second-class carriages, they are responsible for keeping the country together.

'I am a scientist,' said J.P. as the train gathered speed to break from the gravitational orbit of the Howrah Black Hole.

'Really?' I said earnestly. 'What's your area of research?'

J. P. Kamaraj clicked his attaché case shut furtively.

'Very secret project,' he said.

'Oh, I see . . . well, I don't want to pry.'

At that moment the carriage door slid back. The brash young scam-artist was standing in its frame.

'Oh, God, not you!' I said loudly.

J.P. looked up, as if he ought to be introduced.

'Your friend?' he asked.

The child sat in the seat adjacent to mine.

'Certainly *not* my friend,' I said. 'This is a worthless trouble-maker. He's a contriver of the worst kind – he dupes money from the unsuspecting.'

'I gave you back your money,' protested the child. 'I didn't need it anyway. A hundred rupees is nothing to me.'

'Go and leave me in peace,' I said. 'I'm having a conversation with this professional gentleman.'

The child pulled a wad of worn fifty-rupee notes from his underwear. He licked his thumb and counted them with a croupier's dexterity.

'Five thousand . . .' he said. 'Not worthless!'

'Each one of those notes represents someone you've ripped off. You should be ashamed.'

Turning my shoulder to the lad, I told J.P. about my pupillage to Feroze and the journey of observation. As he praised the journey on which I was embarking, the boy cut in:

'I'm coming with you,' he said.

'You most certainly are not.'

'Oh, yes I am, and there's nothing you can do about it.'

'Why don't you go off and defraud a few more innocents and leave me alone?'

'Because I'm staying here with you.'

'All right,' I said. 'See if I care.'

I was certain he would trundle away after minutes. After all, he was very young.

'I'm sorry, J.P.,' I said. 'Before we were interrupted you were telling me of your project.'

Forgetting that he had just advertised the secrecy surrounding it, the scientist explained all.

'We're developing a kind of Habbakuk,' he said.

'Habba-what?'

J.P. slid his reinforced case on to the floor and leant over to me.

'It's another codename for Pykrete,' he whispered. 'We are developing an Indian version . . .'

'What's Pykrete . . . a kind of soap?'

J.P. laughed.

'Not soap,' he said. 'In the war a British scientist called Geoffrey Pyke made an amalgam of ice and wood pulp. It was twelve times stronger than concrete, cheap to make, and it floated. Mountbatten and Churchill used it for "Operation Habbakuk".'

'What was that?'

'Wait, I am telling you,' said J.P. 'You see, their idea was to build huge Pykrete battleships, two thousand feet long – weighing two million tons.'

'So what happened?'

The scientist frowned.

'After successful secret tests in Canada, the Pykrete project was mysteriously shelved.'

'But why?'

'They ran into difficulties,' said J.P. intently. 'You see, they wanted to use the product to make war.'

'Well, the tests *were* being done during World War Two!'

'That's no excuse,' riposted J.P., wagging his index finger at me.

'Well, if you're not intending on using it for war . . . what are you developing Pykrete for?'

A warm, confident smile crossed the scientist's face.

'We,' he said majestically, 'are building a temple on a Pykrete base . . . it will be dedicated to Krishna and will travel around the coast of India. The ship will stop at towns along the way and people will come aboard to worship!'

'That's a stupid idea,' said the scammer, who was listening in.

'Shut up!' I snapped vociferously. But I had to agree, it was an absurd idea.

Bolstered by the audience of sceptics, J.P. ranted on for two hours. He had grand plans for the floating Pykrete *mandir*. The construction would have ice gardens and fountains, a meditation centre, a hospital, lodgings for the staff, a bathhouse, a library and refectory, a spacious assembly hall and a dairy farm.

'Wouldn't the cows get a bit cold?' I asked. 'After all, they would be on a gigantic frozen ship.'

J.P. Kamaraj let out a piercing shriek of laughter.

'Oh, no!' he shouted. 'Of course cows wouldn't get a chill . . . they'll be snug and warm.'

'But it would be absolutely freezing!'

The scientist shook his head. He had worked everything out. Cupping a hand around his mouth, he pressed it to my ear.

'Central heating . . .' he whispered. 'Every cow will be having central heating.'

14

The Secret Army

A few minutes before seven a.m., the scam-artist tugged at my collar, waking me from a deep slumber. He said the train had been held up for five hours in the night; and that Tatanagar, Jamshedpur's station, was a mile or so away.

'I don't need your help, thank you very much!' I snarled.

The delay was fortuitous. Without it, I would undoubtedly have missed the stop. A heifer had been struck by the locomotive on a remote stretch. Obviously a pious Hindu, the driver had alighted to offer prayers to the beast's spirit.

As I was making ready to descend at Jamshedpur's station, J.P. Kamaraj, the Pykrete scientist, wished me luck on my journey of observation. He was proceeding on a connecting train to Hatia to buy wood pulp for his floating Pykrete temple. Before getting down, I looked over to where the mischievous boy had been sitting. But he had gone.

Jamshedpur was a change from the faded pomp and grandeur of Calcutta. Although boasting a population of almost a million, it seemed strangely deserted. Gone were the colonial palaces and the jarring hordes of people. Gone, too, was the iron-black, corrosive air of Calcutta, now replaced by a lighter variety of pollution.

One of the only planned modern cities in India, Jamshedpur was the idea of Jamshedji Tata, Parsi industrialist and pioneer of Indian steel production. Tata realised that with its rich coal deposits and limestone quarries, the site was perfectly suited to heavy industry. Work on the city began in 1908, with the first of Tata's steel hitting the market four years later.

Whereas the majority of Indian towns support a hotchpotch of unrelated businesses and professions, Tata's metropolis is dedicated to the glory of metal. You only make your home there if cast-iron is your passion. For the thousands of workers who reside in the neat lines of white-roofed bungalows, iron is the most magical substance on Earth.

Before seeking out the psychiatric hospital, in search of the godman, I went into town to get some breakfast. As I sat at Quality Restaurant on Main Road, slurping milky coffee and leaning back dangerously on my chair, I made out a familiar high-pitched patter. It came from the far end of the room beside the confectionery counter. Quality's customers were being invited to try their luck in a trick of simple conjury. On offer was a lump of flint-like rock the size of an ice-hockey puck, said by the boy to contain gold.

One or two hopefuls had already parted with their money. The boy's threat to accompany me seemed to have been more than a passing remark. Wrapping the magician's map around my head like an Edwardian bonnet, I hoped to remain disguised until the danger had passed. Five minutes went by, and I sensed the rascal had taken his routine elsewhere. With caution, I peeled the chart away from my left eye. He seemed to have gone. But then there was a tap on my shoulder.

'Are you lost?'

'Oh, no . . . why don't you leave me alone?'

'I told you,' said the boy, slipping easily on to a chair at my table, 'I'm coming with you on your journey. I've already made up my mind.'

'If you don't leave me alone I'll call the police,' I said firmly.

'That's fine with me,' he replied. 'The police are so stupid . . . I make more money from tricking them than anyone else! My name is Bhalu,' he said.

'I don't care what your name is . . . you're a nasty little trickster who should be at school.'

'*Trickster*,' repeated the boy, 'I like that . . . I'm a trickster. From now on I'm the Trickster!'

I paid the waiter and left the café. What else could motivate a junior con-artist but the prospect of liberating my already limited funds? The experience on the Farakka Express had hardened me. No longer was I the gullible, pathetic traveller I had so recently been.

The boy followed me outside. Before insisting once again that he was going to join me, he tossed the precious gold ore pebble into some bushes.

'Wasn't that a bit too valuable to get rid of like that?' I asked.

The child guffawed menacingly.

'No . . .' he cackled. 'I just picked it up before going in there. Those people were so stupid, weren't they?'

When a rickety taxi pulled up, I took it to the mental asylum on the western outskirts of town, alone.

Not having called at an institution for the insane before, I was, I must admit, rather apprehensive. The nature of my visit further added to my anxiety. This being India, anything could happen, the worst case being that I would be mistaken for an inmate and pushed into a padded cell.

A refined group of what looked like respectful pilgrims had clustered on a strip of grass outside the asylum's entrance. They stared at the ground sheepishly as my taxi passed them.

Twenty minutes after arriving at the small psychiatric hospital, I had managed to get access to the building. The overriding problem was that no one spoke a word of English. I began to mime out what a luminary might look like, but soon curtailed such gesticulations, for fear of being thought to be insane myself. I repeated the name of the godman – Gupta – four times, to a man who was typing at an old Triumph. He hunched his shoulders and rolled his lower lip downwards, revealing a set of rotting teeth.

My own stupidity had brought me to the institution without a translator. I turned to leave the reception. But someone was standing in the doorway. It was the Trickster.

'How did you find me here?' I yelled. 'Why the hell are you spying on me?'

'You need someone to talk to the officials?'

'Yes . . .'

Addressing the typist respectfully, Bhalu the Trickster explained who I was looking for. The official glanced at me, then at the ceiling and the floor. Then he laughed.

'Guptaji!' he cried.

'Yes, he knows the godman,' said the Trickster. 'I can translate for you if you want.'

Before I could protest, the street conjuror was leading the way through the low-security asylum to meet the ascetic. It was as if he had been there before. Perhaps, I mused, he was a former inmate.

The sanatorium was crowded with middle-aged men. Its white-washed corridors stank of extra strength bleach and what appeared to be musk aftershave. Dormitories led off to the left and right, confined rooms with six or seven beds, a single barred window and a bare light-bulb. Most of the doors, although wide open, were fitted with twin locks. There were no guards to be seen. As I passed them, the patients

The tomb of Jan Fishan Khan, Burhana

LEFT The widows of Varanasi waiting to die
BELOW LEFT The 'burning' *ghats*, Varanasi

LEFT One of Calcutta's baby dealers and…
ABOVE A client who hires her baby for three rupees a day

A *rickshawalla* plying his trade
in Calcutta's busy streets

Temple of Kali – a supplicant ties
flowers to a tree in a fertility rite

Park Street Cemetery, Calcutta –
where I spent the night under
Topu's watchful eye

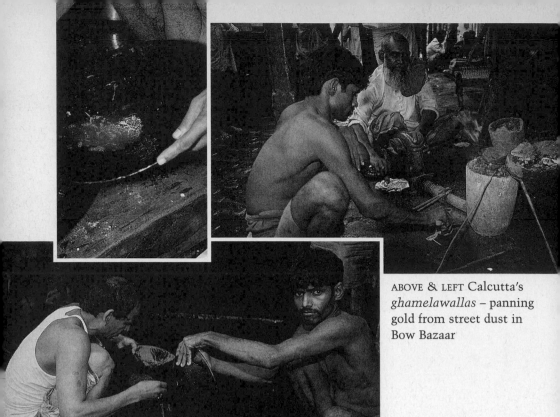

ABOVE & LEFT Calcutta's *ghamelawallas* – panning gold from street dust in Bow Bazaar

BELOW The noxious chemicals vital to the sorcerer's art are readily available over Calcutta's counters.

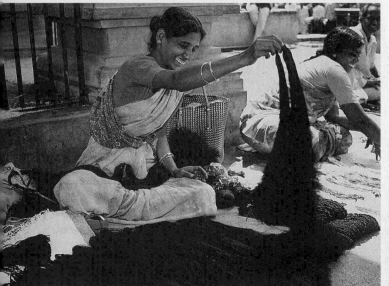

ABOVE Wig maker of Tirupati – making a living from the shorn locks of devotees from the temple at Tirumala

TOP & ABOVE A snake-swallowing *sadhu*, or holy man

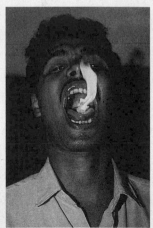

ABOVE & LEFT Men from the Rationalist Movement exposing con-men

LEFT The Gowd brothers, Hyderabad, proponents of the asthma-curing fish miracle

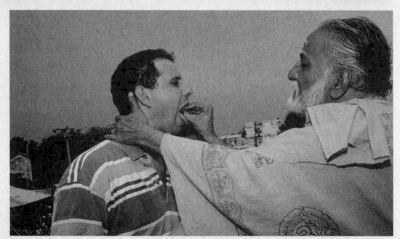

LEFT The author receiving a dose of the fish miracle cure

BELOW A small section of the throng awaiting the cure – each with fish in hand

A typical Indian street healer – with a cure for every known ill

A Bombay café – with a strict policy
on the behaviour of its customers

A godman plying his trade for
passing custom

A modern undertaker's in Bombay

stared at me, giggling and laughing out loud. Some had an air of despondency; others, a silent acceptance of their situation.

The godman was sitting cross-legged in a shaded gravelled square, formed where four of the dormitory buildings came together in a cross. A dozen or so other patients were dotted about nearby. Some were reading; others chatting to each other or themselves.

I observed the *swami* attentively. He was exceedingly old; his features gnarled and mutated, like a sculptor's putty model. He wore a simple white *lungi*, a shabby string vest, and a leather amulet around his neck. Venky's information was, I suspected, extremely out-of-date.

The asylum's clerk bent down and tapped the master on the shoulder. The mystic did not move.

'Is he dead?'

'No, he's in a trance,' explained Bhalu.

Again the clerk tapped, and this time the ancient stirred.

Bhalu translated his frail words:

'Visitors?' he puffed. 'You know I don't like visitors!'

'But, *swami*, this man has come from *Englezabad*, the city of English!'

'All the way from the city of English?'

The clerk nodded.

'From the Bangladesh border?'

'Yes,' said the clerk, 'all the way from the border with Bangladesh.'

There seemed to be some confusion. I had come from the country of England, not the former British trading post called Englezabad, or English Bazar, near Malda in West Bengal. Surely it was obvious I was not a Bengali? I corrected the clerk. He informed the *pandit*.

Drawing his fingers through the dirt beside him like the prongs of a rake, the sage gestured for me to sit.

'Oh great *swami*,' I said reverently, 'I am on a journey of observation, sent by my respected teacher, Hakim Feroze.'

The godman did not respond. Emitting a feeble cough, he slouched his head forward. There was little life left in him.

'Exalted *swami*,' I said to Bhalu, expecting the boy to translate, 'I have come in search of miracles. You are a mystic of great repute . . . I have heard about the wondrous feats which you perform. Could you demonstrate a miracle to me?'

Opening his eyes no more than a crack, the guru choked out a string of words.

'He's asking if you doubt his abilities,' said the Trickster.

'No . . . no,' I said, 'but I have come a long way to see his miracles.'

'Yes,' said the *swami* solemnly, 'you have come from Englezabad. That is a long way.'

Without further conversation, he pulled something from his *lungi*. It was a nail. But this was no ordinary nail. Crafted from twisted steel, it was about five inches long, and as wide as an HB pencil. Tilting his head back, he rammed the sliver of metal up his right nostril. Inch by inch, it disappeared. One or two inches would be understandable. Every schoolboy has experimented with sticking hair-pins up his nose. Two inches, perhaps three, is the extent of a child's ability. But the godman's proficiency went far beyond a child's experimentation. Five inches. Where did it go? How could it have avoided puncturing the brain? The *swami* withdrew the nail with his fingertips.

'That's no miracle,' whispered the Trickster. 'I have done it myself so many times. The nail just goes up into the sinus. It's a street trick!'

Bhalu was probably right. This was a simple illusion.

The sage seemed pleased at the praise which I lavished upon him. He confirmed the nail had not killed him outright because of a miracle of notable potency.

As I applauded, the godman performed another trick.

'Now,' he explained slowly, 'I am going to stop my heart beating.'

He called for the clerk to fetch a doctor's stethoscope from the sanatorium's surgery. The typist, who was enjoying the demonstrations, hurried away, returning a few minutes later with the well-worn apparatus.

The *avatar* pulled up his string vest, revealing a torso ridged with deep horizontal lines. He pressed his thumb to his chest, indicating that the contrivance was to be applied to the skin over the heart. The clerk passed me the stethoscope. I put the earpieces in place and pressed the cool metal of the sound receiver to the guru's chest. As we crouched on the gravel of the asylum's courtyard, in the comfortable shade of *champa* trees, I realised I was examining a man who ought to have been dead.

'There's no heartbeat at all.'

The *swami*, who had closed his eyes again, seemed to have slipped into unconsciousness. His heart appeared to have stopped. Was the miracle done in the same way as Feroze's walnut trick? I searched for walnuts. There were none.

'I think he may have actually died,' I said anxiously. After all, I had come in search of miracles, not to kill the inmates.

The clerk seemed quite blasé about the godman's condition.

'He always recovers,' he said lackadaisically.

'You mean he performs this miracle often?'

'Oh, very frequently.'

As he spoke, the *swami* emerged from his coma. The sound of his heartbeat grew from the faintest whisper to that of a healthy man.

The *avatar* stared at the dirt on which we sat.

'I first developed miraculous feats when I was just a boy,' he explained.

'That was no miracle,' proclaimed the Trickster in English.

'But there wasn't any heartbeat at all,' I said. 'I know how to stop the pulse in an arm with a walnut, but this is quite something else.'

Bhalu, the street conjuror, looked at me with disgust.

'Look at the illusion,' he said.

'What illusion? What am I missing?'

The scam-artist explained:

'When you raised the stethoscope to the old man's chest, did you notice how he filled his lungs very full of air?'

'Yes, I did observe that.'

'Well,' said Bhalu, 'the air is like a cushion . . . it soaks up the force of the heartbeat. In any case, he's an old man, so his beats are not so strong.'

I had to admit, the Trickster was very observant. And yet it was I who had embarked on the journey of observation.

I wondered how Guptaji had landed up in the clinic in the first place.

'Oh great master,' I said, oozing with adulation, 'why do they keep you here? What deranged behaviour do they accuse you of?'

Twisting his neck in slow motion like that of a turtle, the godman faced me.

'No one keeps me here,' he replied. 'I'm not mad, you know.'

I prodded the Trickster. He looked at the clerk.

'Of course he's not demented,' said the typist. 'Half the patients here are totally sane – they have been cured. They even have certificates to prove it.'

'But then why don't they leave?'

The clerk shook his head.

'They have nowhere to go,' he responded. 'Most have been disowned by their families. Many don't even know where their families are. When they move house, they don't inform us. People consider it a curse to have an insane relative.'

'But when was the guru remedied and permitted to leave?'

The typist scratched his head and thought for a moment.

'In 1969,' he said.

*   *   *   *

The encounter with the ancient *swami* came to a premature end. Exhausted after performing only two miracles, he fell into a deep sleep. The clerk advised me that, now in his nineties, the mystic was finding it difficult to perform the feats which had brought him fame.

The Trickster led me back through the hospital's corridors to the main gate. I sensed that he was hoping to muscle in on my journey. As before, I was distinctly distrustful of his motives. Like a member of the Thuggee brotherhood, he was, I felt sure, prepared to spend as much time as necessary in gaining my trust. Then, when I least expected it, he would relieve me of my few belongings. My conscience warned me of the danger. He may have had the appearance of a child, but this was no meek schoolboy; he was a walking crime wave.

At the hospital gates I thanked Bhalu for his help in translating. The service had been recompense for the inconvenience of tricking me in Calcutta. Our arrangement was now at an end. Thank you and goodbye.

As it was a fine afternoon – warm air scented with fir trees – I grasped my bag and started to walk the three or four miles back to Jamshedpur. The asylum, which attracted few visitors, had no need for a taxi rank.

Bhalu asked again if he could accompany me on my journey. He said he'd pay his own way and keep out of trouble. Replying that he could not tag along, I pressed on down the long, dusty trail heading east. Stepping in my footprints, the Trickster followed.

After half an hour we were nearing Jamshedpur. I was regretting the choice of walking, for my bag was quite heavy. Bhalu was still treading in my footsteps, about ten paces behind.

As we approached a bend in the road, he suddenly ran up and pushed me into the ditch which ran alongside the road. I fell head-first into a layer of fermenting filth.

'Damn you! You horrible boy!' I scolded, clambering out. 'I'm covered in muck. I'm going to kill you when I catch you.'

One would have expected him to have scampered off after waging such an unprovoked attack. But Bhalu stood his ground. He was pointing to something on the side of the road. It was the severed body of a large toffee-brown scorpion. Picking up the tail-end in one hand, he displayed an unwieldy hunting knife in the other.

'You were about to stand on this scorpion,' he said. 'There was no time to explain.'

'But I've got shoes on, the sting wouldn't have penetrated their soles.'

'Haven't you ever heard of jumping Bihari scorpions?' he asked.

I looked at the boy, the knife, and what was left of the scorpion. He had certainly acted with honed reflexes. Who knows what would have happened if I had been taken unawares by a jumping scorpion? The Trickster threw the arachnid's tail into the ditch. He shuffled back into line, preparing to stamp forward in my footsteps again. His eyes were focused on the ground; his features frozen in a pathetic expression exuding meekness.

'All right,' I said coldly, 'you can accompany me for a while. But any trouble and that's it.'

My attitude may have been brusque, but I was adamant I would not fall victim to my customary myopia again. Even as I agreed to let the scam-artist tag along, I was having grave doubts.

*   *   *   *

Over breakfast the next day, I filled Bhalu in on my catalogue of misfortune. First, I told him of how as a student I was deceived in southern Spain. Then of how my belongings were pilfered in Brazil. Then I explained how I was drugged and robbed on the infamous Farakka Express. All over the world people were travelling on my passports, driving on my licences, spending my money; and whole communities were kitted out with my belongings. I had had enough.

'Ah, *chakotra*,' said the Trickster fondly, 'that's a great one, I use it often.'

'You mean *you* have drugged people on trains and then robbed them?'

'Many times,' said the boy casually, lighting a *biri*.

'Stop smoking! You're much too young to smoke. How old are you anyway?'

Bhalu scrunched up his eyes.

'I'm seventeen.'

'You're nothing of the sort. You're not even through puberty!'

'Well,' he brooded, reviewing his answer. 'People often think I'm seventeen.'

'How long have you been tricking people, living on the streets?'

'About six years . . . I ran away from that stupid orphanage when I was six.'

'You've spent half your life on the streets of Calcutta?'

'Yup . . . and I make a good living, too.'

There could be nothing more fat-headed than a Calcutta-born

trickster flaunting his successes. One after another, Bhalu advertised his deceptions, boasting like a playground bully. Many were illusions of a sort, but illusions executed to gyp the unsuspecting.

From card tricks and simple sleights to advanced feats of escapology and mind-reading, the Trickster's inventory was one to marvel at.

But, as well as a straightforward con-man, Bhalu had achieved extraordinary success as a salesman. Give him anything and he would have a go at hawking it.

'Let me see,' he said, shading his young eyes from the early-morning sunlight, 'I have sold bottles of dirty water: say it with enough confidence and everyone believes it's Ganga water. Once I took out the microphone discs from twenty telephones in Howrah and sold them on the trains. Old men always believe they're special sex aids. Put them under the pillow and they send out invisible rays to make any wife passionate!'

As Bhalu laughed, I put my head in my hands.

'Then,' he continued, 'I've sold rat tails as lucky charms; cigarette ash as a special "miracle" beauty treatment, and soap pellets as aphrodisiacs. Women,' he went on, shaking his head in disbelief, 'they'll buy anything. Slip into the Ladies Only carriage of a commuter train, offer fake beauty products to the ugliest women – you make a fortune. They lap the stuff up!'

The Trickster may have had entertaining tales, and was amiable enough when he wasn't ripping people off. But still I was wary. I felt certain that – any time now – when I least expected it, he would strike like a disturbed adder in long grass waiting for his moment. Why had he selected me? Out of all the people on platform nine of Howrah Junction, why me? When I put such questions to him, Bhalu replied that our meeting, and this journey, was fate.

'Don't you want to meet the "Petrol Man"?' he asked abruptly, changing the subject.

'Who's he?'

Bhalu rolled his eyes.

'He turns water into petrol, of course. He's just south of here, at Rourkela.'

A man who could actually transform ordinary water into petrol certainly deserved a visit. So we went back to Tatanagar Station and boarded the slow train heading south. The Trickster had already cottoned on to my prime weakness – I'll drop everything in search of oddity.

We took advantage of the free window seats. A salubrious middle-aged figure squashed up beside me. There was no reason to get so close so soon, as the coach was still almost empty. So I stared at the man sternly, and grunted, warding him off. He held his ground. I looked over at him again. On his nose was balanced a pair of oversized glasses; like a welder's goggles they masked much of his face. His eyes were enlarged fourfold, giving him a meek, trustworthy mien. On his lap rested a brand new reinforced plastic VIP Luggage attaché case. Another member of the Secret Army.

Before long, he introduced himself.

'P.D. Roy is pleased to meet you,' he said, running his fingers effortlessly through his bushy toupée, as if it were his own hair.

'Happy to meet you, too. Are you from Jamshedpur?'

'No, no . . .' he responded. 'I am salesman . . . I'm in vigs.'

'Excuse me, but I didn't catch your line of business.'

'Vigs.'

'Figs?' I looked at the Trickster.

'He's in *wigs*. He sells wigs!' the boy sniggered. 'You know, for *taklu*, baldies!'

Since hair loss is a sensitive subject in any country, I would rather have progressed to another topic. But launching in at the deep end, Bhalu interrogated the salesman on his profession.

The passenger had all the accoutrements of a member of the Secret Army – the VIP case, the red coral ring on the little finger of his left hand; the stainless-steel ball-point poking from his shirt pocket. However, P.D. was a salesman with a difference.

At one time, he recounted, he had travelled India's local railway lines touting braking assemblies for auto-rickshaws. Every year he endured months away from home: months spent on trains, with their balding, attaché-case-carrying salesmen. Brake assemblies were a product line devoid of emotion. Either you need one or you do not. P.D. was tired of talking brakes. He yearned for merchandise which people could get passionate about. It was then that he had a brainwave.

Why not create a special product, suited specifically to the Secret Army of salesmen who peddle their wares on India's local line trains? After all, VIP Luggage had done it. No self-respecting sales executive would be seen dead without VIP's finest. So, P.D. came up with his 'Director Brand' wig.

The true brilliance of the product is not that it covers a bald patch – the secret is far more subtle than that. Fashioned for businessmen, P.D.'s toupées are all the same colour and shape. Director Brand wearers are proud of their splendid hairpieces. They sport them with pride, wearing them like a medal, rather than an accessory for the follically-challenged, and take comfort in owning what they consider is a membership card to India's most exclusive club.

I asked the wig merchant when he had first gone bald. It was a delicate question which, I hoped, would divert the conversation from the mercenary subject of the used-hair business.

P.D. tugged the Director Brand toupée from his head and held it out at arm's length towards me. It resembled a miniature three-toed sloth. I stroked the length of its back with my palm, for fear of offending the executive.

'You don't understand,' P.D. Roy responded when I had petted his hairpiece. 'I'm not a baldie.'

A close glance at his scalp corroborated this.

'I shave my head,' he went on. 'You see, the best thing a salesman can do is to use his own product. I don't need the product I sell . . . but this is irrelevant. When customers see me proudly sporting a Director's Brand – even though I don't require one – they are even more eager to snap one or two up!'

'You ought to be put up for an award!' I roared. 'It's brilliant.'

Even the Trickster had to admit that P.D. Roy was taking salesman-ship to new heights.

'Where do you get all the hair from?'

P.D.'s answer was a single word:

'Tirupati.'

'Where's that?'

'In Tamil Nadu, just north-west of Madras. It's where the Temple of Lord Venkateshvara is located.'

'What's that got to do with wigs?'

P.D. Roy, salesman extraordinaire, smiled broadly.

'Tirupati is India's only "vig temple".'

As the local train pulled away from a station of uncertain name, en route to Rourkela, the chief executive of Director Brand toupées revealed the legend:

'At Tirupati, in southern India, the people were always unhappy,' he said. 'They had no gold mines like the nearby towns; they couldn't grow wheat as the ground was too stony; and the drinking water was naturally salty. In their misery, the townspeople gathered together for a meeting. They looked at their poor situation and at the prosperity of their neighbours. Tirupati, they thought, must be cursed by an evil spirit. The only thing to do was to construct a vast temple at Tirumala,

in the hills above the village, and implore the help of the gods. So this
was done.

'When completed,' P.D. Roy went on, 'the temple was impressive in
every way. Its walls were faced with shining white marble. Its floors
were scattered with rose petals. The people were so happy they spent
every spare moment worshipping there. But still their fortunes didn't
improve. The water was saltier than ever; the ground seemed more
stony now than before; and there wasn't a gold mine in sight. Then
someone had an idea.

'The people of Tirupati would spread the word that praying at their
fine temple at Tirumala could cure even the most debilitating
disease. Anyone who sought divine help at their temple would be
made well again. The news spread like wildfire. Soon there was a line
of ten thousand cripples wending its way to the temple. As the first
lame person prepared to step over the shrine's threshold, the priest
threw his arms in the air. He ordered that each pilgrim must have
their head shaved in honour of Lord Venkateshvara. The afflicted
agreed, and barbers set to work shaving the ten thousand heads. Every
day another ten thousand handicapped pilgrims turned up. Each had
their head shaved. Weeks went by, and the people of Tirupati met
again. They congratulated themselves, for their temple had become
very famous. But someone pointed out that – as the sick were
permitted to pray for free – the community was still impoverished.
Then a child at the meeting had a bright idea. Why not bundle up all
the hair which had been sheared from people's scalps and sell it for
vigs?

'Hair from Tirumala became very sought after,' P.D. Roy continued.
'These days most dark-coloured vigs in the world are made from hair
shaved off at the temple. The once-impoverished village is now a
thriving town; and the people who live at Tirumala are wealthy beyond
their dreams . . . all because of the vigs.'

'I have to see this for myself,' I said, circling Tirupati on the Master's
chart. 'I'll go there straight away.'

Leaving the wig merchant to his case of toupées, Bhalu and I
descended at Rourkela, in search of the man who turned water into
petrol. As we stepped on to the platform, the Trickster nudged me in the
ribs.

'Tirumala's famous for all the hair that's shaved off the pilgrims,' he
said. 'And wigs *are* made from the hair,' he said. 'But as for the story . . .
he's made most of it up. Take it from me: it's pure sales pitch.'

So, I pondered, as we walked into town, even the used-hair business has sharp-talking salesmen these days. Whatever is the world coming to?

* * * *

After a night killing mosquitoes at the Aspara Hotel, the Trickster led me into the maze of Rourkela's back-streets. Like all industrial towns, Rourkela is a miniature world . . . a world of interminable shifts. Day or night you can buy a tin of local fertiliser, get your watch repaired, or gorge yourself on a street stall meal. Barbers were busy snipping hair, or running ice cubes across newly shaven faces. Their wives were hanging out the washing; their children sieving dirt through their infant fingers as if it were gold dust. A man was touting a cart of yellow plastic sandals. An old crone rambled by with a dried mango seed balanced on her head. A swarm of union workers followed somewhere behind, protesting their right to protest with garish banners, like a flank of Janissary warriors heading to war.

One shop was doing particularly brisk business. It was more of a specialised booth than a full-scale emporium. Off-duty barbers, sandal-sellers and hags were wrestling forward, desperate to reach the counter. The lucky ones hurried away clutching blue and white tins.

'Looks like a dispensary to me,' I warned Bhalu. 'We'd better stock up with whatever it is while stocks last.'

Bhalu pushed his way to the front, fighting off the droves of barbers and crones. Without asking what the tins contained, he bought two. They only cost ten rupees each. Snatching one away from him, I scrutinised the label.

'Shellac,' I read, '"Pure shellac flakes" . . . I've never heard of them before. Must be a new kind of liver tonic or something. We can try it out later.'

Bhalu gave me a restless glance.

'One spoon of this stuff and you won't have a liver,' he said.

'Nonsense! Look at those women over there; the mere thought of it has given them a new lease of life.'

'You haven't got a clue what shellac is, have you?'

I stuck my nose in the air. It was usually I who doled out medicinal information.

'So what is it, then?'

'It's made from the waxy gum which oozes from the female *lac* beetle's back.'

'That doesn't sound like much of a liver tonic . . .'

'Don't be stupid,' said the Trickster, 'it's a not medicine . . . it's a varnish. Where do you think the word "lacquer" comes from?'

Before I could answer, Bhalu was proceeding down the lane. Minutes later, he had located the petrol maker's workshop. It seemed impossible that he could have located the place with such ease. I asked how he knew the man's whereabouts, but he declined to reveal his sources.

The workshop's door was crafted from a single sheet of copper. A series of religious symbols had been etched into the verdigris. Among those I recognised were a swastika, a cross, a crescent and a Star of David. At the base of the door was a pile of about ten broken beer bottles. Someone had placed a dozen chicken's feet in the middle of the glass. Was it a mysterious offering to the gods? There was only one way to find out.

I knocked twice. As the door swung inwards, I wondered whether the dilapidated shed was indeed the workplace of a man claiming miraculous powers. Surely, anyone with a bona fide system of turning water into petrol would be working out of a modern, high-tech laboratory.

A single beam of blinding sunlight bisected the chamber. Three or four forty-gallon drums were lined up against the back wall. A number of dirty tea crates filled much of the room. The walls, which had been painted a rich shade of magenta, were etched with more crude diagrams, almost like pharaonic hieroglyphs. Standing in the centre of the shack, bathed in the brilliant shaft of sunlight, stood Mr Jafar.

Bandy-legged and with skin as dark as ebony, Mr Jafar fluttered his nimble fingers in the light. His breath was heavy with garlic; his countenance one of greedy anticipation. He wasn't surprised we had come. Indeed, it was almost as if he had been awaiting our arrival. I presented him with a tin of shellac, as a token of goodwill. Thanking me courteously, he begged me to sit on an upturned oil drum.

Then he told of his amazing discovery.

'You may think that I am telling lies,' he announced gingerly, in a voice as shrill as a piccolo. 'Sceptics always prod fun at me: but I understand their suspicions. My process is one of high chemistry. Why should the ignorant be capable of understanding?'

Mr Jafar gazed over to me with his piercing eyes, as if warning me not to doubt him. As he stared, he disclosed a little more:

'I sat in this room experimenting for fifteen years,' he said. 'Every day I drew closer to my aim: to turn simple drinking water into petrol. Only when I was at the end of my tether did I finally chance upon the answer . . . the key to turn in the lock of nature.'

'What *is* the answer?' I asked, bidding Bhalu to translate my question.

'The answer!' shouted the scientist. 'That's what the whole world wants to know. Of course I can't reveal the formula.'

'Well, can you describe the process?'

Mr Jafar picked up a glass beaker and filled it with water from the tap. He held it up to the light. The colour of milk, it had a fluorescent green tinge. I suspected run-off sludge from the steel plants of Rourkela had already given the local drinking water a high octane level.

'This is the raw ingredient,' said the chemist. 'Pure water.'

'What do you do with it?'

'First,' he replied, 'the water is filtered through a pad of hay; then it's mixed with the juice of bark extracts and berries, like this . . . When the solution has been stirred for a few minutes, it's warmed under a naked gas flame.'

Jafar paused to light a gas burner. Within seconds, the liquid was foaming.

'Now for the magic!' said Jafar, beaming. 'Can you see what I'm doing? I'm adding the special ingredient. It's a blend of fifteen more herbs and spices.'

The chemist was beginning to sound like a commercial for Kentucky Fried Chicken.

'Is that petrol now?'

'No . . . before it can be used to power a vehicle, it has to be stored in a cool aluminium tin for thirty days.'

'Thirty days? But I can't sit here for a month waiting for your liquid to mature . . .'

'Well,' snapped Jafar, 'luckily I have some to show you that's been brewing for more than a month.'

Stepping over to one of the forty-gallon oil drums, he siphoned off five gallons into a more manageable petrol canister.

'Here you are,' he said, handing me the plastic container. 'That will be six hundred rupees.'

'Six hundred rupees? That's far more expensive than ordinary petrol. In any case, I don't have a car to use it in.'

Mr Jafar seemed very displeased.

'Fifteen years I have laboured in this chamber,' he thundered. 'I have achieved something that scientists in your country could only hope to accomplish. Look me in the eye and tell me again you are turning down the chance of buying what is nothing short of magic!'

With great reluctance I pulled six hundred rupees from my shoe and handed it to the chemist.

'Here's the money.'

Mr Jafar jerked the wad of bills from my hand and inspected them for irregularities. As he stuffed them into his shirt pocket, I sensed him snorting to himself with laughter. He opened the door for us to leave. The interview was at an end.

'Get out quickly,' he lisped, 'or the dogs will get in.'

'What dogs?'

'Dogs! Dogs! All kinds of dogs! They're lured by the smell of my ingredients. It drives them mad! They stand here at the door, waiting to sneak inside. That's when they fall victim to my trap.'

'Trap?'

'The chicken's feet . . . they're too much of a temptation for them . . . then the glass cuts their feet!'

Mr Jafar let out an abhorrent guffaw.

'Have a good journey. Oh, and you had better be careful,' he murmured through a crack in the door frame. 'My special petrol doesn't travel well.'

Not long after Bhalu and I had tramped off with the leaking container full of Mr Jafar's magic potion, another petrol-making chemist hit the headlines. Scientists across India stepped forward to back the farmer and his process.

The man, named Poonaiah Pillai, from a village in Tamil Nadu, alleged that while on a picnic in the 1970s, he watched a spark from a stove ignite a low-lying bush. After years of primitive scientific testing, he refined a chemical process by which the herb could be transformed into petrol.

First, the leaves of the mystery plant were boiled in water for about ten minutes. Salt and lemon juice were added, and the mixture – a kind of seasoned broth – was left to settle. As it cooled, certain chemicals were mixed in. Soon after, the herbal fuel rose to the surface and could be siphoned away.

Despite the similarities with Mr Jafar's process, Pillai's product – which only cost about one rupee a litre to make – was in hot demand. So much so that Pillai was kidnapped by brigands and tortured. Even though the bandits burned him with cigarettes and suspended him from a ceiling fan, the farmer refused to reveal the secret formula.

In his native Tamil Nadu, Pillai became a folk hero overnight. Everyone, from *rickshawallas* to ministers, was discussing the mysterious chemical process, speculating what the secret herb might be. The state government awarded him a hefty grant with which to continue his research. Petro-chemical multinationals dispatched representatives to India to learn the secret. Diplomats were briefed by their governments to solve the mystery. The Nobel Foundation was put on alert for a possible candidate for their next chemistry award.

Then came the big demonstration. India's most respected scientists filed into a hall in Delhi. A nervous anticipation filled the room. If the farmer could once again prove his process to be genuine, India might soon find itself to be an economic superpower.

Poonaiah Pillai arranged the apparatus. The audience waited with bated breath. The failure of an initial experiment was put down to the new apparatus. Before the second attempt, Pillai asked to use his own stirring rod. The request was granted. Moments later he turned a blend of herbs and water into a thin form of petrol.

But as the audience applauded, someone noticed a key point, which had been overlooked. Pillai's own large stirring rod was hollow. It appeared to have been filled with a petrol solution and then plugged with beeswax. When immersed in the hot soupy, herbal water, the wax plug melted, releasing the motor fuel.

As red-faced experts scuttled back to their laboratories, sceptics suggested that the chicanery had been clearly visible all along; the most obvious indication being that Pillai had asked the audience whether they wanted him to make diesel or petrol. A simple selection of the right stirring rod would guarantee either.

*　　*　　*　　*

Bhalu and I spent two more days at Rourkela. We poked about the steel mills and I wrote to Feroze with details of my journey. I told him of the godman's illusions at Jamshedpur; of the Pykrete and the wigs from Tirumala; and about Mr Jafar's ability. Even the Master, I mused, could not fail to be impressed by these observations.

Next morning, before the sun had risen above the smoke stacks, Bhalu woke me with a loud cry.

'Leave me alone!' I protested, 'I was planning on sleeping in.'

'But we have to go,' said the Trickster. 'The lorry's leaving in twenty minutes.'

'What lorry?'

Wheeling-dealing and, I suspected, picking pockets since dawn, the boy had negotiated a ride heading south, towards Tirupati. My decision to take the train had been overruled. For Bhalu had been struck by an idea. The five gallons of precious herbal-based petrol could be part exchanged for passage as far as Sambalpur, about a hundred and fifty kilometres south-west of Rourkela.

As I struggled to lace up my shoes, I heard the screech of brakes outside the hotel. I peered from the window. A tangerine-orange Ashok Leyland truck, piled high with sugar cane, was waiting.

The driver grabbed the five-gallon jerrycan and stashed it away for later. He seemed more than pleased with the deal. Bhalu was also satisfied. Chance had found us an Ashok Leyland which ran on petrol, rather than the more common diesel.

We ventured out into the web of potholes, the laden hulk huffing like a bloodhound in pursuit. Three hours passed, and the Ashok Leyland lorry had fishtailed its way as far as Sundagarh, about halfway to Sambalpur.

Bhalu selected one of the poles of sugar cane and chewed its end. As he did so, the Ashok Leyland spluttered to a halt. It had run out of petrol. The driver emerged from his cab and, wasting no time, funnelled the freshly brewed herbal petrol into the vehicle's tank. Bhalu sucked at the sweet-tasting stem. I stretched out on the bed of sugar cane, soaking up the sun. Things could not have been better, thanks to Mr Jafar and his miracle mix.

The driver fired up his wagon. But no longer was it huffing merrily. The engine was groaning like a great tusker run through with a lance. No petty growl induced by wear and tear: this was the last wail of a dying beast. Like a *mahout* whose elephant was expiring before him, the driver leapt, howling from his cockpit. Half-paralysed by shock, he comforted his beloved Ashok Leyland in its dying moment. When it had wheezed its last grim sigh, the driver turned his attentions to Bhalu and me. Accusing us of administering a lethal potion to his beloved steed, he climbed up on to the crest of sugar cane and routed us from the back of its carcass.

15

Witch

Marooned at the side of the road, Bhalu and I waited for a fresh tangerine-orange Ashok Leyland truck. But nothing came. The driver of the defunct cane-laden vehicle had chased us away, swearing that he would cut off our ears if he caught us. We walked a couple of miles southward and waited. Well, I reflected quietly to myself as we dug in for a long wait, although the price was exacting, at least we now knew that Mr Jafar's preparation was an expensive imitation of the real thing.

Two hours had passed. Every so often a jalopy would clatter by in the opposite direction. But there was no traffic heading south. Another three hours went by.

Bhalu befriended a girl his own age who was selling wicker baskets at the side of the road. Her face was young and innocent, its complexion a soft amber brown. An embroidered headscarf veiled her plaited hair; a profusion of hefty silver bangles and anklets weighed down her limbs. For now the jewellery was no more than an encumbrance; but one day, not far off, it would form her dowry.

When it came to philandering with local maidens, the Trickster was an expert. One flutter of his eyelashes and any girl was putty in his hands. I watched as, turning his back to the girl, he slid a dark object from his pocket and slipped it up his left sleeve. Meanwhile, the lass had seen a vehicle approaching. She picked up a wicker basket and stepped towards the road. Bhalu took advantage of her distraction. He tossed the henna-coloured object on the ground between him and the road. When the vehicle had driven into the distance, the girl walked solemnly back towards us. As she did so, Bhalu yelled at her not to move. Drawing the hunting knife from its sheath on his belt, he strode over to where his belle was standing. With dramatic flair, he plunged the blade into the back of a toffee-brown scorpion lying at her feet. The girl may have been overjoyed at having her life saved so gallantly. I, on the other hand, was enraged. Unlike her, I had seen the stunt before. Only the most devious scam-artist would stoop to carrying a dead scorpion around, ready to be deployed for the purpose of endearing himself to others. After castigating Bhalu for his dishonesty, I told the basket girl all about the deception. But as she didn't speak English, she had no idea what I was going on about.

Fifteen minutes after saving her from certain death, Bhalu was serenading the child with a distorted rendition of Elton John's song 'Goodbye Yellow Brick Road'. She masked her mouth with the palm of her hand to hide her laughter.

Edging closer, he took her hand in his and kissed the knuckles as suavely as he could. He may have only been twelve or so, but the Trickster was a fast operator. Moving with the serpentine determination of a python, his right hand slunk its way up across the girl's nubile form. Her giggles turned to wonder as she realised that the stranger was moving in for the kill. The maiden leapt up, declaring she had to return home. Her parents would be wondering where she was. Offering to accompany her, Bhalu said he would go in search of sustenance. I feared that a hurried liaison with a local lass was inviting disaster.

As the last rays of light dissipated around us, I made out the rumbling of a truck. By the grating sounds of its bodywork writhing on a battle-worn chassis, I suspected it was a trusty Ashok Leyland. Sure enough, a great pumpkin-orange lorry was veering around the bend and heading straight for us. Bhalu and I leapt up and waved our arms, screaming as loudly as we could. The vehicle slowed to walking pace. Then it stopped. We hurried over. But just as we about to clamber aboard, it accelerated at high speed. This was no ordinary lorry: it was a vehicle which had returned from the dead. At the wheel, tormenting us, the driver gnashed his teeth. He had resurrected his charger.

If the Trickster was going to kill me and plunder my belongings, he would have done it on that inglorious night, spent in an Orissan ditch. Even a veteran Thug would have given his front teeth to be alone with his quarry in such a remote spot. Bhalu was eager to track down the basket girl's village. He filled my mind with fantasies of food, silk bed sheets . . . and loose women.

'Come with me to the village,' he whined, 'and I'll teach you the secret to get Orissan girls.'

'You mean kiss their knuckles and choke out a couple of old Elton John songs?'

'No . . . no, that was just the start . . .'

'What comes next?'

'Why should I tell *you*?'

'You don't have to . . . I wouldn't trust your advice for a second!'

'OK,' retorted the Trickster, 'I'll tell you . . . but only if you promise not to tell a soul.'

'It's a deal: I won't tell.'

'The way to get any woman is simple . . . You have to rub honey into their toes, of course.'

After a night fighting off red ants and scorpions, I woke to the smell of roasted manioc. A smell I had known while travelling in eastern Zaire, manioc, or cassava as it's known in Africa, is a staple. Bhalu had unearthed several of the roots and toasted them until they were charred. Preparing breakfast had taken his mind off the basket weaver's daughter. I was surprised by the boy's aptitude for survival in the countryside. Until now, he had struck me as an urban creature.

At six-thirty a works employee from the nearby Hirakud Dam made an emergency stop when Bhalu threw himself at the bonnet of his vehicle. Recovering from the severity of the deceleration, the driver agreed reluctantly to take us all the way to Sambalpur, located at the southern edge of the Hirakud Reservoir.

A few miles before reaching the destination, we caught a glimpse of the Hirakud Dam. One of the largest of its kind, it's formed from the damming of the Mahanadi River. Illuminated by the morning sunshine, the reservoir stretched westward like an unending silver blanket. With the car's windows wide open, I closed my eyes and filled my lungs with wonderful undefiled air. At that moment, it seemed as if Orissa was the richest, most fertile spot in all India. Yet nothing, as we were soon to find, could have been farther from the truth.

At Sambalpur I checked into the extravagant Hotel Uphar. Having cut costs the night before I was ready to splash out. I made straight for the bazaar to look at the famous *ikat* weaving. Bhalu, who had heard tall tales of the diamonds washed up in the Mahanadi River, hurried off in search of card sharps. By midnight, with no sign of Bhalu, I went to bed. An hour later, the window was pulled open from outside, sending a draught of cool nocturnal air through the room.

'Who is it? Who's there?' I called out, as the curtains ruffled about.

'It's me, it's Bhalu. I'm back!'

As in Rourkela, the Trickster had climbed into my single hotel room in an effort to avoid paying the bill. In any case, he preferred to sleep on the bathroom floor. He said the cool tiled surface reminded him of his dormitory at the orphanage.

'Go to sleep, Bhalu . . . I'm planning on heading on to Tirupati tomorrow.'

'No chance of that,' said the Trickster, in a loud whisper.

'I'll go where I like,' I said sharply.

'A woman's being tried as a witch near Bolangir.'

'Where's that? Where is Bolangir?'

'Three hours away by train,' replied Bhalu, shuffling through the darkness to the bathroom, 'Don't worry . . . leave it all to me.'

The second-class carriage heading south was brimming with chickens, chickens and more chickens. With their feet manacled together, trussed up as if the birds were convicts, they filled all the luggage racks, the aisles, and every inch of corridor. The Trickster watched me as I thumbed a copy of Houdini's *Miracle Mongers and their Methods*. He seemed especially agitated. He couldn't still be thinking of the basket seller. Girls were a quaint frivolity to him. Only one thing could give a con-man such an expression – as sour as rhubarb. Money. I suspected he had been devoured in the low-life gambling den, the wrong side of Sambalpur's railway tracks.

'So, how did you do?' I asked from behind my book. 'Show me the bag of diamonds!'

Bhalu remained taciturn. He didn't need to say a word. His miserable expression said it all. The diamonds had not materialised. Neither had the good hand of cards he had planned on acquiring. The Trickster had been cleaned out. They say there's no one more doleful than a bankrupted millionaire. That may be true. But take a Bengali scam-artist, swindle him of his cash, and he soon bounces back. To survive in Calcutta, a con-merchant has to get back on his feet . . . fast.

As I returned to Houdini's wisdom, Bhalu sprang up and hurried off to the next carriage. For him, a train journey was not a time to relax, or immerse oneself in a good book: it was a time to get down to the big sale.

Fifteen minutes went by, and the carriage door slipped open. Ignoring me, the Trickster called out for the passengers to view his remarkable wares. I glanced over to see what he had on offer. Bhalu had stripped down my hotel room while I had been settling the bill. Curtain rings and bed springs, miniature bars of soap, mothballs and hotel stationery. The entire stock was on sale at knockdown prices.

*

At Bolangir we wasted no time. Bhalu had heard that the witch trial was taking place in a village off the main road running west between Bolangir and Patnagarh. As we took a series of rides on passing vehicles, I began to wonder if we would actually find the witch's village. It seemed unlikely.

About twenty miles out of Bolangir, Bhalu and I first witnessed the severe drought that was crippling Orissa. Crops were almost non-existent: the remains of dry plants, blanched by the relentless sun. The local people had largely deserted the area – heading for Bolangir and other towns in the region. Their children looked thin and sickly. Their mothers, veiled in the bright tie-dye for which Orissa is famous, nursed the infants listlessly, as if waiting for the end to come.

The authorities had done their bit to counter the mass migration. But with their efforts hardly leading to a tangible improvement, it was easier to deny that the drought existed. Curbing the panic of frightened, thirsty people is an insurmountable task. As we waited for the next, infrequent vehicle to edge us a little closer towards Patnagarh, I questioned whether we ought not to follow the evacuees – and return to the town.

Bhalu spotted a group of figures working in the open, a little less than a mile north of the main road. I suspected that they were over-zealous farmers who had refused to leave their lands. The Trickster led me over to where they were toiling. He said they would have water to share with us. Rather than tending crops, the group, of three men, two women and a child, were making coarse bricks from the chutney-brown soil.

Bhalu greeted them. As soon as he heard their voices he seemed troubled.

'What's wrong?'

'They aren't farmers,' he said. 'They are bonded labourers.'

Straining to understand their dialect, which must have been related to Oriya, Bhalu asked the youngest of the men where everyone else had gone.

'They left about two months ago,' was the reply. 'There's no water here and the crops have failed. All the animals are dying. We would leave, but we have nowhere to go. We haven't got any money or food.'

'What about your master?'

'Well, he went away,' retorted the man, whisking a fly from a sore near his eye. 'He told us not to leave. So we are continuing to work.'

'How long have you been working for the master?'

The man's mouth twitched, and for a moment I expected him to smile. He was obviously not used to discussing with strangers the details of his arrangement.

'My father . . .' he said softly, 'it was my father who was in debt. He borrowed five hundred rupees, for his sister's dowry. When he died I had to start work to pay off the loan.'

'When was the money borrowed?'

The man shook his head.

'I don't know,' he intoned forlornly. 'A long time ago.'

'Are the rest of them bonded as well?'

'Yes, all.'

'Why don't you run off? Now's your chance, the master has gone away.'

The labourers looked up together. Their eyes spoke of fear, a great and unknown fear. Their expressions told of the terror: that their master would hunt them. Their features hinted at the indescribable pain they would endure once caught. When he had made examples of them, he would surely sell each one on to an even more despicable lord.

'Why are *you* bonded?' Bhalu asked the child, who must have been about ten or eleven.

The lad blinked nervously.

'I was caught on the train without a ticket,' he explained. 'A policeman at the station took me home to work at his house. He said he would send me to prison if I did not obey him.'

'What happened then?'

'The policeman's brother owed a lot of money to a money-lender,' the boy went on. 'As he didn't have the money to repay the loan, he sold me in exchange for his debt. Then the money-lender sold me to the brick-maker.'

I found the situation almost unbelievable. When I told Bhalu that in the West people had no idea that bonded labour still exists, his usual jocund approach to life disappeared.

'This is slavery,' he said. 'There's little hope for these people. None of them will ever pay off the interest owed to the master. Labourers like these end up selling a kidney or an eye to pay back what started off as a tiny debt.'

Like me, the Trickster was moved by the labourers on the Patnagarh road. I forced them to take some money; and Bhalu handed them each a miniature bar of hotel soap. In a place in which there was little water to drink, let alone wash, the gift was an odd one. But it was the gesture that mattered.

After a second night sleeping rough, bartering soap bars for food, we finally arrived at the witch's village. The journey had led us through half a dozen other villages and hamlets, most of which were all but deserted. As we persevered on foot, hiking north of the Patnagarh road, the Trickster asked an assortment of farmers, labourers and wood-gathering girls if they had heard of the witch. Invariably, they greeted us with bewilderment, waving a hand ahead.

Each mile brought new signs of famine. All the rivers in this once lush basin had run dry. The parched trees were being felled by those who had not yet left their ancestral lands. Once they had chopped up the timber they, too, would be away, hauling it to Bolangir for a sure sale. Orissa is well known for its famine. Eighty per cent of its people live below the poverty line. Disturb their finely-tuned existence by a fraction, and they cannot survive.

No one Bhalu spoke to could remember a drought such as this. In one hamlet we met a widow who had refused to accompany her entire family on their migration to the city. Her skin was creased and swollen with sores. She had not left her home since her marriage, decades before. Even now, in the face of certain death, she had decided to stay behind.

At another village we heard that a young mother had sold her infant daughter. With six other children to feed, she had resorted to the most drastic measure conceivable. Four other women, supporting the first – who was too ashamed to show her face – declared that they, too, would give their daughters away if they had a chance. We continued on, more depressed with every step. And as I entreated Bhalu to give up the search and lead me back to the main road, we reached the witch's village.

Surrounded on all sides by dusty ancestral fields, the community could never have housed more than fifty farmers and their families. Most of the simple mud houses were empty. Their owners had already left. Some of the buildings had begun to collapse, their walls crumbling like dry Oxo cubes. The few villagers who had stayed were loath to admit their community was home to a witch. After prolonged negotiations, Bhalu discovered the wattle-and-daub dwelling in which the woman, an aged widow, was held.

With great unwillingness, the self-appointed head man related the case.

The widow's children had fled the village some two months before, journeying to Cuttack in search of secure jobs. The old woman had always acted strangely, but only when her sons departed did she resort to actual witchcraft. For two years in a row the village's crops of jute and ground nuts had failed. The widow had been seen pacing the fields at night, soliciting evil forces. A neighbour said she observed her transform into a wild dog. Someone else noticed that some seeds she had planted had actually grown in the parched soil. Another purported that the ancient had turned a tank of water sour merely by glancing at it. A fourth claimed she had made three eggs disappear into thin air. The remaining villagers had gathered together to decide a course of action.

Fortunately for the widow, many of her neighbours had departed the village for nearby towns. Had there been a full turn-out, the general state of mass hysteria would certainly have found her guilty without even the most simplistic of trials. In Orissa, a woman condemned as a witch is customarily stoned to death on the spot. Whereas a man – or even a younger woman – accused of sorcery might use it to his advantage, claiming to be a godman, a widow with magical powers is invariably considered to be a witch.

Fortunately for her, the lack of senior villagers had led to indecision. Now that the sorceress had been arrested, no one was quite sure what to do next. The hesitation proved the extraordinary force of mass hysteria. An enraged mob of amateur witch-hunters spontaneously derives solutions.

With no need for me to prompt him, Bhalu instructed the head man that we had been sent to decide the fate of the witch. The arrival of a twelve-year-old boy and a foreigner, both ready to adjudicate, must have seemed implausible. But surprisingly, the head man nodded once and opened the door to the communal store-room where the witch was being held.

Blinded by the daylight, and cringing as if she were about to be guillotined, the widow was pulled out and thrown on the ground. Her head was shaven, her lips were caked in dried white foam, her arms were covered in putrescent lesions, and her torn *sari* was stained with blood.

The woman was as fearful of me as the head man was. She appeared not to have set eyes upon a foreigner before. Bhalu tried to explain that we had come to judge her case. We would listen to the evidence against her a point at a time.

The first witness was called.

A man in his fifties, he had spied the witch strolling in the fields beneath a full moon. She had been speaking to hidden spirits.

'Bhalu,' I said, 'please ask the widow why she was in the field at night, talking to herself.'

The Trickster translated my question and, with distinct difficulty, her reply.

'She says she had been unable to sleep. Her sons had left her all alone. She was miserable because the family's crop of jute had not grown. So she went out into the field and asked *Varuna* to bring rain.'

'There's no witchcraft in that,' I said. 'Move on to the next point. Ask her if she turned into a wild dog.'

The scam-artist enquired if the widow had indeed transformed herself into a 'werewolf'. Ducking her head to veil her face with the hem of her white *sari*, the woman mimed out an answer.

'Bhalu, can you understand what she's saying?'

'Yes . . . she says the whole village knows the problem of wild dogs. Last year two children were killed and eaten by the hounds. But on both occasions, she was with her neighbours in the village.'

'Ask the head man if this is true.'

Bhalu interpreted the question and, grudgingly, the chief villager nodded.

'Next point . . . tell her to take us to the place where her seeds grew.'

Bhalu helped the widow to her feet. Stumbling forward, she led us, and the frantic crowd which had gathered, to a spot at the eastern edge of the village. As her shadow fell over a row of limp green shoots, the woman pointed to the bed of cultivated soil. Curiously, the area of ground was damp. Yet the surrounding earth was cracked and dry. I was about to ask Bhalu for his opinion when he pointed to a pair of water drums at the back of a nearby hut. Without saying a word, the Trickster went over and lifted the edge of the barrel. The soil beneath it was dark with moisture.

'It's got a slow leak,' he said, calling us over. 'The ground over there's wet because of this barrel of stagnant water.'

Accepting this as a plausible explanation, the head man asked the huddle of villagers for their opinion. Most remained silent. They were obviously fuelled by jealousy: the widow had succeeded in germinating a few seeds while all the other village crops had withered.

'If she's a witch,' I said, 'why didn't she make her family's field prosper instead of this pathetic patch of waste ground?'

The villagers stared at their leader and shuffled their feet. They had hunted and caught the witch and now wanted the satisfaction of punishing her.

A man called out from the back of the group.

'What's he saying, Bhalu?'

The Trickster listened to the man's protest; which was repeated several times in a loud, heckling voice.

'He says that you can explain why the seeds grew, but he wants to know why the village water soured when the witch looked at it.'

'Take us to the tank of undrinkable water.'

The inquisition crossed the village in silence.

A group of young women, each with large silver bangles on their wrists, were taking it in turns digging a well-shaft at the other side of the settlement. Their scant frames were, we were told, best suited to clambering down the narrow well-shaft. As the women ferried away dishes of the parched Orissan earth on their heads, we approached a large free-standing water tank next to the well.

'Is this the cistern of sour water?'

The chief villager and the heckler agreed that it was.

Bhalu removed the heap of chipped bricks holding down the water tank's cover. He signalled to three men in the mob, who helped him heave away the steel lid. As soon as I set eyes on the brackish water, I understood why it was the source of numerous afflictions. The swollen bodies of seven grey-backed bandicoot rats were floating on the surface.

At that moment a man with a club-foot hobbled over to where Bhalu, the head man and I were standing. One hand was straining to manage a crutch. In the other was an enamelled mug, filled to the brim with water. The liquid was crystal clear; the chipped mug identical to that which had hung from Feroze's belt. The drink was as translucent as water from a mountain stream. When it was offered to him, I noticed that the Trickster refused courteously. Touched by the club-footed man's kindness, and parched with thirst, I took a long, satisfying draught.

Bhalu explained to the rabble that the rats had soured the water, not the widow's glance. The facts were all well and good, but the villagers were eager for a less scientific trial. The heckler called for the old woman to be subjected to the traditional tests which would prove her guilt.

Orissa is well known for its witch trials. The procedure is usually the same. A local *Jan-guru*, a witch-hunter and amateur exorcist, is summoned. Often he starts by shaving the sorceress' head to eliminate her evil powers. Then, when the entire village has assembled, the testing begins.

Isolated from the outside world, officials find it near-impossible to regulate the trials. In any case, the authorities regard trial by ordeal as crude entertainment, and as a way for a solitary community to vent its emotions.

Before starting his elaborate inquisition, the *Jan-guru* whips up the wrath of the mob. Like hounds frenzied before a hunt, they long for the kill. The exorcist shouts the order, and the suspected witch is brought out.

Any number of tests follow. To go free the witch must pass each one. First, she may be given a *talwaar*, sword, to hold out in front of her. If the blade wavers, she's definitely a witch. Next, her mouth may be filled with dry white rice. If it's still dry when she spits it out, she's guilty. The crowd tend to overlook the fact that one's mouth is likely to dry up in the face of death.

Back in the village, the heckler was again jeering from the rear of the crowd. He was asking for the disappearing eggs to be explained.

I asked Bhalu to take a poll. If I could explain how three ordinary eggs could disappear, would they pledge a solemn oath, permitting the widow go free? The mob fell silent. At first they seemed uneasy. What if I, too, was a witch – who had come to save my fellow sorcerer? This, the unthinkable, was brushed aside. A whispered undertone rose above the hush. The head man asked his fellow villagers for their decision. Enthused at the prospect of testing me, they agreed.

Three fresh hen's eggs were brought forward by a young child. The audience gathered in an arc and watched my fingers. Some sat down, others shaded their eyes from the sun. The heckler pushed his way to the front. Beside him stood the Trickster, who wished me luck. Like the villagers he, too, fell silent. I waited for the moment. Fifty pairs of eyes gazed at me as I remembered all those hours in the Master's study. We had performed sleights so many times. Three eggs was a breeze for someone hardened by swallowing stones almost as large. I sensed Feroze watching the spectacle from a great height. Beside him, I imagined Hafiz Jan peering down at me in the centre of that dusty Orissan village. The Master was betting the Pashtun that I would fail. 'Go on!' I seemed to hear Hafiz Jan command. 'Do it for Jan Fishan Khan!'

A pye dog hobbled from the shadows of one of the houses. It was obviously concerned why the entire village was lined up. Taking advantage of the situation, the dog meandered over to a child on the extreme left of the arc and sank its fangs into the infant's arm. The boy let out a piercing cry. The murderous rabble lost concentration as they turned in unison to behold the child's injuries. Seizing the moment, I flung my arms backwards and dropped the eggs down my collar. A split second later, the mob's gaze was on me again. But the eggs were nowhere to be seen.

16

No Little Girls

Only a madman would have ingenuously accepted a mug of drinking water in a drought-stricken Orissan village. Without pausing to question from where the thirst-quenching liquid had come, I had gulped it down. Now that I think of it, the refreshing water had been flavoured with that certain *je ne sais quoi*, otherwise known as the tang of grey-backed bandicoot.

But by the time my alarm systems were activated, it was too late.

Bhalu and I were waiting for an Ashok Leyland to ferry us back to Bolangir when I collapsed. Somehow, the Trickster managed to transport me to one of Bolangir's more sordid rest-houses, hidden down an unlit alley. For ten days I lay on a *charpoy*, weak and dehydrated. I must have dreamt every dream in the world. Yet the only dreams I can remember were of elephants. No longer were the tuskers swigging tequila from the bottle. This time, they were in ancient Egypt.

A cohort of elephant slaves hauled great slabs of stone to the crack of a tyrant's whip. One by one, the massive honey-coloured blocks were piled high on each other, forming a mighty pyramid. Not far away, in a lustrous palace whose walls were bedecked with hieroglyphs, the Queen of all Elephants lay on her back, while an elephant maid servant dropped peeled grapes into her open mouth. Two tuskers stood guard at the door. A dozen infant calves scurried about with urns of fresh buffalo milk for the royal bath. As the team of servants hastened to and fro, the sweet melody of a lone minstrel elephant radiated out from behind a filigree screen.

As I drifted in and out of consciousness, I could make out the young street lad's face. He left my side only to fetch medicine and mineral water with which to restore my health.

On the eleventh day, after a night of unprecedented sweating, I found myself sitting bolt upright, wide awake. I knew the illness had come to an end. Bhalu was squatting on the edge of the *charpoy*, his Charlie Chaplin smile leering at me, a bottle of sterilised water in his hand.

'Why did you look after me?' I rasped once the strength had returned to me. 'What's your reason? You're not my guardian angel . . . are you?'

The Trickster smiled broadly, like a Cheshire Cat, telling me to lie still and rest.

A week later and we were on the road once again, heading south in the general direction of Tirupati. I was almost back to normal, except for the occasional spasm of stomach muscle. Our route passed some of the most spectacular scenery I had come across in eastern India. Dense forests gave way to wide vistas. Yet still everything was tinder dry. One carelessly discarded match would surely have set the entire region ablaze.

We stopped at the quiet town of Titlagarth to wait out the heat of early afternoon. Recognising my continued weakness, Bhalu insisted that I took no chances. Our pace had slowed to a crawl. Indeed, with my prolonged recuperation at Bolangir, there was a danger that I would not make it to Hyderabad in time for the asthma cure.

*　　*　　*　　*

It was Bhalu who first noticed the wide, sagging canopy, suspended between two *sal* trees. Pointing to the makeshift tent, he wondered aloud why it was attracting such a crowd. Dozens of men and women were turning up. They would hand a single rupee coin to a grubby-looking man standing guard, and disappear into the hessian tent. The doorman had one leg shorter than the other, leading to a cringing gait. His face sneered at the world like a gargoyle, his lengthy neck drooping with vulturine conspiracy.

At first I thought the tent must be a travelling cinema. Judging by the abundance of high-spirited customers, the playhouse was screening a gem of a show. But as we approached the unctuous man on the door and paid our money, I perceived that this was no cinema.

A hundred or so people were pressed up inside the tent like sheep before the dip. Some sitting, others standing, all were focused on a mysterious contraption at the front of the room.

The machine was resting on a collapsible table. It consisted of an electronic casing, a transducer, an undersized QUERTY keyboard and a viewing monitor. Beside it stood a low-quality hospital couch. Casting an eye around the tent, I noticed a row of seven or eight women crouching on the ground. Two were visibly pregnant. I suspected that the others were also expecting.

The filthy man who had been collecting the entrance fees moved over to the sophisticated apparatus. He flicked a couple of switches, turned a dial, and pulled the recoil cord of a small generator. As the tent filled with dense diesel exhaust fumes, the man raised his voice above the noise of the engine.

'What's he saying, Bhalu?'

'He's welcoming everyone . . . and now he's calling for the first patient.'

'*What* patient?'

Before the Trickster could answer, the first pregnant woman stepped forward. She greeted the man – who appeared to be some sort of physician – and slipped him a wad of rupee notes. Only when the money had been counted, and each bill had been checked for perforations, did the clinic begin.

The woman was assisted on to the couch. A lattice screen was then pulled in front of her abdomen, and the machine's monitor was tilted towards the audience. The doctor described what he was doing:

'This machine has the power to tell whether the patient will have a boy or a girl baby,' he explained. 'I am applying an electrode to the stomach. Watch the screen carefully. You will see the unborn child!'

The doctor's contraption was an undersized ultrasound unit: a more common fixture in a hospital than in a playhouse-clinic. As he spoke, the first hazy images could be seen on the black and white screen. Instinctively, the audience lurched forward like cattle in a pen. They had paid good money for the sight. I made out the silhouette of the expecting mother's abdomen through the lattice screen.

Peering into the monitor as though it were a space-age crystal ball, the quack drew a deep breath. Then, screwing up his face, he looked out at the audience and shook his head from left to right.

'Does that mean the baby's sick?' I asked Bhalu.

'No . . .' he responded. 'It means she's carrying a girl.'

A wave of tense energy surged through the crowd. The pregnant woman broke down in tears. To hear she was expecting a daughter was the worst news she could have anticipated.

'What happens now?'

Bhalu wiped his nose.

'She pays the doctor another fifty rupees for an abortion.'

'The same man?'

'Of course . . . but the audience don't watch that part. They just like to hear whether it's going to be a boy or a girl. Look at those men over there . . . they're placing bets with the doctor's sidekick.'

Bhalu was right. At the far end of the tent four men were handing over their stakes to a fifth. Betting on the gender of a foetus was too low even for Bhalu.

The next pregnant woman, aged no more than about fifteen, handed over her money and took her place on the couch. Without wasting time the doctor squirted a little Aquasonic gel® on to the girl's belly and applied the transducer. Like the expectant mother before her, she must have been praying that the murky image on the monitor was that of a son.

Ultrasound may have been designed to check for abnormalities in the unborn, but the apparatus has found a new and far more puissant role in India. Sex determination is now illegal across the nation, but it's bigger business than ever. Worn out Western ultrasound units criss-cross the sub-continent, making a fortune for their untrained operators.

Only a skilled gynaecologist can accurately determine the gender of a foetus using ultrasound. So much of the time the quacks tell the patient that they're expecting a daughter, even when they aren't. This disposes of any embarrassment later, and secures them the lucrative bonus of performing the abortion.

Ultrasound is just the latest weapon in the war against female children. But the concept is nothing new. Communities throughout India have long perfected their own ingenious methods of eliminating unwanted daughters. The Kallar tribe from Tamil Nadu, for instance, can only afford to pay the dowry of one daughter. So when a mother gives birth to a second, third or fourth girl, it's fed milk laced with the white sap of the madder shrub. The baby soon expires from nausea and diarrhoea. Other clans suffocate the infant, or feed it the juice of oleander berries, or the milk extracted from the *erukkam* flower.

The use of the American-made ultrasound at Titlagarth was shocking. Its villainous operator had been no innocent illusionist. He was playing with a device so powerful as to affect the very balance of nature.

Only later, when Bhalu and I were rambling our way towards Bhawanipatna, did the full horror of Indian child-killing become apparent. I was scribbling a report to Feroze, detailing my latest observations. As I wrote, I pondered what effect ultrasound would have on the society. I stared out across the parched fields of Kalahandi. Three boys were throwing stones at a dog; another group of lads were rolling their hoops in the dust. A father was showing off his new-born son to a neighbour. Then it hit me. The future – a land without little girls – had already arrived.

I scouted about, urging Bhalu to ask fathers how many daughters each had. Grinning with calm satisfaction, most replied that they had only sons. There were virtually no daughters aged six years or below, anywhere. With time, perhaps the lack of women will turn the system on its head – with men paying women for the privilege of their hand. But as it stands now, the problem of dowries has led to a stripping-down of the system. The warped logic is clear: dowries are paid by the bride's family to the groom's . . . Instead of doing away with dowries, why not do away with women?

*   *   *   *

Hoping to refocus my attention, Bhalu suggested we travel to a village near Nandul. He wouldn't say why the diversion was necessary. But I had a hunch the boy was on to something. How my travelling companion maintained his source of precious information, I had no idea. Names of significant places, contacts of key importance, little-known data and fascinating lore . . . it all just came to him. Bhalu's education on Calcutta's streets had provided him with a sixth sense for survival. His knack for navigation, and luck at bumping into the right contacts, was more than merely impressive. It was uncanny.

We travelled by ox-cart, rode pillion on passing bicycles, and hitched lifts on the ever less frequent supply of tangerine-orange Ashok Leyland trucks. The roads went from rough, to rougher, to almost impassable. As we crossed spectacular expanses of open country, Bhalu swore he would never return to Calcutta. Despite being gripped by his city, I agreed that its pollution and frenetic pace of life were no match for the wilds of the Orissan country.

At the town of Sargigora a man with a red shoe on his left foot and a green one on his right told of a seer working at Nandul. The man's clothing was a jumble of New York City's hippest costume and Hawaiian beachwear. He seemed very contented with the look. From the unusual combination, it was evident he had been fitted out with clothes donated to a Western charity. He spoke of Nandul as if it were a great city.

By the time we arrived at the town, the Trickster and I had guessed that the odd-shoe man had never been there himself. Rather, he had been weaned on the exaggerated rumours. Located on a small river,

Nandul was a drowsy agricultural community, affected by relentless drought. India's great industrial cities may be raging hotspots of activity; but the country towns are the complete antithesis. For a start, they're virtually silent. The din of rickshaws, generators and clapped-out buses is replaced by bicycles, paraffin lamps and people walking on foot. Yet the most overwhelming difference is the sense of innocence. The streets of Nandul were teeming with incorruptible souls. In contrast, take any street corner in Calcutta and examine it closely. Lurking in the shadows there'll be three or four agents of the Underworld; a baby-renting beggar; a pickpocket; a couple of boot-leggers; and half a dozen others touting anything from second-hand skeletons to fire-engine bells.

Bhalu took up the trail for the godman supposedly working nearby. Some locals pointed left; others indicated right. One man roped in a lame friend to help, who coaxed another to assist. That man and his associates became involved. Then all their friends turned up. Before we knew it, a teeming concourse had gathered to debate the directions. Tea-sellers, fruit merchants, a palm-reader, a brocade-seller, and a man with a tray of *paan* balanced on his head all hurried over to take advantage of the impromptu audience. Every manner of question was asked. Where were we staying? Were we the police? What were our names? Was I related to Mr Harshad Shah of Mohammed Ali Road, Bombay? How were we enjoying our visit to Nandul? Where had we come from? Where were we going? Would we be needing a taxi? Why didn't we pitch up in town for a few days? The more questions that were asked, the more people came. And the more people who came, the more were drawn. Like a snowball careering down a mountainside, the gathering soon grew from two men and a dog into an entire caravanserai.

A boy of about eight who had a pet mongoose in a cage, pushed his way to the front and befriended Bhalu. He seemed to regard the Calcutta-born Trickster as some kind of god. Widening his eyes in awe as Bhalu lit a *biri*, he told us that the seer moved from one community to another. The boy had seen the mystic at a nearby village two days before. He would take us at once . . . as long as we would buy a handful of meat to feed to the mongoose.

Three hours later, Bhalu and I were crouching at the front of a large audience, assembled in the open air. About two hundred villagers had gathered to watch the godman perform miracles. For such an under-populated village, the turn-out was impressively high. Bhalu's young confidant concluded that the drought had boosted the godman's standing. For he, and only he, had the power to ease the suffering . . . and to bring rain.

Like a stand-up comedian stepping from the wings, the magician appeared from a thatched mud-brick house to begin his show. He announced his name, Narashima; but everyone present already knew who he was and why he had come. They were growing impatient for the magic. As he took up his position at the centre of a tattered drugget rug, I caught my first sight of the godman. One glimpse and it became obvious why the villagers were so keen to place their faith in him. Unlike theirs, the magician's skin was not dark brown. It wasn't even light brown. Rather, it was frosty white, the colour of chalk. His hair was not black, but platinum. And he blinked through watery eyes, devoid of pigment. The seer was an albino.

Before the sorcery could begin, the populace was expected to endure an hour of theological ranting. They waited patiently for the sermon to end, and the miracles to start. Like worshippers the world over, they preferred the worthless mumbo-jumbo to the real message. At last, perhaps sensing that his congregation could not bear much more of the exhortation, the sage announced that, to prove his powers, he would perform a series of miracles. An anxious ripple of electric excitement ran through the audience.

Miracles are more common in Hinduism than in almost any other religion. Indians, I noticed, are far better accustomed to accepting the miraculous in everyday life. Other religions, like Christianity, do put faith in the inexplicable, but their miracles are few and far between.

First, the godman announced that through mental powers he would cook a pot of rice. He decreed that any young woman who swallowed a single grain of the rice would give birth to a son. Unlike the rest of us, the albino had no need for a stove. A large urn was placed on a straw mat before him. Chanting incantations, and swirling the hem of his robe in a figure of eight, he circled the blackened pot of rice seven times. A sinister, unnerving hush had fallen across the audience. They focused on the pot. A few minutes went by. A single wisp of steam spiralled from the vessel. Then the godman began convulsing. All around, the spectators watched in wonderment as their prophet writhed about. The more he squirmed, the more vapour rose up from the pot. Fifteen minutes passed. Then, emerging from his trance, the godman returned to the pot. He fished out a ladle of rice. It was fully cooked.

Next, the magician gathered several brown coconuts from his box of props. Five volunteers were called out from the crowd. The lucky spectators were each handed a coconut and told to break it open. They obeyed, smashing the nuts on a stone. Examining the pieces, they fell back in wonderment. The coconuts were filled with jasmine flowers.

Delighted by the stir his second miracle had caused, the holy man moved on to his next trick. He asked a member of the audience to loan him a banknote. The spectators appeared sheepish. None had any money. In any case few, I suspected, would have volunteered their precious savings to assist a godman; even one of the albino's calibre. The visionary called again for a single note of any denomination. Bhalu stepped forward and handed him a ten-rupee note. The audience breathed a sigh of relief. The last thing they wanted was to enrage the magician.

The serial numbers of the bill were called out. The guru's assistant – a young boy with a straying eye – etched the numbers into the soil with the end of a stick. Next, the godman set fire to the banknote. Soon it was nothing but ash. Calling out to the spectators theatrically, he added the ashes to a cup of water, stirred them in, and gulped the mixture down. The assembly were severely agitated by the demonstration. Ten rupees is a lot of money, especially in the uncertainty of drought. But before anyone could protest, the albino tensed his stomach, retched four times, and pulled the crisp banknote from his mouth. The serial number was identical to that of Bhalu's own ten-rupee note.

With his repertoire of miracles apparently exhausted, the magician asked the villagers what problems were troubling them. They stared at him in disbelief. Surely it was obvious. Their lands were as dry as parchment. Most of their animals had already perished. Forest fires had consumed the little available firewood. Without heavy rain they would soon starve to death. Just as the godman must have known the problem well, he would have anticipated the answer. Clambering back to his position on the rug, he fell into a trance again. For forty minutes he chanted mantras. The audience peered on, open-mouthed and trustful. They genuinely hoped that he could bring rain.

The albino's assistant scurried away, while his master opened his eyes and addressed the audience:

'An evil spirit has come to this village,' he shouted out. 'That spirit has chased away the rains. I can feel the force of evil all around me! Have none of you witnessed phantoms as well?'

The villagers nodded enthusiastically. They had observed many recent signs of evil. Some had seen flames shooting out from the ground on the outskirts of the village. Another said her neighbour's laundry had caught fire while it hung to dry.

The *avatar* raised his arms in the air. He called to the villagers to put their faith in him. He would demonstrate that he could bring the rain. But first, everyone would have to focus their eyes upon him. His power would only be activated if everyone stared directly at his solar plexus. Four hundred eyes converged on the mystic, who had begun to chant mantras once more.

Five minutes slipped by. The spectators' concentration didn't waver. As they gawked towards the seer's chest, almost hypnotised, a remarkable thing happened. It began to rain.

The dust beneath our feet smelt fresh and clean as the spray of minute droplets touched it. I breathed in deep. That haunting smell – of the first rain – can only be understood by one who has encountered it. Some of the villagers, many screaming, licked their arms; others danced about. Their fantasy had come true. But as quickly as it had begun, it stopped.

The *sadhu* announced that he could bring further rains. He, and he alone, could restore water to their arid fields. But the villagers would have to contribute to the procedure . . . which, as most had already grasped, wouldn't come cheap.

As the godman's assistant made ready to collect a donation from all those present, a tall, broad-shouldered man stepped from the back of the audience. Without removing his shoes, he paced over and stood on the magician's hallowed carpet. A shudder of fear undulated through the crowd. Who was this man? Who dared be so disrespectful to the rainmaker?

Before the seer, his aide, or the assembly could question his motives, the newcomer called out to the throng. Bhalu gave me a running translation of his words.

'This man is a hoaxer!' he cried. 'You must not trust him, and I will show you why!'

Claiming to be a member of India's ever more popular Rationalist Movement, he jeered at the holy man, ordering him to step aside. I was surprised that the Rationalists were targeting such unimportant godmen, deep in Orissa's hinterland.

An instant later, three more Rationalists were beside the first. They too dared to stand on the sacred rug. In unison they declared they would expose the albino's miracles. He was, they said, nothing but a con-man.

First, they showed how the godman had secretly slipped a cup of quick-lime into the aluminium pot of rice. When the lime – taken from a kiln – had come in contact with the water, it had started a chemical reaction. The result was enough heat to boil the liquid, and cook the rice. Then, while the seer proclaimed that it was the Rationalists who were corrupt, not he, more miracles were exposed.

The coconuts had had their milk drained through the eyes at the top. The night before the demonstration, jasmine buds had been pushed through the holes into the nuts' cavities. Given a little time, they blossomed in the dampness. As for the ten-rupee note: it was nothing more than simple sleight-of-hand.

By this point, tempers were fraying. The *pandit* was incensed that his livelihood was being attacked by the merciless band of Rationalists. To them, the illusionist was just another target on their National Miracle Exposure Campaign. Surprisingly, the villagers showed little interest in the public debunking. As far as they were concerned, the godman was a miracle-worker of the highest calibre. He had made it rain and would, surely, do so again.

As the slanging match continued, the Rationalists unveiled yet more trickery. The flames which had been seen in the night fields were no poltergeist, they said. They were created by the magician, lying in a ditch, spitting kerosene on to a burning torch. And the spontaneous combustion of laundry? The godman's assistant had, no doubt, dabbed the clothing with a solution of phosphorous and carbon disulphide.

To a Westerner, it may sound dubious that a *tantrik* like Narashima would have a ready supply of such potent chemicals. But trawl any Indian small-town bazaar . . . caustic acids, all types of poison, base chemicals and experimental solvents are all available cheaply over the counter. For India is a land untouched by the West's preoccupation with safety.

Meanwhile, the Rationalists moved on to their *coup de maître*: debunking the rain. Simple enough, they said: the godman's helper had sprayed the audience from behind with a fine jet of water, using a modified bicycle pump.

The albino was not going to be put off by a few allegations of chicanery. He had gathered up his props and was busy setting up his clinic at the other end of the village. He had a mission – to breathe new life into his livelihood.

Godmen who work in small towns and villages are, for the first part, entertainers. They have little in common with the affluent jet-set mystics, with their Western devotees, Rolls-Royces and penthouse apartments. Holy men like Narashima are largely harmless performers, employing simple illusions – about as sophisticated as those used at the time of Houdini. Indeed, I realised that the majority of the tricks regularly performed in India were of Houdini's vintage. Many of the feats of swallowing objects, the sleights-of-hand, and the chemical illusions were developed by the great American conjuror himself. Of course there's one key difference: like all Western 'magicians', Houdini claimed to be nothing more than an illusionist. But here, in India, godmen have taken the feats a stage further: they are passing them off as *actual* magic.

Within minutes of the Rationalists' exposé, the villagers were back in position, clustered round their master, who had started to cure the indisposed.

First, a woman with a displeasing skin condition came up to be healed. Veiling her face with the hem of her violet *ikat sari*, she attempted to conceal the numerous pus-ridden sores. It being a small community, the villagers must all have known the woman well. But they leered forward all the same, for a better inspection of the disease.

She appeared to be suffering from severe vitamin deficiency. A course of appropriate medication may well have expunged the affliction. The mystic examined the woman. Acting melodramatically to the gathering, he proclaimed she had offended Yakshi, the tree goddess, by chopping branches from a tree outside the village.

'But, I had to take wood, to sell,' retorted the woman.

'Do you want to be cured?' snapped the albino.

'Yes, I will do anything.'

The remedy was meted out. A folded *sal* leaf was passed to the diseased woman. It contained a teaspoon or two of potassium permanganate. She must wash her hands and feet with a few grains of the powder each morning. When there was no more left, she was to leave the village at dusk and spend the night meditating beneath the tree from which she had chopped wood. Even before she had paid the ten-rupee fee for the powder, the next client had come forward.

'What's wrong with him?' the magician asked the teenage mother who had placed her baby son at his feet.

'He was bitten by a snake.'

Shrouding the child's head with a scrap of ochre-coloured cloth, the albino murmured incantations.

'The child will live,' he whispered, 'but only if you follow my directions.'

Trembling in the presence of a living god, the young woman agreed to obey the seer's commands.

'Take these special *neem* leaves and mix them with cow's milk,' he explained. 'Warm the mixture and let it stand overnight before you feed the drink to the child.'

The woman was ushered away.

I nudged Bhalu to ask him what was wrong with the godman's next patient. But he had no time to translate. He was making his own way over to the magical carpet, in search of treatment.

'Bhalu!' I called. 'What are you doing? Are you mad?'

The Trickster turned.

'He's still got my ten rupees,' he replied. 'I'm seeing him on account!'

17

Disneyland of the Soul

Almost six weeks had passed since Feroze had ordered me from the house. Although still a daunting duty, the journey of observation was making some headway. I had met a selection of curious characters, including a supposed witch, an albino godman, not to mention many intrepid foot-soldiers from a Secret Army. Each evening, before going to sleep, I scribbled down a few words of the day's encounters. The next day I would post them off to be examined by the magician. Wondering how my commentaries had been received, I decided to telephone Calcutta.

The man at the telephone booth tucked away in Jagdalpur's vegetable market licked the palm of his hand and ran it over the seat of a stool, begging me to sit. Then, tugging a frayed velvet cloth away to reveal a fine Bakelite telephone, he dialled the Master's number. I pressed the receiver to my ear.

A conversation in English was already occupying the line.

'Gangu,' said the first voice, 'how are the preparations going for the murders?'

'Very well, sir,' said the second, 'very well indeed. Everything under control.'

'Who will be doing the killing?'

'The vampires will, isn't that what you wanted, sir?'

'OK. But do the vampires have their own costumes?'

'Yes, sir, affirmative, they are looking very nice!'

'Why don't we hire a dwarf vampire . . . it would be a great touch.'

Vampire dwarfs? What a monstrous idea. I had to tell someone of the murderous plan. But who to inform? I was just about to ask the telephonist's advice when I caught more of the sinister conversation:

'But Gangu, make sure the vampires have very fine, pointed teeth. That's imperative. Everyone will be watching them closely.'

'Yes, boss, they will all be given proper sets of vampire dentures.'

Vampires without their own teeth? I pressed the receiver closer to my ear to make sense of the chat:

'Well done, Gangu, it sounds good . . . what time shall we begin the shoot?'

'Sir, the extras will turn up at eight o'clock, and the lighting crew an hour or so before.'

As I wiped my brow with relief, the telephonist managed to make the connection to Feroze's mansion.

'Halloooo?'

'Gokul, is that you?'

'Yes, it me. What name of your party?'

'This is Tahir Shah . . . Gokul, greetings from Jagdalpur. Can I speak with the Master?'

A pause followed as the jumble of voices encroached again.

'No, Tahir Shah *Sahib*,' Gokul yelled. 'Master not in Alipore . . . Master on journey.'

'When did he leave?'

'He gone for long time . . .'

'Where did he go?'

'Out of Calcutta . . . Master having business outside West Bengal.'

'But has he received my letters, Gokul, can you tell me that?'

'Tahir Shah Sahib,' shouted the elderly manservant, 'Master not read letters . . . he been away long time. Very busy.'

Feroze had not mentioned that he planned to leave Calcutta for an extended trip. As I squatted on the saliva-coated stool, I thought of the cosy study, with its soft carpet, its clutter of trophies and its bookshelves. It seemed a million miles from the telephone booth at Jagdalpur. Thinking of it brought on a wave of homesickness for the mansion and its appalling regime.

The telephonist watched me as I stared into space. He was waiting to be handed a wad of rupee notes, but was in no great hurry for payment.

'What you do now?' he asked.

'Continue on my journey,' I said. 'You see, I'm on a journey of observation . . . looking for the unusual.'

The telephonist nodded.

'Laxmi Circus very nice,' he said.

'Where's that?'

Replacing the velvet kerchief squarely over his precious telephone, he opened a drawer, pulled out a flier and passed it over. It was headed: *Laxmi's Circus and Popcorn.*

'Is it any good?'

The man licked his lips and cackled menacingly.

'First class,' he said.

The telephonist's high recommendation had been an introduction too enticing to overlook. I spent the next day with Laxmi's popcorn chef and the troupe, which was performing to a full house each night. It seemed to enjoy a far-reaching reputation. Even those unimpressed by the routines were won over by the circus' other sly crowd-puller: free popcorn for all.

Bhalu accompanied me, albeit reluctantly. He had spent most of the night guzzling country liquor in a truck driver's drinking hole, and was severely hung-over.

Unsure of what acts had brought such fame to the Laxmi's Circus, I approached their heavily patched, grubby marquee with some trepidation. The Trickster entered the tent to announce our arrival. A minute or two passed. Bhalu emerged, his face pale with dread. Five more minutes went by. Then, slowly, the canvas entrance flap was drawn back by an attractive girl. I smiled, taking in the attributes of her unexpected appearance. Aged about fourteen, she was crouching low on the ground. Nothing odd about that. Yet I couldn't help noticing that the peculiarities ran deeper than her posture. The girl had lovely features. Her lips had been painted with cherry-red gloss; her eyes had been lined with *kohl*; her nose was pierced with a silver pin. And she had two heads. I rubbed my eyes. She still had two heads, four eyes, a pair of noses and twenty fingers. Bhalu was sure his hangover was playing tricks on him. When I jabbed him in the small of the back, he explained that we had come to speak to the troupe's members.

Anila and Amrita had been born to a villager near Nagpur in central India. They were joined by a thick band of tissue at the sternum. On realising she had given birth to conjoined – 'Siamese' – twins, what she assumed to be a monster, their mother had drunk poison. Their father assumed the girls were the incarnation of some malevolent spirit. Fearing the wrath of the supernatural, he resolved not to kill them. Instead, he shoved the new-born babies into a sack and hurried with them to Nagpur. The girls were sold from one unscrupulous freak dealer to the next.

'We were shown at circuses across India,' said Anila, brushing her long hair. 'The owners would burn our arms with cigarettes to make us move.'

'If we cried out,' said Amrita, continuing where her sister left off, 'we would be beaten. If one wept, the other was punished. When we were ten, a circus owner sold us to a brothel.'

'Where was that?'

'In Chennai, Madras,' muttered Anila. 'We were locked in a room not much bigger than the bed. Men would come all night to sleep with us. They found us strange. We screamed every night.'

'When our screams disturbed the other girls,' persisted Amrita, 'the pimp would bring a knife and threaten to cut us apart.'

Amrita paused to rub rouge into her cheeks. Like her sister, she had a soft, feminine complexion. Both their faces appeared to have been lightened with bleaching cream.

'Did you escape from the brothel?'

'After two years,' said Anila, 'its owner said we weren't bringing in enough money. So he threw us out into the street in Chennai. We were forced to beg for a living. Then, one day, Laxmi heard about us . . . he asked us to work with him and the others.'

'Is Laxmi here today?'

Amrita pointed a foot to a very ordinary-looking man standing nearby.

'Go and talk to him,' she said.

So I did.

Laxmi was of average build and very hirsute. His hands were large, but not excessively so. His lower jaw was as angular as a set-square, with a bristly mole on its left side. When I asked him what his performance entailed, he said he ate things.

A man with a digestive tract like no other, Laxmi's stage routine was to gulp down whatever the audience threw up to him. Razor blades, nails, door knobs and shoe horns, they found their way into Laxmi's stomach on a nightly basis. Some items would be regurgitated after the act, others would proceed through his intestines.

As an amateur who had toyed with swallowing stones, I could only pay homage to the true maestro. Laxmi had made an art form out of what was for me a deeply unpleasant activity.

'When I was a boy,' he said, explaining how he got started, 'I used to swallow things for fun. At first I swallowed coins and paperclips to make my friends laugh. Then I tried nuts and bolts, marbles, door hinges, keys and belt buckles. The more I swallowed, the more I liked it.'

Laxmi's expertise at swallowing large or sharp-edged objects was impressive. My ingestion of smooth pebbles paled in comparison. I was about to ask him what his most impressive feat of swallowing had been but, quite suddenly, he excused himself. He had a touch of indigestion.

Noticing that the swallower had disappeared, Anila and Amrita crawled over, and introduced us to two veteran members of the circus.

The first was a turbaned hulk of a man with a walrus moustache. Pressing his hand to mine, he wasted no time in demonstrating his skill. He fell down on all fours and performed twenty faultless press-ups. Then, clambering to his feet, he instructed Bhalu and me to examine his forehead. We did so. Miniature beads of perspiration were forming in the furrowed ridges of his brow. But this was no ordinary sweat. It was black. As the inky droplets joined up and ran towards the great moustache, I examined the man's face very carefully. Although there was no way of telling, I felt sure that this coloured sweat was nothing more than an illusion. Perhaps he had painted his skin with a transparent chemical which reacted with the sweat. I would ask Feroze for his opinion when we next spoke.

The second turbaned man – called Vikram Singh – then demonstrated his expertise. In his left hand he held an illuminated glass light-bulb. The bulb, which was flickering gently, wasn't plugged into a socket. When he handed the bulb to me it ceased giving light. As far as I could see there was no battery concealed in the base. For his second feat, Vikram Singh unbuttoned his shirt. He stooped to remove a selection of household objects from a tattered cardboard box. A couple of spoons, a kitchen sieve, a saucepan lid and a bottle opener: one by one, he pressed the items to his chest. Rather than falling to the ground, the items stuck to his torso. I inspected each of them. There was no apparent sign of adhesive. Even so, I thought that, like his associate, Vikram Singh's skills were nothing but crafty conjury.

As we wandered away from the marquee, Anila and Amrita begged Bhalu to drop by after the show. Both seemed to have taken a fancy to him, and were flirting outrageously. Rather than ignoring their affections, he was thrilled at the prospect of entertaining two girls at once.

'How dare you even contemplate leading them on!' I growled, as we moved away from the marquee.

The Trickster licked his palms and pressed down his dirty hair. Soon he would be locked in a passionate embrace . . . like none other. I reminded him that he was getting himself into hot water. Sordid relations with conjoined sisters might, for all we knew, be breaking the law.

Bhalu twisted round to wave to the girls. Once they had shuffled inside, he turned his attention to me.

'What's wrong with them?'

'Bhalu, look at what you're saying . . . I'm having nothing to do with this.'

'You're just jealous!' he said.

*   *   *   *

The following morning, Bhalu was eager to relate the details of his nocturnal encounter with the conjoined sisters. Insisting I had no interest in his sordid love life, I dressed and left the guest house in a huff. I would be taking the noon bus to Kottagudem. If the Trickster didn't appear at the bus stop, I would be only too delighted to leave without him.

Travelling with a twelve-year-old, who acted like a washed up middle-aged rock star, was not an easy experience. Again, I found myself questioning what had induced the boy to tag along. It wasn't as if I were supporting him. He was always adamant that he paid his way – albeit in black money. And it wasn't as if I was an affable companion. I treated him like a menopausal mother would have done. I shouted him down when he gave his opinion; ridiculed him in public for his manners; and ordered him about as if he were a serf. Sooner or later I knew I would discover the reasoning behind his decision to accompany me.

After an hour of hanging around at the town's main bus stop, a dilapidated Tata bus rolled up. The front two tyres were hissing unnervingly. Never one to let a trivial puncture or two get in the way, the driver set off at considerable speed. Bhalu had not turned up. Maybe, I ruminated, his tryst the night before had been true love. If the relationship led to wedlock, was a marriage to conjoined sisters considered to be bigamy?

The bus pushed southwards, crossing one river after the next, slicing through the fertile agricultural lands of the Sabari Valley. The horrific drought of Orissa was nothing but a memory. Every fifteen minutes the driver would jam on the brakes. His assistant, a fawning reprobate of a man wearing a fine coral necklace, would jump down and pump air into the perforated tyres. The regular stops more than doubled our journey time.

On the few occasions that the vehicle managed to gather speed, I thought about the riddle of coloured sweat. Then I wondered what had happened to the Trickster. Would I ever see him again? Perhaps he had decided to head back to Calcutta, where he belonged.

Shortly before dusk, the bus – which had not been in fit shape to undertake the journey in the first place – had ground to a halt at the town of Borgampad, about thirty-five kilometres from Kottagudem. We were now in Andhra Pradesh. The driver announced that all the passengers were invited to pass the night in the vehicle, because of a major puncture. When I offered to help put on the spare wheels, the driver laughed feebly. Of course, there were no spares.

Descending into the dispersing light, in search of a meal, I found refuge at an outdoor roadside café. A series of paraffin gas burners bathed the area in phosphorescent light. The air was thick with moths. A man in a *lungi* and T-shirt bearing an image of the Mona Lisa swaggered over and slapped a thick *paneer*-filled pancake in front of me.

As I sank my teeth into the fritter, I noticed a robed figure slouching beneath a banyan tree, adjacent to the café. His forehead was masked in a large barberry-red *tilak*, outlined in white; his form was caped in yellow; and his neck was thick with wilting *mogra* blossom. The flowers, the red *tilak* and the yellow dress: all were the emblems of a *sadhu* who follows Rama.

There was something else about the old *sadhu* at Borgampad which struck me. His *kamandal*, the ritualistic water vessel carried by all *sadhus*, was extraordinary. Generally crafted from wood, gourds, brass or steel, the traditional water containers are revered as sacred objects in themselves. But the one held in the hands of the Rama *sadhu* was quite unusual. It was fashioned from a coconut of the enchanting *coco-de-mer* palm.

Native only to the island of Praslin, in the Seychelles, the *coco-de-mer* is one of the most astounding of all trees. The coconuts, which closely resemble the shape of a female pelvis, take seven years to mature. Their similarity to the female form may explain some of the wondrous properties which have been ascribed to them. Well designed to cross the turbulent waters of the Indian Ocean, the distinct double nuts have been washed up on the beaches of India's west coast for centuries.

Ancient legends tell of how the nuts grew on trees beneath the sea. Societies along India's western coastline pounded them up to make medicines, elixirs and potent aphrodisiacs. A cult even developed, dedicated to worshipping the coconut. When General Gordon visited

Praslin in 1881, he declared that the island was the Garden of Eden, and the mystical *coco-de-mer* its forbidden fruit.

*　*　*　*

Late the next morning, after an uncomfortable night spent aboard the stationary bus, the driver turned up with an assortment of inner tubes, for which he had traded his assistant's coral necklace. The auxiliary, who was petulant at having his prized possession swapped for a heap of lousy inner tubes, set about with a jack and tyre levers.

Less than two hours later, the machine was heaving into Kottagudem. Defying the sceptics – for whom I was the spokesman – it negotiated the remaining miles without another stop.

After a wash beneath a standpipe in the market area, I tramped over to the railway station. By a great stroke of luck, a slow train bound for Vijayawada, the last sizeable city en route to Tirupati, was about to depart.

Once I had got comfortable in my second-class seat, I again pondered what had happened to Bhalu. If he had been there on the train, he would already be scamming a small fortune from what he considered to be fresh blood. Maybe I had been too abrupt in dashing off without him. But his behaviour had really begun to deteriorate. One-night stands with Siamese twins . . . what would be next?

At Khammam, the largest of the many stops we made, a portly figure entered the carriage and took the seat opposite mine. The baldness and VIP grey attaché case gave him away as a member of the Secret Army. I was about to suggest that he rush out and buy a Director's Brand hairpiece when he clicked open his VIP.

Pretending to be jolted forward as the locomotive took a sudden bend, I attempted to peek over the top of his case. No good; too slow.

Could I work out his business by observing the signs? His open-toed sandals were constructed from good-quality leather; his shirt was indigo silk; a top-of-the-range Indian-made watch was strapped to his wrist; and the deep scar on his left cheek seemed to have been attended to by a skilful surgeon. He was, quite obviously, an important salesman.

Unable to bear my overt investigation any longer, the man pulled a large, shiny oval object from his case and handed it to me.

'Egg?' he said. 'Would you like an Easter egg?'

'Thank you very much,' I replied. 'That's the last thing I'd expect to see on a train in Andhra Pradesh. Are you sure you can spare it?'

The salesman removed his glasses to rub his eyes.

'Oh, yes, of course I can,' he retorted, 'I've got thousands of them.'

Why were the Secret Army of Indian executives breaking into chocolate Easter eggs? One thing was for certain: their motives had nothing to do with Easter. I examined the egg. Its wrapper advertised a cache of jelly babies inside. I also observed that the egg, from Safeway Supermarkets, was eight months past the sell-by date.

'Excuse me for prying,' I said, 'but are you a member of the Christian Church?'

The salesman clutched his case to his chest, as if I had insulted him gravely.

'Certainly not!' he quipped, 'I'm a Hindu.'

'Then why the interest in Easter eggs?'

I had to get to the bottom of it all.

'Vedding-eggs!' he said, squirming back in his seat. 'They're vedding-eggs!'

'*Vedic* eggs?'

'No, no, vedding-eggs . . . matrimony.'

Clearly, I had missed a key snippet of information. What do chocolate Easter eggs from Safeway have to do with Indian weddings? I asked the executive. He was warming to my interest in his product.

'The bride's family gives one to each guest who comes to the marriage. It's a symbol . . . a bountiful future.'

'Was this your own idea, by any chance?'

The salesman beamed with the smile of a man who had come up with a great invention.

'Yes, all my idea,' he said.

'But where do you get the Easter eggs from?'

'My cousin in Blackburn buys up all out-of-date eggs after Easter and ships them over to me. I supply them to veddings across southern India.'

This was a project on a par with Pykrete and Tirupati toupées. Transmutation of a symbol from one religion to another. An anthropologist would kill for a whiff of this. But the concept of the wedding-egg was far more than an anthropological curiosity. It was an example of Indian genius at the highest level. Easter eggs are made by the million in countries across Europe and the Americas. The day after Easter they're virtually worthless. So, enter the calculating mind of the Indian Secret Army executive.

*   *   *   *

One of eastern India's most ancient cities, Vijayawada nestles on the north bank of the mighty Krishna River. Not far from the coast, set on a great floodplain, and bathed in history: one might expect the city to be a key tourist destination. Having installed myself at an open air tea house near the city centre, I dug out my Cadogan guide to south India. What lavish praise had its writers afforded Vijayawada? Opening it at the appropriate page, I began to read: ' . . . *Vijayawada is a classic textbook example of an Indian hell-hole and should be avoided . . .*' Below the write-up was a line-drawing of a supine traveller, his hand wearily stroking his brow.

Pressing the book to my face, I glanced to the left and then to the right, without moving my head. The place had not seemed as bad as all that. Granted, it was rather stifling, and most of the tourists appeared to have been frightened away, but this was no hell-hole. Then it struck me. Of course, instead of being a classic textbook example of a hell-hole, this was a classic textbook example of a travel-guide writer's infatuation. As the author of a guide myself, I knew well the routine of slandering one's favourite spots. How else can an overworked, underpaid travel writer ensure that the riffraff will stay away? I'll stay here a couple of days, I mused. If it's as bad as the guide insists, it must be terrific.

Leaning back on my chair, I ordered another *idli* and a second glass of tea. Then I withdrew my notepad and dashed off a report to Feroze; he would surely be interested in the wedding-egg business. Even if he was out of Calcutta, I was certain that he would eventually arrange for my letters to be sent on. As I scrawled the details down, a gargantuan Westerner approached the restaurant. He was fifty-something, as tall as an oak, with sagging jowls and a face that bore the scars of tropical illness. Even before he sidled over to my table, I knew he was an Australian. My supposition involved little guesswork. This was a man who must have tramped across the Outback, fought crocodiles bare-handed, and feasted on mealy grubs beneath the stars. His hat gave it all away. It was wide-brimmed and made of tightly woven straw. And corks dangled from its outer edge on strings.

'G'day,' said the man, obviously intrigued that another foreigner had ignored the guide-book warnings to turn back.

'Good afternoon.'

'Don't get many strangers in these parts,' he said, removing his hat. 'Had a couple a Kiwis last month, they decorated my hat with the corks. Keeps the flies away pretty well . . .'

'I'm not surprised there are so few tourists: the guide books are virtually pleading with visitors to bypass Vijayawada.'

As I asked the Australian what had brought him to such an outlying locality, I noticed an odd scar, a sort of pock, about an inch above his brow. The advanced state of his baldness drew my eyes to the mark. Although healed, it was as if the wound had originally been quite deep: far more than a superficial break of the skin.

'I'm researching earth eaters,' he said, answering my question.

'Earth eaters? What do they do?'

Even before the words had left my mouth, I was blushing at the stupidity of my question.

'Earth eaters . . .' replied the man with an ominous inflection, 'eat earth.'

'Golly . . .' I said, hoping to claw myself back to the realms of credibility.

The Australian had more to say:

'Unusual cravings, they're my line,' he said, introducing himself as Fisher. Like everything in the Antipodes, his name had been abbreviated, to 'Fish'.

'Earth eating sounds more like a sign of derangement than a craving,' I said.

My attitude to the unusual appetite had not pleased the Australian.

'Geophagy, earth craving is rare in Asia,' he said coldly. 'I've discovered a local pregnant woman who eats more than half a pound of earth a day.'

'Maybe she's starving,' I said.

Fish, who had taken on a pseudo-scientific air, was not impressed with my hypothesis. Pulling out a pair of bifocals, he twirled them around his index finger. I imagined he had condescended to speak to me only as no one else in Vijayawada was in the least bit interested in earth eaters.

'So, why do people eat earth?' I probed, hoping to conclude the conversation. 'It can't taste that good, or everyone would be gorging themselves on it.'

Fish sucked on the arm of his spectacles.

'More people eat it than you think.'

'Really?'

'Oh yes,' he said, straining forward to pass on what he knew. 'In Ghana, five thousand tons of clay are mined each year . . . not to be made into pots, or to build houses, but to be eaten. It's sieved and mixed with water to form a kind of dough.'

'Yes, but all kinds of amazing things are going on in Africa . . .'

'Well, what about Mississippi?'

'What about it?'

'There's a well-known earth-eating tradition there. People near the river say their soil tastes like sherbet. And what about the slaves in the New World? Everyone knows that when they were brought to the Americas, they ate earth out of fear. They got addicted to it.'

'Are there any similarities between the earth eaten in Ghana, Mississippi and Vijayawada?'

'That's the sixty-four-thousand-dollar question,' he replied.

From the furtive way Fish rubbed his palms together, I sensed he knew more than he was giving away.

'Earth eating,' he continued after a few minutes of silence, 'is probably the most primitive side of our brain somehow kicking in. What if one could activate this area of the mind in everyone? Think what it could mean for marketing!'

'Fish, I don't want to denigrate earth eaters,' I said, 'but I really don't think the business community's going to get too worked up about them.'

The Australian called the waiter and asked for a cup of milky tea.

'You don't understand,' he sniffed. 'The implications are tremendous. Find out how these ancient, primeval brain patterns work – why some individuals are ruled by their cravings – and you can control the way people think . . . then you can determine what they buy.'

'But who'd want food that tasted like earth?'

'Forget earth-flavoured anything,' said Fish. 'That doesn't even come into it. The earth eaters are just the key!'

Had Fish been dressed in a Savile Row suit, sitting in a swish Los Angeles office, I might have been reeling in awe at the ramifications of primeval appetite. The fact that he was lying low in Vijayawada, discussing his plans with random foreigners, made me suspicious. Perhaps he was himself an undercover earth eater. For a moment I wished Bhalu was still around. He would have cut straight through to Fish's real intentions.

As far as I was concerned, anyone investigating unusual cravings on the banks of the River Krishna had to be a little eccentric, irrespective of their motives. The more the Australian and I conversed, the more convinced I became that a maniac was sitting before me.

The majority of Westerners one meets in India are on a quest. They're searching for truth, for enlightenment, for themselves, or, like Fish, are hunting for the bizarre. Unlike the West, India – a country dedicated to assisting those on a journey – comforts them, nurturing their peculiarities.

*

Fish and I discussed all kinds of subjects, and spoke of distant places, until late into the afternoon. He came across as a man of considerable acumen, but whose brilliance was marred by disturbing undertones. He claimed to speak six languages, including Tagalog; to have written extensively on the Japanese board-game *Go*; and to play the marimba. Impressive stuff. I didn't doubt any of his accomplishments. But Fish ought to have stopped with the marimba.

Fired by the Master's order to observe at all costs, I bombarded the Australian with questions. He, goaded by my insatiable curiosity, lifted the veil on his deep and peculiar past.

Before dispatching me on my journey of observation, Feroze had instilled in me an important rule of thumb. Never, he said, disclose too much at the first meeting; rather, extract information from your interlocutor. At the time, I had wondered what exactly the magician had meant. But my lengthy conversation with the headstrong Australian was a good example of how not to behave.

Having deliberated on the flavour of Ghanaian soil, the merits of the marimba, and the winning strategies of *Go*, Fish shifted the conversation into the Twilight Zone of his youth.

I asked whether he had been to the sub-continent before.

'I certainly have,' he said languidly. 'It was in the early seventies. Went to Goa, to Kashmir and West Bengal . . . you can't beat this country. Or we couldn't then.'

'Why not? What was so special about India?'

Fish made fists with his hands and banged them together.

'Because,' he called out, 'we were on a quest . . .'

'A quest for what?'

'For a third eye. You see, in the seventies, India was Disneyland . . . it was the Disneyland of the soul.'

The waiter circled our table like a shark. We had not ordered anything for a long time, and the management were ready for us to leave. With the Antipodean just opening up, I had to stall. So, pulling out a hundred-rupee note, I rustled it in my hand like a dry leaf.

Speaking at full speed, Fish revealed a deeper obsession . . . trephination.

His tale began with an interest in the work of the Dutch physician Dr Bart Huges. While at a party in 1962, Huges had seen a man stand on his head. The act had given him a flash of inspiration. Surely, he thought, the more blood you have in your brain, the higher your consciousness? So Huges experimented by standing on his head, and by pinching the veins draining blood from his neck. The results were encouraging. But Huges yearned for a more permanent increase in consciousness. He longed to return to the consciousness of infancy. For this, he thought, the skull would have to be unsealed, like a child's. He realised a third eye could be created by excising a small disc of bone from the head . . . using an electric masonry drill.

Huges was carted away to an asylum when he went public with his ideas. But an Englishman called Mellen took up the gauntlet. He bored a hole into his skull, using a high-speed electric drill. It was uneven, so he drilled another. His friend, a woman called Amanda Fielding, began noticing improvements in Mellen's character. So persuaded was she by the development that she drilled a hole in her own skull. Amanda Fielding grew so thrilled with the operation that she saw it as her duty to campaign for trephination for everyone with only two eyes. She stood as an independent candidate in the 1979 and 1983 parliamentary elections. Her central manifesto pledge was to get head-drilling free for all on the National Health.

'So, where did you get yours done?'

Fish probed the inner reaches of his mouth with his index finger. He suddenly seemed contemplative. But then, one would expect anyone who had applied a high-speed masonry drill to their skull to take the subject seriously. Three or four minutes passed. He said nothing. Perhaps my question had brought back painful memories. Fish was staring into space.

'Sydney in 1976,' he whispered, without changing his focus. 'We were high as kites and looking for stimulation . . . the permanent kind.'

'Golly,' I said, gulping.

'A group of us had heard of Huges and Mellen, and thought we'd have a go ourselves. You see, we had all been to India in search of the third eye, but had left with nothing but diarrhoea.'

'What did it feel like when the drill went in? Did you reach higher consciousness? Do you recommend boring out a third eye? How does it feel now?'

Fish drew a hand across his chin, and paused as my rapid volley of questions struck him.

'There's only one answer I can give,' he responded gently.

'Yes . . . yes, please tell me.'

'If you're so interested,' he replied defensively, 'drill a hole in your own skull . . .'

18

The Yogi's Last Breath

The ravens in the rafters of Vijayawada's railway station were very large indeed. Passengers and red-shirted luggage bearers hurried about, all laden with packages wrapped in greasy newspaper. The coal-black birds peered down, secure in the knowledge that they were untouchable. A herd of boot-boys weaved through the crowds, rapping their brushes together like the keys of a glockenspiel to attract customers. A madman hopped about on one foot, swearing. Fifteen clocks all advertised a different time. A bewigged Secret Army executive spat *paan* against a wall and coughed. Hawkers jostled from one platform to the next, selling padlocks and lavatory chains, rubber gloves and rolling-pins. Just another morning in the railway Black Hole.

Muttering something about making a long-distance telephone call, Fish had left me to find a room for the night. I had risen at dawn and made for the railway station. After an hour of waiting, the ticket officer had sold me a seat on the 0810 service direct to Tirupati. The second-class carriages were full, which meant I would have to travel south in third-class.

Twenty minutes before the train arrived, I observed a crowd gathering at one end of the platform. Always enthusiastic to see another performance, I went over and made my way to the front of the throng. But this was not a new trick. It was one that I knew well. For it was being performed by none other than Bhalu.

'Ah,' he said loudly, 'I was wondering when you'd turn up!'

'I thought you had run off with the twin sisters.'

The Trickster grinned his Charlie Chaplin grin and followed after me as I walked away.

'How have you managed without me?' he chirped. 'You must be missing me a lot.'

*

Hafiz Jan had once told me that my ancestor, Jan Fishan Khan, had burst
out laughing on hearing that India's first railway had been built. That
was back in 1853. The thirty-four kilometre track stretched between
Bombay and Thane. Rising up like a Siberian bear, the great warlord had
poured scorn on the preposterous Western invention. He had proclaimed that railway tracks would never be laid in his homeland,
Afghanistan. 'Your trains may suit you in Europe,' he thundered, 'but
Afghans would never keep to the tracks!' While Jan Fishan's prediction
remained true in his homeland – Afghanistan has no railways – rail
travel caught on in India . . . in a big way.

Even for Bhalu, the third-class train heading southward to Nellore
was unpleasant. I made a big song and dance about the drop in comfort,
until, that is, I realised that the really destitute travellers were sitting
on the carriage's roof. Crowded with dark, silent faces, the compartment had hard wooden benches and an oily layer of mud on the floor.
Until now, the Trickster had preyed on middle-class travellers. As far as
he was concerned, they made the perfect customers. They had just
enough money to splurge on cut-price products – such as cigarette ash
beauty powder – and were too new to the business of luxury to doubt the
effectiveness of his wares. Now presented with the lower-income
echelon of south Indian society, he would need a fresh patter with
which to entice our impecunious companions.

But as the Trickster contemplated his vast repertoire for an ingenious
money-making scam, a stocky man leapt at the train as it was passing a
small station. Defying all laws of physics, the man caught hold, and
pulled himself aboard. It was a remarkable feat of strength and
recklessness. Stumbling through the cabin, he began to tout a single
item.

Bhalu was anxious that another was trespassing on his patch. He was
about to hound the man away when I called him to heel. I wanted to
inspect what the pedlar had on offer.

One by one, the dim faces twitched, dismissing the hawker. Within a
few minutes, the man was standing before us. He was dressed in a
heavy-knit pullover and canary-yellow trousers. His eyes were the
colour of egg yolks; a dark plume of hair sprouted forth from his nose.

'Can you ask him what he's got on offer, Bhalu?'

The Trickster gritted his teeth and translated my question. The man
with egg yolk eyes blinked once and withdrew a half-size vodka bottle
from his pocket. The bottle was empty.

'He says he's a follower of Yogi Radhakrishan, and that he has
something very unusual to give away . . . for a donation.'

'What is it? What's he trying to give away that no one in a third-class carriage wants?'

Bhalu put the question and juggled with the unwieldy response.

'What's he selling, tell me, Bhalu!'

The Trickster seemed gravely impressed; not by the merchandise, but by the story which went along with it.

'This man spent fifteen years at the foot of Yogi Radhakrishan, the famous *sadhu* from Madhya Pradesh,' Bhalu explained. 'His master practised many *tapasya*, austerities. For the last thirty years, the *yogi* consumed nothing but milk. He was ninety when he died, but he never changed his routine. He had spent twenty years in another penance, *ek-bahu*, his arm raised up, propped by a crutch. Then, in his youth, he had tied a thick cast-iron chain around his genitals, to destroy all feelings of lust. And,' continued Bhalu, 'the *sadhu* was said to have had supernatural powers. This man standing here was with his master when he died.'

'That's all very well,' I said, 'but what's in the bottle? It looks empty to me.'

The Trickster asked the disciple to go over the key points again. Then he informed me of the contents of the bottle.

'You're right,' he winced, 'there's nothing in the bottle . . . just air . . . but it's *special* air. It's the *yogi*'s last breath.'

*　　*　　*　　*

Only once before had I heard of a dying breath being bottled. Even then it wasn't for sale on the open market. Unlike the *yogi*'s voluminous exhalation, it was a far more dainty sample. The American automobile magnate Henry Ford was a known admirer of Thomas Edison. He was said to have bought anything connected to the great inventor's life. His collection included all manner of personal and scientific objects. But pride of place was devoted to a small glass vial, labelled 'Edison's Last Breath'.

I would have forked out a hundred rupees for the holy man's last exhalation, but, as ever, my funds were too low for such luxuries. Bhalu could easily have afforded the bottle and its contents; but he was horrified at my gullibility. Wads of tattered rupee notes were stashed in each of his pockets, in a pouch around his neck, and in the folds of his underwear. He had been minting money since the trip began. Nothing was easier than fleecing unsuspecting citizens in the provinces. Such profitability must, I mused, have been the motivation behind the Trickster's eagerness to embark on a grand Indian tour.

There was little to observe on the train journey south from Vijayawada. Not that the landscape was dull; it certainly wasn't. But my face was pressed up against a crate of over-ripe mangoes for most of the journey. The third-class carriage had a stupendous agitation of life. Gone were the wig-wearing, VIP-case-carrying salesmen of second-class. They had been replaced by another Secret Army . . . of astrologers.

India is the most capitalistic nation on Earth. The Western world may think it has a fine tradition of commerce, but sadly, it's quite mistaken. Give any executive from Frankfurt or London a dessert spoon, drop him down in Andhra Pradesh, and he would be starving inside of a week. But present an Indian with such a simple item of cutlery, and he has a foolproof way of supporting his extended family, for life.

Two other ingredients aid capitalism in India. The first is people. The sub-continent has a billion potential customers for any product. The other is an unquestioning belief in the supernatural. Put the two together and, as I found out, a dessert spoon is more than enough to reap the rewards of a market economy.

When the train stopped at Ongole, a stone's throw from the Bay of Bengal, the carriage swelled into a makeshift bazaar. Boot-boys and peanut-sellers pushed each other aside, vying for custom. Hucksters, touting Rubik's cubes, whistles and water pistols, showed off their wares. Blinking through milk-bottle-glass lenses, the mob of largely, elderly passengers seemed nonplussed. They had no need for water pistols or Rubik's cubes. At their advanced stage of life, they were far more concerned about another matter . . . their destiny in the next life.

Then, as the train surged from the station, the tide of pedlars ebbed away. Seizing the moment, the fortune-tellers revealed themselves.

The infantry of astrologers appeared to be members of one extended family. Each had perfected a different method of peering into the unknown. One would read a person's shadow; another could interpret the pattern of flies landing on a mango seed; a third deciphered a strand of one's hair; and yet another would describe one's horoscope merely by taking the pulse.

Before I could select which method of divination most appealed to me, a man with an enormous frothy white turban, gnarled features, a patch over one eye, and a large amulet bound to his arm had pushed a dessert spoon at my face. In its bowl I glimpsed the distorted reflection of carriage life. Like upside-down spectres, the fray of mendicants, mangoes, and boss-eyed travellers loomed up behind me. The medium spoke in a thick, raspy tone. Although the accent and appearance were unfamiliar, there was something recognisable about the clairvoyant. It was his smell. He smelt of lavender, a fragrance favoured by Feroze. And his hands . . . they were very much like the magician's. For a foolish moment, I wondered if my teacher had resorted to following me on my journey. No, I reasoned, Feroze would not have bothered himself with that. A mendicant's life was not for him . . . *he* would never have endured the ragged costume and third-class travel.

But this was not the time to question the man's appearance or the Master's schemes. The polished dessert spoon, which was being thrust back and forth towards my face as sharply as a piston, was in danger of blinding me.

'What's going on?' I bleated. 'Get that spoon away from me!'

But the implement did not move away. Instead, it began to fluctuate more wildly than before, from side to side. Was this a crude form of hypnosis? Had the mystic lost his own eye in practising the specialised system of divination? I asked Bhalu what was happening.

'The man is saying that he can tell your fortune,' he explained. 'Stare into the shiny spoon and he will read your eyeballs.'

'I don't want my eyeballs read. They're private!'

But the reading had already begun.

Chanting mantras and pressing his bristly face closer to mine, the astrologer stared deeply into my eyes. He paused to lick the spoon with his tongue. Then he choked out my fate a few words at a time.

Bhalu translated the reading of my destiny:

'You came to India to study illusion,' he declared, interpreting the seer's words. 'After visiting the tomb of your ancestor, you travelled to Calcutta to begin an apprenticeship with Hakim Feroze, the master illusionist. And now you are on a great journey . . . of observation.'

'That's impossible,' I scoffed. 'How could he know all that just from my eyes?'

The Trickster, who appeared blasé at the man's information, continued with the translation:

'Now you are travelling to Tirupati and then to the temple at Tirumala. After that, you plan to venture to Bangalore and then up to Hyderabad, for the mysterious cure . . . for your asthma.'

Again the astrologer licked the spoon with his eel-like tongue. Without a coating of saliva, the magic did not work. As before, he studied my eyeballs with considerable attention.

'All right,' I said, 'enough of my past and my plans, tell me the details of my actual future!'

Bhalu leaned a little closer to heed my fate.

'The destiny,' he said, 'is to bring many good things. But if you know in advance what they will be, your actions may change. The result could send you on another path . . . leading to a different, less pleasing fate.'

'Can't he tell me a single thing that's going to happen? He doesn't have the right attitude . . . after all, he *is* a fortune-teller.'

The spoon was licked for a third time.

'All he will say is that your journey will end with a tremendous conclusion.'

I handed over a rupee for the pleasure of having the man peer into my eyeballs. Then I launched into a studious analysis of the reading. Certain that this was nothing more than simple deception, I broke it down bit by bit. Since a blind dwarf fortune-teller and his accomplice had once hijacked my wallet to learn all about me in Bombay, I had become far more sceptical in the face of supposed clairvoyants. Even so, I had no idea where the lavender-scented mystic had acquired his data. An hour after the man and his family had moved on from our carriage, the Trickster was tiring of my dissection. He couldn't understand why I was taking the spoon-reading so seriously.

'Let's go through it one more time,' I blustered.

Bhalu, who had been eyeing a girl sitting opposite, glowered at me.

'Will you try to act normally?' he snapped. 'You're scaring away my little friend over there!'

*   *   *   *

Ten hours after leaving Vijayawada, train 8079 heaved into Tirupati. Very often, when the locomotive screeched into a station, I couldn't be certain whether it was my stop or not. The signs were either in an unfamiliar script, or were obscured by the general mass of porters, forlorn travellers and soda-water-sellers. But this time it was different. As soon as the hailstorm of porters threw themselves suicidally at the arriving train, I knew we had reached Tirupati. It was an easy deduction.

Because everyone was bald.

We alighted and pushed down the platform through the jam of pilgrims. I found myself staring at each one. Their shaven heads were powdery white, their expressions sorrowful and drawn. They looked like human guinea-pigs at a concentration camp, waiting lethargically for orders. The air was heavy with melancholy; one might have concluded that the departing pilgrims were sad. Far from it. Each had achieved a lifetime ambition: to pray at the temple of Venkateshvara.

When travelling about India, it always seemed that everyone, except me, knew what was going on . . . rather as if the entire population had mugged up a set of crib notes which I hadn't seen. But Tirupati was different. We were all strangers, all anxious. All, that is, except for Bhalu. As others trembled with trepidation, he shifted into a new gear of mercenary activity. I observed the unending supply of bald pilgrims around us. I was touched by their self-sacrifice, moved that they should have journeyed to Tirupati to worship Lord Venkateshvara. The Trickster's sight was not tinted by the same rose-coloured lens of compassion. Instead of bald devotees, he saw an infinite stock of clients.

Next morning, as we boarded the tattered old bus bound for the temple complex at Tirumala, I asked Bhalu for his impressions.

'Great, isn't it?' he said.

'It certainly is . . . I'm pleased you're so uplifted.'

'Going to make a lot of money here . . .'

'Bhalu! How can you be thinking of money at a time like this? This is a place of pilgrimage . . . look at these people. They're dressed so simply. Most of them are barefoot.'

The Trickster was too busy planning to pay much attention.

'There's plenty of money, don't be deceived,' he said. 'No one's as generous as a pilgrim who's surrounded by other pilgrims.'

P.D. Roy's tale of Tirupati and his line of Director's Brand wigs had been an appealing enticement. But now we had actually arrived I was, I must confess, rather embarrassed. For the other passengers taking the hour-long ride up to the hilltop temple, the head shaving was only a fragment of what was a profoundly religious experience. Although I was trying to appear appropriately sombre, I had been lured by the idea of wigs. Bhalu wasn't even bothering to keep up my meagre level of pretence. He was in it for the money and nothing else.

The road from Tirupati to Tirumala was formed from one hairpin bend after another. The bus jolted obliquely to the left, then the right, throwing us about like astronauts in a space capsule. Lazy visitors – like Bhalu and myself – risked life and limb driving by bus to the shrine. Pious pilgrims wouldn't have been seen dead taking the bus. They made the journey on foot – barefoot – or even on their knees.

Grinding and moaning like a battle-worn Panzer division, the turmoil of shuttle buses to Tirumala destroyed what might have been a harmonious experience. As they strolled, or crawled, through the wooded groves of mango and sandalwood, the pious must have been cursing us for shattering the peace.

Tirumala was a pristine community built in what must once have been a sublime glade in the forest. The air was clean and warm. The place was as orderly as a military cantonment. There was no litter, no pye dogs, no sound of Hindi pop music, no stench of *biris*, and no one was spitting *paan* on to the ground. It wasn't like real India at all.

The passengers exited the bus like conscripts arriving at the base for the first time. They were eager to be part of the brotherhood, but they didn't know what to do or where to go. They stuck out from the throng of initiated pilgrims. For they still had hair.

Instead of following the newly arrived acolytes straight to the barbers' hall, Bhalu suggested we first get our bearings. I sat beneath a mottled tree in a communal area, taking in the almost carnival atmosphere. All types of products were on offer, none of them any practical use. Balloons on bamboo sticks, cuddly toys with button eyes, yellow and pink candy-floss, plastic flowers, yo-yos and fairy lights – the range was certainly impressive. Bhalu hurried about from one stall to the next. Anyone else might have thought he was looking for a bargain. I knew otherwise. He was searching for a gap in the market.

'So, what's it going to be?' I asked him.

'Nice and warm, isn't it?' he said.

'You're right, it's only nine-thirty and it's baking already. Imagine what it's like for all these people with shaven heads. Their scalps must be frying.'

'Exactly,' said Bhalu. 'Frying scalps means one thing . . .'

'A soothing lotion to stop the burning?'

Bhalu cupped his hands and clapped them together.

'You go and work on your potion,' I said. 'I'll meet you later on.'

Several thousand pilgrims had lined up to have their heads shaved in the barbers' hall, which was set apart from the main temple complex. Up to fifty thousand people have their heads shaved at Tirumala every day. Most spend months growing their hair as long as possible. The

longer the hair, the greater the sacrifice, and the more raw material
there is for wigs. I queued up with the neophytes, hoping to sneak into
the tonsure chamber with them. After about an hour, the line had only
moved a few feet. The man behind me was keen to pass on details of his
unlikely devotion for Wycombe Wanderers Football Club. He had spent
ten years running a corner shop in High Wycombe but, beset with
arthritis, had recently returned to India. The pilgrimage to Tirumala
was his last hope of assuaging the affliction. We talked football talk.
Great tackles, fouls and memorable scores, conditions of the home
pitch . . . we even discussed the stitching of the club strip. Another
hour dragged by. For someone with no more than a passing interest in
football, an hour on tackle-talk was an eternity.

The queue had hardly moved. By my estimation, there was at least
six hours to go of football purgatory. Unable to take a second more, I
pretended to have forgotten my money. The Wycombe supporter
replied that a full head shave was only two rupees. As a gesture of
charity from one football supporter to another, he was willing to pay
for my haircut. I responded with a catalogue of implausible excuses. I
had spotted a long-lost friend at the back of the line . . . I was about
to have a nosebleed . . . I was claustrophobic. Once away from
Wycombe Wanderers Man, I hurried to find a back door into the
barbers' hall.

A flight of steps led up to the chamber's back door. The stairs were
guarded by a uniformed *chowkidar*, watchman. He caught me sneaking
in, against the one-way flow of bald pilgrims. I explained that I was not
intending to have a tonsure, only to see the bundles of hair. I persisted
that I was solely concerned with the buying and selling of old hair . . .
my regard was for the shrine's part in the wig business, rather than its
religious role. It was obviously the wrong thing to have said. The guard
ordered me to leave. To him – and to everyone else – I was a sick-minded
voyeur.

I sat at the foot of the steps wondering how to get past the sentry.
Bhalu, who was running a scam near the exit gate, came over to see
what the problem was. He had brewed up a pot of some foul-smelling
liquid.

'Get that away from me', I said.

'Rub in a spoon of it and your sunburn will disappear.'

'But I don't have sunburn.'

'Well, it'll cure all other skin problems too.'

'What's in it?'

Bhalu disliked revealing the exact recipes of his potions, fearing a copycat scam-artist might be listening in. I stared into the pot. It was certainly attracting a great deal of attention from Tirumala's flies.

'Got something sweet in it, has it? The flies love it . . . so do the bluebottles.'

Only after considerable persuasion did the Trickster lift the veil on his concoction. Even for him, it was particularly inventive. Among the main ingredients were a kilo of sugar, two teaspoons of salt, a knob of *ghee* and a litre of stolen creosote.

Bhalu said he would get me past the *chowkidar* if I promised to publicise the sunburn lotion. I agreed to do what I could to help. Without wasting a moment, he showed me the secret. He waited for a knot of newly shaven pilgrims to exit and, choosing the moment, told me to walk backwards into the chamber. Everyone, he said, would assume I was leaving rather than entering. He was right.

There were actually several tonsuring halls arranged beside each other in a line. All were severely unpleasant. Marble-floored, with strip lighting, no ventilation, thick with flies, and strewn with haystack-like heaps of black hair, they were like a cross between a sheep-shearing shed in the Australian Outback and a rundown Turkish bath. Along one wall of the main chamber were the barbers – about fifty of them. Squatting on low wooden stools, they chattered away to each other, wielding cut-throat razors like boy scouts with bowie knives. Before them, cross-legged on the floor, heads tilted forward, arms by their sides, fifty pilgrims sat frozen to the spot, as the razor blades pared away every strand of hair.

There was no question of a bit off the top, a light trim, or even a short back and sides. The standard cut being dished out was a zero on any scale. Spend a few minutes observing the shrine's barbers, and you realise what frivolous stuff hair is. We preen ourselves like macaws, pampering our mops with expensive shampoos, conditioners and oils. We fling ourselves at the mercy of coiffeurs in upmarket salons. But forty-five seconds before a Tirumala barber shatters even the most outrageous delusion.

The head is first dipped in a bucket. When the barber's waxy palm has fondled the water into the scalp, the shearing begins. The blade begins at the crown, sweeping down to the brow in a single dextrous movement. Then back towards the neck. Four more strokes in quick succession and it's all over . . . total baldness.

At one end of the chamber an army of haggard men were gathering the hair into a single heap. Exceptionally fine locks were ferreted out by a special foreman. They were kept aside to be put in one of the frequent hair auctions. Yet many of these never reach the international wig trade. Instead, they're bustled away to the black market outside. P.D. Roy had told me that his team of craftsmen would regularly visit Tirumala for the pick of the crop. Because nothing less than the best, he had said, would do for a Director's Brand wig.

Remembering my promise to Bhalu, I waylaid a group of hairless pilgrims who were preparing to leave the hall. I advertised the miraculous potion, saying that a limited supply was available outside. They asked a string of questions. Was it suitable for sensitive skin? How much did it cost? Was it made from the purest ingredients? Did it protect the scalp from the harshest sunlight? I fielded the enquiries with appropriate inventiveness and went back over to the barbers. Perhaps, I thought, it would be worth drawing people's attention to the potion while they were lining up.

My sales pitch, which had started as a shy apology, soon turned into a merciless harangue. Before I knew it, I was claiming wide-ranging applications for the brew. It was, I said, a panacea . . . it would protect against sunburn, dandruff, scabies, lice, ringworm, and any known diseases of the head. Apply it once and your scalp would be as soft as suede, but protected from the elements like the tarred hull of a brigantine. Any unsatisfied customers, I went on, would be given a full refund. As I congratulated myself for an effort worthy of the Secret Army, Bhalu charged into the tonsuring hall and grabbed me by the collar.

'We've got to get out of here right now!' he said.

'What do you mean? Listen to my pitch . . . I've got really good at selling.'

'Well, maybe you've got too good,' riposted the Trickster. 'Everyone's demanding their money back . . .'

'What's wrong with the potion? I thought it was the best stuff around.'

For the first time Bhalu appeared genuinely nervous.

'It's the flies,' he said, once we had made our escape from the hall. 'They loved the stuff . . . they stick to it like glue.'

19

Real Power

Only those who have been sucked down in the maelstrom of an ecstatic south Indian crowd can understand the hateful nature of the sensation. Intoxicated with zeal, and fanatic beyond all reason, the mass of devotees waiting to hear *swami* Sri Gobind speak pressed around. Some were cackling – gripped by the laughter of lunacy. Others were wailing for no apparent reason. Bhalu and I fought to stand upright, snatching at air. Around us, three thousand of the godman's supporters surged forward. Conceiving that their need was, quite obviously, greater than ours, I called the Trickster back. We would attend an audience with the famous Madrasi guru another day.

By way of consolation, I suggested we visit a special festival, being held at a local sanctuary.

When I had heard that a shelter for mistreated cattle was having an 'Open Day', I thought it was a joke. Bhalu was the first to rebuke me for finding humour in what even he considered to be a sacred creature. For, in India, cows are taken very seriously indeed.

A great painted banner welcomed us to the annual bovine Open Day. Beyond it, the modest sanctuary was showing off its work, and encouraging visitors to express their affection for cows. About seventy cattle were being cared for at the shelter. Some had been hit by vehicles and left for dead; others were the victims of starvation, disease or stress. But the centre was far more than a simple resting place for recuperating cattle. It offered a variety of complementary therapies for the sacred creatures. Massage and acupuncture, light therapy and Ayurvedic treatments, each had been adapted for the bovine community.

Most of the shelter's cows were the familiar zebu cattle: the powerhouse of India. Long-horned and with a distinctive hump, the country's two hundred million zebu cows do the work of fifteen million tractors. But they do far more than hauling carts and ploughs. They provide milk and dung for fuel, and play a central role in the religious spirit of the nation.

After greeting a number of convalescing cattle, a tall, rather severe young lady apprehended me. She had dressed up for the bovine fête. A mazarine-blue frock hung from her slender form. Very swish, I thought, tucking my grimy shirt into my trousers. We exchanged pleasantries. When I told her that I had spent much of my time in England, her initial courtesy turned to hostility.

'Murderer!' she shrieked, as other respectable members of Madras society craned their necks to see what was going on.

'What do you mean? I've never murdered anything in my life.'

'Bovine spongiform encephalopathy,' she snarled. 'You Britishers treat your cows so ruthlessly that they're dying of plague!'

It seemed a bit unfair to blame the so-called 'mad cow' scare on me. After all, I hadn't eaten British beef for years. Long before the scandal had hit the headlines, a journalist friend had slipped me a rather unnerving dossier, warning of the risks. The confidential report would have put a butcher off beef.

But the woman had set her sights on me.

'The deities are now punishing you damn Britishers!' she announced, before the respectable audience of socialites and abused cattle. 'You're all getting infected from eating our holy animal. It serves you bloody well right!'

There was nothing I could say to quell the woman's fury.

'When will you people stop messing with nature?' she barked, prodding my solar plexus with her index finger. 'That's what's at the root of the problem . . . your meddling.'

'Please understand, I'm not involved in this, I'm innocent.'

'First you mistreat cows, next you test cosmetics on rabbits, you're evil! Why do you think the poor zebu cow is losing its hump?'

The woman pushed her crimson glass bangles up her arms, as if she was spoiling for a fight.

'Vanishing hump? What are you going on about?'

'The hump! The hump! It's disappearing . . . a few more years and there won't be a zebu hump left in India!'

I had heard of the famous case of the zebu's vanishing hump. The problem had begun when 'unholy' European cows were brought to India and bred with sacred Hindu zebu cattle. The project, which was supposed to lead to a higher yield of milk, worked better than anyone had dared to hope. But it had never crossed the scientists' minds that the famous zebu hump might be lost in the new gene cocktail. The loss of a cow's hump doesn't sound like much, but it's a catastrophe of unimaginable proportions.

For three thousand years India's zebu cattle have drawn carts and ploughs. The simplest form of yoke – a straight wooden bar placed across the hump – is used as standard from Amritsar to Alleppey. Without the hump, farmers can't plough their fields. With eighty-three million ploughs and carts to be redesigned, the very future of India seems suddenly in jeopardy.

I apologised to the militant bovinophile. I had been blinkered until that moment. Henceforth, I explained, I would dedicate my life to saving the zebu's hump. I would go and live in a mountain monastery and tend dear zebu cattle, drinking nothing but milk.

The radical woman was not pleased with my facetious attitude.

'How dare you make fun of milk?' she lisped. 'It is a miracle . . . it is the Milk Miracle!'

'*Miracle?* What are you talking about?'

'Ganesha drinking milk . . . I saw it with my own eyes!'

The Milk Miracle: it was all coming back to me. In England, fish have been found to rain from the sky; in the United States, people regularly spontaneously combust. And in India, deities drink milk. Well, to be more exact, effigies of the four-armed elephant god Ganesha quaffed milk in temples and homes around the world on a single day in 1995.

The day Ganesha drank milk was a curious one. It began with a man in Delhi claiming he had seen an idol of the deity drink a spoonful of milk in his neighbour's house. News of the miracle spread . . . first through the back-streets of Old Delhi, then across the capital, throughout India, and on. By dawn, Hindus across the known world were hurrying to feed cow's milk to their statues. Temples were mobbed by the pious, all clutching tablespoons of milk. Millions of Indians, from Calcutta to California, reported having witnessed the miracle themselves. By the end of the second day, Ganesha had had enough, he would drink no more.

Mad cow disease, milk miracles, and a tale of the vanishing hump: there was much to explain. But the militant lady at the cow shelter was in no mood for scientific deliberation. Thrusting her bird-like wrist up in the air, she ordered me to leave. I was unwelcome. My hands were stained with bovine blood.

*   *   *   *

I spent much of the afternoon ferreting about at the back of

Higginbotham's Bookshop on Anna Salai Road. Amid the racks of turgid textbooks and biographies on the first-floor, I came across a volume extolling the pleasures of lavatory seat collecting. I have a passing interest in obscure collections. A snippet which later began to obsess me was this: before President Nixon departed for China in 1972 on his ground-breaking journey of diplomacy, he sent a special covert team ahead. Presidential missions regularly necessitate such reconnaissance units. But the squad's job was not to search for concealed bugs in hotel rooms, or to make sure the red carpets weren't motheaten. Their brief was to double-check every lavatory seat to be used by the President. The book divulged a little-known fact – many Chinese loo seats are made from the poisonous *sumal* tree. When a tender Western posterior engages the wooden seat, an allergic reaction can occur.

Think of it. The President's bottom gets an embarrassing rash: what humiliation. One thing leads to another. The CIA is sent in to defame the Chinese Premier's own behind. Tit-for-tat expulsions from each other's embassies follow. Then massing of troops, the launching of spy planes, AWACS and extreme-depth submarines. Before you know it, someone's pressing the nuclear button. Armageddon, all because of a lavatory seat.

As I was deliberating how the Cold War might have been, I felt a tap on my shoulder. It was Bhalu. He was beaming expansively.

'OK, I've set it all up!' he announced, folding his arms.

'How did you find me here? What have you *set up*? Look, have a listen to this story about Nixon's Chinese trip . . .'

'We must leave right away,' maintained the Trickster.

'Where?'

'To Sri Gobind . . . he's waiting to see you.'

*　　*　　*　　*

The forecourt of the luminary's *ashram* was choked with even more devotees than before. Thousands had travelled across India merely to catch a glimpse of the man they revered as a deity. Others were in search of salvation. More still yearned to be healed: to cast away crutches or rid themselves of their white sticks, neck braces and bandages. Knotted together like a knitted quilt, they stood firm; an impassable barrier between us and the *ashram*.

'Bhalu,' I said, as we approached the crowds, 'look at them, we'll never get through!'

But the Trickster apprehended one of the guru's cronies and whispered something to him. Mysteriously, the concourse of infirm and fanatic acolytes parted down the middle, like butter carved with a heated knife. Calling for us to follow, the godman's henchman led the way into the compound.

The activity of a large *ashram* is quite bewildering. In some respects it's like a military encampment. Sentries are posted at the gates. Staff supervise the serving of meals, meditation sessions, seminars, and workshops. The place is a closed unit, run along strict, unwavering lines. Yet, in other respects a spiritual *ashram* couldn't be less like a battalion's camp. No one speaks in normal voices; they go about whispering. Neither do they frown, gloat, whinge, like real human beings. With bare feet and faces rapt with dreamy expressions, they list about like lotus-eaters.

Far too twisted to appreciate the compassionate atmosphere, my instinct was to escape. But the henchman beckoned us forward to a private apartment within the compound. As we snaked through corridors lit with yellow light, past offices where main-frame computers were crunching numbers, I questioned how Bhalu had gained us such easy access into the nerve centre of the cult. When I asked him what falsehood he had dreamt up, he grinned and pointed ahead.

A male secretary with a shaven scalp led us through a carpeted conference room, replete with a tortoiseshell-veneered table, into a modest-sized library. The walls were lined with dozens of exquisite volumes, most bound in turquoise leather with finely tooled spines. Mounted high on one wall was a pastel portrait of the *yogi*, his palms pressed together, his expression oozing meekness. Twin garlands of marigolds had been tied across the sketch. The secretary directed us to a chintz-covered sofa. Then he left.

I tugged the Trickster's shirt-tail as the aide tottered off to bring refreshments.

'What did you tell them, Bhalu?'

The boy had no time to reply. The door was swept back by a hulkish American bodyguard, who towered up like a *jinn*. Two young women scurried in, sprinkling pink rose petals on the carpet. Another girl followed closely behind, strumming her manicured nails across a lyre. Each was clothed in a simple pink-coloured cotton garment. After the maidens came the *avatar* himself, with the same airy expression as his admirers. Behind him, a dozen or so factotums, yes-men, secretaries, bearers and acolytes gambolled in. All of them – male and female – were

attired in orchid-pink raiments. By the time the entire entourage had
filed in, the library was close to capacity.

Amid the scent of rose petals and the mellifluous harping, the *swami*
paced over to where Bhalu and I were sitting.

His skin seemed to have a purply-brown glow; the unusual tinge
complemented a voluminous mantle of lavender silk in which the guru
was wrapped. A white polka-dot *tikka* was painted squarely on his
divine brow. I studied the features of his face. They were not unlike
those of Bhola Das, the indefatigable hangman of West Bengal.

Taking his time, the *sadhu* greeted us:

'Tahir Shah,' he said, cheerily, 'it is a great honour to meet you at
last.'

Perplexed at how the godman might have heard of me, I replied that
the honour was all mine. After all, it is not every day one meets a god.
The guru clustered the fingertips of his right hand together. With a
dextrous swivelling of the wrist, he had materialised something from
thin air. I raised an eyebrow. This was a sleight which Feroze had made
me practise feverishly. The godman pressed the object into the centre of
my palm. It was cold and hard. I looked down at the gift – a miniature
silver effigy of Ganesha.

I thanked Sri Gobind. Waving my praise aside, he flicked his fingers at
the entourage. He gave no direct instructions yet, like automata, they
each performed their own duty for a moment or two. The bodyguard
flexed his back; the rose-petal girls sprinkled; the lyre-player
strummed; the factotums ducked their heads sycophantically; the yes-
men agreed; the secretaries scribbled on shorthand pads; and the bearers
bore.

Gosh, I thought to myself, that's real power.

'You will stay with us for a few days, of course . . .' said the holy man.
'If there is anything you need, please ask for it. Tell my secretary where
to collect your belongings and they will be fetched.'

Bhalu twitched his fingers restlessly. The notion of having all his
wishes catered for was one which pleased him. No sooner had the
swami strolled away – preceded by the backward-walking sprinklers –
than Bhalu began a long, uncompromising list of requests.

Still bewildered as to why we were being given preferential
treatment, again I urged Bhalu to come clean. As before, he refused to
reveal the lies. Ignorant of the nature of our alibi, I resolved to make use
of the circumstances. I would study the sage's methods first-hand.

Three hours after our arrival, the *ashram*'s members entered the
central heart-shaped auditorium in single file. Most were barefoot; all

were dressed in the association's symbolic hue of orchid pink. The believers appeared to have come from many backgrounds, across the sub-continent. There were foreigners too. I heard them whispering in Japanese, French, Spanish, Arabic and Russian. Wherever they had come from was irrelevant now. Their allegiance to Sri Gobind transcended national boundaries. Each devotee wore a thin pinkish cotton band around the left wrist; a simple yet earnest token of their obeisance.

I scanned the assembly hall for Bhalu, who was absent. He was, no doubt, making use of the fraternity's mixed bathing pool. To the Trickster, the idea of naked rose-petal-sprinkling girls was far more intriguing than a public audience with a deity in human form.

Before the *swami* entered the hall, his disciples clasped hands, forming a single chain. In unison they chanted a short mantra, over and over. At first the verse was slow and distinct. But with each repetition it became a little more blurred by the acceleration of the delivery. To the words were added lurching, writhing movements of the torso. One by one, the followers broke the daisy chain of hands, veering off in their own directions, their bodies quivering. Some rocked their heads back and forth; others rubbed their hands lasciviously over their thighs. All seemed well practised in the obscure ritual. Like any group with its own traditions, they drew strength from what was alien to others, but central to themselves.

Again, the flower-sprinkling maidens heralded the arrival of the *yogi*'s retinue. As the first wilting petals touched the central dais, an ominous hush fell across the hall. The master was surrounded by those who worshipped him. Rather, he was above them, seated on a golden throne, up on the dais. Placated by the presence of their leader, the disciples' frantic expressions were calmed.

It was then, at that moment, that I understood the key aspects of the cult environment. Give people a symbol – whether an emblem, a movement of the hand, a secret word, a colour, or an amulet. Tell them to hand over all their worries, and place absolute trust in you. Better still, never actually say this, but imply it. Preach lessons which no one can fully understand. Exhort notions that contradict everything the followers have ever learned. Fill a hall with five hundred people; but don't let them forget that each communicates with the other through you. Without you, they are blind, deaf, and dumb. But, most importantly, prove your occult competence in real terms . . . through miracles.

Concoct the right blend of the mysterious, and the disciples will follow you anywhere. You can laugh, cry, rant, and rave; or merely sit for hours in silence. Hone that balance and you can do what you like: for the equilibrium of mystery has made you a god.

On that first evening, half a dozen Chinese businessmen were attending the *darshan*, the service. They had, I heard later, been dragooned into visiting the *ashram* by a local politician. Once he was comfortable on his golden throne, his hands stroking the panther-head arm rests, the *yogi* called out for the Chinese, and then for me, to join him on the dais. As visitors to the commune we stood out by the nature of our dress. Only the initiated were permitted to wear the orchid pink robes of the clan.

The Chinese and I scrambled up on to the platform, which was positioned at the acute end of the heart-shaped auditorium. I perched on a pink satin cushion to the left of the holy man, slightly further back than his throne.

When we were in position, the lyre player strummed a few chords, and as she did so, the followers prostrated themselves on the floor and prayed. Sitting on the stage, I understood how a guru feels when his acolytes pay homage. My instinct was to thrust up my arms and plead with them to stop. I would, I mused, not make a good godman.

Standing, the lyrist began to play again; this time she was accompanied by a *sitar* player. As the chamber filled with soft, soothing music, the *swami* began his oration. He spoke of love, of truth, hope and peace. His language was sugar-sweet like the messages on greeting cards which make you cringe. He rambled on about the merits of free love, invincible joy and faith. The Chinese sat stony-faced, staring at the cushions before them. Perhaps sensing that the concentration of his guests was waning, Sri Gobind began a series of superb miracles.

No explanation was given why the illusions were done at all. If this was a god standing before us, why should he need to prove his abilities? Nonetheless, in the most devoted disciple lies a kernel of doubt.

Circling his wrist three times, the *yogi* created *vibhuti*, as if from nowhere, and sprinkled it on the cupped palms of the Chinese executives and myself. Then, lifting his left hand up to his ear, he pulled out a shiny oval object. It was about three centimetres high and made from milk chocolate. It was an Easter egg. He handed it to me, telling me the egg was a symbol of new life and purity. The devotees applauded rabidly. Far more cynical than they, I checked the sell-by date. As I suspected, it was three months past due. The wedding-egg salesman had obviously found another outlet for his products.

When the Chinese had been presented with eggs, the godman moved on to the next illusion. He asked someone from the audience to come up and give him a coin. The smaller the value, the better, he said. A voluptuous Bavarian woman leapt to her feet and bounded up on to the stage. She presented the *pandit* with a ten-*paisa* coin. He held it up to the devotees, like an amateur magician would do at a child's party. The followers squirmed with delight. Chanting mantras and twisting about on the platform like a disco dancer in slow motion, the mystic fell into an impromptu trance. A moment later, the coin had vanished and reappeared. Touching it to his brow, Gobind returned it to the disciple. The Chinese narrowed their eyes. The devotees drew a deep breath. I craned my neck to scrutinise the guru's hands.

Suddenly, the German lady screamed that the coin was secreting ash. She had witnessed a miracle and wanted everyone to know it.

Back in Calcutta, Feroze had demonstrated the 'ash from coins' illusion on several occasions. He had mentioned that the routine was popular with Indian godmen.

The secret is very simple. A five-, ten- or twenty-*paisa* coin must be used. They are the only aluminium coins circulated in India. Distracting his acolytes by dancing around, the guru rubs the coin on a sponge concealed in a pocket of his robe. The sponge has been dipped in a saturated solution of mercuric chloride. When it comes into contact with the soft aluminium, a chemical reaction begins. After a moment or two on the warm palm of the follower, the aluminium metal sweats ash. Even if it's washed in water, it continues to give off heat and grey ash.

The Bavarian woman buzzed through the hall like a spinning top, showing off her ash-covered coin to anyone interested. Another handful of miniature Easter eggs were materialised and thrown to the audience to halt feelings of jealousy. Unlike the Chinese and I, who had scoffed our eggs, the followers clutched theirs reverentially, as if they were holding divine objects.

With another prolonged discourse at an end, the *yogi* called for a volunteer. Fifty devotees jumped to their feet, begging to be selected. Snapping his fingers at a short, rotund Indian, Sri Gobind instructed him to draw an image on a blank card. He did so, and the card was placed in an envelope. Sellotape was used to secure the pouch. The participant scrawled his signature across the seal. He handed it back to the guru. Staring at the cushioned floor of the dais, Gobind went into deep and introspective thought. Again, the auditorium fell silent. Could he reveal what had been written on the card without unsealing the envelope? The Chinese and I, who were hoping for another hand-out of

Easter eggs, were sceptical. The followers knew that another miracle was on the way.

As I had practised tricks under Feroze's guidance, I had recognised that without showmanship, even the most dazzling conjuring was two-dimensional. For the first time I was witnessing illusions being carried off before a large audience, by a formidable Thespian. The prosaic air of the Master's study had been replaced by a hall crammed full of believers.

Sri Gobind manipulated his spectators like a true professional. He moulded their emotions; feeding them with his magic. I sensed the expectation, then the surge of rapture as a second miracle was delivered. This was a performance which might have stirred even Feroze. Indeed, the more I considered it, the more I realised that the godman's conjury was very similar to that of my own teacher.

So while his devoted brethren twitched like wind-up toys, the showman did his stuff. When five or six minutes of chanting were at an end, the *yogi* announced the nature of the unseen symbol. The fanatic had drawn a Hand of Fatima. A potent sign, which appears in numerous religions, the Hand was a favoured emblem of the cult.

Tearing through the envelope, the godman displayed the card to the followers. It did indeed bear a large, crudely drawn Hand of Fatima.

The auditorium echoed to the sounds of crazed applause. A woman at the back of the hall began to rip at her locks ecstatically, screaming out her adoration. She pulled out two handfuls of thick mouse-coloured hair. The tall Anglo-Saxon man beside her was similarly awe-struck. Prostrating himself on the floor, he declared Sri Gobind to be 'the True God'. But he was preaching to the converted. Even the sceptical Chinese businessmen were now being swayed by the godman's magic.

I was the only unbeliever. From my position on the stage, I had scrutinised the miracle at close quarters. The meeting hall's shape – a heart – was obviously more than symbolic. The design, with the dais at the pointed end, ensured that no one could position himself behind Sri Gobind. From where I was sitting, on the sidelines, the second miracle had melted away into illusion. But even I, a hard-bitten sceptic, could not fail to applaud the mastery with which the *yogi* had performed.

With deft-handed artifice, he had furtively wiped the front of the envelope across one corner of his mantle. The fabric had probably been treated with ordinary lighter fluid. When the oil came in contact with the paper of the envelope, it turned it from opaque to transparent

– allowing the *pandit* to glimpse the symbol inside. A couple of minutes later, once the lighter fuel had evaporated, the paper was opaque again.

When the *darshan* was at an end, I searched out the Trickster. He had raided the cult's hospitality stores, and was stuffing all manner of booty into a pillowcase in his suite. Disposable Bic razors, shower caps, toothbrushes and sachets of *eau de toilette*: they represented loot of the most valuable kind. We had been invited to stay as honoured guests; and all he could do was steal from the host. Did he feel no shame? Bhalu, who was busy unhooking a shower curtain in the bathroom, told me he had no choice. Theft was in his blood.

By the next morning, the Trickster had filled eight pillowcases with booty. They were stacked like sandbags in his cupboard. Again, I rebuked my young companion. But to him, a thousand sachets of *eau de toilette* represented spoils gained on a subversive mission. The plunder would, I suspected, turn him into the premier trading magnate of the railways overnight.

As I hurried off to another public audience with Sri Gobind, Bhalu pondered how to convey his sacks from the compound unseen.

Like the audience hall, the *ashram* itself was constructed in a heart shape. For, as the guru said so often, everything we know and have is created from love . . . hot love. Five heart-shaped buildings formed the backbone of the compound. In their heart-shaped rooms devotees meditated and read, slept and ate. When not swimming in a heart-shaped pool, they were encouraged to explore the heart-shaped maze, or sit beneath the great heart-shaped water-clock to consider the *swami*'s teachings.

As I strolled over to the compound's heart-shaped auditorium, I noticed a number of modest stone shrines dotted about the paths. One could not help noticing them; for each one – about three feet high – had a follower sitting in meditation beside it. Rather than sheltering a miniature effigy, the shrines housed something far more precious: the hand-print of the *yogi*.

All godmen and godwomen are expected to be eccentric. The more worshipped and wealthy they are, the more outlandishly they are supposed to behave. Some religious leaders have drunk their own urine; others have advocated unthinkable sexual practices or have swanned about in fleets of Rolls-Royces. An anthropologist friend once suggested to me that godmen are like politicians. Articulate and well-dressed, they travel first-class, invent new rules, amass great fortunes at the public's expense and, given half a chance, cavort about with licentious abandon.

When it came to divine eccentricity, Sri Gobind was no exception. His followers took great pride in the tales of their teacher's irregularities. Every so often, gripped by an insatiable desire, the guru would jump naked from his bed. Running into the heart-shaped gardens, he would relieve himself in the bushes. Or, in the middle of an address, he had been known to rip off all his clothes and anoint his flabby belly with buffalo-milk butter. Each morning, his fans averred, the holy man would douse himself in a bath of potassium permanganate. The immersion gave his skin its exotic purply-brown tinge. He would dress his hair with a pomade of seasoned egg whites; dab his earlobes with witch hazel; and spray his nether regions with his own blend of catnip cologne.

Several hundred followers, with frozen lotus-eater smiles, were loitering at the heart-shaped meeting hall by the time I arrived. As well as the hard-core devotees, hundreds of others turned up to be cured and blessed. The sick and ailing, each rapt with expectant hope, reminded me of the psychic healer in the Calcutta marshes. But here, in Madras, the stakes were far higher. Sri Gobind was no two-bit village prestidigitator: he was the helmsman of an immense money-making operation.

Like some sublime ruler, he didn't travel in search of partisans; he waited for them to attend him. And they came in their droves, prostrating themselves at his feet. Politicians and scholars, Hollywood actors, ageing hippies, and ordinary folk, they embraced Sri Gobind with equal zest, bringing him all their woes. Questions of religious identity, marriage problems, financial difficulties, or relief from illness: nothing was beyond the expertise of their lord.

With the sun high above the heart-shaped theatre, packed with pilgrims and adherents, the faint whisper of a hand rasping at a lyre's strings hinted that the godman's retinue was approaching.

First came the pink petal girls; then the stooping factotums; the amiable yes-men and nodders followed; and on their heels hastened the farrago of secretaries, bearers and bodyguards, *punkhawallas* and bandsmen. At the centre of the multitude, cooled by a dozen heart-shaped fans, was the *yogi* himself.

The retinue advanced to the dais. As the mystic stepped up on to the platform, the first marvel occurred. Two banks of red tulips – in tubs either side of the stage – bowed their heads in honour of the omnipotent god. The effect of this feat was awesome. A woman with turquoise nail varnish threw her arms in the air and exclaimed her devotion. A contingent of Uruguayan beatniks gaped wide-eyed at the miracle. Unable to contain himself, an old Punjabi scrambled on to the podium, crawled over to the godman, and began to lick his feet. The *jinn*-like henchman grabbed the ancient by the neck and flung him into the crowd.

Feroze had demonstrated the 'flowers bow down' routine in the laboratory. A concealed jet sprays chloroform over the blooms. Like humans, they are susceptible to anaesthesia, and quickly droop.

As before, Sri Gobind beckoned for me to join him on the dais. Once on the stage, I greeted him. He looked me in the eye and wished me boundless hot love. Returning the remark anxiously, I noticed that the godman's eyes had changed colour overnight. The day before, they had been a dusty brown. Now they had mutated to a deep shade of royal purple. The tint complemented the guru's lavender shot-silk robes rather well. I glanced down at the spectators. They seemed blasé at their deity's astonishing eye colour. What significance is a spontaneous change of eye colour to an immortal capable of far greater feats? I had heard of another godman who would tour Indian villages wearing mirror-like contact lenses. Who would doubt that a man with reflective eyes was not a deity?

Every Thursday, Sri Gobind treated the ill and dying. Those who could walk would congregate at one side of the dais. Others, too sick to stand, would be lined up on the stage on stretchers. That day about eighty patients had been admitted to the *ashram* to be healed. None would be charged for the treatment, which was laid on more as a public-relations exercise than an organised clinic. In any case, I suspected Sri Gobind had little need to accept petty fees from the infirm: his coffers must already have been brimming over with donations from his disciples.

Before the healing could commence, the *yogi* performed a selection of miracles to put the ailing at ease and to titillate the audience.

First, he materialised *vibhuti* and sprinkled it into the palms of the infirm. Then he pulled a gold bracelet from nowhere and offered it to the wife of a wealthy businessman. She had come to have her angina treated. As the guru moved to his next miracle, four large church candles at each corner of the dais lit themselves spontaneously. Sri Gobind said it was hot love, not he, which had ignited their wicks. I knew differently. Feroze had taught me the trick. The wicks are dipped in a solution of white phosphorous, mixed with carbon disulphide. When the solvent has evaporated, the wick catches light.

The last miracle was the most intriguing. Although certain that it was achieved by illusion, I couldn't see how the deception was done. A rusty tin chest – the size of a school tuck box – was carried to the centre of the dais by the *swami*. The box appeared light enough. It was filled with heart-shaped sweets, which were distributed to the infirm. Once in position, the purple-eyed godman invited members of the congregation to lift it up and carry it away. Twenty impatient fanatics scrabbled up and tried their luck. None could wrest the tin tuck box from the floor. Warning his devotees that only true hot love could provide real strength, Gobind went over to the box and raised it effortlessly above his head.

Over the next three hours, Sri Gobind cured one patient after the next. Cancer, emphysema, angina, intestinal haemorrhaging, and tuberculosis: all were assuaged without medicine or surgery. Such methods, the guru insisted, were the tools of quacks. He merely waved half a coconut over the head of each patient. An assistant followed, tying a pink cotton band around the left ankle of those who had been treated. The string was, they were told, an amulet. It would protect them as they recuperated from the *avatar*'s therapy.

Early that evening, when the disciples and pilgrims had hurried away to frolic in the heart-shaped pool, I returned to the heart-shaped auditorium and examined the dais. First, I noticed a series of inconspicuous nozzles located where the tulips had stood, presumably used to spray the chloroform mist. On the left side of the stage was a trap door. Making sure no one was watching, I prised it open and climbed down into the chamber beneath. Enough daylight was filtering through the cracks between the floorboards of the stage to provide illumination. In the middle of the room stood an electrical contraption, the top of which was connected to a sheet of metal on the dais. The device was wired up to the electricity mains, and consisted of two magnets, cables and some wire coils. The metal chest must have been held to the floor using this, a crudely made electromagnet. When the *yogi* had wanted to pick up the box, a lackey had obviously switched off the power supply, disabling the magnet.

Unlike the small-time godman working in an Indian village, Sri Gobind had a fully developed magician's stage at his disposal. The facilities permitted complex illusions to be carried off faultlessly. However tempted I was to condemn such illusionists – who pretended their tricks were miracles – I had to admit it: this was impressive stuff.

*

Later that night I told Bhalu what I had found. He was more interested in recounting his own exploits than listening to the details of my investigation. While I had been scrutinising miracles, he had smuggled his pillowcase sacks out of the *ashram* in a workman's truck. The loot was now stashed in the bushes behind the compound. He pleaded with me to take flight while the going was good.

Reluctantly, I scrawled a simple letter to the *swami*, thanking him for his hospitality and blessings of hot love. There was no point in disturbing him again. More importantly, I was unsure whether the cult had discovered that their toiletry supplies had been plundered. Handing the note to the sentry at the main gate, we slipped from the *ashram* before dawn the next morning.

Despite arriving at Chennai Central Station before breakfast, the first express to Bangalore wasn't due to leave until 1330 hours. The seven hours of waiting were spent taking it in turns to protect the pillowcases. When train 6023 arrived we struggled aboard with the swag. Once we were aboard, I secured a window seat for myself. In the luggage racks above me were lodged eight pillowcases of booty. Promenading up and down the aisle, proud as a bulldog, was Bhalu. The usual fraternity of salesmen, with their potato-peelers and pinking shears, had shied away. None could compete with the Trickster. After all, who would buy a potato-peeler when they could spend their savings on a sachet or two of cut-price Givenchy aftershave?

Shortly before midnight, the express screeched into Bangalore City Station. Virtually every descending passenger had an assortment of newly acquired goodies tucked away. Hand-towels and shower caps, talcum powder and tiny sewing kits, shoe horns and sun block, moisturiser and French perfume: none had resisted Bhalu's tantalising sales pitch. Stuffing a fortune in coins and paper money into another pillowcase, the Trickster grinned his Charlie Chaplin grin. Even he had never known a sale quite like it.

20

The Penniless Billionaire

Bhalu, who had not owned many belongings before, was fast learning the drawbacks that assets bring. Travelling with the pillowcase sacks of valuable cargo was a nightmare. For the first time, he had become paranoid about falling victim to thieves. For this reason – and the late time of our arrival – he talked me into staying at the Bangalore City Station's retiring rooms.

All next day, the Trickster sat in the railway suite, crooning over his hoard. I invited him to accompany me to see the town. He sniffed at the idea. Why would someone who had just cornered the miniature soap market want to go sight-seeing?

Bangalore has been described as the Silicon Valley of India. Much of the world's cutting-edge computer software is written in air-conditioned bunkers around town. News magazines are always pointing to the foreign companies relocating to Bangalore in droves. Stirring as this was, I had come in search of the city's more archaic sights. First on my list was the Bull Temple on the south-western corner of Bangalore, at Basavanagudi. Its grey granite statue of Nandi, Shiva's bull, was rumoured to be growing in size.

I made my way south from the station down Bhashyam Road, and on towards the southern extremity of town. It was a stifling day. Before I knew it, sweat was pouring from my brow and I was feeling faint. Better get some pills, I thought. So I meandered into the Gandhi Bazaar area in search of a pharmacy.

Sandwiched between a video rental shop and a cloth merchant's, I found an impressive-looking chemist's shop. A flight of steps led up to the door. I ascended and entered. The emporium was like the den of corsairs who had knocked off a hospital ship. Medical equipment was piled up in stacks. Stretchers, wheelchairs, and irrigation syringes; drip-stands, forceps, and clamps. With such an impressive inventory of medical accessories, I could only imagine what the pharmaceuticals were like. I hurried over to the sales desk. Before I put in my order, the chemist slapped a kilo tin of potassium permanganate crystals down on the counter.

'This is it,' he said.

'No, you misunderstand . . . I'd like some pills, please.'

'Only having potassium permanganate.'

The shop-keeper, who stank of liquor, waved his arm in a grand arc across the display cabinets behind him. They were filled top to bottom with identical tins of potassium permanganate.

'I see, you're a specialist shop, are you?'

The chemist grunted, swaying back and forth on the balls of his feet. An open bottle of Mohgul Monarch whisky on the counter hinted at how he had spent the morning.

The thought of a potassium permanganate bath was, for some inexplicable reason, suddenly very tempting. After all, Sri Gobind appeared to favour it greatly. Why not follow his example? Or that of my own paternal grandfather, Sirdar Ikbal Ali Shah. Like the Madrasi godman, my grandfather had been very keen on potassium permanganate. He used it to kill germs in the food, a habit which began when he was living with the Bedouin in the 1930s. Everything he ate was washed liberally in potassium permanganate which, he said, cleaned out his digestive tract as well as disinfecting food. Whatever he ate – from chicken to strawberries – was dyed sludgy brown.

The chemist had begun to wrap the tin in newspaper. His movements were extremely disjointed.

'Are you drunk?' I enquired.

'No, *Sahib*, not dlunk.'

'By the way, how much is it?'

'How much what?'

I pointed to the wrapped tin.

'Two hundred twenty rupees,' the shop-keeper slurred.

'That's an awful lot. Can't I get a discount?'

The chemist shook his head violently from side to side in a savage sweeping motion. Then he threw up over the counter. The sudden swivelling movement had been too jarring.

'Yuk! Why did you do that?'

'Sorry, *Sahib*,' wheezed the shop-keeper, 'feeling not well.'

'Why don't you take some medicine?'

Again, the chemist shook his head.

'Indian medicine rubbish,' he said. 'No working. Potassium perman-ganate good.'

'You've got the wrong attitude,' I retorted, dabbing at the residue of half-digested egg which had splattered on to my shirt. 'I happen to be a great fan of Indian potions and pills . . . actually, I can't resist them. That's my trouble!'

I pulled a few crumpled notes from my pocket and held them out in front of me.

'Look, I haven't got a lot of cash,' I said. 'Bit impoverished . . . you know.'

Mopping a splash of vomit from my purchase, the pharmacist let out a great hoot of laughter.

'Not like Krishnan!' he cackled.

I didn't understand what he had meant.

'Who's Krishnan?'

The pharmacist stared at me bleary-eyed and disbelieving.

'Richest man in world,' he said.

'*Really?* Where does he live?'

'Round the corner, Bugle Rock Lane.'

'Are you sure?'

'Why not?' said the chemist. 'Everyone's knowing him round here.'

If I were the richest man in the world, I would move into a cliff-top palace in Monte Carlo, or to a tropical island paradise in the Caribbean. For this reason I found it odd that the world's wealthiest tycoon should live in a secluded lane in Bangalore.

The pharmacist passed me the telephone directory. I flicked to 'K' and scanned the columns.

'There it is . . . *Krishnan, B* . . . Bugle Rock Lane . . .'

'Are you sure he's got more money than anyone else?' I quizzed as I dialled the number.

'Of course not,' riposted the pharmacist, taking a swig of his whisky. 'Krishnan is having no money at all!'

Feroze had once said that riches and deception always go hand in hand. Where you find one, you're sure to find the other. So, praising Mr Krishnan's legendary philanthropy, I strained to arrange a rendezvous.

Thirty minutes later, I found myself sitting straight-backed and correct at a secret location in central Bangalore. My clothing stank of the chemist's alcohol-pickled vomit. My shoes were disintegrating, and my hair needed cutting. I was in no state to meet the wealthiest man in the world. What if he had intended to fly me to his desert castle for dinner? The private jet might be refuelling at that very moment. My eyes glazed over at the thought of wealth beyond my wildest dreams. Then Mr Krishnan arrived.

Taking both his hands in mine, bowing acutely, I greeted him with dutiful respect. Such veneration seemed appropriate. After all, the rest of my life might hinge on the meeting; and first impressions are rarely revised. Krishnan waved me to a seat and sat back. He was a short man, about five feet four. His face, although engaging, bore many wrinkles – no doubt gained through weighty responsibilities. And his attire was decidedly modest. Indeed, it was almost as shabby as mine. He was wrapped in a ragged beige blanket. On his feet were carpet slippers. This man, I puzzled to myself, is so rich he can dress as he likes. He doesn't have to impress people. To act like this, he really must be as rich as the rumours say.

Sipping a glass of sweet mint tea, Mr B. Krishnan swept back his silvery hair in his hands and told the extraordinary tale of how he became the richest man on Earth.

The son of a penniless farmer, he was born a little over sixty years ago into an impoverished village family on the outskirts of Bangalore. Determined to seek fame and fortune, he fled the countryside in his youth, adamant that he would carve out a career for himself in the big city.

'My ancestors were direct descendants of the ancient Vijayanagaram kings,' Krishnan began, in slow and precise English. 'Our family was once in the ruling class. Heirlooms were passed down from one generation to the next. Seemingly worthless objects, but nonetheless each was worshipped by our family for centuries.'

The old tycoon paused to wipe his mouth with his hand.

'A special room was set aside in the farmhouse,' he said, continuing with the story. 'Inside was a variety of icons, idols and other objects. My father used to worship those things in the ceremony room. Amongst the items there were four odd-shaped black lumps. On all auspicious occasions they would be taken down and worshipped with great reverence.'

Krishnan explained how one generation after the next performed rituals in respect of the mysterious black lumps.

'Nobody knew exactly what they were,' expounded the billionaire, with a glint of excitement in his eye. 'All that was known was the lumps were very special. They were always protected and worshipped.'

The years passed. Krishnan went off to Bangalore, where he began his career as a legal advocate. He moved into a tiny apartment. He married, had four children and, after thirty-two years of practice, retired due to ill health. His life, which had been very ordinary, in no way prepared him for the events that were to come.

Krishnan had never been a religious man. But when his parents and the other children of his generation had died, he inherited the room filled with icons, objects, and the four black lumps. He was far too busy and impatient to perform the *pujas* necessary to keep the gods content. Instead, he shut the heirlooms up in a cupboard and forgot about them.

'My wife used to nag me for locking the relics away,' moaned Krishnan. 'She has always been much more religious than I. So, to please her, I agreed we would donate the artefacts and the four lumps to the temple of Nanjundeswara, at Nanjangud, south-west of Bangalore.'

At the temple, Krishnan was met with endless forms and bureaucracy.

'Being an advocate,' he said authoritatively, 'I knew how to make an application, and that getting through all the red tape was not worthwhile. I had no intention of getting permission from the High Commissioner just to donate some old heirlooms.'

So Krishnan took his family back to Bangalore. On the way his wife pestered him again. She feared ill fortune would prevail if the objects were not worshipped at all. But Krishnan, whose mind had set to work, had other plans.

'As we made our way home,' he carried on, staring at me without moving, 'it struck me that the black lumps were very heavy. Perhaps, I thought, they might contain gold. Even if there was a trace of gold, it could be extracted . . . and I would make some money. When I told my wife, she was horrified at the idea of desecrating the sacred objects. She pressured me not to melt down the lumps or change their shape.'

The thought of the gold nagged at Krishnan's conscience. He tried to forget about it, but was unable to do so. Everything reminded him of the possible ore, the gold, the instant wealth. So one night Krishnan sent his wife and daughters off to the cinema. Then he set to work.

'I embarked on an investigation,' he began softly, speaking in formal English. 'There was a thick black crust of soot and grime covering the lumps. I took an old toothbrush and a bar of soap and began to wash. At first, I assumed I was washing metal. The dirt was so hard that only some came away. After a lot of cleaning with the toothbrush, I held the lumps up to the light. In one I could see specks of red, and in another blue specks. It was then I realised these were not metal, but minerals, and that they might be very valuable indeed.'

For months Krishnan kept his discovery secret. He immersed himself in the study of gemstones from books and articles borrowed from Bangalore's public library. He was dogged by worries that news of his find would leak out. No one could be trusted with the secret.

'I thought,' he went on, 'if I took them to a jeweller, I might be hoodwinked and misguided. Such people might try to work for their own benefit. So I studied the gemological sciences for a year or two.'

Gradually the retired advocate learned the experiments necessary to identify a precious gemstone. In the seclusion of his book-lined chamber, he performed the vital tests. At last he could pronounce with certainty the minerals' true identities.

Three of the stones were enormous rose-coloured double-star rubies; the fourth was a colossal sapphire.

How did four of the world's biggest gemstones end up in Krishnan's cupboard in the first place? They may have been passed down through generations, from his ancestors – the Vijayanagaram kings. For safe keeping, the gems could have been dyed black, then covered in soot and dirt. Over time, members of the family may have forgotten exactly what they were, remembering only that they were important religious artefacts.

Krishnan's discovery filled him with fear for his safety. Constant anxiety, long hours of gemological study, not to mention his diabetic condition, hampered his health. But still he could confide his great secret to no one. Having read a little about the art of lapidary, the advocate bought a hand-driven grinding wheel. One evening, in the darkened study at his home, he set to work with the grinder to remove the top portions of the stones himself.

For months, Krishnan continued to maintain his secrecy. He would attend to his chores by day, and study gemology by night. One by one, he had the three rubies and the sapphire cut by a trusted professional. Over the next months and years, he announced their existence to the world.

All the gems were cut in India. Krishnan himself admitted regret at rushing into having them cut. His knowledge, about how some of the biggest and most priceless gems in the world should be faceted was very limited indeed.

Krishnan amazed the gemological world by first producing a colossal ruby of 215 carats. A second great ruby was the next to be put on show.

It weighed 650 carats: having been cut from the original stone of 1,125 carats.

For two more years Krishnan kept silent. Then, quite unexpectedly, he announced his ownership of a ruby of truly phenomenal proportions. It weighed 2,475 carats when fully cut.

'It's about the size of a tennis ball,' mumbled Krishnan, draining his cup of tea.

Had the heirlooms been a few gold coins, or even a hoard of smaller gems, the ageing advocate would have found it far easier to cash in his fortune. Rubies and sapphires the size of tennis balls are worth a lot of money. So much money that no one on Earth can afford them. For starters, calculating their value is no easy matter.

Krishnan used the rule of the celebrated French traveller and jeweller Jean-Baptiste Tavernier to estimate the value of his gems. Tavernier said that the value of a precious stone is directly proportional to the square of its weight. So, if one carat of a ruby is worth £2,000, the value of Krishnan's largest ruby would be £2,000 x 2,475 x 2,475 – more than £12 billion. Krishnan said that the rarity value of the stone would double its price, to about £24 billion.

But Krishnan's treasure did not stop with rubies. His collection was also home to one of the greatest sapphires in existence. Weighing 1,370 carats, according to Krishnan, it was worth up to £3 billion.

'They say I am the richest man in the world!' he exclaimed, counting the billions on his fingers. 'Next comes the Sultan of Brunei, Bill Gates, and others. These people have money, so let them come forward and buy my gemstones!'

B. Krishnan, the billionaire who lives in a rented flat for about one hundred and fifty rupees a month, was willing to sell his gems off at bargain-basement prices. He needed the money. His daughters were soon to be married, but the solicitor-turned-penniless-tycoon, was worrying about their dowries. 'A wedding in India is very expensive these days,' he grumbled. 'It costs good money – money which I don't have.'

One morning the press got word of the advocate's priceless gems. Only then did his obsession with *The Guinness Book of Records* begin. It's an obsession which seems to grip many Indians. After months of correspondence he gained an entry into the columns of the hallowed book. Nothing could have made him happier. Indeed, he appeared more interested in his Guinness record than in the actual value of the gems.

Krishnan was a confused man. Sick of poverty, of the threatening telephone calls, and worrying about the safety of his family, he was trapped in a no-win situation. He could cut up the gems into smaller and more affordable sizes: but then his most prized possession – the Guinness entry – would be lost.

He had begun to wonder whether the gems were a divine test. The tale smacked of irony. It was a resolute disbelief in the divine which helped Krishnan unveil the gems in the first place.

His conversation was peppered with references to God and supernatural energy. But Krishnan had good reason to believe in angelic powers. A strange incident many years ago had returned to haunt him.

'When I was a young man,' he recalled, 'I was once taken by a friend to a famous astrologer. The man read my future and told me that all mundane things in my life would fail. He asked me to pick a card inscribed in Sanskrit.

'It was written that solar power is dominant in me. Rubies are associated with solar power. The fortune-teller told me that this solar power would bring me fame and fortune. Before I went away, he prophesied that in my late fifties I would become famous and extremely wealthy.'

So where was this billion-dollar fortune of gems? Perhaps they didn't exist – was that the deception? Krishnan side-stepped all questions of their whereabouts.

'They are locked away in bank vaults, but even I am not knowing where they are right now,' he disclosed, pulling out a couple of scratched transparencies of his treasure. 'Look at that!' he croaked. 'They are the rarest of the rare gemological phenomena! What a great thing I have achieved!'

Shaking his head slowly to and fro, Mr Krishnan got up and shuffled away in his bedroom slippers. His wife would be waiting. Under one arm was clutched his bible: *The Guinness Book of Records*. In his hand nestled the two blurred slides of the hoard which had brought so many worries.

'Oh, by the way,' he called back as he left, 'do you know anyone who could afford my gems? Please bring buyers to me. If they are serious I could take them to see the stones. We could negotiate on the price.'

21

Take One Live Murrel Fish . . .

For fifteen hours the Trickster brooded over how he might relieve Mr Krishnan of his hoard of gems. He considered it criminal that such wealth should have fallen to a man with so little foresight.

We were aboard a bus, heading north towards Hyderabad. Bhalu, whose sacks had been strapped to the roof of the vehicle, was busy scheming.

'I'm going to dress up as a buyer, and then you're going to take me to Krishnan . . . then I'll snatch the gems,' he explained, plotting aloud.

'You're going to do no such thing! Besides, you're only twelve years old. He'd never take you as a serious buyer.'

To the Trickster, the idea of becoming a gentleman gem thief was very appealing. I told him about Raffles, the infamous aristocratic jewel robber. He liked the sound of it very much. While the world scorned a Calcutta-born pickpocket, they would surely fall at the feet of a thief with breeding. Imagine the perks of such a profession . . . the fine clothes, the opulent estates, and, most importantly, the bawdy women of the court. For Bhalu, the dream was an easy one to picture. But then, Raffles had been at least twice his age. And in any case, Bhalu was no gentleman.

By the time the bus entered Kurnool, on the banks of the Tungabhadra River, it was extremely late. Taking charge, Bhalu clicked his fingers twice. A clapped-out rickshaw appeared from nowhere. Loading the filthy pillowcase sacks aboard, like bags of coal on to a tender, we clambered up. Bhalu exchanged a few words of Telugu with the driver. The boy never ceased to surprise me. He had an unrivalled gift for languages. Lowering his head as if he were an accomplice in some vile misdemeanour, the driver revved his vehicle and sped away.

Rather than heading towards the city centre, the rickshaw slalomed down dim back-streets. One dark, rat-infested alleyway led to another. With each turn the streets became dingier and more deserted. As if taking care to select the dirtiest building in the most abhorrent corner of the suburbs, the driver brought his vehicle to a halt. We unloaded the booty, the *rickshawalla* explained what seemed to be directions, then careered away.

'Bhalu,' I whispered, 'I don't think the driver understood your instructions. This is the most ghastly, forsaken place I've ever been. It's even worse than Hotel Bliss in Delhi.'

'Relax,' replied the Trickster, motioning for me to be silent. 'He understood exactly what I meant.'

'Are we at a hotel?'

'Well, it's a sort of hotel,' he murmured.

We staggered ahead under the weight of the three remaining pillow-cases of loot, and my own more modest luggage. Bhalu led the way round to the back of the building. The path which encircled the ramshackle squat of a building stank of ripe urine. Although I had seen no other patrons making for the hotel, the trail was remarkably well trodden. It was so late that everyone must already have been inside, tucked up for the night.

Once at the back of the inn, Bhalu fumbled around in the darkness. He found a Fanta bottle on the ground.

'What's going on?' I griped impatiently. 'Let's just knock.'

'Do you have a coin?'

'Is it for a tip?'

'Just give me a coin, any coin.'

I handed over a one-rupee coin. Bhalu zipped its edge across the grooves in the bottle. A whirring sound was created.

Then a queer thing happened.

A sizeable trapdoor, leading to a cellar beneath the building, was opened from within. A young man ushered us down. The bottle and coin had been the hotel's doorbell. But as my eyes adjusted to the candlelight of the subterranean chamber, I realised that this was no hotel. And what I had taken for a bell was actually a password.

The cavern was very big. Its brick walls were dappled with damp rot; its ceiling was low and caked in soot from the candles. Sixty or so men sat about. Some were moving bottle tops across home-made chequer boards; others merely sat in silence, staring at the array of candles.

The Trickster led me to a pair of old car seats at one end of the underground saloon. My lungs filled with the cavern's intoxicating smell. I shook Bhalu by the arm, suggesting we ought to leave and find a proper place to spend the night. But the Trickster took no notice. He was delighted with the surroundings. As he coaxed me to relax, a tall figure swanned over and clinked two glasses of fluorescent green liquid down in front of us.

It was impossible to avoid breathing in the asphyxiating vapour which was rising from the surface of the brew like mist from a peat bog. My eyes began to water, and I felt an asthmatic attack coming on.

'What's going on, Bhalu? I want a hot bath and a filling meal. These people shouldn't be serving alcohol; don't they realise Andhra Pradesh is dry?'*

Bhalu drained his glass in one; then he drank mine.

'This is good stuff,' he coughed, motioning to the waiter for another round.

'I can't believe you're drinking in a dry state.'

'Well, what do you expect?' said the scam-artist. 'This is a chat-slowly.'

'You mean speakeasy.'

In the movies, the American Prohibition always seemed like such a convivial time. Granted, there were plenty of mobsters massacring each other, but everyone else in the old films was having a ball. American speakeasies were wild with ambience. There was always an old bar-back playing ragtime on the piano, damsels dancing, cigar-smoking croupiers, roulette wheels, fancy cocktails, crystal chandeliers, and a genteel clientele with slicked-back, centre-parted hair.

I scanned the cellar. No one was smoking Havana cigars. There was no piano, no chorus line, no croupiers, no cut-glass light-fittings, and no cocktails.

An elderly, cultivated man with almond eyes and fair skin, pulled up a chair and joined us. He leant over and put his arm round Bhalu.

'One taste of this drink and you have an unquenchable thirst!' he said.

The Trickster hissed incorrigibly.

'But drink is illegal in Andhra Pradesh, so everyone here's breaking the law,' I said righteously.

'My friend,' responded the old man, gulping his glass of rotgut as if it were orange squash, 'this liquid is medicine . . . medicine for the soul.'

'Then why does it destroy the body?'

*Shortly after our visit to Andhra Pradesh, the state government lifted the Prohibition order.

The man gave me a cold look.

'I can't help it,' he announced stolidly, 'if elixir for the soul is poison for the flesh.'

As another round of moonshine was dished out by the waiter, Bhalu's drinking partner introduced himself. He was a Christian businessman named A.B. Robert. I asked him what line of business he was in. Swirling the gritty, glowing liquid around his glass, he held it up as if ready to make a toast.

'I'm in this,' he snorted.

'You make moonshine?'

'Make it, supply it, own places which sell it . . .'

'But what about the police?'

A.B. Robert shrugged his shoulders.

'Yes, the police love it,' he said, smirking. 'The problem's the women.'

'Women police?'

'No,' sighed the old man. 'I told you, the police aren't a problem: it's the wives who give us trouble. They thought their husbands would give up drinking when Prohibition came. But the men love this – it's much stronger than the usual stuff.'

'But how exactly do the wives give you trouble?'

Again, A.B. sighed.

'They break all our bottles,' he said. 'They burn down our warehouses and smash our stills. They've become very violent. We tell husbands not to overdo it – but they won't listen. Of course they're going to die if they drink too much. This is strong stuff!'

'What about the people who find your *chullu* too strong?'

'Yes, some don't have the stomach for it,' said A.B. Robert. 'That's why we give them something special.'

'Soft drinks?'

'No . . . not soft drinks!' barked the businessman.

He stared at me acerbically. To him, the thought of a beverage devoid of alcohol was sacrilege. 'Not soft drinks!' he repeated.

'Then what?'

'*Cocktails* . . . we give cocktails to the weak ones.'

Cocktails – it sounded very sophisticated. I pictured a frozen daiquiri with a sliver of lime. A.B. called instructions to the bartender, who presented me with a delicate brown bottle. It was wrapped in a grimy cloth and contained a sludge-brown liquid, which smelt faintly of mint.

'It's a refreshing, smooth little cocktail made locally,' elucidated the liquor magnate.

I peeled away the knotted rag to inspect the orange and white label.

The word MUKUF was written in bold lettering. Beneath that was more writing: 'Herbal Cough Syrup. Take Two Teaspoonfuls Three Times Daily.'

*   *   *   *

Despite my experiences, it was still as an innocent that I arrived dishevelled and gasping for breath at the great Mughal stronghold of Hyderabad. By the time we alighted from the wicked country bus, it was late afternoon. Eight hours of rush-hour traffic had turned the air charcoal grey with diesel fumes. My asthma was now so acute that every breath was a strain. I was panting like a wolf after the kill. I had longed to explore the secret corners of the city; to track down Thesiger's beloved Rock Castle Hotel; to trek out to Golconda Fort. But far more pressing matters first demanded my attention.

Bhalu hailed an auto-rickshaw and commanded the driver to hurry to the Old City. He agreed that in my deteriorating condition, the Gowd brothers' miracle asthma cure might be my only hope. Not once had the Trickster shown impatience with my constant infirmity. A childhood spent on the hidden back-streets of Calcutta had ensured that his was a cast-iron constitution. His own lungs were hardy as a blacksmith's bellows; his stomach was robust as granite; and his stamina was unflagging. My handicaps were the product of the familiar luxuries of our world: central heating, sterilised foods and regular doses of antibiotics.

Even though I was aware of the approximate date of the asthma cure, and the name of its guardian family, I knew nothing more. In any other country the distinct lack of key information would have been a setback. Yet in India, only the barest nugget – in this case, a single sentence from Gokul – is usually enough to go on.

The rickshaw skidded to a halt beside the gateway of Charminar: the four spectacular minarets which loom up, marking the centre of the Old City. Bhalu directed the driver to take us to the Gowds' house.

'We want the cure for asthma,' I explained.

The driver bit his lower lip.

'Fish medicine?' he groaned.

'No, *asthma* cure.'

'*Haa*, fish medicine asthma cure.'

Gokul had never said anything about fish. I've never been one for seafood. The manservant, who was aware of this, had obviously overlooked the fact deliberately.

Before I had time to protest, the rickshaw had veered right, down into the labyrinth of back-streets east of the Charminar monument. A cluster of women veiled in black were haggling for glass bangles on low-set stalls; another knot of wives were wrangling for melons, guava and grapes, piled high like trophies of war. A group of elderly gentlemen were standing in an arched doorway, bemoaning married life; beside them, a goat was gazing affectionately at his owner, a butcher, oblivious to its fate. Everywhere children ran through the dirt pulling kites and hoops and home-made toys on strings. As we ventured on at break-neck pace, down one passage after the next, the secret lanes of the Old City revealed themselves. Then we turned into Dood Bholi, the street where the Gowd brothers lived.

As we turned the corner, the *rickshawalla* slammed on the brakes and emitted a demonic shriek. Never one to show surprise, Bhalu also released a piercing cry of terror. Unlike the others, I made no sound. The shock had turned me dumb.

Before us lay an ocean of people. Tens of thousands of them, packed together like grains of salt in a sack. Every inch of cobblestone was thick with feet. Arms thrashed upwards, as the strong trampled the infirm down into the quagmire of mud. People everywhere jostled like bees around their queen. All were gasping for breath; gripped by an ecstasy of hyperventilation. All knew their objective – to reach a mottled cloisonné-blue door, which led to a tiny whitewashed home at the centre of the lane.

There was no question of the date . . . and we had certainly come to the right place. I sent Bhalu to gather background information for a preliminary report. He returned with the gossip, which read like a ticker-tape bulletin: the treatment would begin the next day, with the first sighting of the Margashirsa Karthe star. Special trains, buses and flights had been laid on to ferry people to Hyderabad from the furthest reaches of India. More than half a million people had already turned up. Many had staked their life savings to make the journey. Others were arriving with their entire families for the expedition of a lifetime. In a rare show of solidarity, Muslims, Buddhists, Jains, and Hindus, from every caste, were gathering at the Gowds' house. Every hotel and guest house in town was full to bursting. Mosques and temples, wayside cafés, bus depots, and railway stations were cluttered with panting asthmatics from far and wide.

I indicated to the Trickster that a little queue-barging would be in order. When on a journey of observation, one is occasionally required to get straight to the point. We climbed up on to a roof at one end of the lane and, scurrying on our hands and knees, made a beeline for the Gowds' refuge.

Harinath Gowd was sitting in the courtyard of the family home, casting an uneasy eye at the main entrance. The battered blue door bent inwards as the half-million-strong crowd pressed against the other side. The Old City's narrow streets were clogged with asthmatics for miles around. Second eldest of the five brothers, Harinath greeted us cordially, without questioning why we had leapt into his house from the roof.

He was busy attending to last-minute arrangements. Two hundred kilos of a magical paste had been prepared, concocted according to a secret Ayurvedic recipe. *Pujas* were taking place around the clock to appease malevolent forces. The air, thick with incense, aggravated my breathing difficulties. The police had been briefed in case of rioting. Astrological tables had been checked and double-checked.

Harinath asked us to sit, before excusing himself. The tattered door urgently required reinforcing with a plank of wood. Once he had taken his seat on a *charpoy* in the courtyard, he clarified the central details of the cure.

'Every year more and more people come,' he declared, swaying from side to side. 'See how popular is this miracle of miracles! It all started with my ancestor.'

'Which one?'

'My great-great-great-grandfather. You see, he was a very generous man,' winced Harinath. 'He was known throughout Hyderabad for his good deeds. During the monsoon of 1845, he saw a *sadhu* sitting in the pouring rain. The mystic was cold, hungry, and abandoned by the world. So my ancestor – Veerana Gowd – brought him here, into this house. He fed him, and nursed him back to health. Weeks passed. Then, just before the *sadhu* was about to go on his way, he revealed the fish miracle to my forefather.'

'*Fish* miracle?' I mumbled. 'Where exactly do the fish come into it?'

Harinath Gowd recited a string of orders to his son.

'The holy man,' he continued, evading my question, 'said that from henceforth the well in the courtyard would be full of magical water . . . we were to use it to make a special paste. The water, the ingredients of the paste, and the astrological timing together form the magic of the miracle. The *sadhu* said my family were to serve a free cure for asthma on the first day of the monsoon. If any fee was charged for the remedy, it would have no effect . . . charge money, and the magic would be broken. That was about a hundred and fifty years ago. True to our word, my family have never charged for the cure.'

Initially, news of the miraculous remedy was slow to spread. In the first few years, asthmatics from the back-streets adjacent to the Gowds' house turned up. But as the years passed, more and more people heard of the miracle. And as more heard of it, and tried it, word spread faster and further.

In any other country, if half a million patients arrived at your house appealing for a miracle, the authorities would demand forms to be filled and permits to be signed. But in India, where miracle remedies are a way of life, things are far more straightforward.

Watching a Hindi movie on television the night before the asthma extravaganza, the five Gowd brothers seemed remarkably relaxed. Didn't it bother them that five hundred thousand asthmatics were pounding on the door?

Shivram Gowd, the eldest of the brothers, stretched out to turn up the TV's volume, to drown out the frenzied groans of asthmatics in the street.

'Of course we're not worried,' he said. 'Remember: this isn't a feeble allopathic medicine . . . but a miracle cure!'

The sheer number of patients demanding the unconventional prescription has meant that, in recent years, the Gowds have had to take on extra staff. More than five hundred volunteers were ready to make sure things went smoothly. Hundreds more were at action stations, preparing to hand out free drinking water and custard creams donated by local businesses and charities. Whereas sufferers were all once treated in the Gowds' ancestral home, now special stalls were erected in neighbouring streets to administer the physic to the maximum number over the twenty-four-hour period.

The *sadhu*'s directions ensured that the Gowds make no profit from their miracle cure. But it was obvious they enjoyed being the centre of attention for one day a year.

'We are proud to be helping people in this way,' intoned Shivram Gowd warmly.

Would he prefer the miracle cure to be handed out on more than one day a year? Shivram Gowd paused to take in the cries of the half-million patients outside. Rolling his eyes, he whispered, 'No, one day a year is quite sufficient.'

Bhalu and I had no hope of leaving the Gowds' home, which was totally besieged by asthmatics. Hyperventilating and bent double after the arduous journey, the majority were planning on spending the night standing upright, crushed in the crowd. All night, mantras were repeated over the great basins of mysterious beeswax-coloured paste, which had the consistency of marzipan and the smell of purifying offal. We bedded down on the flat roof of the Gowds' home.

As dawn rose over the Mughal city of Hyderabad, a prolonged ritual began in the confined courtyard of the Gowds' ancestral home. The five brothers sat on a raised platform surrounded by their families, as their forefathers had done before them. Dressed in sacred saffron robes, they blessed the tubs of oily ointment. Out in the maze of winding lanes, the asthmatics and their families were jostling about with restless anticipation. The miracle was near.

Shortly after seven a.m., I poked my head out into the street. At the front of the queue was an aged farmer from Orissa. He said his name was Krishna Punji. In his hand was a transparent plastic bag. In the bag was a live grey fish.

'I've been here six weeks,' he announced feebly. 'I wasn't sure when the miracle was to be held. So I came a bit early. You see, I've got very bad asthma.' He let out a loud wheeze to prove his point.

'What's the fish for, though?' I asked.

Krishna Punji scratched his head. 'This is a miracle *fish* cure . . . that's why I have murrel fish.'

I scanned the crowd. Everyone was clutching an identical polythene bag. In each bag was a live fish. Like children bringing goldfish home from the fair, they held them up to the light.

Unable to get a clear explanation from anyone, I pulled my head back inside. I sidled up to Harinath, who had been so helpful. I tried to ask about the significance of the fish; but he had no chance to respond. Like his brother, Shivram, he was also too occupied, praying at the family shrine. Bhalu was of no use either. Having spied an attractive girl trapped in the throng, he had hurled himself over the wall to be with her. So I stood next to the shrine, in silence, waiting for the miracle cure like everyone else.

On the stroke of eight, Harinath Gowd made it known that the crucial moment for the annual miracle asthma cure had arrived. The members of the extended family hustled around the elder brothers. Shivram declared that the Gowds always started by taking the medicine themselves. As a guest, I could go first. Great, I thought to myself, I've got ahead of five hundred thousand others. This is what I call *real* queue-barging.

The sense of elation was short-lived.

Shivram juggled with a polythene bag for a moment or two, emptying a live three-inch murrel fish into his hand. The creature's miniature jaws were prised apart. A pellet of the foul-smelling yellow paste – the size of a walnut – was forced into the fish's mouth and around its head. The Gowds' extended family strained closer to watch my moment of joy. One of them indicated for me to stick out my tongue. The fish and I exchanged a troubled glance. The murrel seemed to be demanding an explanation. Alas, I was as bewildered as he. What came next was a new experience for both the fish and me.

In a single, expert movement, Shivram Gowd thrust his hand at my face. Having a grown man's fingers lunging to the back of one's throat is deeply unpleasant. But it's nothing in comparison to the sensation of a live and terrified murrel fish – bearing fetid miracle ointment – swimming down one's oesophagus.

As my torso folded at the waist, my throat retching uncontrollably, the battered doors of the Gowds' home were pulled inward. A great surging tidal wave of asthmatics flooded into the courtyard. At its crest was Krishna Punji. Still gagging as my poor murrel fish fought to swim upward – like a salmon returning to its spawning waters – I watched as the Orissan farmer handed over his fish. Obediently, he opened his toothless mouth as wide as he could and, before he knew it, the speckled murrel fish was slithering south towards his stomach.

Nervously, I voiced my disapproval at the medicine. But supporters were reserved in backing my campaign. Rather than being appalled by the unorthodox treatment, the half a million asthmatics couldn't seem to get enough of it.

Out on the street every urchin was crying out, 'Machhi! Machhi!', 'Fish! Fish!' The competition between sellers kept the prices down. The emphasis was very much on size, everyone believing that the larger the fish, the better it would clean out the throat as it went down.

'The wringling of the fish is very beneficial,' Harinath Gowd called out to me, as he shoved his complete hand into a south Indian woman's mouth. The patient began to choke. Her fish was almost seven inches long – far too large to negotiate anyone's throat. A harsh thump on her back dislodged it. The murrel fish could be seen amid rows of teeth, frantically trying to swim backwards, towards safety. Engulfed by the waves of asthmatics, Harinath Gowd again jammed his fingers down the woman's throat. The seven-inch fish headed into the dark abyss of the patient's oesophagus, never to surface again.

If you recoil at the prospect of swallowing an oversized antibiotic, forget the Gowds' miracle cure. It's traumatic for the patient; and is no easy remedy to administer. Every step of the procedure had its own hazards. When removing it from the bag, the fish tended to flail about and fall into the mud underfoot. With the throng so tight, bending down to search for a lost fish was distinctly hazardous. More difficult still was the business of levering the murrel's jaws apart and inserting the nugget of paste. Even when this had been achieved, the creature had to be propelled head-first down the sufferer's throat. Administering the medicine a single time would be an achievement worthy of praise. But performing it half a million times in a single day was a miracle in itself.

Every city, town and village of the sub-continent seemed to be represented at the Gowds' tiny home. Buddhist monks, Assamese tribesmen, businessmen from Bangalore, Goans and Tamils, Pashtuns and Sikhs: all had congregated together into a whirlwind of life, all frantic for the miracle. Many were gasping for breath, seized by asthmatic attacks brought on by the swarm of bodies pressing tighter and tighter. Others were screaming hysterically as they were separated from their children. Every moment the turmoil heightened to a new pitch. The mob was compressed like liquid injected through a syringe. Then, suddenly, it was rife with rumours. *The stocks of fish are running out. The supplies of miracle paste are almost at an end.* Stampede followed. Babies were clutched above heads to prevent them from being sucked down. Pots of murrel fish were held high in the air. Moments later, the half-million murrel fish were not the only casualties of the day. Two elderly men were killed in the stampede, trampled underfoot.

With news of the Gowds' medication spreading throughout India, and abroad, a regular stream of fraudsters have tried to capitalise on the miracle cure. Quacks and charlatans in every large city advertise a similar antidote on the same day each year. Most claim to be related to the Gowds. Unlike the five brothers from Hyderabad, they charge handsome sums for their medicine.

'It's expected that fakes will try to make money from this,' said Harinath Gowd pragmatically. 'We have been offered millions of rupees by multinational drug companies for the formula, too. But we don't have any fear of the con-men, or of people copying our recipe through reverse engineering. They can copy us all they like, but we have one thing they can never have . . . the magical blessing of the *sadhu*.'

Not surprisingly, the Gowd family's miracle cure for asthma is the laughing stock of the medical establishment. Gulping down live fish may sound like nothing more than mumbo-jumbo. But the remedy could have a scientific grounding after all. Scientists at the Royal Prince Alfred Institute of Respiratory Medicine in Sydney recently published a possible cure for asthma. And it happens to be – *very* fresh oily fish. Fresh fish, they say, has anti-inflammatory properties which can soothe an asthmatic's airway passages.

Back outside the Gowds' ancestral home, the local police officers had all but given up trying to keep control. Pickpockets from across India were busy taking advantage of the crowds. Amongst them somewhere, I feared, was the inimitable Bhalu.

Hour after hour, thousands of asthmatics received the treatment. All through the day, the afternoon, and then the night. By six a.m. the next morning, the short-lived shantytown around the Gowds' two-room house began to break up. The pickpockets were boarding trains for other cities. The balloon-sellers, beggars, and most of the five hundred thousand asthmatics had disappeared. By seven a.m., the fish merchants were frantic to get rid of their supplies. The bottom had fallen out of the murrel-fish market for another year.

22

Lord Elvis

My asthmatic condition had improved overnight. But I was quite unsure whether the Gowds' ancient prescription had anything to do with my recovery, which may have resulted from Hyderabad's pleasant climate. Now the murrel fish was swimming about inside me, I considered what to do next. Should I hasten back to Calcutta? Surely the magician would be back from his trip by now. I could pick up the Madras Mail and be back in time for bed the next day. It was a tempting option. I had much to report on to Feroze . . . everything from trephination and earth eaters to petunia-coloured contact lenses, vast gemstones, and now miraculous murrel fish.

But a nagging insecurity pushed me on. If I arrived back at the mansion without crossing the sub-continent – from the Bay of Bengal to the Arabian Sea – the Master would doubtless feel it necessary to humiliate me. He had not ordered me to traverse the nation, but I had a feeling he expected it. Having borne the brunt of his animosity so often before, I pledged to continue westward . . . to Bombay. Maybe I would be in time to watch the monsoon break over Back Bay. It may be a mad dash, I reflected, but I will return to Calcutta with my head held high.

As always, the Trickster was enthusiastic about continuing the journey. We had developed a curious symbiotic relationship. I needed him to translate and listen to my tedious stories; and he relied on me as the one trusted person who would haul about his pillowcase sacks of swag.

As we went to Nampally Railway Station, to catch the train to Bombay, I exchanged a quizzical glance with Bhalu. 'Tell me your motives,' it said. The Trickster rubbed his nose, smiled, and looked away. He had secret reasons for accompanying me: reasons which I hoped, one day soon, I would learn.

*

Shortly after three-thirty, the Minar Express heaved westward from Hyderabad, bound for Bombay. By breakfast next morning we would be strolling down Colaba Causeway, breathing air fresh from the Arabian Sea.

I crouched forward on my seat and peered out through the open window. Within minutes, the train was carving its way through the endless shanties. I watched rag-pickers and goats foraging for scraps in the rotting piles of waste. Three boys, who had made crumpled kites from plastic bags and string, were running through the sludge with their arms high like triumphant athletes. Not far away, a veiled corpse was being conveyed at waist height by mourning relatives. The light paled to platinum and silence followed. The whining of the locomotive faded. The air outside chilled very slightly . . . the leaves of a *jamun* tree rustled like crisp crêpe-paper. The indigo storm clouds grew a little darker, the wind whipped up, the light turned bluer. Then, and only then, the first bewitching drops of the monsoon burst forth.

I thrust my head from the carriage window into the downpour, whooping like a rodeo star. By the time I retracted, a foreign couple were sitting adjacent to me. I knew instantly that they were from the American Deep South. Even before I heard their accents, I had read the clues. Both were dressed identically: neat London Fog raincoats, Reebok running shoes, and waterproof money belts. There was no hint of Californian ostentation about them; nor was there the crumpled, carefree clothing favoured by New Yorkers. Both in their late fifties, the couple were sensibly dressed. Their large physiques implied a diet rich in fried food. These were not finicky *nouvelle cuisine* vegetarians from the coasts. An entirely different strain of human altogether: they were catfish folk. During my time in Tennessee, I had developed a great fondness for deep-fried fish. And only a Southerner understands the joys of catfish.

As I scanned their shirt-fronts for tell-tale stains of catfish oil, they smiled in time with each other. Friendliness to fellow travellers is a hallowed rule of the South.

'I'm Jake Dorfman, and this here is my wife, Matilda,' intoned the man warmly.

I surrendered my name. As always, it was awkward for untrained vocal cords to create the sound. Jake and Matilda repeated my name numerous times, as if they were learning a foreign language using a cassette tape.

'No catfish here!' I blurted out, hoping to jump straight into a conversation.

In hindsight, I agree it was an odd opening gambit.

'Thank God for that,' laughed Jake, as he straightened his maroon cloth cap. 'We're vegans, can't stand catfish . . . it's horrible stuff.'

'You don't eat meat?'

'Nope, we don't believe in killing animals for food,' cooed Matilda.

'Oh, I love meat,' I muttered, without thinking. 'Can't get enough of it. And catfish – all deep-fried and crunchy – it's the only fish I like. I lived on it in Memphis.'

The couple exchanged a solicitous glance. They seemed troubled at my lack of tact. Whenever I'm planning ahead to say the right thing, I put my foot in it. Somehow, I had to back-pedal enough to steer the conversation towards safe ground. I prayed no one would ask what had taken me to the South in the first place. But I was too slow off the mark.

'What brought you to Tennessee, Turhur?'

'Um, er, um . . . I was writing about something there.'

'Oh?' winced Jake, leaning across expectantly. 'What might that have been about?'

'Um, er, well . . . I was writing about the local social issues . . .'

'Oh, yeah? What aspects of social life?'

'Um, well . . .'

I stared out of the window and prayed the train would plunge off a cliff, or that a freak plague of locusts would engulf us. But the cliff and the locusts didn't come in time. Jake and his wife were waiting for their answer.

'I was writing about a group of people in Pulaski,' I said.

'Oh, yeah? Who would that have been?' snorted the vegans together.

'The Ku Klux Klan,' I said.

Jake comforted his wife, who had begun to sniff into a tissue. Her reaction seemed rather excessive. After all, my magazine articles had brought the full wrath of the KKK upon me.

'Honey,' moaned Matilda, 'I told you – people always think of the Klan when they think of Tennessee!'

'That's not true,' I retorted. 'Tennessee's got so much more than the Ku Klux Klan.'

Jake pecked his wife on the cheek.

'What?' he asked. 'What else does Tennessee have?'

It was a difficult question. Bhalu, who had returned to grab another handful of mini soap bars, shrugged his shoulders. The other travellers in the second-class carriage looked at their feet nervously. Like me, their knowledge of the American Deep South was, at best, sketchy.

'Well,' I declared, 'you've got catfish!'

'What else d'we have?' probed Jake.

Again, I deliberated hard. Then it came to me.

'You've got Elvis!' I shrieked. 'Well, you *had* him.'

An expansive grin swept across Jake's face. He jabbed Matilda in the ribs, and she started to smile as well.

'How did you know?' they chortled. 'How d'you know 'bout Elvis?'

'Um, Elvis – everyone knows about him.'

'No, no, how did you *know* 'bout Elvis and us?' gasped Matilda. 'You like him? Is that it?'

One could not be sure. After all, Jake and his wife were vegans. I had never known a Tennessean to condemn catfish before. But Elvis is different. No one from the 'Volunteer State' would dare to speak against the King.

'Like him?' snarled Jake. 'We love him!'

The Southern couple held each other's hands and cooed like turtle doves. Then they revealed the reason for their visit to India. A friend of a friend had sent them a clipping from an Indian newspaper. Reaching into his back pocket, Jake withdrew the article. It told of how a man called V.N. Gajarajan, living in a hamlet near Bangalore, worships a photograph of Elvis Presley at his family shrine. Gajarajan also gained public attention recently for his monograph entitled 'Why My Daughter Married Michael Jackson'.

I handed the article back to Jake.

'Funny, isn't it?' I exclaimed. 'Just like that temple – Karnidevi, near Bikaner – where they worship rats. I've heard there're thousands of the little fellows. Devotees flock to the temple from across India. They feed the rats great trays of food. Only when the rodents can devour no more, do the pilgrims eat what they've left.'

'Worshipping rats?' quipped the Southerner. 'That's not the same as venerating the father of world music.'

'You mean . . .?'

I gave the couple a sharp, anxious look.

'Yes,' said Jake portentously, 'I'm referring to none other than Mr Elvis Presley.'

Jake and Matilda Dorfman had travelled across eleven time zones to pray at the shrine of Lord Elvis the Divine. It was more than a pilgrimage.

But first things first. Had they brought an offering to leave at the shrine?

Jake Dorfman squinted at his wife. She gestured back to him. Only then did he pull a scratched tobacco tin from his money belt.

'This is our humble contribution,' he said. 'It's a small token, but we feel it's appropriate.'

He handed me the tin. Taking it from him reverently, I slipped off the rubber band. Then, very cautiously, I prised away the lid.

Whatever I had expected to be inside, was not what I found.

'It's soil . . .' I said.

'That's right,' agreed Jake tenderly. 'But it's not ordinary soil . . . it's from Graceland.'

23

Duel of Miracles

At Gulbarga, the American couple shook my hand, clenched their faces in courteous smiles, and stepped off the train. I would have enquired why they were taking such an unconventional route to Bangalore, but I had asked enough questions already.

The Minar Express rumbled across the border to Maharashtra, Bombay's state. Drifting off to sleep, I filled my mind with images of the city, recently rechristened as 'Mumbai'. I saw Churchgate Station and the Chateau Windsor Guest House, the Eros Cinema, and my cherished restaurant, Gaylord's. As I slipped into a deep slumber, I felt something tugging my earlobe. Without even opening my eyes, I knew who it was.

'Bhalu, go and sell your damn soap bars and leave me alone!'

'Sorry,' said the Trickster, 'unexpected stop. We're getting off at the next station . . . Sholapur.'

'What are you talking about? What about Bombay? Only ten hours to go now . . . let's go on to Bombay!'

'Hurry and get off the train – it's slowing down for the station.'

'I'll meet you in Bombay,' I said. 'I've got nothing to do in Sholapur.'

But the Trickster had already made the decision for both of us. He was hauling his grubby pillowcase sacks down from the luggage rack, and pulling them to the door. With great reluctance I followed him down on to the platform.

After hiring a convoy of taxis at enormous cost to bear our combined luggage to Hotel Khajuraho, Bhalu disappeared, leaving me to pay off the drivers. It was unlike him not to pay his way, and was even more unusual for the Trickster not to insist on supervising his loot himself. Without giving his irregular behaviour much thought, I checked into the hotel. As it was late I was forced to pay an eighty per cent surcharge.

*

Next morning the door of my room arched inwards as a fist struck its outer side. The overly zealous bell-hop announced that a guest was waiting for me in the reception. I wondered who it could be. It certainly wasn't Bhalu, who had not yet reappeared – he would have come through the window.

After the taxi ride and hotel surcharge, word would surely spread through Sholapur that the world's most gullible man had come to town. My curiosity heightened by the prospect of an unexpected guest, I hurried down to the reception.

Before I could ask for the visitor, a man sidled up and shook both my hands. Aged about forty, he was of average height, average build and average of appearance: except for a rather splendid Vandyke beard.

'Hello hello hello,' he said, continuing to waggle my hands in his, 'I have come to meet Mr Shah.'

'I am Mr Shah.'

The Vandyke beard twitched with delight.

'Can we sit together?' asked the man, gargling as if there were marbles in his mouth.

'Excuse me for being so forward . . . but do I *know* you?'

Vandyke twitched again.

'I am Goadbaba,' he said.

I ran the name around my mind. Even with my inexpert grasp of Marathi – the language of Maharashtra – I could decipher the name.

'That means Mr Sweet,' I said.

'Precisely!'

Goadbaba lured me out on to the terrace of the Hotel Khajuraho. A contingent of gardeners and their lackeys were watering plants, scrubbing the flagstones and repotting seedlings. With the monsoon well under way, it was a busy time in the garden. Goadbaba and I sat in silence under a large parasol, shading our eyes from the bright morning sunlight.

A waiter pranced over, laden with a tray of tea. He unloaded the teapot, spoons, two cups, slices of lemon, and a jug of milk. As he stooped to place the sugar bowl at the centre of the table, the man with the Vandyke beard brushed him away.

'Do you mind?' I said pertly. 'I'd like some sugar.'

Goadbaba wrung his hands together. I had the feeling I was about to learn the reason for his visit.

'How many spoons do you take?' he asked.

'Two . . . I like two spoons of sugar in my tea.'

Without hesitation, the self-invited guest dipped the thumb and forefinger of his left hand into my tea. In the East, where it's important to observe conventions of courtesy, a guest can get away with a lot more than in the West. But in the East, there's another convention that's followed rigorously. Everyone wipes their posterior with the left hand. This second custom led to distinct misgivings. Where had Vandyke's left hand been?

As his fingers were withdrawn from my tea, I craned my neck to inspect the man's fingernails. An ebony-black crescent of dirt was concealed beneath each one.

'Go on!' sniffed Goadbaba. 'Try it. Taste your tea!'

I mumbled a range of feeble excuses. The guest lifted the cup to my lips like a chalice of Eucharistic wine. I gulped down half a mouthful of the straw-coloured liquid.

'Darjeeling,' I said. 'I like Darjeeling very much.'

'But what about the sugar?' said the stranger.

'You're right: it tastes very sweet – maybe it's a freak batch.'

'No, *Sahib*.' Goadbaba sniffed again. 'This is not freaky, this is my *talent*.'

'What talent's that?'

The man dried his fingers on his beard.

'I make things sweet!' he said.

My fears had been realised. Word had spread that Tahir Shah – the most ingenuous person in the world – had arrived in Sholapur.

Goadbaba touched everything on the table and begged me to verify his skill.

'Taste this spoon,' he said, 'or taste this, the cup, or the table itself!'

I licked a couple of random objects. Sure enough: they were all unusually sweet.

'So, how did you acquire this *talent*?'

Goadbaba pressed his magic fingertips together and explained:

'I was an office clerk here in Sholapur. Last year, after a big meal, I picked something from my tooth. To my surprise, I tasted sweetness. Suddenly I realised that anything I touch goes sweet.'

'What other things have you touched?'

'I have touched so many things,' he said innocently. 'I touched a bowl of rice, a loaf of bread, a cigarette, my friend's shoe, a wallet, a car . . .'

Goadbaba's list was certainly extensive.

'And?'

'And . . . they all went sweet . . . like sugar.'

Mr Sweet pulled up his sleeves in the middle of the conversation. He was keen to prove there were no sugar cubes hidden up his arms. This put my mind at rest. I had expected the talent to be nothing more than a sleight-of-hand illusion, like *vibhuti* pellets.

'Thank you for sharing this,' I said. 'But what do you want *me* to do?'

Like the man with the Midas touch, Goadbaba stretched up and pressed his thumb to the parasol . . . turning it sweet.

'I was hoping you could take me to London,' he said optimistically.

'What ever for?'

'I want to prove my skill to *The Guinness Book of Records*,' said Goadbaba, breaking out into a broad smile. 'I am thinking they will be liking me very much!'

Not again, I mused. Why can't I get away from the Indian preoccupation with *The Guinness Book of Records*? Every other person one meets in India seems to be perfecting an outlandish skill, in the earnest hope of getting their name into the venerated book.

One fifth of all Guinness' mail comes from India. The records book is deluged with material from the sub-continent on a daily basis. One can only sympathise with the chaps at Guinness. What could life be like at an office bombarded day and night with letters from deserving Indians? One single 'greetings' fax sent by a Delhi man to the Guinness headquarters was supposedly a hundred metres long. There's so much interest that *The Guinness Book of Records* is published in four Indian languages.

But whereas many nationalities concentrate on breaking the more sombre records, Indians prefer to perform extraordinary feats. The obsession may, I suppose, have resulted from the tantalising records of endurance set by the nation's holy men.

Dozens of ordinary Indians are world record holders. Surendra Apharya, for instance, has the record for inscribing a grain of rice. He burned 1,749 characters into a single grain using a magnifying glass. Others hold records for limbo dancing on roller-skates (5 1/8 inches); for crawling (870 miles); for milk bottle balancing (more than 64 miles); for continuous standing (17 years); and for needle threading (11,796 times in two hours).

Con-men tour small Indian towns masquerading as agents from the sacred *Guinness Book of Records*. For a steep charge they judge the applicant's entry, promising to include it in the book.

I told Goadbaba I would inform Guinness of his exceptional talent. He was thrilled and, clenching my hand in his, shook it up and down vigorously. When he was gone I licked my palm. It was very sweet indeed.

*

Soon after my meeting with Goadbaba, I was talking to an Indian journalist. When I mentioned the queer skill, the reporter cited half a dozen other Indians claiming the same ability. He told me how the trick was done. Most Goadbabas, he said, were nothing more than copycat illusionists. They wash their hands in a strong solution of saccharin – which is five hundred times sweeter than sugar. Within seconds they go from being ordinary people to men with the Sweet 'N' Low touch.

*   *   *   *

Bhalu had still not reappeared. He often vanished for a day or two at a time. But this time he was gone much longer. Six days passed. Each day I became more and more irritated, especially as he had coerced me into stopping at Sholapur in the first place.

At dawn on the seventh day, I rose early to get ready to take the bus to Bombay. As I emerged from the shower a rustling noise startled me. I spun round. It was Bhalu. He was climbing in through the window.

'Come on and follow me,' he called, climbing back outside and shinning down the outside of the hotel.

'Bhalu, where have you been?'

'I'll tell you later. Just follow me.'

With great unwillingness, I followed the Trickster out of the window. My room, which was on the third-floor, enjoyed a fine view across the southern portion of Sholapur. But as I grappled for a hand-hold, the city's sights were the last thing on my mind.

'What the hell are you up to? You don't just turn up after a week away and get someone to risk life and limb scurrying down a drainpipe. Why don't we use the stairs like everyone else?'

'Don't be lazy,' he retorted, lighting up a *biri*. 'There's something you'll want to see.'

Bhalu led me at break-neck speed through the main area of the town. As we hastened past boarded shops, stand-pipe bathers, and tea-stall attendants, I wondered what the *scam du jour* was to be. The week without Bhalu had been a welcome break from my new role as a con-man's accomplice. Every day, the Trickster encouraged me to turn my hand to another and more unlawful activity, hissing that such knowledge might be useful to me in the future. But when would I need to concoct beauty products from lavatory bleach, spent tea leaves, and grease scraped from the door hinges of a first-class railway carriage? Or, for that matter, when would anyone ask me to create aphrodisiacs from dried mango skins; turn all-purpose miniature bars of Lux soap into medicated suppositories; or pass putrescent drainage liquid off as holy Ganga water?

Bhalu's childhood had moulded him into an incorrigible con-artist. He may not have known the key dates of Indian history, or the correct way to eat peas with a knife and fork: but he had no need for such profitless information. A professional scammer requires far more practical expertise. The Trickster's qualifications were unsurpassed for life on the street. He had a salesman's tongue, a forger's fingers, a gambler's nerve, the million-dollar smile of a chat-show host, and the mathematical artifice of a Nobelist. He spoke faultless English, passable Italian and German, and could communicate in a dozen Indian languages. On their own, none of these attributes may have been enough to survive on the streets of Calcutta. But Bhalu had been blessed with a far scarcer virtue – natural charisma.

And so, as on many other occasions, I found myself hurrying behind him, wondering what depravity was to be next on the agenda.

Twenty minutes after being bundled from the window of the Hotel Khajuraho, we were walking on grass. Bhalu had brought me to a wide hockey pitch on the outskirts of Sholapur.

As I was about to declare my disapproval, I heard voices coming from the far end of the hockey ground. To be more precise, I heard what sounded like a gargantuan, bloodthirsty demon. Screeching as if its baby demons had been snatched by another monster, it was severely distressed. Bhalu said to take no notice of the noise. We had come for a far more important encounter. More important than a female demon robbed of her babies? The Trickster nodded ominously. The demon was trifling in comparison to what he had arranged.

The monster's shrieks did not subside. Instead, they became louder and more aroused. I peered over to where the sound was coming from. Even when narrowing my eyes to focus better, I could see no demon. The pitch was flat, with a large, dense bush bordering it. Telling Bhalu to send for help if I were attacked, I went over to investigate.

When it comes to bewilderment, India has its own scale. No other country on Earth can mystify a foreigner so utterly. Sometimes, when travelling in the sub-continent, one has no choice but to concede total defeat. This was one such instance. I leant forward to peer round the shrub, prepared for anything. Standing behind the bush there was no weeping demon: but something far more unexpected.

Ten men and women, each dressed in sports clothes, were exercising.

Yet instead of performing familiar training drills, they were laughing. It was no timid tittering . . . rather, it was a puissant, hostile form of laughter.

'Excuse me,' I said, 'what are you doing?'

Hearing my question, the leader of the group abruptly stopped guffawing. He pulled up his white cotton ankle socks.

'We're members of the Sholapur Laughter Club,' he said grandly.

'Members of what?'

'The Laughter Club . . . We meet here every morning to laugh.'

'Forgive me for my ignorance . . . but *why* do you laugh?'

The team leader gave me a stern look.

'For exercise, of course! Laughter is the best way to keep the heart and lungs in trim. A powerful spate of early-morning laughter is equal to a three-mile jog.'

'Is that so?'

'Yes, it is,' replied the class in unison.

'Who tells the jokes, then?'

'We don't use jokes,' called out a scrawny woman at the back of the group. 'They're forbidden.'

'Forbidden? That seems a bit hard going – especially if you're doing laughter exercise.'

The team leader seemed keen to get on with the routine.

'Sooner or later a joke would offend someone,' he said. 'So we've outlawed them. In any case, we can laugh on cue.'

He clapped his hands twice. Within an instant, the sound of the wailing demon echoed out across the hockey field. I would have thanked the fitness fanatics for their time. But they were too busy laughing.

*   *   *   *

At eight o'clock the first spectator arrived.

'Is *it* going to be here?' he asked.

Bhalu dipped his head in a nod. He pointed to the centre of the hockey pitch. The man handed the boy two rupees, then sat down in the middle of the field.

'Is *what* going to be here? Why did that chap give you two rupees?'

The Trickster told me to be quiet.

By nine o'clock the sun was high. Five hundred people had turned up to watch the mysterious spectacle. On arrival, each dropped two rupees into a large empty paint can held by Bhalu. Whatever it was for, the audience seemed to feel it was money well spent.

An hour later, a thousand people were loitering about on the hockey pitch. More were turning up all the time. Each obediently dropped their two rupees into the tin. I had never seen Indians so willing to pay money for anything before.

'Bhalu,' I snorted, 'what are you up to? You could get into a lot of trouble for this.'

The Trickster waved me out of the way. He had entrance fees to collect.

At ten-thirty, an official in a tattered uniform accosted Bhalu. A weighty pouch was handed over. The man turned on his heel and hurried away.

I was growing increasingly alarmed. Always at the cutting-edge of fraud, my travelling companion was now navigating in uncharted territory of deceit. I warned him of the consequences. Again, he brushed me aside.

Then, promptly on the stroke of noon, a man and a woman pranced over to the hockey pitch. Both were heavily laden with accessories and equipment. They appeared to be ignoring each other. Their arrival was greeted by a resounding cheer from the audience.

'You've got to tell me what's going on,' I hollered at Bhalu, who appeared relieved at the couple's arrival.

'Prepare yourself for a fantastic show,' he said. 'I heard two gurus were trying to "control" a group of villages near Tirth – just west of here. Both claim supernatural powers. I went to meet them on your behalf.'

'Why didn't you take me along?'

'Because,' said the Trickster, running his hand through the paint can of coins, 'they wouldn't have agreed if a foreigner was around.'

'Agreed to what?'

'Agreed to a duel.'

'Are they going to kill each other?'

'Of course they aren't,' snapped Bhalu. 'They're going to have a duel of miracles.'

'How ever did you get them to trek all the way over here?'

The Trickster stuck his nose in the air haughtily.

'They're letting me referee,' he said. 'As the judge, I said the duel must be held on neutral ground.'

'And what about your tin of cash?'

'Well,' he replied derisively, 'you wouldn't begrudge me my wages, would you?'

*

The crowd was getting agitated. They were ready for the duel to commence. Bhalu had taken great care to advertise the special form of combat. He had hired an army of street children to spread the word in the villages surrounding Sholapur. Potential spectators had been advised that one of the godmen would undoubtedly suffer terrible humiliation. There is only one thing an Indian villager enjoys more than a miracle: and that's to see someone publicly embarrassed. The Trickster had made a considerable cash profit on the entrance fee alone. But one would not expect a fraudster from Calcutta to stop at that.

To Bhalu, the crowd was not merely a potential audience, but a captive market in itself. The *avatars* had been ordered to delay for as long as possible. That is, until the referee gave the word. As the spectators waited for the singular blend of miracles and humiliation to ensue, the army of street urchins scurried about selling wares from the Trickster's pillowcase sacks. Soap bars and shower caps, hand-towels and sachets of French perfume: all were touted at knock-down prices.

Even after the entrance fee, and snapping up a few bargain toiletries, Bhalu noticed that some of the spectators still had money left. And so he turned his hand from soap-bar magnate to bookmaker. The ability to swap one profession for another in a split second is a gift which turns humble entrepreneurs into billionaires. Bhalu had that gift.

I went over to have a look at the godmen. They were both unquestionably odd.

On the left was Sri Kasbekar. Probably in his fifties, he had the appearance of someone who had been dragged round the keel of an eighteenth-century sloop. His features were gnarled; his apparel bedraggled beyond description; and his hands crudely tattooed with indistinct symbols. Yet there was something far more unusual about the guru. He was polydactylic: he had six fingers on each hand. Polydactyly is not uncommon in India. From time to time one sees people with a sixth digit protruding from another finger. Sri Kasbekar's condition was far rarer – for his two extra digits were perfectly formed.

Without counting his fingers individually, one might not have noticed the difference. Rather, without counting them, *I* might not have noticed them. The two thousand bystanders observed them immediately. While in the West people are wary of genetic mutations, in India an extra appendage has an uncanny significance. Hindu deities are frequently portrayed with an additional set of arms and hands. To many in the Sholapur district, a perfectly formed sixth finger on each hand suggested miraculous powers.

On the right side of the makeshift arena was Srimati Kulkarni. Svelte in a butch kind of way, she had long auburn hair, a square mouth filled with square teeth, and alluring midnight eyes. She was dressed in a vibrant fuchsia cotton *sari*. But, it was her ears which first attracted one's attention. Their outer edges were thick with neatly clipped hair. The bristles were about the size and shape of an eyebrow. It looked as if a hairy caterpillar was crawling up into each ear.

The Trickster addressed the gathering, whipping them up into a frenzy. He announced the ground rules. Each seer would be permitted to perform four miracles. No member of the audience would be allowed to participate, although props were admissible. The referee could disqualify either dueller at his discretion. The guru with the best miracles would be permitted to offer divine salvation in the villages near Sholapur.

Seething with anticipation, the spectators swayed forward. I sensed that many villagers' fortunes were riding on the contest. Bhalu curled two fingers around his tongue and whistled.

The duel of miracles began.

First up was Srimati Kulkarni. Brushing back her hair, she addressed the audience in Marathi. She told them she did not like to use her abilities frivolously; but she had to prove her competitor was a fraud. Indeed, she claimed he was worse than a mere con-artist – he was *Shaitan*, the Devil.

Srimati Kulkarni's oration went down very well. Bhalu paused from translating for me, and noted down half a dozen last-minute bets.

Without hesitation, Kulkarni began to weave her magic. She pulled a hundred-rupee note from her blouse, dipped it in water, and then set it alight. Remarkably, the paper did not burn, although it was engulfed in flames. This was the first miracle.

Feroze had taught me variations on the illusion. It can be done with most kinds of paper, cloth, or even wood. In this case, the paper was probably treated with a solution of carbon disulphide and carbon tetrachloride.

For her second act of wonderment, Srimati Kulkarni announced that the *Shaitan* had created an unfavourable atmosphere. If she, a divine being, did not alleviate the hex, a plague would strike the audience down. Such side-comments of impending destruction proved very popular with the assembly. Delighted, they nudged each other in the ribs, and jostled a little closer to the godwoman.

To assuage the evil forces, Kulkarni took up a large brown coconut, and held it above her head. Wailing incantations, she called for the demons to stir from their hiding places and flow into the body of the nut. No place, she said, was safe for them but the confines of the coconut. Then, crouching over, she crimped the nut between her *sari*-covered legs. As two thousand eyes scrutinised her, the mystic held the coconut at arm's length, towards the gathering. A minute passed. The same thought went through everyone's mind: had the miracle failed? Such failure would spell divine disgrace. Another minute passed. As the audience held their breath, the end of the coconut blew out. Like some kind of schoolboy's bomb, a jet of flame and oily smoke issued from the hole. We all stared in wonderment; this was impressive stuff. But there was more to come.

Seizing the nut in both hands, Srimati Kulkarni flung it at a stony patch on the arena. It split open. A quantity of what looked like blood soaked into the ground. Raising her frame to its maximum height, the godwoman cried that the villagers were safe now from her competitor's evil: for the blood had been that of the demons.

Only later did I work out how the illusion had been achieved. Coconuts have three eyes at one end. One of these is soft, and can easily be bored out. The guru perforates the soft eye and fills the nut with a saturated solution of potassium permanganate. From a distance, this resembles blood. The hole is sealed with wax. For the explosion, the mendicant surreptitiously inserts a pellet of sodium through the soft eye. As it reacts with the water in the potassium permanganate solution, it causes a violent eruption.

After Kulkarni's two miracles, the spectators were beside themselves with enthusiasm. A live display of what they considered to be real magic was even better than the special effects of Bollywood movies.

To further exacerbate the sense of tension, Bhalu ordered that Sri Kasbekar should now present two miracles. This was a popular decision. The godwoman was led away to the sidelines, and the polydactyl addressed the villagers.

He told them he was not their god, but their servant: he would heal them, not dictate to them. If they selected his opponent, they would live below a sky made dark with malevolence. The recitation, which carried on for about fifteen minutes, sounded like a party political broadcast.

Cautioning both duellists to refrain from bad-mouthing the other, Bhalu commanded Sri Kasbekar to get on with his routine.

Before the performance began, the polydactyl waved his fingers at the crowd. Titillated like old women at the sight of a naked man, they edged forward for a closer look of the mutation.

For his first miracle, Sri Kasbekar carried a bucket full of greenish lemons into the centre of the arena. Next, he held up a needle and thread and removed his shirt. Grabbing a chunk of flab on his stomach, he stabbed the needle through it, and sewed on a lemon. The audience watched nonplussed as the *yogi* sewed one lemon after the next on to his belly. Instead of grimacing with pain, he chanted mantras, and maintained an airy smile.

'Isn't that hurting him?' I asked the Trickster.

'Don't be so stupid,' he replied. 'Watch how he's pinching the fat tightly with his fingers before jabbing in the needle. Do that and it doesn't hurt . . . it hardly even bleeds.'

Bhalu was right. There was no blood. Within ten minutes, Sri Kasbekar had a dozen fruits hanging from his abdomen like spiders on silk. He seemed in no discomfort at all. Fluttering his fingers once more, with the lemons still dangling, he moved on to his second feat.

With great care he pulled a three-foot viper from his bag of props. Dazzled by the sunlight, the snake reeled about as its owner explained to the bystanders that this was an extremely poisonous reptile. The serpent, he told them, came from the wastelands of the Great Thar Desert. One drop of its venom would bring an agonising death.

The spectators listed backwards. Twisting the viper about his twelve fingers, the godman induced a brave villager to come forward and try his luck with the snake.

The referee shouted out from the perimeter of the arena that volunteers were prohibited under the rules. A communal sigh of relief swept through the audience. The macho villagers had had their pride saved by officialdom. For Bhalu's part, the rule had been a shrewd calculation. If one of the spectators had been struck down by a Rajasthani serpent, he would have had hell to pay.

With no takers allowed, Sri Kasbekar waved the snake around his head like a lasso. Then he prised its mouth open and forced its fangs on to his neck. A stream of blood issued from the *swami*'s jugular. He then threw the viper on the ground and stamped on its head. It might have been a harsh move, but the reptile could have killed the godman, who was none the worse after the encounter.

From where I was standing, the snake bite was plausible. The crowd had also been impressed by the stunt. As they applauded wildly, I remembered something Feroze had told me in Calcutta. Standing one morning at the window of his study, he had declared that ninety per cent of Indian snakes are non-venomous. Ignorant of the many species of serpent, most villagers assume that any snake bite is fatal. For his illusion, Sri Kasbekar had used a harmless snake. It didn't actually have fangs. As its mouth was pulled from his neck, he had squeezed a blood-filled sponge over the area.

Two miracles each. The score was even. Anxious to keep up the tension, Bhalu called for Srimati Kulkarni to perform her next feat.

Taking her place in the circle, she informed the audience that her twelve-fingered rival had used an innocuous species of serpent for his demonstration. The godwoman had hoped to secure victory through denouncing the opposition, but the villagers were far too astute to declare a winner halfway through. Having paid two rupees each to watch the duel, they expected value for money. In their eyes, value meant quantity.

For her third miracle, Kulkarni pulled up the hem of her *sari* and washed her feet in a bucket of water. As she sloshed about, she emitted a series of shrill gasps. The spectators were unimpressed by the woman's manner. I sensed the tide was turning against her: largely for her outbursts against Polydactyl Man.

After three or four minutes of washing, Srimati Kulkarni jerked her body about as if it were being entered by angelic forces. She then pushed the bucket away, and walked calmly down a long piece of dusty yellow cloth. Moments later the miracle was visible. Distinct rusty-red footprints had been left where her feet had stepped. The material was held up to the audience. Their reaction was sober. The miracle had none of the anguish of a snakebite or of sewing fruit on to the skin.

As with so many other illusions I had seen on my journey of observation, Feroze had accommodated me with a faultless rendering of the trick at his mansion. The deception is very simple. The feet are not washed with ordinary water. It's a mixture of slaked lime and water. Shortly before use, the cloth is dipped in a light turmeric solution and dried. As the seer's holy feet press against the fabric, a chemical reaction occurs. A red mark is left where the turmeric and lime meet.

Sri Kasbekar's third miracle was one I shall not readily forget. It wasn't that the feat was so impressive; but the response it drew touched me. Like a stage magician of the old school, Polydactyl Man walked into the arena in silence. He had removed the lemons from his belly and replaced his shirt. A thousand people surrounded him, but none said a word. I sensed that they were now truly awed by his presence.

Frivolously, he withdrew something from his *lungi* and placed it on the ground. It was a thick black ball-point pen, with four small buttons up the side. Chanting a cryptic mantra beneath his breath, the godman walked around the pen in a figure of eight. When he had completed the circuit in one direction, he repeated it the other way. He did this seven times. Only then did he pluck the pen from the ground.

I was ready for the implement to squirt blood, or to write with invisible ink. But what happened was totally unexpected. Polydactyl Man held the ball-point out before him in the way a fencer holds a foil. Then, as the mystic closed his eyes in concentration, the pen began to speak. It was no random voice, but that of the godman. Sri Kasbekar was speaking through the pen.

The audience went apoplectic. This was surely proof that he was a higher being. Even Bhalu recoiled at the feat. By chance, I could explain the miracle. About a year before, I had been glancing through an airline's in-flight magazine when I spotted the same ball-point 'Memo Pen'. Advertised as the gadget that every weary executive needs, the pen has a microchip which stores a few seconds of one's voice. Perfect, the ad had claimed, for the businessman on the move – make a note of that brilliant idea when driving, in a lift, or when out and about. I wondered whether the American manufacturers had dreamt their executive toy would ever become a divine object.

The villagers had already made up their minds. They liked the oracle pen and Polydactyl Man. But a heckler at the back of the crowd was calling for the last two miracles.

The referee clapped his hands. As he was riding on a high of public adulation, Sri Kasbekar was allowed to go first.

A shallow pit had been dug in the hockey pitch and filled with red-hot coals. I had warned Bhalu that he could get into trouble for defacing city property, but he waved my outburst aside. Calling out a fantastic set of magical words, Polydactyl Man approached the coals. Then, with great self-control, he stepped on to them. Halfway across, his face seemed to buckle from pain. But he continued, without giving voice to his discomfort.

Firewalking has occurred in the East for thousands of years. It's recently been introduced in the West, too. Tired Memo Pen-carrying executives now hurry across hot coals as part of special bonding seminars. Contrary to popular belief, firewalking is dead simple. The skin on the soles of the feet and the ash which covers the coals are both poor conductors of heat. Anyone can do it. But the villagers didn't know this. For them, Polydactyl Man was the hero of the day.

A quick glance at his feet proved he was indeed the hero, but for another reason – sabotage. While his back was turned, the godwoman had stealthily sprinkled sugar on to the coals. The sugar melts and sticks to the feet, burning them.

Determined not to be beaten by subversion of any kind, Sri Kasbekar took the pain. After all, he was passing himself off as a living god. As more and more godmen earn a living from healing and performing miracles, an increasing number are falling victim not to Rationalists, but to sabotage from their own kind.

When the time came for her last miracle, Srimati Kulkarni crawled beneath a heavy blanket positioned at the centre of the arena. I could sense the spectators wishing her to fail. Very slowly, her head, and then her body, began to leave the ground. An inch at a time, it rose above the grass. The seer paused at about three feet, her body quivering slightly under the blanket. This was the first time I had seen a full levitation performed.

Just as I was going to ask Bhalu how he thought the illusion was done, something rather embarrassing happened. Embarrassing, that is, for the godwoman. The thick wool blanket which had covered her slipped away. In an instant the secret of full body levitation was revealed. The secret was that there was no levitation. Srimati Kulkarni had been standing under the blanket, her arms outstretched, holding two chipped hockey sticks by the handles. The sticks' blades had been pointing upwards, giving the impression of feet.

Her face red as a beetroot, she proclaimed that Sri Kasbekar – the Devil – had bewitched her with a curse. But no one listened. The villagers were far too preoccupied with something else to pay attention to a fraudulent goddess. Besotted with Polydactyl Man's miracles, they yearned for more revelations from his miracle of miracles . . . the sacred oracle pen.

24

Jimmy, the Part-Time God

The glass-fronted cabinets were filled with neat rows of disintegrating volumes. Labelled with yellowed tags, and stained with damp, most of the books had not been opened for decades. The tables, chairs, wainscot, floor, and even the reading lecterns had been anointed with liberal coats of furniture oil generations before. Dusty marble busts loomed down from their plinths like those of Roman emperors; a free-standing brass fan churned the dank monsoon air; and, mounted on the far wall, an antique regulator clock, its burr walnut inlay severely warped, recorded the passing of time. Nothing had altered for years in this, the reading-room of Bombay's Native General Library.

Favoured by the city's dwindling Parsi community, the library is a mysterious sanctuary where Parsi elders lounge away the afternoons as if reclining at a gentlemen's club. They talk of the good old days, when their existence was not under threat. They speak of their formidable heritage; their belief in Zarathustra, and how they came from Persia long ago.

When the duel of the godmen had come to an end, Bhalu had scooped up his sizeable takings and accompanied me on the Netravati Express to Bombay. He spent most of the journey counting his new fortune, all of which was in small change.

Returning to a city that one has known and loved fills you with a delicious sense of warmth. Unbridled greed had brought me to Bombay some time before. Like the Trickster, I had hoped to make a fortune from others' naivety. Unlike him, I had a distinct handicap. I had not grown up on the streets of Calcutta. My conniving idea – to buy up European antiques in Bombay's infamous Chor Bazaar, the Thieves' Market, and sell them back in England – had come to nothing. Now, returned to the city which I had hoped once to take by storm, I castigated myself. How could I have been so foolish? How had I expected to bamboozle Bombay's hard-bitten antique dealers into selling their artefacts cheaply?

As Bhalu went in search of an old pal from Calcutta, I waited in the Parsi reading-room for D. Blake to turn up.

Friend, confidant, and mentor, Blake was an American musician who had made his home in Bombay. He had first come to the city in search of a teacher of Indian music. Years spent in Bombay had shown Blake many things, and he was now a mine of city's most arcane information. I felt certain that he could direct me towards the unusual.

Unfortunately, Blake had become detribalised beyond recovery. Tell-tale signs of his degeneration popped up in many forms – the most notable being that he was always extremely late for an appointment.

As the regulator clock chimed three, a white-haired Parsi gentleman sat down in the tattered armchair beside mine. He must have been in his nineties. I wished him a pleasant afternoon, and said I thought it would rain. The man drew a long, deep breath into his lungs, and let out a sharp cough. Whatever his condition was, it was obviously very advanced.

'Got asthma, have you?' I chirped. 'If you do, I can recommend a wonderful cure in Hyderabad. The treatment was a little distressing, but it's cured me.'

The old gentleman thumped a fist on his chest.

'It's not asthma,' he grunted. 'I don't have asthma.'

'I'm glad to hear it. Then you're probably in fine shape.'

Coughing phlegm into a handkerchief, the old Parsi continued the inane conversation.

He introduced himself as Mr Sodawaterwala. It was an unlikely name, but the Parsi community used to take their job titles as a surname during the British Raj, and some of the stranger surnames have endured.

'Do you want to hear something?' he asked.

'Of course, what?'

'Well,' said the wrinkled mouth, 'when I was a baby, my parents took me to have my horoscope read. The astrologer foretold my future in great detail. He said that I would become an industrialist, which I am. And he said I would have three sons, which I have. But he prophesied that I would die by drowning.'

'Oh, dear, I hope you can swim.'

'I can't,' replied Mr Sodawaterwala. 'My parents were so fearful of the prediction, they made sure that I never learned. They thought that if I could swim, I might be tempted to go near water . . . and the astrologer's horoscope would come true. So,' the old gentleman continued, 'I have spent my entire life avoiding water. I have never paddled in a river, bathed in the ocean, splashed about in a swimming pool. I've never even taken a bath. Imagine what a curse the astrologer's horoscope has been all these years!'

'But avoiding water so cautiously sounds very sensible to me.'

Mr Sodawaterwala regarded me for an instant.

'Maybe not so sensible,' he said. 'You see, I've just come back from my doctor. I have a heart condition. This means my heart doesn't work as well as it should. It *should* be pumping hard enough to drain the fluid from my lungs. But it isn't. The result is my lungs are filling with water. In short – I'm drowning.'

When D. Blake finally turned up more than three hours late, I told him about Mr Sodawaterwala, who had gone home.

'Don't you just love this place?' he said. 'It's the greatest hang-out in town. There's never a dull moment when there are Parsis around.'

Blake had altered little in appearance since my previous visit to Bombay. He was still dressed like a Cuban revolutionary: black beret, dark glasses, and scraggly beard. His conversation was the same florid blend of sardonic remarks and witticisms.

'So, what's all this about studying illusion?' he sniffed, when we had done with pleasantries.

'You know, I've always been fascinated with illusion and conjuring. Always – since the guardian of Jan Fishan's tomb got me interested as a kid.'

Blake removed his dark glasses and waved them around as he spoke. His emerald eyes flashed subversively.

'Oh yeah?' he cracked. 'So pull a rabbit out of my beret then!'

'I'm not here to practise illusions,' I said, 'I'm here to observe. You see, I'm on a journey of observation.'

Straightening his beret, Blake thought for a moment.

'Who told you to go on this journey then, man?'

'Feroze did, of course.'

'*Feroze!*'

'Yes, Feroze, he's my teacher.'

D. Blake's face dropped. He was obviously taken aback. For he had himself been my mentor.

'Feroze is an illusionist,' I said. 'He's instructing me in the illusory sciences.'

'I know when I'm not wanted,' Blake whimpered. 'I'll just go back to my rooftop.'

'Listen to me, Blake! I need help. What's going on in town? You know . . . unusual stuff.'

Blake perked up a bit. Like me, he had a penchant for the bizarre.

'You know there's no shortage of oddballs here,' he said. 'What about the guy who's spinning spider's webs into silk for bullet-proof jackets? Or there are the street kids who're being kidnapped and shipped to the Persian Gulf to work as under-age camel jockeys. Or what about the dude who's making dolphin-milk cheese? Or,' cried Blake, flailing his arms about briskly, 'what about Jimmy, the part-time god?'

D. Blake told me that as far as he knew Jimmy held a *darshan*, a session of worship, every second Tuesday. Thousands of devotees from across town flocked to the meetings held in north Bombay. When I had asked Blake what motivated the part-time god, he had replied that such matters were for me to find out.

A brawny male masseur at the secret Iraqi *hammaam* off Mohammed Ali Road revealed that Jimmy's sign was a cobra, and that he had at least one *lakh*, a hundred thousand, followers. The masseur sent me to a labourer in the nearby Fighting-Kite Bazaar. As he blended a paste of powdered light-bulbs and glue, to cover the strings of fighting-kites, he disclosed that Jimmy was always accompanied by his adoptive mother: an elderly goddess named Gururani. He disclosed, too, that Jimmy had worked as a clerk in a bank, until his position became untenable. The bank manager, who himself was a follower of Jimmy's, felt obliged to crawl past the clerk on his hands and knees. Since leaving the bank, Jimmy had started his own business making 'Jimmy Brand' incense. The information seemed to have the hallmarks of fabrication. Only a face-to-face encounter with the deity would, I was sure, shed light on the truth.

From the Fighting-Kite Bazaar, I made my way to the Chor Bazaar, to meet an old associate. He was a shop-keeper with a cavern of European artefacts. His name was Anwar Sadat.

Anyone in Bombay in need of a rusty World War I dental drill, an HMV gramophone, an old set of golf clubs, or a tuba from Berlin knows to drop in on Anwar. For two hundred years his family have been purveyors of European antiques. Now almost lost in time, his wares lie like an attic of souvenirs from Bombay's past. I adored glancing around the cluttered shelves, imagining the private histories of Anwar's paraphernalia. Each object, encased in oil and dust, hides a tale.

Stethoscopes and tinplate toys, sextants and barometers, chandeliers of Belgian crystal, plate cameras and warped violas, a scale model of a four-masted barque, a set of silver fish knives, a Meissen figurine, and a doll's house with a damaged roof.

Years had passed since I last sat and chatted to Anwar Sadat. He was a soft-spoken man, a jewel in a trade which tends to attract the more mendacious members of Bombay society. But then again, as I always reminded myself, this *was* the Thieves' Bazaar.

With two pots of hot sweet tea inside us, Anwar called for his young son to come down from the attic room above the shop. The sound of infant footsteps on the precipitous staircase followed. A moment later, the boy's hand squeezed mine in a strong greeting, and I wondered how I could have forgotten about him. For his name was Saddam Hussein.

Anwar listened to my enquiry. When I had finished, he stared at the floor tiles of his shop and thought hard. If anyone knew where Jimmy held his meetings, I felt sure it would be Anwar Sadat.

A third pot of tea came and went. The pet goat, Rustam, gambolled over in search of food. Anwar rubbed the sides of his bristly face, furrowed his brow, and pondered the riddle of Jimmy, the part-time god. As a pious Muslim, the shop-keeper might have derided the notion of a less than full-time supreme being. He might too have scorned the thought of a god in human form. Although not condoning the godman, he was willing to help me seek him out.

'I don't know what life's coming to,' he lisped. 'All sorts of unlikely things are going on. Look at this . . .'

Anwar held up the morning's newspaper. He pointed to a report about a Western doctor's work on implanting pigs' hearts into humans. It might be a life-saving operation, but for Muslims the very idea is monstrous.

'First pigs' hearts and now a god called Jimmy,' moaned Anwar Sadat. 'I don't know where the world is going. But then,' he said, squeezing his son's cheek, as Hafiz Jan had once done to me, 'we are just observers, aren't we?'

Anwar shooed Rustam away from nibbling volume nine of a rotting *Encyclopaedia Britannica*. He scribbled something on a corner of his newspaper. Tearing it off, he handed the scrap to me.

'Go and see this man,' he said. 'He deals in freight, but I have a feeling that he will know your god.'

*

The directions took me to a building in north Bombay, near the city's domestic airport at Santacruz. At first, I felt sure I had misread the address. The business was not a freight or haulage company. It was an undertaker's. Coffins were stacked up either side of the doorway like crates at the dockside. A number of seasoned carpenters were squatting at the back of the room, smoking *biris*. I handed the fragment of newspaper to a rather dapper character inside the office. There were seven telephones on his desk, each a different colour. He shook my hand.

'Are you a friend of Anwar Sadat?' I enquired.

'Ah, Anwar,' he said warmly, 'I haven't visited him for a long time. And how's little Saddam Hussein?'

'He's very well. Anwar told me you were in the freight business. So I am a little puzzled to see so many coffins.'

'But I *am* in shipping,' said the man, scanning his telephones. 'I'm a corpse shipper. Ship them all over India, and abroad, too.'

When pleasantries were at an end, I asked the undertaker what he knew about Jimmy.

'Sri Jimmy Nagputhra and Gururani Nagkanya,' he proclaimed. 'Of course I know them. A couple of my employees follow them.'

A pair of elderly carpenters were called from the workshop. Both wore a badge depicting a multi-headed cobra. The older of the two artisans invited me to the Tuesday-evening *darshan*, in two days' time. All were welcome to hear Sri Jimmy speak. The meeting would commence at eight p.m., and would continue well into the night.

The corpse shipper snapped his fingers, and his employees slipped back to the workshop. Unable to contain my enthusiasm, I reflected aloud.

'This sounds wonderful,' I said. 'Imagine a part-time god called Jimmy, whose symbol is the cobra, and whose devotees number over one hundred thousand!'

The corpse shipper straightened the telephones on his desk. Then, very slowly, he shook his head from right to left.

'Why?' he asked acerbically. 'Why do you waste your time with these fly-by-night gods?'

*   *   *   *

Tuesday night eventually came. By the time darkness fell, I could hardly contain my enthusiasm. After a slap-up meal at Gaylord's – most of which was spent press-ganging Bhalu into joining me – we took a taxi to Lalbag in north Bombay. I never thought I would be imploring the Trickster to follow me.

As the vehicle stop-started its way through the ever-denser traffic, I stared out at the apocalyptic clouds. The monsoon was well under way. Its storms had been pounding the city's streets nightly. All the elements were there: a tip-off from Blake, a secret location, a considerable following and, best of all, a part-time god.

We arrived at the Samaj Mandir Hall some time after nine p.m. There was no doubt that this was where the *darshan* would be held. About four thousand people – representing a cross-section of society – were milling about. All the women were wearing headscarves; all the men had plain white handkerchiefs tied over their heads. Bhalu and I copied them, for fear of standing out. The deities had obviously not yet arrived, for an electric wave of apprehension seemed to bind all the devotees. Some chatted together; others flicked through pamphlets bearing a cobra's image. Still more stood in silent meditation.

Soon after ten p.m. the followers flew into a panic.

An Indian-made Pal car was approaching. The vehicle – bedecked in marigold flowers – had taken on the aura of an emblazoned chariot. Some of the devotees shielded their eyes; others prostrated themselves as the motorcar drew up to the red carpet. Very slowly, the car's doors opened, and the gods descended.

Gururani got out first. She looked rather ordinary. Aged somewhere between sixty and seventy-five, her face bore an apathetic expression, like a rock star tired of the road. Numerous garlands weighed down her fragile neck; a sensible handbag dangled from her wrist. She was cloaked in a shimmering raspberry-coloured mantle.

Jimmy followed her from the vehicle on to the crimson carpet. Bhalu pulled me to the front of the crowd to get a good view. Tall, robust, and no more than about forty, he had a great square-shaped face, most of which was obscured by beard. Like Gururani, Jimmy was resplendent in a garish silvery-blue robe; and, as with his adoptive mother, he wore a golden filigree crown.

The deities swaggered on platform shoes into the hall. I took a deep breath. It was a moment to savour. Rose petals were scattered from baskets clasped by a row of onlookers. Adoring devotees fell to the floor as the gods made their way past. When the deities had entered the capacious hall, the followers scurried barefoot behind.

Once inside, the supreme beings ascended a dais; their followers taking their places on the main floor beneath. On the left side of the room sat the men; on the right, the women. No more than five hundred of the most respectable acolytes were permitted inside. The rest, who by this time must have numbered more than eight thousand, occupied a sizeable football field outside.

The Trickster and I took our places with the men. I wondered whether I might have a chance to chat to Jimmy. As if reading my thoughts, an elderly Parsi behind tapped me on the back.

'The Divine Lights are the purest of all godly creatures,' he said. 'Of course no one can speak to them directly, except for those who've been cleansed.'

'Is that really true?'

The Parsi agreed it was.

'Could I be cleansed?' I asked optimistically.

The gentleman looked me up and down and grimaced.

'Certainly not!' he fumed. 'But you can think clean thoughts. The Divine Lights can read what you're thinking.'

'Divine Lights?'

The man gave me an austere glance.

'Their holinesses,' he said. 'They're powerful . . . their energy can unlock a man in chains . . . it can release the ignorance of the soul.'

It sounded like strong stuff.

Jimmy and Gururani were alone on the dais. Behind them rose up an extraordinary scene. Like some backdrop to a Hollywood – or, rather, a Bollywood – fantasy, it depicted ice mountains, forests, mythical creatures, and ten-headed cobras. Directly above the deities' crowns loomed an oversized rotating parasol, emblazoned with the words 'Jimmy', and 'Gururani'. Behind their holinesses heads were mounted immense glitter-encrusted golden halos. With sharp serrated edges like great circular saws, they, too, rotated, emphasising the couple's divinity.

The prohibition from speaking to, or even greeting, Jimmy directly hindered the interview process. Fortunately, the devotees were more than willing to surrender fragments of background about their god.

When he was aged only seven years, Gururani had seen Jimmy emanating divine light. She adopted the boy and raised him as a deity. Like Gururani, Jimmy was a Parsi. But the couple seemed not to condone or condemn any creed. One of their faithful explained this by saying they were above religion. Another imparted that, as deities, they never wore the same set of robes twice. Re-using garments was beneath them. A film producer who I met later suggested the duo rented their tawdry mantles from a costume-hire firm in Bollywood. He swore the very same gowns had been worn in the popular Indian television soap opera of the *Ramayana*.

While the disciples took their places, the deities attended to the more mundane business of preparing for the show. Sitting on their thrones, they were greeted by a stream of aides and sycophants. Some seemed to be holding up letters which needed answering; others may have been hoping to place bulk orders for Jimmy's special brand of incense.

The goddess Gururani opened her sensible handbag and whipped out a scarlet lipstick. When her lips were suitably adorned, the festivities began.

An accordionist ran a set of manicured nails across his instrument's keys. The hall was filled with the soothing sounds of Hindi music. A primitive system of wires and loud-speakers broadcast the music to the devotees outside. Poised on their thrones, with the electric halos whirring behind them, Jimmy and Gururani held their right palms towards the back of the hall, like Native American chiefs offering a greeting. Then they did what they did best – sat quiescently as those around them prostrated themselves.

The night's ritual was long and elaborate. When the band had warmed up, Gururani took a microphone in her right hand, stepped into the centre of the stage, and began to sing. An Arab friend of mine says that, to his untrained ear, Italian opera sounds like the wailing of she-camels. In the same way, my ears failed to appreciate the goddess' ability.

For almost an hour I endured an agonising cross-legged position. When Gururani had returned to her throne, and her halo had been reactivated, Jimmy grabbed the microphone. A deep, rhythmical voice streamed from his mouth. The words blared from speakers mounted on every wall.

Outside, it had begun to rain: not a modest April shower, but a full-blown monsoon downpour. I peered out. The eight thousand adherents were sitting cross-legged and obedient as the water soaked them. They might have left, but the powerful strains of Jimmy's voice wafted around them, soothing them in their discomfort.

The shimmering blue robes and the music – which was not dissimilar to an early Elvis ballad – would have delighted the Dorfmans. Jimmy could certainly pound out the tunes. Although I understand no Gujarati, I was mesmerised by the sheer force of his voice. For a split second I entertained the thought of getting Sri Jimmy a recording contract. His alternative clothing, his mellow attitude to life, and his incense know-how would have gone down well at any Los Angeles record label. But communication would be the stumbling block. What record producer would sign a man who was too pure to speak to him?

The solo ballads came and went. After the music, each devotee lit a miniature *ghee* lamp. These were handed to footmen, who bore them up to the dais on silver trays. When the gods had blessed each tray, the lamps were conveyed back down to the followers. Only then did the audience participation ensue. With the lamps balanced precariously on their laps, the devotees swayed back and forth ecstatically. Every so often a member of the congregation would jump up and run all around, gripped by the divine light. In the commotion a woman's *sari* caught alight. She flapped her arms back and forth frantically like a moth's wings. Eventually those around her realised their companion was all but a ball of flames. The inferno was quietly extinguished.

Outside the hall, the eight thousand weather-worn disciples were still struggling to light their *ghee* lamps with damp matches. The monsoon and the winds were not making the task any easier.

When all the lamps had been blessed by the deities, the band struck up again. I leant back and savoured the encounter. The folk music, the headscarves worn by all, the flaming colours of the robes, the flickering lamps, the scenic backdrop – they were all reminiscent of a gypsy encampment. I nudged Bhalu and asked him what he thought of my analogy. He had not been to a Romany encampment and so refrained from commenting. But the bearded man beside me was more than willing to offer his opinion. He told me that if I denigrated Sri Jimmy further, he would take me outside and deal with me.

The last thing on my mind was knocking the part-time god. It would have been wrong to vilify Jimmy and his group. Certainly, international cults with their multi-million-dollar turnovers may be fair game. Yet here was a man who was taking nothing from his disciples. He wasn't even performing pseudo-miracles. His followers seemed content with a selection of gypsy ballads. Granted, they provided him with opulent gowns, but there were none of the tell-tale signs hinting at a big business dynamic. The hall was rented on an *ad hoc* basis. The robes were, supposedly, hired when needed; and I didn't hear the swiping of credit card donations or the nervous laughter of foreign supporters.

Jimmy's incense was on sale at a stall outside the auditorium. Priced at ten rupees a box, it was cheaper than competing brands; as were the key fobs and badges which bore the haunting image of the five-headed cobra.

Jimmy's extravaganza ended abruptly at three a.m. As Bhalu and I made our way from the hall, I felt deflated. At first I wondered why I had been hit by the sudden change of mood. Was it that I had been lured by the prospect of deception, and found none? Or had my twisted alter ego been craving to make fun of the deity? Perhaps it was a little of both. On reflection I had to admit the truth: Jimmy, the part-time god, may have been a showman of unparalleled expertise . . . but he was no laughing matter.

*   *   *   *

Sitting in the doorway of Jan Fishan's tomb, Hafiz Jan had recounted all he knew about the Anglo-Afghan Wars. He had told me of the blood and gore; and he had deliberated on how the British had been routed on three occasions from Afghan soil.

The British may have forgotten the three wars they fought in Afghanistan. But in a neglected corner of Bombay a memory of the sanguinary encounters remains. It was Hafiz Jan who had first mentioned the Afghan Church, located at the southern tip of Colaba. I remember our conversation well. I had said an Afghan church was a contradiction in terms. Almost all Afghans are followers of Islam. The guardian of Jan Fishan's mausoleum had rolled about with laughter. The Afghan Church was, he had said, a nickname. It was there, overlooking the Arabian Sea, that the British war dead from the Anglo-Afghan campaigns had been honoured.

Before my triumphant return to Calcutta, I had an afternoon to spare. A second meeting with Blake had reminded me of Hafiz Jan's conversation about the church. Bhalu had no interest in inspecting the names of dead colonials carved into floor slabs. And so I set out by myself.

Colaba may be part of Bombay's bustling downtown area, but its southern expanse, towards Cuffe Parade, is seldom visited by well-dressed professionals or by the city's share of emaciated, low-budget tourists. I meandered down Colaba Causeway. It was still early. Street vendors were setting up their stalls. Visitors from the Arabian Gulf, who favour the district's sea-front hotels, were still in bed. On Strand Road a ball-point-pen-seller was displaying his new range of Japanese pens. He demonstrated the subtle clicking action of their mechanism. When I rejected his wares, the merchant threw stones at a three-legged pye dog. It was a dastardly retaliation. Like everyone else, he knew that Westerners cannot stand to see a dog in pain. I bought a biro and strolled on.

On past the Sassoon Docks and the Koli fisherwomen. Fine-boned, with baskets of pomfret on their heads, they hurried about in the early-morning light. Fish is a scarce commodity in the monsoon. The strengthened currents and the seasonal rains are the bane of fishermen across Asia.

Very soon the tarmac road was wending its way through groves of palms and lush vegetation. It was hard to imagine that the turbulent streets of Bombay were only a mile or so to the north. Turning a corner, I set eyes upon the so-called Afghan Church.

Officially known as the Church of St John, the Neo-Gothic building is topped by a formidable steeple, reaching over two hundred feet into the sky. Its coarse buff basalt facing was in excellent condition, considering it was over a hundred and thirty years old.

As I pushed open the gate to the enclosure, large irregular droplets of rain started to fall: warning that a far heavier monsoon downpour would soon follow. I rushed to the church's main door, twisted the iron handle. Within moments I was transported back in time.

The interior of the Afghan Church was silent and austere. It reeked of an era when the sub-continent was in the grip of the British Raj. Walking on the cool flagstones at the back of the nave, one could almost sense the survivors of the Anglo-Afghan campaigns praying there. The air was stale and dank. Dim monsoon light filtered through the stained-glass friezes of the chancel. The church was like a remote isle, sequestered from the clamour of modern Bombay. It was as if the spirits of the dead haunted the place, unwilling to relinquish it.

Tiny, insignificant reminders of their presence were all around. The scuff of a hobnailed boot on the skirting; the initials of an infantryman, etched into a lacquered frame; and, most poignant of all, the actual British battle standards from the First Anglo-Afghan War. Shrouded behind antique glass like anatomical specimens, they were at the point of disintegration. Delicate as dragonfly wings, they hung like medieval pennons from a knight's lance. Had my own ancestor – Jan Fishan Khan – ridden against these standards during the battles of 1842?

Outside, the day's first monsoon deluge was well under way. Drops of rain were splattering on to the granite flagstones through multiple perforations in the roof. I ran a hand over the row of lacquered chairs at the back of the church. Each had a notch for a soldier's rifle – insurance against being taken unawares, instituted after the Revolt of 1857. As my fingers progressed over the glossed wood, a chill ran down my spine.

A man was sitting in the front row.

From where I was standing, I could just see the back of his head. His hair was pigeon-grey and brushed back. At first I thought it might be a ghost. Perhaps one of the soldiers. Had he been slain by Jan Fishan and, realising who I was, come for retribution? My forebear would, I was sure, have wanted me to face any ghost head on. And so I marched down the nave to confront whatever spirit it might be.

Five rows before the altar, and I felt a sharp pang at the base of my stomach. Was it a warning to turn on my heel and flee? Three more rows and my nose warned me of a well known aroma. One more step. I was inches from the figure. Just as I was about to touch him on the shoulder, he swivelled sharply to face me.

No face – living or dead – could have filled me with a greater sensation of astonishment.

It was Feroze.

Delighted that I had collapsed into the chair behind his, the Master stood up.

'Surprised to see me?' he sniffed.

'Well, er . . .'

Feroze swished an 'F' in the air with his reliable bull's pizzle riding crop. He was obviously jubilant.

'There's no time to dilly-dally,' he said. 'Haven't heard from you in ages. Thought I'd better come and check you hadn't run off.'

I wiped the perspiration from my top lip.

'How did you know to find me here? Wait a minute – how did you know I was in Bombay, let alone *here*?'

The magician tilted his head back and stroked his Adam's apple. He was relishing the moment.

'You underestimate me,' he said.

'I could never do that,' I answered. 'But this was the last place I expected to see you . . .'

'Why haven't you posted any reports in the last two weeks?'

'I'd given up. I called the house . . . Gokul said you were away. He said you'd been gone for a long time.'

Feroze gazed up at the rafters.

'Yes . . . I've been on a journey myself,' he said absently.

'Really? What kind of journey?'

Clicking his heels together like a sergeant on the parade ground, the Master faced me in profile.

'I've been on a journey of observation,' he said.

It was a familiar phrase.

'What do you mean?'

'*You* tell *me* what I mean . . . With one eye examine the detail, with the other look at the entire picture.'

I thought hard and, as I thought, a second frozen chill shot down my spine.

'Your *journey*,' I said. 'Did it by any chance have anything to do with my own journey?'

Feroze licked his lips with furtive anticipation.

'Had your eyeballs read recently?' he asked, bending over to tie a shoelace.

'Eyeballs? Yes, as a matter of . . .'

I looked across at the Master, who was looming over me with folded arms like an executioner. His brilliantined hair had been miraculously concealed beneath a giant off-white turban. A moth-eaten patch was covering his right eye. He fished a dessert spoon from the welt pocket of his waistcoat, and licked it.

'The eyeball-reader at Ongole . . . that *was* you!'

Rising up on tiptoe, the Master smiled wryly. Without a word, he waited for me to ferret out the truth myself. Feroze always disliked doing someone else's thinking for them.

As I sat there in the draught of the church hall, I began to understand.

'The journey, *my* journey, was really *your* journey of observation, wasn't it? It was designed for you to observe me.'

Hakim Feroze tugged off the eyeball-reader's disguise and stuffed away the spoon.

'Had a very lucky trip, meeting so many interesting people, haven't you?' he said, without answering my question.

'What do you mean?'

'You tell me . . .'

I contemplated his words. He had a point. Even for India, with its constant stream of improbable characters, I had crossed paths with an excess of sages, *swamis* and eccentrics.

I thought back to the many unlikely episodes of the expedition.

'Sri Gobind in Madras . . . is that why he welcomed me so hospitably? And the duel at Sholapur?'

Feroze narrowed his eyes and smiled.

I scrolled back, remembering the other outlandish characters.

'Mr Jafar and his lousy over-priced herbal petrol . . . did you have anything to do with him? And what about the godman at Nandul . . . and the witch and, for that matter, what about Goadbaba?'

Climbing up on to the church's altar, the Master rubbed his hands together and burst into laughter.

'We all need a little help from time to time,' he said.

'Help?'

Feroze smacked his hands together five times in a slow clap, until the nave echoed like a belfry at midnight. Outside, the rain was still pelting down. The church door seemed to open and slam. I assumed it was the wind.

'What's all this about help?'

As usual, the Master wasn't listening to my question. He was staring at something behind me. I turned round to face the aisle. Then came the morning's second moment of perplexity.

Behind me, standing to attention in the church's nave, was Bhalu.

In silence he went over to Feroze and greeted him. Then he turned to me and scratched his ear.

'What would you have done without me?' he laughed.

Like a Grand-Master who has checkmated the opponent in four moves, Feroze bathed in the satisfaction of it all.

'I don't believe this,' I stammered. 'It's impossible!'

'*Impossible* as your chance meeting with Guptaji at Jamshedpur?'

'What *are* you talking about? That was Venky's idea,' I said, biting my lip at revealing my own secret weapon.

'Ah, yes, Venkatraman the *rickshawalla*,' spat Feroze. 'Nice chap, isn't he?'

'You *know* him? You know Venky?'

The magician raised an eyebrow.

'Next thing,' I said, 'you'll be telling me you were responsible for Vatson and the Aghori *sadhu* in Varanasi.'

Feroze looked at the floor bashfully. He descended from the altar and sat down on the chair beside mine.

'So you knew all along I was coming to Calcutta? That *chance* meeting at the Albert Hall . . . it wasn't chance at all, was it?'

The sorcerer remained tight-lipped. Instead of replying, he took a deep breath, timing the inhalation with his trusty pocket-watch.

'I suppose,' I said astringently, 'you *arranged* for me to be robbed on the Farakka Express as well.'

At that, Feroze leapt to his feet.

'My friend,' he responded, 'don't blame me for your own negligence.'

'But what do I do now?' I asked, hoping to break the awkward silence which followed the Master's outburst. 'What's the next part of the course?'

Feroze Hakim hurled his beloved bull's pizzle riding crop to the floor. Then, seething with fury as I had never seen him before, he yelled:

'The course is over!'

'*Over?* So suddenly? Is that it?'

'Am I obliged to forewarn you of my decisions?'

'Have I passed?'

'How dare you denigrate this work by speaking in terms of pass and failure,' said the magician with characteristic iciness. 'The pursuit of illusion is not about studying for prizes, or for study's sake. There's no right or wrong, no pass or fail. I have revealed to you the basic principles, and shown you what to look for. The rest is up to you . . .'

The Master was interrupted by a rapping at the church door. A second later it came again, louder than before. Strange, I thought, because when Bhalu had entered, the door hadn't been locked. I asked Feroze who it might be. A fist struck the door a third time.

'Curious, aren't you?' he said. 'Better go and have a look.'

I stood up and paced back down the nave like a sleep-walker. Of course I was inquisitive. But after the events of the Afghan Church, little could surprise me. I twisted the handle clockwise, and wrenched the hefty oak portal inwards.

There was no one waiting on the outside. Slamming the door shut, I went back into the nave and marched back down the central aisle to the altar.

But Feroze and Bhalu had disappeared.

I called their names. There was no reply.

Glossary

Aga: sir; term of respect; loan-word from Persian and Turkish.

Aghori: one of several specific kinds of *sadhu* found in India, traditionally said to have been cannibalistic. Close to traditional shamans in their beliefs, they are thought to have the power to control spirits.

Anglo-Afghan Wars: three wars fought on Afghan soil between the British and Afghans – waged between 1839 and 1919 – in which the British were defeated conclusively each time.

Aquasonic gel®: gel solution applied to an area (especially of the abdomen) before an ultrasound examination. See ultrasound.

areca: nut from the betel palm (*sopaari* in Hindi); essential ingredient for the preparation of *paan*.

Ashpaz, Khalifa: the master chef of the Hindu Kush, renowned for his colossal feasts, employed by Jan Fishan Khan.

ashram: centre for spiritual learning.

avatar: the incarnation of a Hindu god, usually Vishnu; a godman.

Ayurvedic: the ancient art of Hindu medicine, relying on the use of herbs, massage and meditation.

Bandicota indica: infamous grey-backed bandicoot common in India; one of the largest and hungriest rats in the world.

barafwalla: ice merchant or haulier; common sight in Indian cities and towns, where refrigeration still relies on blocks of ice.

Berndorf: town in Austria (south-west of Vienna) famous for its metal works and shell-casing factories at the time of the World War I.

bezoar: reddish stone found in the entrails of animals; concretion like a kidney stone. Also said to be extracted from an aged toad's head. Forms a powerful amulet or talisman; especially against poison.

bhang: (*Cannabis indica*); preparation of pounded marijuana, from the hemp plant which is used in offerings at temples – such as Calcutta's Kali Temple.

bharh: miniature fired clay cup used to drink tea in Bengal and other regions; afforded no value and disposed of after a single use.

bhishtiwalla: one who sells drinking water carried in a goat hide; popular sight in Calcutta.

Bihari: person from the state of Bihar in north-eastern India. Many menial jobs in Calcutta are performed by impoverished Biharis.

bindi: dot – usually vermilion – frequently worn on the forehead of Hindu women. See tikka.

biri: small hand-rolled tobacco cigarette, popular in India. Often made by bonded labourers in Tamil Nadu.

Black Hole of Calcutta: prison cell where 146 British captives – held by the Nawab of Bengal – were incarcerated on the night of 20TH June 1756; all but 23 suffocated.

Bollywood: India's most famous film studios, responsible for making hundreds of three-hour movie extravaganzas each year.

Brahmin: highest caste in India.

BSE: *bovine spongiform encephalopathy*; a neurological disease occurring in the brain and spinal column of infected cattle.

Cagliostro, Alessandro: 'Prince of Quacks'; celebrated eighteenth-century Italian mountebank, magician and illusionist.

Cannabis indica: hemp plant commonly found in India from which marijuana, or *bhang*, is prepared.

chai-i-sabs: green tea; a popular drink frequently served in Afghanistan, Pakistan and northern India.

chaitan: the 'devil's tree', the bark of which is powdered and burned by magicians to stupefy an audience.

chakotra: grapefruit, popular citrus fruit in India.

champa: (*Michelia champa*); low tree sacred to Hindus bearing fragrant creamy-white flowers.

chandni: silver.

chapatti: unleavened wheat bread.

chappal: slipper; used to mean 'sandal'.

charpoy: literally 'four legs'; simple rope bed without a mattress commonly seen on the streets of Indian towns and villages.

Chennai: original Indian name for Madras.

chilam: ritual clay pipe, as used by *sadhus*; regularly used for smoking marijuana or hashish.

chloroform: colourless sweet-smelling liquid formerly used as an anaesthetic.

chowkidar: watchman.

choolah: small stove.

Chor Bazaar: Thieves' Market; the area in Bombay where antique European and Indian objects can be found.

chor: thief.

chowk: square, market area.

chukka: ankle-high laced boot, usually crafted from suede, resembling a polo boot, hence the name.

chullu: bootleg liquor, generally made from distilled grain.

coco-de-mer: mysterious nut of the coco-de-mer palm, which takes seven years to mature; native only to the island of Praslin in the Seychelles; wondrous mystical and medicinal properties have been attributed to the nuts in eastern Africa, the Middle East and in India.

daal: dish of cooked lentils popular throughout India.

dada: literally 'Big Brother'; used to refer to gangster leaders and members of the Mafia operating at street level in Calcutta and other Indian cities.

darshan: audience with a holy person.

das: ten.

dhobi: laundry; also person who does laundry, usually by hand.

dhobi's **itch**: unpleasant eruption of the skin, particularly that of the inner thighs.

dhyaan: literally 'concentration', state of trance entered by Hindu mystics.

diazepam: sleeping pill and muscle relaxant containing benzodiazepine.

dom: person infamous in West Bengal for stealing skeletons. See: *konkalwalla*.

doxology: the study of hymns.

drugget: coarse hair and cotton woven rug.

ek: one.

ek-bahu: ritual penance as performed by a *sadhu*; such as standing on one foot or holding an arm upright for a number of years.

Englezabad: town on the border with Bangladesh, founded by the British in the late seventeenth-century as a trading post; also known as English (or 'Ingraz') Bazar.

erukkam: plant, the poisonous milk of whose flowers is used as a preparation to kill unwanted (female) new-born babies.

fakir: Muslim holy man.

fenny: distilled drink made from cashew or coconut, especially popular in Goa.

Ganesha: Hindu deity – especially popular in Maharashtra – usually represented with the head of an elephant and the body of a man.

Ganga: River Ganges; sacred water obtained from the river.

Gardiner: type of teapot named after an Englishman who founded a legendary ceramics factory in imperial Russia.

geophagy: condition whereby humans eat earth.

ghamela: crude shovel used by *ghamelawallas*.

ghamelawalla: person who buys dirt from a jewellery workshop's floor and extracts minimal amounts of gold from it.

ghanti: literally 'bell'; especially the small bell carried by all *rickshawallas* in Calcutta to announce their presence so that people to move out of their way.

ghat: steps leading down to a river or waterline; especially those in the holy city of Varanasi at which Hindus descend to the River Ganges.

ghee: clarified butter used in numerous Indian dishes.

Go: Japanese board game for two players, similar to draughts, but exceedingly difficult to master.

Goadbaba: literally 'Mr Sweet'; person who claims the ability of making anything taste of sugar merely by touching it.

godman: holy man claiming divine and miraculous powers, typically resorting to dubious methods to create illusions.

Grey-backed bandicoot: see *Bandicota indica*.

guru: teacher or mentor; literally 'he who dispels darkness'; also *guruji*, where *-ji* is a suffix denoting respect.

haa: yes.

Habbakuk: codename used during World War II for Pyke's invention 'Pykrete'. See Pykrete.

Haji: Muslim who has been on the pilgrimage to Mecca.

Hammaam: Turkish-style steam bath.

Hand of Fatima: symbolic outstretched hand, commonly found across the Islamic world, associated with Fatima – daughter of the Prophet Mohammed – signifying his family and the duties of every Muslim.

Herizi: relating to the Heriz region of Azerbaijan, known for its fabulous coarse tribal rugs, usually displaying geometric patterns and a central medallion.

hilsa: medium-sized salt-water fish which spawns in freshwater.

Hindi: one of the most widely spoken languages in India; especially in the north of the country.

Hindustan: India; literally 'Land of Hindus'.

Hobson-Jobson: dictionary of colloquial Anglo-Indian words and phrases, first published in 1886; renowned for its lore and extraneous information.

Houdini, Harry: legendary American illusionist and escapologist (1874-1926); credited with devising hundreds of illusions, as well as exposing mediums and others (claimed by him) to be fakes.

Hydra: ferocious nine-headed water monster of Greek myth.

idli: steamed rice-cake popular in southern India.

ikat: highly specialised system of weaving, perfected in India, where the warp, weft, or both threads, are tie-dyed before being woven; creating subtle designs on the cloth.

ipecac: (*Cephaelis ipecacuanha*); South American shrub, a preparation of whose root is used as an emetic. Correctly called *ipecacuanha*.

jabba: (*Hibiscus rosa-siensis*); red hibiscus or China rose, whose large red flowers are popular adornments at temples.

jadoo: magic.

jadoowalla: magician; person said to have miraculous powers.

Jain: peaceful religious group in India, whose founder – Mahavira – broke away from Hinduism during the sixth-century BC.

Jalasayin: *ghat* at Varanasi where the deceased are cremated on enormous funeral pyres on the banks of the Ganges; also known as 'Burning Ghat'.

jaldi: hurry up; quickly!

jalebi: deep-fried syrupy batter snack, yellow-orange in colour, popular throughout India.

jalousie shutters: slatted shutters built into a window-frame or door, the angle of whose horizontal slats can be adjusted to admit light and air, but to exclude sun and rain.

jambiya: curved Arab dagger, often with a silver scabbard and a rhino-horn hilt; the most prized examples are produced in Yemen.

Jami'a Masjid: great mosque near the Red Fort in Old Delhi; the largest mosque in India.

jamun: (*Stzygium cumini*); java plum tree, found throughout India, especially abundant in the south. Known for its rough bark, oval leathery leaves and white flowers.

Jan-guru: witch-hunter and exorcist whose trials (especially in remote Indian villages) supposedly detect 'genuine' witches.

Janissary: member of an élite military unit of the Turkish army, formed during the fourteenth century, and famed for their marching band – the oldest in the world.

jinn: spirit, especially a kindly or mischievous one.

Kaaba: cubical building standing in the courtyard at the central mosque in the holy city of Mecca, containing a sacred black stone; the central focus of pilgrimage for Muslims.

Kabuli: relating to Kabul, capital city of Afghanistan.

Kali: devouring, destructive goddess (meaning 'black' in Sanskrit); depicted as a vile woman bathed in blood, with a protruding tongue.

Kalighat: name from which 'Calcutta' is derived.

kamandal: ritualistic water vessel carried by many *sadhus*.

kanji: starchy water in which rice has been washed.

Kashi: name for the holy city of Varanasi, sacred to Hindus, situated on the River Ganges.

kelim: pile-less tapestry-woven rug frequently produced in bright colours; crafted in Turkey and other Near Eastern countries.

Kellar, Harry: American illusionist and conjuror, contemporary and great friend of Harry Houdini.

kishmish: mixture of nuts and dried fruit popular in Afghanistan, Pakistan and northern India.

Kiswah: immense black cloth mantle, embroidered with gold calligraphy, crafted each year for the Kaaba at Mecca.

kohl: antimony; brittle, silvery metal used powdered as an eye make-up.

Koli: traditional fishermen of Bombay.

konkalwalla: literally 'skeleton-man'; i.e. someone engaged (especially in Calcutta) in the business of selling human skeletons. See: dom.

kundalini: yogic idea of a divine energy coiled like a serpent at the base of the spine, which is activated by exercise.

lakh: one hundred thousand.

lungi: loincloth, worn in India and some neighbouring countries; loan-word from Persian, in which it correctly means 'turban cloth'.

machhi: fish.

Mahabharata: ancient Sanskrit epic poem consisting of more than 220,000 lines, recounting the war between the Pandavas and the Kauravas.

mahout: person who trains, keeps, or drives an elephant.

maidan: open space, especially a grassland, in a town.

mandir: temple.

Marathi: Indo-Aryan language spoken in the state of Maharashtra.

Margashirsa Karthe star: star in the Hindu solar system whose appearance in early summer marks the start of the Gowds' miracle asthma cure in Hyderabad.

masjid: mosque.

mattar-paneer: spiced dish of peas and curd cheese.

mehendi: reddish-orange preparation made from the leaves of the henna shrub (*Lawsonia inermis*), used to dye the hair and hands, especially at time of marriage.

mogra: (*Jasminum ambac*); fragrant off-white flower of the Arabian jasmine plant, used in garlands for a woman's hair.

moksha: salvation, spiritual liberation, when the soul ascends to Paradise.

monosodium glutamate: white crystalline powder used to enhance the flavour of savoury food, (chemical formula: $HOOC.CH(NH_2)CH_2CH_2COONa$).

muezzin: the Muslim call to prayer.

Mughal: dynasty of Mongols, of the line of Genghiz Khan, who conquered India and were its Emperors immediately before the British advent.

mujahed: one who fights in a holy war (literally 'struggler'). According to traditions, there are two kinds of Muslim Jihad: the Lesser, armed struggle, and the Greater, with the mind and tongue.

Mumbai: original Indian name for Bombay.

murgh mussallam: spiced chicken dish especially popular in northern India.

Mutiny of 1857: major revolt of Hindu and Muslim troops within the British Army; known as the 'Sepoy Mutiny' by the British, and the Revolt of 1857 by Indians.

naan: unleavened bread popular in the northern areas of India, as well as in Pakistan and Afghanistan.

Naga: people from several distinct warrior tribes from north-east India, known traditionally for their head-hunting practices.

namaskar. Hindu greeting of bowing the head and placing the palms together.

namaste: common Hindi greeting (literally 'I salute all divine qualities in you'); often accompanied by *namaskar*.

naswar. green-coloured snuff favoured by those living in the Himalayas.

Nawab: landowner or governor of an area of land; title relating to 'prince'.

neem: (*Azadirachta indica*); a large evergreen tree common in India, used in the preparation of medicinal oils; its twigs are used to clean the teeth.

obsessive-compulsive disorder: anxiety disorder in which a person is preoccupied by recurrent activities or habits.

Oriya: Indo-Aryan language spoken in the state of Orissa, in eastern India.

ossuary: chamber in which bones are stored; especially those periodically exhumed from a small cemetery.

paan: leaf of the betel palm, combined with an astringent mixture of areca nut, lime, tobacco, etc.; the concoction – which is chewed – is very popular in India. The remains are generally spat out after chewing, staining the ground crimson.

pabda: small salt-water fish popular in West Bengal.

paisa: one hundredth part of a rupee; also used to mean 'money'.

palanquin: covered litter suspended from four poles, borne by attendants; common in India until late nineteenth-century, superseded in Calcutta and other cities by the rickshaw.

panch: five.

Panchganga: one of the *ghats* at Varanasi.

Parsi: Persian Zorastrians, who settled in Bombay in 1670 at the invitation of the British. Parsis fled Persia during the seventh-century AD and settled in what is now the Indian state of Gujarat.

Partition: process of the splitting of the Hindu-Muslim India, in 1947 to form what is now Pakistan, Bangladesh (then East Pakistan) and India.

Pashtu: language of the Pashtuns (incorrectly called 'Pathans'); the most common language in eastern Afghanistan.

Pashtun: mountain people numbering about twelve million, fabled for their bravery, located mainly in eastern Afghanistan and north-west Pakistan.

Phansigar: one of the secret fraternity of Thugs who strangled travellers in honour of Kali; known as 'the People of the Noose'. See: Thuggee.

pilau: (more correctly *'palao'*); Central Asian spiced rice dish, popular in northern India, Pakistan and Afghanistan.

pipal: (*Ficus religiosa*); large long-living fig tree common in India; the tree under which Buddha is said to have been sitting when he attained enlightenment.

pognophobia: the fear of facial hair, especially beards.

pomfret: flat fish of the *Stromateidae* family, abundant in the Arabian Sea; common dish in Bombay.

pongamia: (*Pongamia pinnata*); commonly seen tree in avenues and along river banks throughout India, with pale bark and wide sprawling branches.

puchkawalla: person who prepares snacks on street stalls and sells them to passers-by.

puja: rites performed in worship of the Hindu deities.

pandit: religious scholar versed in the ancient Sanskrit texts who oversees religious ceremonies and rites.

punkhawalla: person responsible for fanning others before electric fans or air-conditioning were available.

puri: small circular fried wheat bread.

Pykrete: amalgam of wood pulp and ice said to be twelve times stronger than concrete; the brainchild of eccentric British inventor Geoffrey Pyke, who enthused Mountbatten and Churchill with the idea of constructing 2,000-feet-long Pykrete battleships, during World War II.

Raj: rule; commonly referring to the British colonial rule of India.

Rajput: princely rulers whose dynasties reigned over much of north-west India, especially Rajasthan.

Rama: seventh incarnation of Vishnu, the heroic son of King Dasaratha of

Ayodhya, dedicated to ridding the earth of evil-doers. See: Ramayana.

Ramasi: secret language of the brotherhood of Thugs.

Ramayana: ancient Sanskrit epic describing the deeds of Rama, the seventh incarnation of Vishnu; also popular Indian soap opera based on the ancient text, renowned for its lavish costumes and flamboyant portrayals of the deities.

Rationalist: national movement in India seeking to curb the rise of mendacious godmen.

rickshaw: (correctly 'jinrickisha'); two-wheeled passenger cart pulled by one person, brought to India in 1880s by the Chinese; now only found in Calcutta, they are being phased out. Motorised version popular across India, indeed across Asia, is known as an 'auto-rickshaw', or simply 'rickshaw'.

Robert-Houdin, Jean-Eugène: French stage magician (1805-1871), regarded as the father of modern conjuring. Harry Houdini named himself after Robert-Houdin but later sought to expose his former hero.

ruddiwalla: 'rag-picker'; person who searches for rags or other scraps to be recycled.

rumaal: handkerchief; especially a knotted one, as used by Thugs to strangle their victims.

rupia: rupee, the currency of India.

sadhu: holy man or sage.

sahib: honorific title of address, meaning 'sir' or 'Mr' in India; Arabic loan-word, it signifies friend, owner and sir in various usages.

sal: (*Shorea robusta*); evergreen hardwood tree prized for its timber; second in importance only to teak.

salwaar kameez: lose-fitting shirt and trousers, popular in northern India, Pakistan and Afghanistan.

samadhi: state of profound meditation.

sari: long piece of cloth worn by women in India as a robe.

sati: custom of a Hindu widow immolating herself on her deceased husband's funeral pyre, supposedly in emulation of Siva's consort; literally 'a virtuous woman'.

Sayed: honorific title borne by descendants of the Prophet Mohammed.

Shah: title (literally, 'king') borne by descendants of the Prophet Mohammed, who also trace their ancestry to the Sassanian emperors. In India, the name occurs as a surname in Hindus, particularly those from Gujarat, although they are not from the Prophet's family.

Shah-Saz: 'King-Maker'; the epithet of Nawab Jan Fishan Khan.

Shaitan: the Devil; Hindi loan-word taken from Arabic; derived from *shatn*, 'opposition'.

sitar: Indian stringed instrument, similar to the lute, with a long, fretted neck.

sopaari: see areca.

sukto: Bengali dish of fried, diced vegetables.

sumal: tree from mainland China whose wood irritates sensitive skin.

swami: a Hindu religious instructor.

taklu: 'baldie'; derogatory slang term in Hindi for a balding person.

talwaar: long Indian sabre.

tandoori: food cooked in a *tandoor*, a cylindrical clay oven, especially bread and meat marinated in yoghurt and spices and threaded on to skewers.

tantra: religious texts laying out the path to enlightenment.

tantrik: practitioner of *tantra*; a holy man.

tapasya: self-inflicted regime of austerity or penance employed by Hindu holy men.

Telugu: Dravidian language spoken across the state of Andhra Pradesh in south-east India.

thali: metal tray in which an array of grains and vegetables are placed; originally from south of India, now found across the country.

Thuggee: cult of ritual murderers dedicated to the goddess Kali, who strangled tens of thousands of travellers until their persecution in the mid-nineteenth-century. See: *Phansigar*.

tikka: vermilion powder smeared on the forehead by Hindus during religious ritual as a symbol of the divine; now used by women as a decorative accessory; also known as *'tilak'*.

tilak: see: *tikka*.

transducer: sensitive probe arm attached to an ultrasound unit which scans a pregnant woman's abdomen when detecting the development of a foetus.

trephination: adaptation of trepanation – conceived by Dutch physician Dr Bart Huges in 1962; to drill a 'third eye' above a patient's forehead using a high-speed masonry drill.

ultrasound: electronic medical unit designed to detect the development of an unborn child by use of a transducer; commonly used in India to ascertain the gender of a foetus, so that unwanted female foetuses can be aborted.

yogi: a person on a mystical path; one who practises yoga.

Vedic: relating to the Vedas, the ancient sacred Hindu texts.

vibhuti: grey-coloured ash commonly produced from nowhere by Indian godmen, and sprinkled on to the hands of devotees.

Vyasa: 'the Compiler'; poet of the great Sanskrit epic, the Mahabharata.

Yakshi: goddess who represents the forces of nature, especially trees. Felling a tree rouses the anger of the deity.

Zarathustra: (also 'Zoroaster'); deity revered by Parsis, who lived as a sage in Persia during the sixth century BC.